SECTIONALISM IN VIRGINIA
FROM 1776 TO 1861

WEST VIRGINIA AND APPALACHIA
A Series Edited by Ronald L. Lewis

Volume 7

OTHER BOOKS IN THE SERIES:

Transnational West Virginia
Edited by Ken Fones-Wolf
ISBN 0-937058-67-X [HC] • ISBN 0-937058-76-9 [PB]

The Blackwater Chronicle
Edited By Timothy Sweet
ISBN 0-937058-65-3 [HC] • ISBN 0-937058-66-1 [PB]

Clash of Loyalties
By John W. Shaffer
ISBN 0-937058-73-4 [HC ONLY]

Afflicting the Comfortable
By Thomas F. Stafford
ISBN 1-933202-04-1 [HC ONLY]

Bringing Down the Mountains
By Shirley Stewart Burns
ISBN 978-1-933202-17-4 [PB]

Monongah: The Tragic Story of the 1907 Monongah Mine Disaster, The Worst Industrial Accident in US History
By Davitt McAteer
ISBN 978-1-933202-23-7 [HC ONLY]

SECTIONALISM IN VIRGINIA FROM 1776 TO 1861

BY
CHARLES HENRY AMBLER, PH.D.

SECOND EDITION

WITH A NEW INTRODUCTION BY
BARBARA RASMUSSEN

MORGANTOWN 2008

West Virginia University Press, Morgantown 26506
© 2008 West Virginia University Press
All rights reserved.
First edition 1910 published by The University of Chicago Press; rpt. New York 1964
Second edition 2008 with "Introduction to the Second Edition" by Barbara Rasmussen, published by West Virginia University Press
Printed in U.S.A.

15 14 13 12 11 10 09 08   8 7 6 5 4 3 2 1

ISBN 978-1-933202-21-1 [paperback]

Library of Congress Cataloguing-in-Publication Data

Sectionalism in Virginia from 1776 to 1861
p. cm. —
1. West Virginia–Politics and government–History. 2. Virginia–Politics and government–1775-1865. 3. West Virginia–History. I. Title. II. Ambler, Charles Henry, 1876-1957. III. Rasmussen, Barbara, 1947-
IN PROCESS
Library of Congress Control Number: 2008922136

Cover design by Rachel Rosolina

Printed in U.S.A. by BookMobile

TABLE OF CONTENTS

	INTRODUCTION TO THE SECOND EDITION	VII
	LIST OF MAPS	LXI
	PREFACE	LXIII
I	INTRODUCTION	1
II.	REVOLUTION, CONFEDERATION, AND THE CONSTITUTION, 1776–90	24
III.	FEDERALISTS AND REPUBLICANS	61
IV.	THE ERA OF GOOD FEELING AND THE RISE OF THE NATIONAL REPUBLICAN PARTY, 1817–28	100
V.	THE CONSTITUTIONAL CONVENTION OF 1829–30	137
VI.	INTERNAL IMPROVEMENTS, NEGRO SLAVERY, AND NULLIFICATION, 1829–33	175
VII.	PARTIES IN THE WHIG PERIOD, 1834–50	219
VIII.	THE REFORM CONVENTION OF 1850–51	251
IX.	SECTIONALISM IN EDUCATION AND THE CHURCH, 1830–61	273
X.	HISTORY OF POLITICAL PARTIES, 1851–61	300
	BIBLIOGRAPHY	339
	INDEX	351

INTRODUCTION TO THE SECOND EDITION

The birth of the state of West Virginia, as the only territorial adjustment to come because of the Civil War, is unique to the nation and poses the question of whether there would ever have been a West Virginia without that dark passage of 1861–65. From the perspective of historian Charles H. Ambler, almost certainly there would have been a rending of Virginia no matter the war. His thesis holds that an aristocratic minority in Virginia resisted democratic pressures for so long that when western economic might coalesced with sectional crisis the state could not hold itself together. Deadly dull studies of the West Virginia statehood conventions of 1861–62 and the state's rejection of slavery once were the lynchpins of eighth grade West Virginia history classes, and often these perspectives dominated college study as well. This approach, however, tended to overlook the real genesis of the new state movement.

West Virginia statehood was long in the making and had its start in politics driven by economic interests, not abolition. Dr. Ambler's 1910 study of sectionalism in Virginia clearly shows how the East and West of Virginia were always destined to separate. His work underpinned state history for more than sixty years until the mid 1960s and 1970s, when the study of the topic expanded to include the full array of social class relations, distribution of resources, and legislated economic realities. Historians of new inclinations targeted these aspects of West Virginia history. Neo-colonialists, Marxists, Cultural Determinists, and contrarians all weighed in on West Virginia, largely leaving behind the statehood movement to look at the state's misery and sorrow during the early twentieth century. Nearly all of these new historians had one thing in common. To a soul, each of them had read and digested Dr. Ambler's *Sectionalism in Virginia, 1776–1861*. Skeptical of the Cultural Determinism that the local color writers injected into the history of West Virginia during the early twentieth century; many of these new historians followed Ambler's lead and turned their attentions to the political causes of the state and regional economic difficulties.

From Ambler's perspective, West Virginia statehood was the final blow to a weakening aristocracy's eighty-five year long unsuccessful effort to preserve itself in the face of powerful economic and political demands from a boisterous western democracy flush with resources sufficient to a kingdom. From another perspective, frustrated middle class western leaders fomented their own rebellion in the style of Crane Brinton's *Anatomy of a Revolution*, wherein a sitting government thwarts an able and ambitious middle class, fails to collect taxes, and sees its own authority erode.[1]

Both perspectives boded ill for the Tidewater planter class that looked with great trepidation at the growing population and economic potentials of the West. They surely saw and noted the nascent, but growing, cities of

[1] Crane Brinton, *Anatomy of a Revolution* (New York: Vintage Books, 1965), 65.

Ohio, Kentucky, and Pennsylvania, toward which western Virginia's rivers flowed. They also must have seen the early winter frosts and rugged terrain that largely precluded tobacco, and therefore plantations. Instead, there was salt, iron, coal, whisky, hogs, apples, lumber, and pottery, and north or west flowing rivers to carry it all out of Virginia. Relatively few slaves toiled along side their farmer masters, however industrial slaves contributed to the production of salt, iron, and coal. Try as they might to legislate against this potential, the aristocrats were only temporarily successful. West Virginia, as a political entity with a coherent agenda, gained its identity in the 1818 debate over the nation's tariff. From that early date, Virginia's leaders were so protective of slavery that they ignored the pleas of iron makers and salt makers in Virginia's West who sought a tariff that would protect their fledgling industries from British competition after the conclusion of the War of 1812.[2] Virginia, at this time, was a place of many places, a culture of many cultures. Professor Ambler's study of the political behavior of the many sections of the state has become a mainstay in the study of West Virginia history as well as Virginia history. Still pertinent one hundred years after it was written, this work is now being re-issued by the West Virginia University Press so that more generations of historians may have easier access to its wisdom.

When planters trounced western interests because they preferred to purchase cheaper English iron tools for their slaves rather than to nurture Virginia's own in-

---

[2] Charles H. Ambler, *Sectionalism in Virginia 1776–1861* (Chicago: University of Chicago Press, 1910), 118.

dustrial potential, the West and the East, no longer able to ignore each other, began to clash. By 1833, the legislature was nurturing the infant Tredegar Iron Works in Richmond at the expense of the Ohio and Monongahela valleys' iron industries. This early expression of sectionalism in economic interests was just the beginning of two phenomena in antebellum Virginia. First, the state was growing and diversifying at an astonishing rate. Unlike the rest of the slave-owning south, Virginia in the years before the Civil War was not in a general decline. Some sections were; most were not. According to Daniel W. Crofts, "Late antebellum Virginia was a land of paradox" that contained the largest population in the south, and an economic and social character that was distinctly different from the Deep South.[3] Secondly, Virginia was hurtling recklessly toward war with itself. Far from being the decadent aristocracy of the eighteenth century, most of Virginia was experiencing the "same dynamic economic and social development that characterized the country as a whole," according to William G. Shade.[4] Crofts and Shade argue that Virginia's political leaders "exaggerated the Old Dominion's affinity for Deep South particularism. Even though economic and social trends indicated otherwise, Virginia Democrats liked to pretend that their state was as southern as any."[5]

[3] Daniel W. Crofts, "Late Antebellum Virginia Reconsidered," in *The Virginia Magazine of History and Biography.* 107 (Summer 1999): 253–286, 253.

[4] William G. Shade, *Democratizing the old Dominion: Virginia and the Second Party System: 1824–1861* (Charlottesville and London: University of Virginia Press, 1996), 3.

[5] Crofts, *Late Antebellum Virginia Reconsidered,* 253.

Such a perception, real or contrived, led to disaster by 1861.

Actually, the Virginia House of Delegates absolutely did not presume to hold the affections of their citizens. These aristocrats also did not over-estimate Virginians' love of Tidewater chivalry and cavalier governance; rather, they well and truly knew what kind of political disaster awaited them in the future. As the population of the state grew and the center of population shifted westward, the patrician elite of Virginia saw their own minority lifestyle seriously threatened. Their aristocracy became a shrinking percentage of the population that would suffer under a democratically elected government. Thus, by 1818, they were fighting tooth and nail to forestall the inevitable decline of their traditional planter-based society. In the process, they went to extremes, setting up conditions that allowed secession and, subsequently, the division of the state.

In 1776, American Patriots cajoled reluctant Tidewater planters into supporting the American Revolution after Governor Lord Dunmore's offer of freedom to their slaves, but they wanted nothing to do with the democracy that was hiding in rebellion's pocket. It was never clear to the planters that severing ties to England meant also ending Virginia's aristocracy. Most of them shared William Byrd's belief that illiteracy among the general population was a sure way to keep the aristocracy secure. By the end of the War of 1812, these elites had already lost the political majority—or would have under a more democratic apportionment of the statehouse. While the population of Virginia grew and diversified, and its economy moved away from dependence on any one crop, much like the rest of the nation, the aristocratic Virginia state government did not evolve at all. The sectionalization of Virginia gradually was hewing a hardened cadre of northwesterners who were determined to partition the state. Another cadre anxious to see them go flanked them on the east.

Political acrimony increasingly laced the years between 1818 and secession that deepened the sectional issues. Over time, the debates identified the line that, in 1863, formalized the schism. The tariff issue was the first time that the state legislature acted so boldly against the interests of their fellow Virginians, but it was not the last. The constitutional convention of 1829, the ensuing slavery debate, and the frustrated pleas for banking, internal improvements, and universal white male suffrage were equally disappointing to the West. The Tidewater resisted with every tool available the growing fervor for widening the democracy within the Old Dominion. As a result of this resistance, four sections of Virginia grew more clearly identifiable during these years. Defined by their geography at first, the Tidewater, Piedmont, Shenandoah Valley and the West soon became recognizable for their differing political perspectives as well. Eventually, politics sharpened and the discourse became less and less amiable. From the beginning, "the West" meant "democracy," and that was a problem for Virginia.

We have learned these things from Ambler's *Sectionalism*. It was the first history of Virginia to look carefully at the formation of public opinion on controversial issues in Virginia and the nation. Ambler's tome remains the seminal work of West Virginia history. This book is important because it talks about politics, not culture. All of the subsequent state history rests upon his thesis, and a few works expand on his interpretations. Scholars who followed Ambler found many ways to broaden his thesis to explain state history. Freed from the false burdens of Cultural Determinism, the historians of the late twentieth century applied a similar sharp eye to newer political issues: What were the dynamics governing labor relations in the coalfields? What was behind the feudalism of clan warfare in the hinterland? What were the new fathers thinking when they wrote the West Virginia Constitution of 1872? Why make whisky instead of corn meal? Why should a governor overawe a school system?[6]

Ambler's respect for long historical perspective predated the French Annalist historians' *longue duree,* but they would admire him for starting his story at the beginning of Virginia's settlement. In the early seventeenth century, western Virginia began at the line of the waterfalls that halted upriver navigation, separating the Tidewater from the rest of the commonwealth. The coastal areas were dominated by a relatively few wealthy

---

[6] Ronald L. Lewis, *Coal Iron and Slaves: Industrial Slavery in Maryland and Virginia 1715–1865* (Westport Conn.: Greenwood Press, 1979); Lewis, *Black Coal Miners in America: Race, Class and Community Conflict.* (Lexington: University Press of Kentucky, 1987); Ed Steel, *The Courtmartial of Mother Jones* (Lexington: University Press of Kentucky, 1995); Altina Waller, *Feud: Hatfields, McCoys and Social Change in Appalachia, 1860–1900* (Chapel Hill: University of North Carolina Press, 1988); Thomas P. Slaughter, *The Whisky Rebellion, Frontier Epilogue to the American Revolution* (New York: Oxford University Press, 1986); John Hennen, *The Americanization of West Virginia: Creating a Modern Industrial State, 1916–1925* (Lexington: University Press of Kentucky, 1996).

individuals for whose interests everyone else toiled. By the 1660s, new arrivals from Europe and the sons of Tidewater families were marching that line westward to the Blue Ridge. Fine plantations characterized the gently rolling hills of this Piedmont, offering a seductive and lush landscape that included moderate holdings of slaves. Thomas Jefferson and James Madison lived here in wonderful plantation houses that survive to this day as beloved American treasures. However, Piedmont planters never lived in the sumptuous and powerful style of the low country that was home to such planters as Charles Carter and William Byrd.

By 1754, the western frontier had further advanced to the Shenandoah Valley. At its mouth, the level terrain spanned a distance of about thirty miles, east to west. Prosperous farmers who practiced a mixed agriculture there flourished on large farms, not plantations. Ultimately, there were many slaves in the valley, but there were never as many as in the Piedmont and the Tidewater. Called "Washington country" because the brothers of George Washington settled there, the mouth of the valley housed, by 1786, the town of Charles Town, named for the future president's younger brother. An early settler built the oldest structure there in 1754, along Evitts Run. It was a sixteen-foot-by-sixteen-foot log cabin that still stands. That year, in carrying out his orders to evict French trespassers at the forks of the Ohio River, George Washington assembled the Virginia militia near this place. His conduct in this assignment triggered the French and Indian War, which had the effect of moving many more people farther west, including a few slaves.

Beyond the western edge of the Valley, a daunting wilderness rolled on until it reached the Ohio River. The formidable Allegheny Front of the Appalachian Mountains slowed, but did not stop, westward settlement. By the end of Washington's war, frontiersmen, immigrants, and an occasional deserting soldier moved west—pushing upstream along the Monongahela River deep into the heart of the mountains. Long before the American Revolution began, adventurous Virginians of every sort were making their way across this mountain range and pressing hard upon the Ohio River. This Transmontane region featured smaller farms, more rugged land, and sparse numbers of slaves because the steep mountains and cool climates could not reliably offer the necessary frost-free days to support the growth of tobacco. Instead, the early mountain farmers grew corn for whisky, hogs, and apples, which they exported to market via the great interior waterway of America. One leg of that system originated at the top of Rich Mountain in Randolph County, in western Virginia, and flowed north through the Tygart Valley. This Tygart Valley River joined with the West Fork River at present-day Fairmont, forming the Monongahela, one of the forks of the Ohio. Thus, from deep within the mountains, farmers could float their canoes, flatboats, and pirogues to New Orleans and world markets, thereby connecting the interior of Virginia to the world economy at an early date. This waterborne commerce was durable, if not voluminous; Monongahela Rye Whisky graced the palace at St. Petersburg, Russia, prior to the writing of the U.S. Constitution. Foodstuffs from western Virginia fed Europe during political strife in the 1780s. Western Virginia also produced salt and iron. This section of Virginia was very different from the Tidewater. Mountain Virginians who looked away looked not to Dixie but to the West, because the Allegheny Front blocked the eastward view, at least from a political standpoint.[7]

In 1776, planter and speculator Patrick Henry replaced the fleeing Royal Governor to become Virginia's first American governor. The political changes that would ultimately come with nationhood were not compatible with Virginia's slave based aristocracy so Henry sought ways to subdue democracy in Virginia. The first state constitution, written by the elites of the Tidewater assembled as a legislature, was a tour de force from this perspective; it cloistered political power along the seacoast where it remained until the Civil War. This constitution assigned representation in the general assembly on a county basis, loading it with a majority of representatives from the small seaside counties, at the expense of the larger and more populous counties in the other three sections of the state. There were only three counties in the West: Ohio, Monongalia, and Yohogania. Grumbling about such a disparity in representation began almost immediately. Calls for constitutional reform in Virginia began in earnest in 1784, when the general assembly received a petition calling for the abolition of slavery. Many Virginians believed

---

[7] Joyce Appleby, "Commercial Farming and the 'Agrarian Myth' in the Early Republic, *Journal of American History* 68 (March 1982): 839; Allan Kulikoff, *The Agrarian Origins of American Capitalism* (Charlottesville: University Press of Virginia, 1992), 103.

the institution was incompatible with the Declaration of Independence, but slavery also repressed Virginia's economic development because the slaveocracy would not tax themselves to provide the infrastructure needed for economic diversification.

The governmental changes asked for by the West increasingly threatened the economic interests of the East. As early as 1790, more than one hundred thousand Virginians lived in the Transmontane, a fact likely interpreted by Frederick Jackson Turner to mean that there was a rise of "an unusually intense individualistic spirit."[8] Historian William Shade agrees, describing a politically vibrant, reasonably well informed electorate in Virginia that was not at all at peace with the patrician Tidewater aristocrats.[9] By this time, the West contained the majority of the state's population, but the Tidewater contained the majority of the state's political leaders who resisted a more equitable reapportionment. The general assembly did not acknowledge the complaints of the West until 1829–30 when a constitutional convention addressed the matter of representation. There is a robust literature about this period in Virginia's history, and all of it agrees that the event was important, but not all agree on why it was important. Ambler saw the convention as a focusing of sectional interests within the state. The slaveocracy and the public hysteria that followed in the wake of slave preacher Nat Turner's bloody uprising in 1831 that left fifty-five white people dead dashed all hopes for reform at that time. Instead

[8] Ambler, *Sectionalism*, 43.
[9] Shade, *Democratizing the Old Dominion*, 1–7.

of attending to representational problems in Virginia, in 1832 lawmakers tightened the slave codes to an unconscionable level of oppression. By standing firmly against constitutional revision or reapportionment, the elites protected their aristocracy at the very real expense of the democracy. The West gained nothing from the 1830 convention and Nat Turner forced public attention in the direction of racial fears thereafter. Western newspapers and politicians continued to rail against the unfairness of the system and to demand a reallocation of the political power within the state. Until reapportionment, nothing would ease the western plight. As the aristocrats well knew, such a step ultimately would mean the demise of their slave-based power.

The four areas of Virginia became smaller political entities with specific agendas that were increasingly difficult for the general assembly to ignore. By the 1830s, The Tidewater, Piedmont, Valley, and Western regions were distinct sections. They became the four pillars of Virginia's history and set the agenda for the study of West Virginia history for the next one hundred years. Ambler looked closely at the political divisions over key issues in the Old Dominion during the years between American Independence and the start of the Civil War. This scrutiny enabled him to point out the nature and substance of the differences between the regions.

The shores of Virginia's Atlantic coast are broad and flat and the shores of the Ohio River are narrow. Strictly speaking, Virginia's boundaries did not stop at the river, they originally extended to "the great south sea" or Pacific Ocean; however, conditions along the Ohio shore and in Kentucky County in the 1770s were a constant source of grief for the Crown and the Virginia colonial government. Powerful speculators and ruthless settlers in this western territory set up conditions that were beyond the control of any authority, even Governor Lord Dunmore, who did much to cause the chaos.[10] By the end of the American Revolution, speculators and land companies made up of powerful politicians who could influence the direction of political tides largely claimed the territory of northwest Virginia and Kentucky. Reluctantly, Virginia compromised with the other twelve former colonies and yielded her western lands to the nation in 1787. Later, Virginia bent to strong pressure from interested parties in Kentucky County and consented to its statehood in 1792. Thus, Virginia tacitly acknowledged that there never had been and never would be a satisfactory way for the Old Dominion to govern as much territory as the original colonial charter gave it. The Ohio River was about as far as Virginia governance could reach.

Because of the state's complicated and varying geography, the life ways of Virginians varied according to their locations. These observations, however, do not ex-

[10] Barbara Rasmussen, "Anarchy and Enterprise on the Imperial Frontier: Washington, Dunmore, Logan, and Land in the Eighteenth Century Ohio Valley" in *Ohio Valley History* 6:4 (Winter 2006):1–26; for a somewhat different interpretation see Stephen Aron, "How the West Was Lost: The Transformation of Kentucky from Daniel Boone to Henry Clay," (Ph.D. diss., University of California at Berkeley, 1990), and Christopher Waldrep, "Opportunity on the Frontier South of the Green," in Craig Thompson Friend, ed., *The Buzzel about Kentuck: Settling the Promised Land* (Lexington: University Press of Kentucky, 1999), 153–172.

plain the state's history of sectionalization in quite the precise way that Ambler's powerful analysis set about to do. He quantified the subtler, but important, political differences among Virginians that sprang from the geographical realities of the state's terrain. Virginia's geography virtually guaranteed that the state would never remain whole and would be partitioned, yielding to the pressures of sectionalism. Sectional contentions were not only inevitable they were also an extremely rational expression of enlightened self-interest.

Ambler's explanation of the sectional nature of the popular vote on select issues also revealed that the state's contemporary newspapers were accurately reflecting their readers' passions on controversial matters, and Ambler used them as sources for his study. He analyzed voting patterns, quantified the votes, and placed their outcomes upon maps of the state, thus drawing multiple pictures of the growing fissure within Virginia. His research articulated the nature of the varying interests and assessed their respective influence in the state. Over the years, the differences grew larger and the chasm between East and West widened. Because the West was quickly growing more populous than the East, a truly democratic Virginia would have produced a state government well attuned to the legitimate needs of the West. Although the Southwest and Valley were securely allied with Richmond in the matter of slavery, substantive reform that would have empowered the Northwest was never a real option. The infrastructure needs of the West would have required increasing the state's revenue stream. The necessary taxation would have addressed slavery in the interest of internal improvements, which the aristocracy would not risk.

Virginia's population was growing rapidly in the three western sections but not in the Tidewater. Planters nevertheless retained a firm grip on the state government. Ambler explains that at the heart of America's first colony, a small faction was willfully entrenched against the democracy that resulted from the Revolution. In the seventeenth century, the prospect that commoners would learn to read horrified Governor Berkeley; by the eighteenth century, their grip on power slipping, the planters trembled at the prospect of yeomen gaining the vote. Many of the planters were descendants of the royalists recruited to America by Berkeley between 1641 and 1676, when Oliver Cromwell seized power in England. Others came from families in the upper ranks of English society who gave up careers in commerce to become American planters.[11]

By pointing to the economic and political basis for the differences in Virginia, Professor Ambler created a historical process for studying West Virginia history that asked clearer questions and shunned cultural biases. This first political history of western Virginia is unequaled. Interestingly, Ambler wrote it in the same era of the "local color" writers who did so much to marginalize the culture and people of Appalachia. Yet, by delineating the various sections of old Virginia according to how they voted on issues, Ambler described the

---

[11] David Hackett Fischer, *Albion Seed: Four British Folkways in North America* (New York: Oxford University Press, 1989), 216, 347.

political realities in the state. Antebellum Virginia put on an outward face of unity for the nation, but her citizens were deeply divided, and inexorably grew more so. Opposing social myths, to borrow a term from historian and journalist Theodore White, played a large role in the nation's sectional crisis, but Ambler's analysis of voting patterns in antebellum Virginia presents a view of opposing economic realities: West Virginia statehood was as inevitable as the Civil War that birthed her. Far from being "the bastard child of a political rape," as Virginia Governor Henry A. Wise called the new state, West Virginia was the slumbering industrial dynamo that loomed powerful indeed: With slavery in the breach, Virginia's leaders could never bring themselves to treat the West democratically. Historian James C. McGregor wrote, "Nothing illustrates better the domineering spirit of the Tidewater planters than the fact that each new community as it established itself in the west gave unmistakable evidence of chafing under a political tyranny." He branded the apportionment of representation in Virginia as a "system of representation that was only a degree less antiquated than the English rotten borough system, a small eastern clique was enabled to put through such legislation as it pleased."[12]

As the situation worsened, cries for severing the Old Dominion replaced cries for reapportionment of the statehouse, which did prompt the 1829 acquiescence. Although the West accrued no gains at that con-

---

[12] James C. McGregor, *The Disruption of Virginia* (New York: The Macmillan Company, 1922), 27.

vention, historian Alison Goodyear Freehling contends that the event identified the real agenda in Virginia, and revealed the intertwined relationship between power and slavery. Only by maintaining this aristocracy of slave wealth could the planters protect their way of life. By contrast, the western sections were democratic and resented the injustice of having to suffer at the hands of an aristocracy when no other Americans were similarly constrained. Only when real war loomed, and the western population soared, did the lawmakers offer meaningful concessions. While the general assembly reapportioned the legislature in 1851 to give the West universal white male suffrage and a white-based representation in the lower house, they put off reapportioning the senate. Promises of senate reapportionment in 1865 temporarily soothed the West, but by then, the world had changed. Constitution writers aimed at retarding the further development of the West by slipping in language that restricted the size of new counties to six hundred square miles. It was seemingly an innocuous step, but upon analysis, it was an astute attempt to staunch the rise of new towns, which brought more voters, more politicians, and new gentry, all of whom joined the ranks of an increasingly vocal opposition to the eastern establishment. Before 1851, white male suffrage had required landownership so westerners rushed to claim the minimum amount necessary to participate in the electoral process. This trend led to serious confusion with the land books as did the formation of new counties that western growth prompted. Land claims overlapped like shingles on a roof. This rapid growth foretold an ultimate alienation of the land, but many decades would lapse before the tragedy of that phenomenon would become widely known.[13]

Population growth in the West numbered the days of the Old Dominion. The attempt to block new counties to slow western population growth did not work. Ironically, out-of-state entrepreneurs joined wealthy Virginians in their rush to erect new counties. The William Parker Foulke family of Philadelphia shared the same vision as the Virginian Deakins brothers, Henry Banks, Henry O. Middleton, and Wilson Carey Nicholas, all of whom became active in land acquisition in Western Virginia soon after the American Revolution. They may have been protecting their interests against a collapse of the aristocracy by purchasing mineral rich lands in the West.

Contending with a terrain that made a trip to the seat of court arduous, county-builders amassed the necessary one thousand petitioners and sought boundary changes that would assure most people of a courthouse within one day's ride. Citizens continued to petition successfully for the formation of new counties. The 1851 concessions to the West were too little, too late, to save Virginia if such was even possible. From Dr. Ambler's meticulous work, modern students of West Virginia history can readily appreciate the inevitability of West Virginia statehood.

---

[13] Otis Rice, *The Allegheny Frontier, 1730–1830* (Lexington: University Press of Kentucky, 1970); Barbara Rasmussen, *Absentee Landowning and Exploitation in West Virginia, 1760–1920* (Lexington: University Press of Kentucky, 1994).

INTRODUCTION TO THE 2ND EDITION	XXV

Ambler coupled his analysis of voting patterns with an explanation of the role played by the mountains, rivers, flat lands, coal, oil, gas, and limestone. His work points out that it was easier for Thomas Jefferson and James Madison to forge a nation than to mend a state. The great Virginians were successful in helping to bind thirteen states into a sovereign country, but the vast economic potential of the West so frightened them that they were unable to reunite a sectionalized Virginia. It was not for lack of trying, however; Ambler takes great pains to explain the efforts expended by Madison, Jefferson, and James Monroe in the interests of Virginia state politics. In discussing the Virginia Constitutional Convention of 1829, he demonstrates that prestigious Virginians—Monroe, Madison, John Randolph, John Marshall, L.W. Tazewell, and Governor William Branch Giles—despite their loyalty to the Old Dominion—could not come to grips with the economic potentials of its West.[14] In between the lines we see the inevitable problem of slavery that beleaguered all Virginians, those in the West most of all. Without a tariff and without transportation enhancements the iron and salt industries soon were in decline, undone by competitors who could rely on the Ohio River to move their production. Tied to the interior, the Ellicott family's iron works along the Cheat River and Ruffner's salt industry in Kanawha County were out of business by 1847. On the Ohio, Wheeling's industries were flourishing from the northern demand for railroad iron, nails, and

---

[14] Ambler, *Sectionalism*, 150.

glass.¹⁵ Water transportation was the key to successful manufacturing. Yet, the transportation improvements that the western industries required would have been extraordinarily expensive. In the 1780s, George Washington pondered a canal to link the Monongahela River and the Potomac River. He also proposed a road/canal link between the James River and the Kanawha River. The enormity of the projects doomed them—geography again—but it is instructive to remember that long ago Indians, French, British, and Americans each coveted the vast wealth promised by the West. Such an empire as this was worth fighting for, and no one shied away from that prospect except the Quaker-led state of Pennsylvania. It is a brutal irony for West Virginia that even as the low country lawmakers were refusing democratization of the state government, many of them were acquiring vast land holdings in the West, committed to the idea that the best way to control an empire is to own it. This is an example of the "many defiles" that historian John Alexander Williams sees woven into the history of West Virginia.¹⁶

Ambler completed his dissertation in 1908 under the direction of frontier historian Frederick Jackson Turner. Ambler acknowledges the assistance and support of southern historians Ulrich B. Phillips, W. E. Dodd, and W. L. Fleming. Ambler's original manuscript has apparently been lost; only the published version ap-

---

¹⁵ Crofts, "Late Antebellum Virginia Reconsidered," 256.

¹⁶ John Alexander Williams, "The New Dominion and the Old: Ante-Bellum and Statehood Politics as the Background of West Virginia's 'Bourbon Democracy'" *West Virginia History* 33:4 (July 1972): 317–407.

pears to exist, so we do not know how far the published version strays, if at all, from the student submission, although he added two chapters when the University of Chicago published the work in 1910. Ambler's professors were eminent early craftsmen of American history whose writings were highly successful in pointing scholars, including Ambler, in many new directions in the study of American history. Their eyes and their pens, except for Turner, were focused clearly and exclusively on the American south. Interestingly, Ambler's papers contain carefully typed outlines of Turner's lectures at Wisconsin.[17]

Dodd was Jefferson Davis's principal biographer, and wrote *The Cotton Kingdom—a Chronicle of the Old South* (Philadelphia, 1907). Ambler met him in person only after his own work was completed.[18] Fleming was a southern Reconstruction historian. His *Documentary History of Reconstruction, Political, Military, Social, Religious, Educational and Industrial from 1865 to the Present Time* (Cleveland, 1906) was available to Ambler the student. The influence of these historical philosophies is readily evident in his work, although he cites only one article each by Phillips and Fleming in his bibliography. Ambler does not cite Turner, who perhaps influenced him the most, at all.

Sectionalism makes some breathtaking departures from the doctrines of Ambler's masters. Ambler says very little about slavery, outside of discussing the con-

---

[17] The Papers of Charles H. Ambler, A & M 1010, West Virginia and Regional Collection of the West Virginia University Libraries.

[18] Ambler Papers, A & M 1010, Box 35, Folder G.

temporary opposition to the slave trade, and western rejection of the institution, yet Dodd was an apologist for the practice. Ohio-born Ambler originally intended to write a history of West Virginia, but he became captivated by the sectionalism he discovered in voting patterns and instead concentrated on analyzing the political struggle that led to the division of Virginia. Late in his career, Ambler did write a complete history of the state. Although sixty years out of date, it is the best such work that exists.

We know by Ambler's comments in the forward to *Sectionalism* that these scholars and West Virginia's first archivist, Virgil A. Lewis, were instrumental in helping him formulate the thought that led to his work. Lewis wrote a history of West Virginia in 1901, but his major contribution to Ambler was in helping the scholar to navigate the state archives. Over the decades, multiple scholars have cited Ambler in their studies dealing with frontiers, political dissolution, the rise of cities, the settling of the West, the American frontier, and the American Revolution. He also wrote on those subjects prolifically. Although he, himself, never explicitly pointed fingers about the misery that grew in West Virginia because of the rapid industrialization of the late nineteenth and early twentieth centuries, he laid a very strong foundation for subsequent scholars who did. Armed with *Sectionalism*, later historians revisited West Virginia history and challenged much of the earlier traditional written history of the state, consciously molded, in fact, by twentieth-century politicians, beginning with Governor J. J. Cornwell, who looked to the public school curriculum to train a patriotic West Virginian, not necessarily a thinking one.[19] Soon thereafter, Governor Homer A. Holt institutionalized the gubernatorial practice of concealing industrial disasters and coddling the extractive industries.[20]

Writing in a time when industrialization was king in the state, Ambler did not examine the history of taxation patterns, immigration, working conditions, or industrial hegemony. He only subtly assigned causality to West Virginia's conditions; he noted the engrossment of landownership, but that was enough for his successors. His political history helped to unearth new sources for West Virginia history which by the 1970s and 80s resulted in more studies that probed the state's economic torpor, labor history, industrial abuses, and corrupt politics as well as its heroic citizens, spectacular beauty, and rugged wilderness.

Ambler's scholarly roots reached deep into the perspectives of the Old South, but his wings took flight in a different direction. Modern students of West Virginia and of the Appalachian region rely heavily on his studies of Thomas Ritchie, Waitman T. Willey, Francis Pierpont, and John Floyd, because these four men each made unique contributions to the formation of the new state of West Virginia. Only someone as well-grounded in the state's history as Ambler was would know how

---

[19] Hennen, The Americanization of West Virginia.
[20] Thomas, Jerry B. "'The Nearly Perfect State': Governor Homer Adams Holt, the WPA Writers' Project, and the Making of '*West Virginia: A Guide to the Mountain State*,'" *West Virginia History* 52 (1993): 91–108.

very influential these four individuals were.

Ritchie was the editor of the *Richmond Enquirer* who spent his career injecting "leaven" into the Federalist, aristocratic society of the Tidewater that dominated Virginia. He often wrote about the conditions of the West and the undemocratic ways of Virginia's government. He could get away with it because he was himself a member of the Richmond aristocracy, which often derided but could not muzzle his newspaper. Willey, a lawyer from Monongalia County, was the state's first U.S. senator and helped construct the new state's reluctant position against slavery—a requirement for statehood. Pierpont, a founder of what became Consolidated Coal Company, became the governor of loyal Virginia and secured permission from the mother state for the formation of West Virginia. John B. Floyd, as governor of Virginia and as a Confederate General, influenced the West in numerous ways, not always prudently. His military caprice ultimately contributed a great deal of real estate to the area that became West Virginia.

Ambler placed West Virginia history in the context of national history and national political influences. He examined voting records on the ratification of the federal constitution, the Virginia Resolves, the tariff of 1828, the presidential elections of 1824 and 1828, the slavery debates of 1829–30, and other important referendums, which delineate very clearly that the political and economic perspectives of the Tidewater were diametrically opposed to those of the West.

One of the most contentious issues between the sections was the paucity of banking services in the West.

The conservative easterners preferred to increase the capital of the Bank of Virginia, not charter new banks. Not until the Whig legislatures after 1838, did banking come to the West. By that time, western entrepreneurs had strong financial ties to Baltimore, Philadelphia, and Pittsburgh, not Richmond or Norfolk.[21] This early alliance served post-statehood industrialists well, because it created a source for the vast capital that they would need to drive the industrial transformation of the West.

It is interesting to speculate on the influences Ambler's teachers exerted over their student, particularly given their deep southern roots. Phillips' *American Negro Slavery* was the first systematic study of the southern labor system. A Georgian by birth, his sense of place informed his social perspectives. Slavery, in his view, was a benevolent social system that brought order and discipline to an aristocratic way of life, while benefiting a less capable race of humans. Economically, he viewed slavery as a disaster for the south, but could not bring himself to set aside a personal racial prejudice. Racism was pervasive in the United States in the early twentieth century, and his perspective on the institution probably reflected broad public sentiments. Besides, he noted, slaves must have been content, because so few of them resisted their bonds. This theory endured in historical scholarship for decades after the turn of the twentieth century, before Herbert Aptheker's *American Negro Slave Revolts* (1943) challenged that premise. Ambler did not take up Phillips' torch. He treated the economic inter-

---

[21] Ambler, *Sectionalism*, 239.

ests of the slaveholders and the mountaineers with an equally dispassionate objectivity. Historian Ronald Lewis sees Ambler's work as significant for what it did, but also for what it did not do.

Still, without Phillips, there could have been no Ambler, no deeper digging, and no challenge to the old presumptions. First, Phillips demonstrated in his work that the power of place is one of the most overarching influences of the human experience. His sense of place drove his sense of history. Secondly, his articulated theories of racial inequality and economic disaster in the south induced skepticism in younger scholars who looked for other explanations and other evidence.

We see these two inheritances in Ambler's work. He too, is a proponent of the destiny of place, and he used sources that challenged existing (1910) interpretations of the creation of the new state. *Sectionalism* illustrates why planters defended slavery and why mountaineers decried it. He shows that by 1818, Virginia was essentially already two places. His discussion of western Virginia's animosity to slavery and eastern Virginia's embrace of it rests largely on questions of economic interest, not social control. Subsequent scholarship by Daniel Crofts and John C. Inscoe challenged that idea. They cited the 1860 presidential election in which many western Virginians yielded to their racial insecurities and voted for the southern fire-eater John C. Breckenridge rather than Abraham Lincoln or Stephen A. Douglas; either Douglas or Lincoln would have been far more likely to gratify the West's need for internal improvements. Many southern mountaineers, generally of the impression that slaves were "vile saucy things," preferred to have their blacks in bondage, if they were to have blacks at all.[22]

Frederick Jackson Turner's contributions to Ambler's philosophy are largely conceptual, providing the idea of "sections" as a focus of study. Ambler likens Virginia's west to a frontier demonstrating that its youth, economic vitality, and democratic outlook posed a very real threat to the eastern aristocracy. Western Virginia, as revealed by Ambler, does not fit seamlessly into a Turnerian definition of a frontier, however. Many national and regional scholars have adopted Turner's Frontier Thesis of American history, but his theories did not convince everyone. His colleagues criticized him for misunderstanding the order of development of the growing American nation. He looked at westward expansion as a uniquely American phenomenon, suggesting that the seemingly endless expanse of unclaimed (except by Native Americans) western territory offered endless blessings—a safety valve against social unrest, unending resources for development, and the kind of environment that created a new man entirely: an American. Quite unlike Europeans, Turner saw a unique destiny for Americans as they rode the waves of frontier westward.[23] Even as life on the frontiers varied according to time

---

[22] Daniel W. Crofts, *Reluctant Confederates: Upper South Unionists in the Secession Crisis* (Chapel Hill: University of North Carolina Press, 1989), 83; John C. Inscoe, *Mountain Masters: Slavery and the Sectional Crisis in Western North Carolina* (Knoxville: University of Tennessee Press, 1996), 110.

[23] Frederick Jackson Turner, *The Frontier in American History* foreword by Wilbur R. Jacobs (Tucson: University of Arizona Press, 1994), xiii.

and place, the fact of the frontier and the endless opportunities it presented was a unifying force in defining the true nature of America, serving to overcome serious sectional differences within the nation's vast expanse. Ambler backed away from that in *Sectionalism*; relentless sectional strife was the only issue he studied.

He learned from Turner to look closely at Virginia's empty spaces. When he did so, Ambler discovered the nearby frontier that so frightened the eastern establishment. Turner taught Ambler to look at the West without the patriotic baggage of "dominion." The economic colossus that was waiting west of the Allegheny Front needed no platitudes about stoic mountaineers and Spartan, fundamentalist thinking. Ambler saw, and measured, the substantial gap between East and West. *Sectionalism* is the foundation document for West Virginia history. Yet Ambler's contributions to history continued long after publication of *Sectionalism*. His participation in the careful editing of the debates and proceedings of the West Virginia constitutional convention in the 1940s helped set aside the popular assumption that moral disdain for slavery drove the statehood movement. He also debunked the myth that "the Methodist Church made West Virginia." In a later article, Ambler allowed as how the Methodists made most of the noise at the statehood convention, but Peter G. Van Winkle, a New York-born railroad tycoon, made most of the decisions.[24] Ambler's interpretations of sectionalism in Virginia encouraged the historians of the

---

[24] Charles H. Ambler, "The Makers of West Virginia" in *West Virginia History* 2 (July 1941): 267–78.

late twentieth century who based much of their interpretations of the state's history on social class struggle and resource allocation. *Sectionalism* gave these historians new angles of sight. James Morton Callahan, Otis Rice, Ronald Lewis, Altina Waller, Ken Fones-Wolf, and John Hennen have used Ambler's perspective to inform their own work. Even those writers who look at other aspects of West Virginia's history do so with the vocabulary of sectionalism that Ambler generated.

Professor Dodd's influence upon Ambler is less easy to see, but we do know that he applauded the younger historian. Writing in a 1910 review of *Sectionalism*, he said that, "though it professes only to review those matters which entered into or bore upon the long sectional quarrel between the eastern and western parts of the state, taken altogether, it is the best history of the Old Dominion since 1776 we have; for the sectional quarrel there, as in the nation at large, was the dominant issue of every crisis, of almost every legislative session."[25] Dodd also praised Ambler's handling of the rise of the national Republican Party, "which must be welcome to students of Virginia history who have not hitherto had the tangled personal politics of the so-called era of good feeling analyzed and cleared up." He also made much of Ambler's "unbiased and detached judgment, devotion to truth, and clear historical insight."[26]

Ambler gets right to the point about sectionalism in his opening paragraph, "The surface of Virginia is

---

[25] William E. Dodd, review of *Sectionalism in Virginia 1776–1861* in the *American Historical Review* 16 (1910): 150.

[26] Dodd, Review, 151.

divided into two un-equally inclined planes and a centrally located valley."[27] He forges on, dividing the eastern plane into the Piedmont and the Tidewater, and dividing the western plane into the Alleghany Highlands, the Cumberland Plateau, and the Ohio Valley section. In between the planes lies the Valley that contains "numerous smaller sections, including the Chinch, Holston, New, and Shenandoah." Subsequent paragraphs dispassionately recite the geology, geography, elevation, and topography of each of the regions he has drawn so that the reader, two and a half pages later, understands which rivers may accommodate large boats, and which require small boats. He understands which of their shores will support crops of grains or grass or fruits or tobacco, and which will not. He understands where there is coal.

In the trans-Alleghany (his spelling), Ambler recounts, there is great and untold natural wealth consisting of minerals, soils, and stone. With navigable rivers to carry this wealth from the section's heart to the Louisiana Delta, and thence to the markets of the world, Virginians, and others, could not resist the lure of western fortune. Ambler identifies a coherent political philosophy in the West that centered on the need for internal improvements and industrial development. The potential economic power of the West had ample capacity to gore the aristocracy. Sectional antagonism within Virginia resulted because of political disagreements about how to reconcile slavery with the state's inexhaustible economic potentials. Ambler further bends the Turnerian ideal by the end of page three, "As population ex-

[27] Ambler, *Sectionalism*, 1.

tended to the westward and became more diverse in nationality, the contrasts and conflicts between the older and newer societies became more pronounced."[28] This is quite a departure from Turner, who saw the frontier as a place of resolution, not conflict. Anticipating historical inquiry into social class relations by more than half a century, Ambler observed that later comers to Virginia, the Scotch-Irish, Germans, and Irish, brought different ways of life with them, and saw themselves differently than the Virginians of English descent. They certainly were of different faiths. As Catholics, Presbyterians, Methodists, and Baptists, they chafed under Virginia's established Episcopalian religion.

In Ambler's view, Virginia's history is comprised of three eras, each of which ended with discord along the western frontier caused by demands upon the legislature to grant political concessions to the region. The first era lasted sixty-nine years, from initial settlement in 1607 until the reforms that followed Bacon's Rebellion in 1676. That uprising occurred largely because Governor Berkeley ignored the aspirations of Virginians living along the Piedmont frontier. The second phase began when settlers in the Piedmont demanded a share in the government of Virginia and ended in 1830, when the constitutional convention refused to apportion the legislature more democratically. The third period began when the Transmontane demanded a voice in government and ended in 1861 with the Civil War and the creation of West Virginia.[29] Ambler's sec-

---

[28] Ambler, *Sectionalism*, 3.
[29] Ambler, *Sectionalism*, 3–6.

tional descriptions also draw some distinctions between social classes in Virginia. On the eve of the American Revolution, the upper class of the Tidewater claimed historical privilege as aristocrats and would not accede to the West's demands. By 1830, he wrote the third phase of sectional strife was largely a struggle between those who lived west of the mountains and those in the East. This division also separated large farms from small farms, new society from older society, homogenous English descendants from the descendants of multiple immigrant groups, and southern economic perspectives from northern ones. This view presaged new areas of historical inquiry that have broadened the discourse. Shade's *Democratizing the Old Dominion* exhaustively explores this context, relying partly on Ambler to set up his own argument that trouble in Virginia was political, not economic. He contends that the rise of political parties in Virginia between the years of 1833 and 1840 exposed Virginians to the Jacksonian Democrats and the Anti-Jacksonians who became Whigs. Heightened political involvement in these years allowed for the growth of partisanship and sharpened political lines on national issues that also had their impact on state issues. Virginia's Democrats were vocally pro-slavery, while Virginia's Whigs looked more to economic development and moral reform.[30] Although Virginia's economy was flourishing on its own, Virginians themselves clung to an unproductive political behavior that ignored the real issue before them. Besotted by slavery, Virginia's Democrats could see nothing else coming.

[30] Crofts, "Late Antebellum Virginia Reconsidered," 270–71.

In the western mountains, politicians grew ever more outraged and shrill in their demand for political equity. Their ultimate brittleness in debate worsened the strife. John George Jackson of Harrison County worked hard to turn westerners into Jeffersonians.[31]

Ambler applauded the rise of the new Virginia leaders "born in the democratic air of the mountains" and their perspectives that were so influential in the movement toward American independence.[32] The nation's Virginia founders, he reminds, were from the Piedmont, not the Tidewater. Thomas Jefferson and James Madison were from Virginia's second families, although Jefferson was the son of Jane Randolph. Jefferson, Ambler wrote, was particularly "fitted for leadership" in the revolutionary era. Many of Virginia's conservatives knew and admired Jefferson and they trusted him at first. "The secret of Jefferson's ability as a leader at this time lay . . . in the fact that he was a democrat of the frontier type. . . . He loved simplicity and equality." As a "precocious child of a frontier surveyor," Jefferson embraced the political outlook of the dissenters, not the Tidewater aristocracy. His contributions to the 1776 Virginia constitution included townships, free schools, and contemplated emancipation of slaves. These suggestions alienated the aristocracy and branded Jefferson as a radical whose ideas ultimately drove Patrick Henry away from the ideas of reform and revolution.[33]

---

[31] Charles H. Ambler, *West Virginia the Mountain State* (New York: Prentice-Hall, 1940), 187.

[32] Ambler, *Sectionalism*, 31.

[33] Ambler, *Sectionalism*, 34.

While studying at Princeton, James Madison became enamored of the principles of religious toleration and opposed many of the changes to the Virginia state constitution in 1776. Their mutual agreement on religious toleration was the beginning of much political collaboration between Jefferson and Madison. The level of resistance that the Tidewater exerted in defense of established religion was fierce, but compared to the political struggle to protect slavery, the remonstrance was nothing.

Ambler explained that the first challenge confronting the Virginia assembly in 1776 was the established church in Virginia. Frontier Baptists, Methodists, and Presbyterians, opposed the established Episcopal Church, but the planters who had renamed their Anglican faith after the revolution defended it. While radical lawmakers were successful in suspending the salaries of the state church in 1776, they were not able to disestablish it until 1779, when Jefferson's tireless efforts to unhinge state religion were partly successful. Final triumph came in 1799. Ambler seems to be suggesting that when people argue about religion, it is really about something else—in this case, taxation. Dissenters loathed paying taxes to support other men's heresy.

Other assaults upon the aristocracy came in the form of eliminating entails, the practice of keeping an estate intact in perpetuity. "It would be almost impossible to overestimate the effect of this law in producing democratic equality in Virginia," Ambler wrote.[34] Jeffer-

---

[34] Ambler, *Sectionalism*, 33.

son's observation that life belongs to the living helped end the practice that would have ensured a hereditary elite—or aristocracy—in America. The Tidewater aristocracy lost many of its prerogatives as the deferential society of Virginia began to change in the years after the Revolution, so protecting their few remaining advantages was extremely important to them, particularly their domination of the legislature. Some reformers in Virginia balked at the end of entails and pulled back into the conservative planter group, which generally had opposed a complete break with England, Dunmore's outrage notwithstanding.

Even the diplomatic Jefferson could not find a way to extract concessions from the East—at least for as long as his former compatriot Patrick Henry was in the legislature to bedevil him. When Henry lost the leadership of the western delegation to the constitutional convention, he became more conservative and allied his interests with those of Edmund Pendleton and Robert Carter Nicholas. Henry's change of heart triggered a permanent breach between himself and Jefferson.

In his 1790 *Notes on the State of Virginia,* Jefferson illustrated that Virginia democracy was appallingly unbalanced, with the East firmly holding on to an inordinate amount of power. Jefferson continued his calls for reform by pointing out anti-democratic tendencies in Virginia that Ambler quantified more than a century after Jefferson wrote his study.

Ambler reminds his readers that although the U.S. Constitution was largely the labor of western (Piedmont) Virginians, Tidewater aristocrats who were very leery of so much democracy guided the state's ratification vote. Concessions, including protections for slavery and a bill of rights, were required before the state accepted the document.[35] The ratification vote in Virginia reflected sectional perspectives. The Tidewater split its vote, but most of the West voted for ratification, an evenly divided Monongalia County being the exception. The Kanawha Valley, Southside, and most of Kentucky, all sparsely populated, rejected the document. These frontier places were teeming with land speculators, settlers, and adventurers, none of whom wanted a government of any kind, let alone a strong one, because they found unique opportunities for wealth and land swirling in the frontier chaos.[36]

The years between 1789 and 1812 saw tumult in Virginia's political alliances. The Jeffersonian Republicans ascended in state affairs as well as national ones, but by 1812, Federalists regained some seats in the Tidewater and along the Kanawha River. This shift tends to reflect the location of wealth in Virginia. Traditionally, the Tidewater planters were wealthy and conservative, but by this time, the great salt industry in the Kanawha Valley and iron furnaces in Monongalia County were also making adventuresome men wealthy.[37]

Western calls for reform most likely came from Federalist voices as well as Republican ones. Internal improvements, banks, greater representation in the general assembly, and universal white male suffrage remained

---

[35] Ambler, *Sectionalism*, 52.
[36] Rasmussen, "Anarchy and Enterprise," 1–2.
[37] Ambler, *Sectionalism*, 93.

the West's enduring demand, transcending other political differences in the region. So persistent were western complaints that some observers saw the Northwest as a serious problem to Virginia. By 1816, the *Alexandria Herald* newspaper proposed dividing Virginia into two states. There were increasingly shrill calls for dismemberment of the state, made formal in the August 19–23, 1816, Staunton convention.[38]

Ambler's skillful development of the concept of sections and his ability to tie them to political action and economic objectives is one of the major legacies of this work. He shows us a Virginia that is articulate, politically focused, and economically concerned within each of the great sections, and demonstrates with great clarity that for Virginia, the center could not hold. The constant struggle of western Virginia for economic and political equality with the East, the steady drone of newspaper editorials castigating the Richmond government, and the constitutional conventions that gave with one hand and took with another tended to instill western Virginians with more resolve and less resignation. Virginians carved their sectional identity as finely as their social class identity. Pittsburgh, Cincinnati, and Louisville, and their appetites for what western Virginia produced in abundance, lured the West toward economic alliances that turned commerce away from Richmond. Because of the continental divide, the navigable rivers of the West flow north and west until they meet the Ohio. Nothing west of the Allegheny Front in Virginia pointed to the Atlantic Ocean, while everything east of the front did. This real-

[38] Ambler, *Sectionalism*, 94.

ity left eastern and western Virginians back to back, their visions opposed, somewhere atop of Cheat Mountain in Randolph County, very early in the nineteenth century.

Ambler's interpretation of Virginia sectionalism echoes in the writing of West Virginia historian Otis Rice, who accepted the concept of sectionalism as a strong explanation for the state's enduring economic difficulty. He built on Ambler's theme in his 1970 work *The Allegheny Frontier, 1730–1830*, and expanded the conversation to discuss some of the troubling aspects of West Virginia history that Ambler pointed to but did not pursue, particularly the "alienation of the land," as Rice explains. In the century Rice studied, Virginia conveyed a great many land grants in the West. This practice perhaps hurt West Virginia more than any other single phenomenon, in his view. Ambler earlier wrote that "engrossment of the most desirable lands" offers a "possible explanation for West Virginia's retarded development."[39] While the state was conveying small parcels of land to settlers and soldiers, it was also conveying huge parcels of unsurveyed territory to a few powerful speculators. The Virginia land law of 1730 stipulated the terms of actual settlement in the West, but provided no means whereby a settler could secure his claim from the rapacious appetites of speculators like Thomas Walker or Andrew Lewis. Rice's argument, based upon the historical approaches of Turner and Ambler, provides yet another example of how the sectionalized perspective of Virginians influenced politics and land law.[40]

[39] Ambler, *Sectionalism*, 44–5.
[40] Rice, *The Allegheny Frontier*, 118–122.

Richard Orr Curry uses the concept of sectionalism to inquire into West Virginia's past from another direction and embellishes the Ambler argument with another intriguing perspective. He includes Ambler in the group of historians he labeled "pro-Union apologists."[41] Pro-Union historians were correct about sectionalism, he wrote, but they did not understand the nature of the sectional divisions that were operating in 1861. By then, the Northwest contained a population of 210,000, far more than the rural southern counties. Curry examined the idea of sectionalism and suggested that its changing pattern was its main characteristic.[42] Yet, looking at the immediate antebellum period, he drew the sectional lines much the way Ambler did, with one important exception. Curry looked at the demographics of the pro-statehood counties, finding that twenty-four of the northwestern counties favored a new state, while twenty-five of the other counties that ended up in West Virginia voted for secession from the Union. That observation, pregnant with possibilities, lies undeveloped in Curry's treatise. Did Virginia abandon the twenty-five pro-secession counties or did West Virginia kidnap them? Moreover, what would have been the reasons?

It is not too preposterous to look at the occupations of the founders and the dates on the geological surveys conducted by Virginia in the 1820s to build an argument that the leading state-makers were industrialists foremost and were preparing for a postwar industri-

---

[41] Richard Orr Curry, "A Reappraisal of Statehood Politics in West Virginia" *Journal of Southern History* 28 (1962): 403.

[42] Curry, "Reappraisal of Statehood Politics," 412.

alization that would not fare well under the plantation mentality of the Confederacy. Mudsill workers would be available also in the event of a Union victory, in the persons of the freed slaves. A Marxist historian would find much to investigate in the statehood proceedings of 1861–62, by which date the mineral wealth of the West was widely known. Governor Arthur I. Boreman of Parkersburg owned a coal mine, as did "Loyal" Virginia Governor Francis Pierpont of Fairmont. New York native Peter G. Van Winkle was president of the railroad that connected the Baltimore and Ohio line to Parkersburg. Whig Waitman T. Willey was "soft" on slavery, which cast doubt upon his loyalty to the Commonwealth. J. N. Camden, initially a southern sympathizer and owner of vast lands in the West, took no part in the statehood proceedings but he watched them carefully and soon sold his oil fields to John D. Rockefeller, retired to enter politics, and spent the remainder of his career defending the interests of the oil industry. Henry Gassaway Davis, a Maryland native and Civil War profiteer, also watched from the wings while quietly using his wife's inheritance to gather land and money. He served in the state's first legislature and soon arrived at the U.S. Senate to replace Willey. Naturalist and industrialist William H. Edwards had already partitioned Nicholas and Kanawha counties to create Clay County, which was ardently pro-Confederacy, yet chocked full of coal. The first Clay County deed book deals with Edwards' ejectment proceeding against a farmer whose family farm was generations old.[43] That farm ultimately

[43] Rasmussen, *Absentee Landowning*, 57–59; Clay County West Virginia

became the property of the Paint Creek Coal Co. Thirty years later, Democrat Camden revealed his colors when he lost an election to the U.S. Senate; he confided to an associate that "at least we'll make a lot of money" with Republican coal baron Stephen B. Elkins representing the state in Washington.[44] These industrialists, though few in number, were supported by others, and were without doubt the most powerful men in West Virginia during the 1860s and 1870s. They also helped to write the West Virginia State Constitution of 1872, which blatantly favors coal, timber, and railroad interests.

Curry emphasized the contemporary cultural disdain low country Virginians held for the northwest counties of Virginia that Ambler did not. As the Shenandoah Valley swelled with slaves, the West remained economically and philosophically isolated from the rest of Virginia, which eyed the west with suspicion. The Northwest had become a threat, Curry wrote, echoing Ambler.[45] Although Shenandoah Valley political sentiments stayed with the West through much of its antebellum history, that loyalty was gone by 1830. On December 3 of that year, The *Winchester Republican* warned its readers that, "dispute the claims of the Trans-Allegheny counties to what they may deem a proper share of the fund for internal improvements and a division of the state must follow." The paper, branding the Northwest as a disaffected region, urged that Virginia let it go. "Let them go. Let

Deed Book 1, p. 343.

[44] J. N. Camden to A. B. Fleming, Nov. 7, 1900, Aretas Brooks Fleming Papers, A & M 40, West Virginia and Regional History Collection, West Virginia University Libraries, Morgantown, West Virginia.

[45] Curry, "Reappraisal of Statehood Politics," 413.

us get clear of this disaffected population. Then prosecute the improvements called for in the Southwest, and that portion of our state, deprived of its northern allies, would give up its desire for a separation." This position acknowledges the sectionalism of Virginia, but carves the west into two sections—a detested one that could handily join with Pennsylvania or Maryland with little harm to Virginia, and the newly loyal Southwest secured for the south by a railroad. The editorial captured the mood of the times; the Southwest got the Virginia and Tennessee Railroad and other internal improvements well before the Civil War. Few additional improvements accrued to the north, other than the Baltimore and Ohio Railroad, completed to Wheeling by 1857. Denied a route through the Shenandoah Valley, the Baltimore and Ohio came through the Northwest, insuring that Baltimore, Pittsburgh, Philadelphia, and Cincinnati became the Northwest's trading partners. The Southwest and the Valley, placated by their own railroad, other concessions, and the pro-slavery stance of the press and the church turned solidly eastward in sentiment. This "iron road to secession" won the hearts of the Southwest to slavery's cause.[46] The Northwest remained "disaffected" or critical of slavery. Historian Kenneth Noe contends that the schism between northwest and southwest Virginia calls into question the entire sectionalism thesis; however, his own study of the Virginia and Tennessee Railroad demonstrates that the loyalty of the Southwest to the Old Dominion was largely bought with a railroad

[46] Curry, "Reappraisal of Statehood Politics," 414.

and other economic attention late in the antebellum period.[47] Had similar attention been given to the Northwest, perhaps that region would have stayed loyal, also. The schism within one section does not negate the powerful influence of sectional perspectives in Virginia; it strengthens the thesis.

Simmering resentment over tax preferences for slavery and a lack of equal representation in the state senate had the effect of further isolating the Northwest from the rest of the state. Although Curry cites abolitionist talk as an important part of the ultimate statehood movement, time has proven that not to be as important a factor as believed for many decades. The first state constitution sent to congress did not outlaw slavery. The Radical congress returned it for correction and amendment, undertaken by the former Whig slave owner, Willey. However, emancipation proved to be a deal-breaker for many pro-statehood Copperheads in western Virginia, most notably John C. Carlile, Sherard Clemens, and John J. Davis who retired from the statehood effort rather than accept a state that would allow free blacks. Race more than slavery played a large role in the political life of western Virginia, with Copperheads uniting with ex-Confederates after statehood to cement their alliance against the freedmen.[48]

Freehling contends that the debate over representation in Virginia's statehouse was mainly a debate

---

[47] Kenneth Noe, *Southwest Virginia's Railroad: Modernization and the Sectional Crisis* (Urbana: University of Illinois Press, 1994), 2.

[48] Curry, "Reappraisal of Statehood Politics," 419.

over slavery.⁴⁹ She contested Ambler's assertion that challenges to slavery in Virginia came largely from the Trans-Allegheny, demonstrating many examples of abolitionist sentiment in the Piedmont and in the cities of the Tidewater. Otherwise, she carries Ambler's argument forward with her interpretive analysis of the slavery debate that Nat Turner's revolt triggered. In her 1982 *Drift Toward Dissolution: The Virginia Slavery Debate of 1831–32*, Freehling used Ambler's sections as the main framework for her analysis. She referred to the "escalating clamor in Virginia's vast Trans-Allegheny where . . . whites increasingly resented slaveholders' hegemony."⁵⁰ Although her discussion focused only on one event in Virginia's history, Freehling's look at the impact of slavery on economic democracy in Virginia carries all of the language and perspective of Ambler's earlier work. She writes that Ambler cast the sectionalization of the state into an east-west divide too strictly. There was no single lone cry from the West to democratize representation in the state; sectional interests became more intricate and gave rise to efforts of "progressive, under-represented counties in all sections of Virginia to end the disproportionate legislative influence of the conservative Tidewater."⁵¹ Although Freehling criticizes Ambler for what she sees as oversimplifying the issue, she still draws much the same conclusion: economic interests of the various sections of Virginia were unable to democratize

---

⁴⁹ Alison Goodyear Freehling, *Drift Toward Dissolution: The Virginia Slavery Debate of 1831–32* (Baton Rouge: Louisiana State University Press, 1982), 47.

⁵⁰ Freehling, *Drift Toward Dissolution*, xiii.

⁵¹ Freehling, *Drift Toward Dissolution*, 39.

the Tidewater aristocracy short of dissolution of the Old Dominion. Both Ambler and Freehling focus their analyses on the attempts of Virginians to equalize political power throughout Virginia. Both scholars use sectional data to make their points. Both scholars make it clear that there was no way to separate political power from slavery. However, Freehling goes farther to assert that slavery was the principal barrier to political democracy in Virginia. Ambler was content to point to a full menu of differences, mostly political.

McGregor looked at the military vulnerability of the Northwest and Wheeling business leaders as a reason for the statehood movement, which he contends the West did not broadly support. "Troops concentrating at Pittsburgh could penetrate into the very heart of western Virginia simply by going up the Monongahela River," he wrote. "The industrial machinery along the Monongahela and Ohio Rivers was extremely vulnerable, and so were the fortunes that they represented."[52] He contended further that if not for a small group of northwesterners, no disruption of Virginia would have occurred—an argument that is difficult to understand.[53] U. B. Phillips reviewed the work in 1923, with the lively observation that "the tail of the Old Dominion wagged off the whole hind quarter," but an unsigned review in the *Journal of Negro History*, citing McGregor's shrill language, dismissed his University of Pennsylvania dissertation as a polemic.[54]

---

[52] McGregor, *Disruption of Virginia*, 70.
[53] McGregor, *Disruption of Virginia*, 70–71.
[54] U. B. Philips, review, Mississippi *Valley Historical Review* 10

McGregor excoriated the first work of West Virginia history, *The Rending of Virginia* by Granville Davisson Hall, as being partisan and "worthless as history—it is misleading and harmful."[55] John Stealey, however points to Hall's work as evidence that West Virginia statehood was a "failure of statecraft" and that "insidious contradictions" among Virginia's leaders led ultimately to the Commonwealth's rupture.[56] Stealey's observation added new grist to the statehood story. The West's political leadership was brittle and inflexible which did not help deconstruct sectional barriers. *The Rending of Virginia*, Stealey wrote, is an important piece of state history because it is the only existing first-hand account of the proceedings in Wheeling. Hall was the reporter who covered the events. He reported from the perspective of a young man who grew up in a slave-free community in Ohio. *Wheeling Intelligencer* publisher Archibald Campbell recruited him specifically for the post.

Hall, who held various political appointments in West Virginia during his lifetime, found statehood to be a "sublime" accomplishment. He wrote with insights that may have influenced Ambler, noting that all of the commerce in the Old Dominion "divides at the watersheds," alluding even in 1901 to the idea of sectional differences. However, Hall blames slavery for the ultimate bifurcation of the state.[57] To him we owe

---

(December 1923): 331–2; author unknown, *The Journal of Negro History* 8 (April 1923): 239–241.

[55] McGregor, *Disruption of Virginia*, xi.

[56] Granville Davisson Hall, *The Rending of Virginia: a History* reprint (Knoxville: University of Tennessee Press, 2000), xi.

[57] Hall, *Rending of Virginia*, 20.

the longstanding misconception that the abolitionists formed the state. That idea has become a sturdy, but indefensible, historical legend. Hall's distaste for the institution is readily evident in his provocative description of it: "The domestic slave trade is active in Western Virginia. Three miles east of Clarksburg, an ex-governor of Virginia owns a Negro ranch where young Negroes from childhood were corralled, ranged, and fed for the Southern market, almost as if they had been sheep or swine."[58]

James Morton Callahan, a distinguished historian at West Virginia University from 1924–1940, embraced the Ambler theory and carried it forward with bountiful examples of the rancor between the sections of Virginia, emphasizing the bitterness felt by the western counties. He also introduced an economic context to the differences between the state's sections. Citing eastern references to the "peasants" of the mountains, the West deeply resented the comfort with which the eastern aristocracy equated the westerners with their slaves. Callahan thus also anticipated social class relations as an area of scholarly inquiry. "Virginia sectionalism was largely a series of controversies between the gentlemen of the eastern counties who owned negroes, and the farmers of the hill and mountain region who owned no negroes but who usually outnumbered their eastern rivals," he wrote. Callahan also remarked also on the importance of new immigrants into Virginia who were not of English origin. "These new communities of foreign stock were quite unlike those east of the Blue

---

[58] Hall, *Rending of Virginia*, 49–50.

Ridge," he wrote. "Instead of devoting themselves to the production of staples, they became self sufficing."[59] With no real dependency upon the aristocratic planters, western farmers had no use for a patrician culture. The diversity of western communities focused upon commerce and cooperative efforts to locate new markets, he explained.

Politically, Callahan said, a minority of aristocrats were devoted to controlling all segments of Virginia's government because "they felt that a loss of this supreme position in the community would mean the overthrow of slavery, which was probably a correct view of the situation." Slavery in Virginia would have been abolished before 1860 if the state had embraced the standards for representation and suffrage that were commonplace elsewhere in the nation. "If Virginia had abolished slavery there would have been no Civil War and no Reconstruction, so fatal to the interests of both South and North," he wrote.[60] In this, Callahan probably assigned too much significance to Virginia; six states seceded prior to Virginia, among them South Carolina, which was not to be mollified.

Callahan concluded that the transportation needs of the salt industry in the West triggered the process that eventually led to the division of Virginia. However, he also saw damaging sectional issues associated with public education and religion. Western commerce, ed-

---

[59] James Morton Callahan, *History of West Virginia, Old and New, in one volume, and West Virginia biography, in two additional volumes by special editorial staff of the publishers* (Chicago and New York: The American Historical Society, 1923), 315.

[60] Callahan, *History of West Virginia,* 315–316.

ucation, and travel—encouraged by the natural flows of the rivers—looked north and west. Western sons attended universities in Pennsylvania and Ohio, not Virginia. He noted that easterners believed that an education in Virginia for westerners' sons would help heal the rift between the sections, yet the East would not fund a highway to bring the boys to school. Many political decisions protected eastern interests, and the routing of the Baltimore and Ohio Railroad was one of the biggest. It virtually severed the West from the Tidewater. "With the building of the Baltimore and Ohio railroad to the Ohio," Callahan explained, "the trans-Allegheny Northwest became independent of Richmond. Trade could no longer be diverted from Baltimore to Richmond." Few western Virginians visited Richmond; they had no business ties there. They were more comfortable in Baltimore, "where they sold their cattle and bought merchandise. . . . The line of business separation was drawn a quarter of a century before the act of political separation was accomplished," he wrote.[61]

Over the years, resentment between eastern and western Virginia deepened, and every slight or woe was a wedge driven even further into the sectional fissures. Because "the western habit of mistrust and hatred had become second nature, the parting of the ways was inevitable," Callahan wrote. According to the son of Waitman T. Willey, greater Virginia was an incongruous assembly of interests. He said, "It is not strange that the two sections parted. It is strange that they remained together as long as they did."[62]

---

[61] Callahan, *History of West Virginia*, 331.
[62] Callahan, *History of West Virginia*, 334.

Perhaps the most important historiographic departure from the importance of sectionalism in Virginia comes from John Alexander Williams, though he also acknowledges powerful differences among Virginians. He sees much significance in the formation of political parties in West Virginia and the attempts of various factions to gain political advantage. Williams' argument focuses on the state-making era and the preceding ten years. However, he does not address the hard evidence of sectionalized economic interests that drove Virginia politics between American Independence and the Civil War. He contends that geography and long-standing institutions in the Old Dominion brought West Virginia to life. Citing "competing political cultures, one based on modern forms of communication and political organization advancing southward and eastward with the spread of industrialism, the other on a blend of Virginia political customs modified by the social and economic conditions imposed by mountainous terrain. . . ." At bottom, this theory nods to the importance of sectional differences as well. Williams' categorization of West Virginia Democrats into "Regulars, Redeemers, Agrarians, and the Kanawha Ring," supplies additional evidence that perhaps one of the most troubling problems with western Virginia were its brittle and self-focused political leaders with sectional loyalties.[63]

Williams has written brilliantly about the industrial domination of the state's developing economy.[64]

---

[63] Williams, "The New Dominion and the Old," 363.

[64] John Alexander Williams, *West Virginia and the Captains of Industry* (Morgantown, WV: West Virginia University Library, 1976).

Many of his insights have triggered subsequent inquiries into the character and particular interests of the state's founders. He does not set aside the importance of Ambler's theories of sectionalism, but he brings new insights to West Virginia history, thus broadening the historiography. Writing at opposite ends of the twentieth century, Williams and Ambler are the two historians who have studied West Virginia statehood the most closely. Taken together, they point the way to new endeavors in the field. Historical conclusions, Williams wrote three decades ago, "are as likely to be shaped by the kinds of questions we ask as by the kinds of information at hand. Because it will be a long time before historians manage to sort out the definitive answers to the many questions surrounding statehood, surely it is time to start asking them."[65]

With the thorough discrediting of the local colorists' approach to Appalachian history, scholars have indeed begun asking new questions. Ronald Lewis's interest in the coal industry and the labor movement has brought new perspectives to the history of the region. The influence of immigrants on the largely homogenous region has triggered many investigations, most recently by Kenneth Fones-Wolf and Lewis. Kenneth Bailey studied the hiring practices of the coal industry in the early twentieth century. The jaws of the Great Depression bit hard in the mountains and Jerry Bruce Thomas does not waiver in his telling of the politics behind the suffering. John Hennen has shed light on the role of politicians in education, while Altina Waller

[65] Williams, "The New Dominion and the Old," 401–2.

put to rest the mistaken perceptions surrounding the state's most famous feud. Reporter Thomas Stafford, whose memoir constitutes the only modern political history of the state, exposed twentieth century political corruption in the statehouse. Each of these writers has taken state history well beyond a simple accounting of statehood, and that is in large part because they have paid attention to what Charles H. Ambler was saying about politics in Virginia a century ago.[66]

Ambler was born in New Matamoras, Ohio, on Aug. 31, 1876, a son of Lutellus and Ella Rebecca Ambler. He grew up and attended school in West Virginia, professing that, "Quite early in my college career I began to inquire about the causes of the dismemberment of the 'Old Dominion.'"[67] After high school, he taught in the public schools of West Virginia from 1894–1900, when he graduated from West Liberty Normal School. In 1904, he received his B.A. degree from West Virginia University, followed by an M.A. in 1905. He taught social science as a graduate assistant there. Moving on to the University of Wisconsin for doctoral study, he received a Ph.D. three years later, in 1908. He was Profes-

---

[66] Ken Fones-Wolf and Ronald L. Lewis, *Transnational West Virginia: Ethnic Communities and Economic Change, 1840–1940* (Morgantown: West Virginia University Press, 2005); Kenneth Bailey, "A Judicious Mixture: Negroes and Immigrants in the West Virginia Mines, 1880–1917" in *West Virginia History* 34 (January 1973) 141–61; Jerry Bruce Thomas, *An Appalachian New Deal: West Virginia and the Great Depression* (Lexington: University Press of Kentucky, 1998); Hennen, *The Americanization of West Virginia*; Altina Waller, *Feud: Hatfields, McCoys and Social Change*; Thomas F. Stafford, *Afflicting the Comfortable: Journalism and Politics in West Virginia* (Morgantown: West Virginia University Press, 2005).

[67] Ambler, *Sectionalism*, v.

sor Dodd's handpicked successor at Randolph Macon College in 1909, a fact that Ambler only learned of after his appointment there. Of Dodd, Ambler later said, "I learned to appreciate his cleverness in getting the essentials of the situation from a Democratic and liberal viewpoint."[68] Ambler was Professor of History and Political Science at the Virginia school until 1917, when he returned to West Virginia University as a professor of history, where he remained until his retirement in 1946, then becoming Professor Emeritus.

He was a charter member of the WVU chapter of Sigma Nu Fraternity and remained active in alumni affairs throughout his life. He was also active in the West Virginia and Monongalia County historical societies, and Wesley United Methodist Church in Morgantown. Ambler found time to serve on the Morgantown City Council, and was president of the Monongalia County Board of Education from 1933–39. He also served in the West Virginia House of Delegates from 1951–54. He died in 1957 at the age of 81. In the view of local historian Dr. Earl Core, Ambler was an "untiring researcher and author."[69] He wrote prolifically about West Virginia, authoring or editing twenty books and twelve articles for the journal *West Virginia History*. Of particular note are his 1936 *George Washington and the West* and *A History of Transportation in the Ohio Valley, with Special Reference to its Waterways, Trade, and Commerce from the Ear-*

---

[68] August 23, 1954, Charles H. Ambler to Wood Gray, Ambler Papers B 35 F G. WVU.

[69] Earl L. Core, *The Monongalia Story, A Bicentennial History, Volume V Sophistication* (Parsons, WV: McClain Printing Company, 1984), 314–315.

liest Period to the Present Time, written in 1932. However, his first work, *Sectionalism*, remains his best work. It is all the more remarkable because he was a clear-eyed investigator bucking the currents of local color writers who were flooding the markets with damning and incorrect accounts of life in the mountains. Fortunately for generations of West Virginians, Dr. Ambler persevered to discredit them all while handing down to posterity a powerful tool for the study of the birth and the history of the State of West Virginia.

LIST OF MAPS

1. VOTE ON THE RATIFICATION OF THE FEDERAL CONSTITUTION 58
2. VOTE IN THE HOUSE OF DELEGATES ON THE RESOLUTIONS OF 1798 71
3. VOTE OF VIRGINIA'S REPRESENTATIVES ON THE TARIFF BILL OF 1828 122
4. PRESIDENTIAL ELECTION OF 1824 131
5. PRESIDENTIAL ELECTION OF 1828 135
6. VOTE ON THE CONSTITUTIONAL CONVENTION BILL OF 1828 144
7. VOTE BY COUNTIES ON THE RATIFICATION OF THE CONSTITUTION OF 1830 172
8. VOTE OF THE HOUSE OF DELEGATES OF 1831–32 ON THE EXPEDIENCY OF LEGISLATING FOR THE ABOLITION OF NEGRO SLAVERY 199
9. VOTE OF VIRGINIA'S REPRESENTATIVES ON THE TARIFF OF 1832 204
10. VOTE IN THE HOUSE OF DELEGATES OF 1832–33 ON RESOLUTIONS MILDLY APPROVING THE COURSE OF SOUTH CAROLINA ON NULLIFICATION . . . 217
11. WHIG AND DEMOCRATIC STRENGTH AS SHOWN BY THE MEMBERSHIP OF THE HOUSE OF DELEGATES OF 1834–35 222
12. PRESIDENTIAL ELECTION OF 1860 330

PREFACE

My interest in things pertaining to both West Virginia and Virginia is due largely to the fact that I was reared and educated in the former state and born of parents who, like all true Virginians, never forgot the latter, the state of their nativity. Quite early in my college career I began to inquire about the causes of the dismemberment of the "Old Dominion." I then planned to write a monograph upon the "Formation of West Virginia." But a casual search into the preliminaries for this study soon convinced me that they were probably more important than the subject upon which I proposed to write. Accordingly I gave up my original plan for a more difficult undertaking, the study of sectionalism in Virginia during the ante-bellum period. As it would require volumes to present every detail of this subject, I have restricted this monograph mainly to the political differences.

Neither pains nor time have been spared to obtain accurate and exhaustive information. In addition to the suggestions and information kindly given me by scores of old men, who remember the last years of the ante-bellum period, I have tried to obtain, by travel and otherwise, a thorough knowledge of the geography of both Virginia and West Virginia. Besides, I have made research in person in the Department of Archives and History, at Charleston, W. Va., in the Virginia State Library, at Richmond, in the Library of the State Historical Society of Wisconsin, at Madison, and in the Congressional Library. But my chief sources of information have been the legislative documents of Virginia and West Virginia and the public prints. I realize fully the treachery of such sources as the last named, but, all things considered, they are the best that are available for a study of this nature.

The first eight chapters of this study were offered and accepted for my Doctor's dissertation at the University of Wisconsin in 1908. For suggestions, criticism, and the care with which he has read my manuscript I am especially indebted to Dr. Ulrich B. Phillips, of New Orleans, La. My acknowledgments and thanks are also due to Dr. F. J. Turner, of Madison, Wis.; to Dr. W. E. Dodd, of Chicago, Ill.; to Dr. W. L. Fleming, of Baton Rouge, La., and to Mr. Virgil A. Lewis, of Charleston, W. Va. To the many others who have assisted me in various ways, I can here extend only a sweeping expression of thanks.

CHARLES HENRY AMBLER

ASHLAND, VA.
September 6, 1909

CHAPTER I
INTRODUCTION
PART I. NATURAL FEATURES

The surface of Virginia is divided into two unequally inclined planes and a centrally located valley. The eastern plane is subdivided into the Piedmont and the Tidewater; the western into the Alleghany Highlands, the Cumberland Plateau, and the Ohio Valley section. The area between them is commonly spoken of as the "Valley." It is subdivided into numerous smaller sections of which the Chinch, Holston, New, and Shenandoah valleys are the most important.

The Tidewater extends from the Atlantic Coast to the "fall line" on the rivers, i. e., to the line connecting the present cities of Fredericksburg, Richmond, Petersburg, and Weldon. The soil contains gravel, sand, shale, and clay. The Chesapeake and its broad arms are doorways to the sea, the Atlantic rivers being navigable for large vessels to Richmond, Fredericksburg, and Alexandria.

The Virginia Piedmont lies in a right triangle. Its base is the northern boundary of North Carolina; its perpendicular the fall line of the Atlantic rivers; and its hypotenuse the Blue Ridge mountain range. The surface varies from rolling to hilly. The soil is of decomposed rocks of the Archean age and contains gneiss, mica, granite, porphyry, and iron. It is well adapted to wheat, corn, fruits, and tobacco. The only considerable rivers of the Piedmont, the James, Potomac, and Roanoke, are too swift and shoaly to be navigable above the fall line except in short stretches, or for small boats bound down stream.

The Valley is a part of the great Appalachian range of valleys. It is not a river basin, as its name might indicate, but a depressed surface some hundred feet below the top of the Blue Ridge on one side and the Alleghanies on the other. Within this area are hilly elevations which set apart slender valleys many of which are unsurpassed for beauty of scenery and fertility of soil. The soil is of limestone formation and is well adapted to grass, fruit, and wheat. The gaps in the Alleghanies and the Blue Ridge at the headwaters of the Kanawha and James respectively give openings to the east and the west. The rivers of the southern portion of the Valley flow toward the Ohio; those of the northern to the Atlantic. Thus two natural east-and-west thoroughfares join in the central part of the state.

The land west of the Alleghanies slopes very irregularly to the Ohio. The Alleghany Highlands, a portion of this section, is a trough-like area lying between the Alleghany Mountains and the Cumberland Plateau. The famous "Glades," or blue-grass country, is a part of this section. The Cumberland Plateau is the northeastern continuation of the Cumberland Mountains and paralleling the Alleghanies stretches entirely across western Virginia. It has an elevation of from one to two thousand feet, and the surface is very uneven. The Ohio Valley section is the hilly slope from the Cumberland Plateau to the Ohio River. The country here is of rugged hills interspersed by fertile river and creek bottoms. The soil of the bottom land is fertile and well adapted to wheat, corn, rye, oats, and buckwheat.

The trans-Alleghany possesses untold natural resources. Both the Cumberland Plateau and the Alleghany Highlands are underlaid by two or more strata of bituminous coal and contain valuable building-stone. The Ohio Valley section has vast stores of natural gas and petroleum, and its pasture lands are unsurpassed in excellence. The rivers of this section are navigable from their falls in the Cumberland Plateau to the Ohio.

PART II. SECTIONAL DIFFERENCES IN THE COLONY AND POLITICAL CONDITIONS ON THE EVE OF THE REVOLUTION

The history of Virginia has been characterized by sectional antagonism. The natural features of her territory and the different elements in her population made such conflicts inevitable. In the early colonial days, even before population advanced into the Piedmont, the frontier settlers chafed under the rule of the older and more aristocratic planters. As population extended to the westward and became more diverse in nationality, the contrasts and conflicts between the older and newer societies became more pronounced.

For the purpose of study, the history of sectionalism in Virginia may be divided into three periods. The first period began early in colonial history and ended with Bacon's Rebellion and the reforms which

followed. The second began when settlement pushed
into the Piedmont and the inhabitants of that section
demanded a share in the colonial government. The
beginning of its end came with the Revolution and the
accompanying reforms, but the end was not reached
until the making of adjustments by the constitutional
convention of 1829-30. The third period began when
the trans-Alleghany and portions of the Valley demanded a voice in the state government. It ended with
the Civil War and dismemberment.

The first phase was a petty contest between the
newer plantations and counties about Williamsburg
and to the east thereof and the older counties and
plantations above on the James. As in subsequent
contests, so in this one, the inhabitants residing between
the two contending sections cast lot with the newer
and more democratic sections. The crisis, Bacon's
Rebellion, forced the concession of the moderate reforms demanded.

The second phase was a contest on a larger scale
between the newer society of the Piedmont and that
of the older and more aristocratic Tidewater. Under
the changed conditions of the eighteenth century the
inhabitants of the former section had need for legislation and public expenditures neither understood nor
appreciated by the older settlements. The petitions
from the uplands for the construction of roads and
bridges, for improved navigation of the rivers, and
for the erection of warehouses and a more adequate
defense were accordingly passed over with little consideration and less legislation. In time the denial of

these requests brought urgent demands for a greater share in the government and a democratic aversion to the rule of the tidewater aristocracy.[1]

The frontier took advantage of the preliminaries to the Revolution to revolt against the misrule and indifference of conservatism. The time was indeed propitious for a change. The aristocrats could not, or at least they would not, take an aggressive stand against the mother country to which they were attached by the ties of affection, the emolument of office, and the returns of a lucrative commercial intercourse. The old families, the Pendletons, Robinsons, Randolphs, Nicholases, Blairs, and Tylers, accordingly forfeited leadership to a new and younger generation. Henry and Washington, and later Jefferson and Madison, each closely identified with the interests of the interior and of new families, as their names indicate, assumed leadership.[2] Their energies were exerted for independence and a democratic government.

The third phase of sectional strife was mainly a contest between a cismontane and a transmontane people. It was a contest between an older society with its peculiar institutions and a newer society fundamentally different from the older and inadequately represented in the law-making bodies. It was a contest between the owners of large estates and the owners of small farms; between a population largely English and one composed of various nationalities; and between a people whose economic interests and relations

[1] Spotswood, *Letters,* II, 93–103.
[2] Rives, *Madison,* I, 170; Randall, *Jefferson,* I, 195.

were with the South and a people whose interests and relations were mainly with the North. Unable to control the action of the state in 1861, as the lower Tidewater and the Piedmont had controlled the colony in 1676 and 1776, most of the trans-Alleghany withdrew from the state and formed West Virginia.

It is the purpose of this study to give an account of sectionalism in Virginia only from 1776 to 1861. But a sketch of the earlier developments is very necessary as an introduction. Accordingly an effort will be made to trace briefly the settlement of the sections and to call attention to their respective institutions and customs.

The industrial, social, and political life of the Tidewater centered in the large estate.[3] This institution had evolved from an abundance of free land, from the nature of the agriculture adopted, and from the financial failure of the promoters of the colony. About 1616 financial embarrassment compelled the London Company to make land grants to individuals instead of waiting for them to be taken by associations of individuals as originally proposed. Subsequently the discovery of means of curing tobacco in large quantities and the use of indentured servants and negro slaves made tobacco-raising profitable and preserved this method of making land grants, thus giving an impetus to the growth of the individual plantation.

The spread of the plantation system was rapid. Following the favorable treaties made with the Indians

[3] Bruce, *Ec. Hist. of Va.*, I, 569; *idem, Social Life of Va.*, chaps. iii, iv.

in 1622 and 1623 so much land was given to tobacco-growing and the consequent extension of the plantation was so rapid that the Burgesses found it necessary to restrict excessive planting by limiting the number of plants which a landowner might grow and by restricting all trade to Jamestown.[4] But attempts at restriction were futile; the plantations continued to increase in size and numbers. The fertile land along the James was soon taken, and population extended thence to the lower York peninsula, to the eastern shores of the Chesapeake, and finally to the Potomac.

By the beginning of the eighteenth century this aggressive agricultural system had extended along the rivers of the Tidewater and occupied an area almost as large as the present state of Massachusetts. But the continued importation of negroes, the successful contests for Indian lands, and the good prices for tobacco made people impatient to push farther into the interior. Tobacco culture necessitated expansion, the plant requiring great fertility of soil and the finest quality growing only on new lands. Thus when Spotswood came as royal governor, he found a land craze on in the colony not unlike those of more modern times. He too caught the land fever, and in response to the popular demand organized "The Order of the Knights of the Golden Horseshoe," composed of adventurers who were willing to cross the mountains. Already many land grants had been made above the fall line; now numerous others quickly followed.[5]

[4] Hening, *Statutes*, I, 163.
[5] Spotswood, *Letters*, II, 1-80; *Va. Magazine*, XIII, 7.

By 1776 the plantation had become the basis of society and industry in the Piedmont as well as in the Tidewater. Indeed portions of the former section had already become exhausted by excessive cropping. It should be observed, however, that in 1776 the large plantation did not reign supreme in the Piedmont; it was simply the basis of the industrial order. As population advanced to the Piedmont foothills and to the elevated lands between the rivers, wheat, hemp, flax, and corn had become staples and the holdings had gradually decreased in size. Although one and two-thirds times as large as the Tidewater, the Piedmont, in 1790, contained a much smaller negro slave population. Immigrants from the northern colonies, who, as will be shown later, had pushed into the Valley, came into the Piedmont from the rear. For the most part they were conscientiously opposed to slave-holding and consequently did not become tobacco-growers. On the other hand, the poorer whites of the Tidewater had been pushed, by the gradual advance of the plantation, into the less desirable lands of the Piedmont. Lack of ability and the presence of conscientious scruples prevented them from becoming large planters. These elements constituted a large and influential democratic and non-slaveholding population in the Piedmont. The Piedmont counties, Orange, Albemarle, Nelson, Amherst, Bedford, Franklin, Patrick, and Henry, were strongholds of Democracy.

The society which developed in the Tidewater and later extended to the Piedmont, in a somewhat modified form to be sure, resembled that of the mother country.[6] It consisted of several strata separated by no clearly marked lines. Along the large rivers there were the great landowners who lived in a style of luxury and extravagance beyond the means of the other inhabitants. Immediately below them were the "half-breeds," persons descended from the younger sons and daughters of the landed proprietors. They had all the pride and social tastes of the upper class but not its wealth. Then came the "pretenders," men of industry and enterprise but not of established families. The opportunities afforded by an abundance of practically free lands and by commercial ventures had enabled them to accumulate wealth and to gain admission to the highest social ranks. Below these classes were the "yeomen," most of whom were very poor. The system of entail and primogeniture operated to preserve these strata intact.[7] A very large portion of the inhabitants belonged to the Anglican church, which was established by law. The industrial system afforded the planter leisure, and he naturally turned to society and politics. Incomes were not such as to create a voluptuous society, but they did afford the means for a generous hospitality. Men frequently indulged in intemperance but never forgot to practice civility. Social virtues occasionally ran to show and haughtiness; but truth was cherished, and honor was a thing to die for.[8]

In theory the government of Virginia resembled

[6] Bruce, *Ec. Hist. of Va.*, II, 163.   [7] Wirt, *Henry*, 32 ff.
[8] Jefferson, *Notes on Va.* (ed. of 1787), 261–70; Tucker, *Jefferson*, I, 19.

that of the mother country. The Governor, Council, and Burgesses corresponded in their respective functions to the King, Lords, and Commons. Like the English government, that of Virginia was based upon a representation of local units and not a representation of numbers. The theory that a member of the Burgesses represented the commonwealth and not the county which elected him was not unpopular in colonial Virginia.[9] In this respect the political theory of the Tidewater was diametrically opposed to the principles of equal representation for equal numbers which became so strong in the northern colonies and in the Valley of Virginia.

The government of the Tidewater and the Piedmont was indigenous to the colony. At each step of the frontier advance it had adjusted itself to the changing needs of the plantation and to the constant necessity of a vigilant defense. Following the Indian massacre of 1622 the four boroughs along the James became judicial and military units, and the plantations were grouped into districts for similar purposes. Soon the name shire, later changed to county, was applied to these units. The official at first intrusted with the military command now became the county lieutenant and other local officials became the county court. As the counties were extended to the westward they were increased in size. The engrossment of lands, the sparseness of population, and the military regulations[10]

[9] Grigsby, *Va. Constitutional Convention of 1829-30*, 50-80.

[10] Each county was required to provide for its own defense (Hening, *Statutes*, III, 284; Grigsby, *Va. Constitutional Convention of 1829-30*, 327-37; Spotswood, *Letters*, I, December 15, 1710, p. 36).

necessitated larger counties. The practice early developed of giving each county two delegates in the House of Burgesses. An early attempt to preserve political equality between the large and small communities by allowing parish representation proved unsatisfactory and was abandoned.[11]

In many respects the plantation was a self-sufficing institution. Planters had among their slaves carpenters, coopers, blacksmiths, tanners, shoemakers, spinners, and weavers.[12] The plantation furnished the raw material for these embryo manufactures; the surplus only went to purchase foreign luxuries and such articles as could not be made on the estate. All the Virginia planter desired was a free market and credit. To him the patronage of manufacturing on a large scale was a secondary and incidental thing designed chiefly to supply luxuries. In this industrial system ocean commerce stood next to agriculture; it was the sole means whereby a market could be found.

The Northern Neck requires special mention. It was that long narrow peninsula bounded by the Potomac and the Rappahannock and a straight line connecting their sources. In 1661 this immense tract was granted to a proprietor. As a proprietorial government it maintained a semi-independence of the colonial government down to the Revolution, the proprietors having their own land office and enjoying special favors

[11] Hening, *Statutes,* I, 545; II, 357.
[12] Tucker, *Jefferson,* I, 9; Rowland, *Mason,* I, 99; Phillips, "Origin and Growth of Southern Black Belts," *Am. Hist. Rev.,* XI, 803.

in taxation.[13] Besides, the area possessed great natural advantages; the fall line of its rivers was far inland; the soil was fertile; and the low and swamp lands were comparatively less extensive than on the James and the Roanoke.

These favorable circumstances caused the eastern portion of this section to be taken at a very early date by the highest class of planters. Accordingly many Cavaliers found homes there in the Cromwell period. For generations a large and important settlement on the Potomac was spoken of as the "Cavaliers of Chotonk."[14] The custom of making grants for "headrights," so prevalent in other parts of the colony, was not followed by the proprietors, who thus excluded a large number of small landowners from this area.[15] In 1776 the society of the Northern Neck was consequently older and more aristocratic than that of the Piedmont south of the James; the frontier characteristics had long since disappeared, the plantation having spent its force in large areas which were now given up to wheat-raising.[16]

Antipathies naturally arose between this society and the newer and more democratic communities south of the James. The state of feeling existing between the two sections is well brought out in the last will and testament of Thomson Mason, brother of George

[13] Hening, *Statutes,* XII, 111.

[14] DeBow, *Review,* XXX, 77.

[15] Bruce, *Ec. Hist. of Va.,* I, 523.

[16] Hening, *Statutes,* VII, 292; *William and Mary College Quarterly,* XI, 245; DeBow, *Review,* XXVI, 616; *Va. Hist. Mag.,* XI, 230; Howe, *Hist. Coll.,* 354.

INTRODUCTION   13

Mason and an old resident of the Northern Neck. He expressly directed that neither of his two sons be permitted to reside south of the James or below Williamsburg before they had attained the age of twenty-one, "lest they should imbibe more exalted notions of their own importance than I could wish any child of mine to possess."[17]

The Valley was settled largely by Scotch-Irish and Germans.[18] The latter constituted so large an element of the population that it was found necessary to translate the laws into their language.[19] German and Scotch-Irish pioneers began to pour into the Valley about 1726[20] and soon extended settlement along the Shenandoah and the South Branch of the Potomac. The arrival of these foreign nationalities on the frontier at a period before the society and institutions of the coast had reached the Blue Ridge constitutes an important epoch in Virginia's history. The westward advance of her peculiar institutions was thereby interrupted, and a new society, naturally hostile to things Virginian, was planted.

Settlement moved into the Valley in communities. A band of congenial families came and occupied one of the many canoe-shaped valleys; necessity for defense made isolated settlement impossible. Each of the

[17] Rowland, *Mason*, II, 77.

[18] Langmeister, *Leben im Valley in 1752*; Schuricht, *German Element in Va.*; Foote, *Sketches of Va.*, 99–105; Wayland, "The Germans in the Valley of Virginia," *Va. Mag.*, IX, X.

[19] Shepherd, *Statutes at Large*, I, 339.

[20] Kuhn, *German and Swiss Settlements in Pa.*, chap. ii.

larger geographic settlements of the Valley had its "Irish corner" and "German settlement."

The society which developed there was quite unlike that east of the Blue Ridge. Here communities became self-sufficing instead of devoting themselves to the production of the staples. The small villages which sprang up in the midst of the community settlement contained wagon-makers, shoemakers, saddlers, gunsmiths, harness-makers, tanners, etc. Strasburg, Zapp, Hamburg, Hinkle, Chrisman, and Amsterdam were centers of these small communities. Around these villages there were many small farmers. The fertile soil and abundant pastures soon created a surplus of farm products and live stock; a market was then sought. Inadequate means of communication made it necessary for the farmer to feed his hay and grain and to sell only those products which could walk to market.[21] To this commercial activity the inhabitants of the small communities soon learned to look for means of subsistence. Accordingly all interests cooperated in the efforts made to secure good markets and means of access to them. The homogeneity of interests between the smaller sections soon brought cooperation on a large scale.

The industrial life of the Valley centered in the small farm. In 1730 Colonel Carter tried to operate, by the use of slave labor, a tract of sixty-three thousand acres located on the west bank of the Shenandoah. Writing of his failure Kercheval later said: "This

[21] *Richmond Enquirer*, February 23, 1820; *Niles Register*, IX, 152.

fine body of land is now subdivided into many most valuable farms."[22] The German settler desired little more land than he, with the aid of a large family, could cultivate. His skill in agriculture enabled him to preserve its productivity and in some instances to enhance it.

In practice local government in the Valley conformed to that east of the Blue Ridge. The political theories, however, differed very widely from those entertained in the east. The Germans and Scotch-Irish brought to the Valley the sacred traditions of years of religious wars, which taught hatred to an established church, antipathy to a government by the privileged, and a love for civic and personal liberty. To the Scotch-Irish, the political leaders, civil liberty meant freedom of person, the right of fee-simple possession, and an open door to civic honors. They believed that free lands made free peoples who had a perfect right to form free governments.

Home life in the Valley was plain and simple.[23] A shabby log hut with numerous children about the door and the absence of servants and slaves were not signs of a lack of comfort and happiness. The wife and children did the spinning and weaving for the family, and little attention was paid to society. Religion held a prominent place in the daily life. Those churches especially noted for piety, the Presbyterian, Baptist, Quaker, and Mennonite, flourished there. It was only with reluctance that these dissenters gave of their means to support an established church.

[22] Kercheval, *Hist. of the Valley*, 68.   [23] Cutler, *Cutler*, 94.

Both spiritually and commercially the Valley and the Northern Neck were more intimately connected with the North than with the South. Live stock and furs found their chief market in Baltimore and Philadelphia, whence came practically all articles of foreign manufacture.[24] Preachers and teachers from Yale and Princeton had been important factors in shaping the intellectual ideas and social customs. Their pious energies had early turned to the establishment of institutions of learning. In this work Samuel Davies, later president of Princeton, was a pioneer. In the west Princeton became an active rival to William and Mary. In 1747 John Todd, of the Princeton class of that year, founded a classical academy in Louisa County. In the same year a secondary school, which later became Washington and Lee University, was founded in Augusta by John Brown, a Princeton graduate. In 1776 Prince Edward Academy, now Hampden-Sidney College, was founded by Stanhope Smith, of the Princeton class of 1769. Many other educational institutions were founded by teachers and preachers from Princeton and Yale.[25]

During the years immediately preceding the Revolution the Valley and the Piedmont formulated an effective opposition to the political rule of the Tidewater, and sectional parties shaped themselves on both

---

[24] *Debates, Va. Constitutional Convention of 1829-30*, 452.

[25] *William and Mary College Quarterly*, VI, 186; *Washington and Lee Hist. Papers*, No. 5, p. 54; *Report of Com. of Ed. 1895-96*, I, 270.

INTRODUCTION 17

local and national issues.[26] The first stage in the breach between the east and the west came in the years immediately following the protest against the Stamp Act. It was then that the corruption and inefficiency of the former section became apparent, and the west found a leader in the person of Patrick Henry.

Many forces operated at this time to bring the eastern leaders into discredit and to precipitate their political downfall. The indifference, credulity, and aversion to detail on their part permitted corruption and barred the way to reform. Dissenters used tellingly the well-founded charges of corruption against the clergy of the established church. Governor Fauquier's genial manners and democratic practices had won the hearts of many, who following his example gave themselves up to gaming and racing. When the governor made his annual visits to favorite planters "dice rattled, cards appeared, and money in immense sums was lost and won."[27] Writing in 1848 Howison believed that the contagion of Fauquier's influence had not then disappeared from Virginia.[28]

The west led a revolt against these conditions. The occasion came when John Robinson and his associates tried to conceal a deficit in the treasury. Robinson was one of the most opulent of the landed aristocracy; for twenty-five years he had been Speaker of the Burgesses; and he had made large loans on private

[26] Grigsby, *Constitutional Convention of 1788*, in "Va. Hist. Coll.," IX, 49.

[27] Howison, *Hist. of Va.*, II, 47–58.

[28] Wirt, *Henry* (ed. 1838), 37.

account to his personal and political friends. "This prolific business had continued so long that Robinson had finally become a defaulter to an enormous amount; and in order to avert the shame and ruin of an exposure, he and his particular friends . . . . invented a device to be called a public loan office."[29] From this office it was proposed to loan money on landed security, by which means Robinson hoped to transfer his private loans to the public, to hide his defalcation, and to save himself from ruin and exposure.[30]

It was under these conditions that Henry became a member of the Burgesses and the leader of the discontented interior. He was eminently fitted for this new duty. He prided himself upon being one of the common people; in dress, manners, and education he was the popular ideal; his family was intermarried with some of the most prominent new families of the interior; already he had championed the popular side in the parsons' cause and in efforts to defeat the election of corrupt Burgesses. A thorough democrat himself, he taught his constituency that government was instituted solely for the benefit of the governed; that the people were the foundation of political power; and that offices and honors were created for them. His ability as a popular leader finds explanation only in the character of the interior of which he was the spokesman.[31]

[29] Tyler, *Henry* (ed. 1887), 56.

[30] *Va. Gazette*, May 17, 1765; *Journal, House of Burgesses* (ed. Kennedy 1766–69), x–xxi; Wirt, *Henry*, 69–75.

[31] For a different statement see Tyler, *Henry*, 52.

The public loan office was pushed as a measure wise and beneficial, and received the support of many honorable and nonsuspecting Burgesses. It was on the point of passage when Henry, ignorant of its true purpose, arose to condemn the scheme on general principles. "He laid open with so much energy the spirit of favoritism, upon which the proposition was founded, and the abuses to which it would lead that it was crushed in its birth."[32] On the final vote he carried with him all the delegates from the interior counties. The following year Robinson died and his deficit became public. It was not until then that the real significance of Henry's victory became apparent. His popularity at once increased, and the cake of custom was soon broken by the repeated blows which he administered to the aristocracy.

It was in this unpropitious state of things, the east divided against the west, that Henry introduced and carried the Stamp Act Resolutions. Though intended mainly to protest against the actions of the mother country, they were in no small degree the product of domestic conditions. They were carried by the vote of the united interior against the east,[33] led by Peyton Randolph, the king's attorney-general, and Edmund Pendleton, the protégé and bondsman of Robinson. Of the activity of the interior on this occasion Grigsby says: "Had the British policy in Ireland been other than it was, those resolutions might indeed have been

[32] Jefferson, *Writings* (ed. Ford), IX, 339.
[33] Grigsby, *Va. Constitutional Convention of 1776*, 43.

offered, but they would have been rejected by a decisive majority."[34]

The advent of the west to power in 1765 marked an important epoch. Young men like Washington and Jefferson then saw the aristocracy exposed and repudiated. Jefferson, then a man of twenty-three, stood at the door of the Burgesses while the vote on the Stamp Act Resolutions was being taken. When they were declared carried, it was with disgust that he saw and heard Peyton Randolph emerge from the door and with an oath exclaim: "I would have given five hundred guineas for a single vote."[35]

These years mark also a formative period in political ideas. The questions raised by Coke on Littleton and by Blackstone were then being comprehended. Ideas of natural and individual rights continued to grow in favor and to master the minds of political thinkers. Meanwhile young men of aristocratic families refused to rest under the opprobium of corruption and inefficiency and joined the ranks of the reformers. Prominent among such were Richard Henry Lee and George Wythe. A large number of conservatives continued however to oppose a stubborn resistance to the democratic tendencies and to take their cue from the English royalty. Under these conditions the natural aversion of the interior to the rule of kings and the privileged became more pronounced.

The differences between the east and the west were

[34] Grigsby, *Constitutional Convention of 1788*, in "Va. Hist. Coll.," IX, 49.

[35] The resolutions were carried by one vote (Wirt, *Henry*, 79).

INTRODUCTION

not, however, wholly theoretical. The inhabitants of the latter section were impatiently waiting to enter promised land bounties beyond the Alleghanies and desired the Burgesses to push their claims. In the Quebec Act, Dunmore's relations with the Indians, and the Royal Proclamation of 1763, prohibiting settlers and traders to pass beyond the Alleghanies, they professed to see acts designed to deprive them of new homes and to call upon them the wrath of the savage. The inhabitants of northeastern Virginia were also aggrieved at these acts. Because of the engrossing of lands this area was now overpopulated, and the inhabitants, averse as they were to finding new homes in southern Virginia, were looking to the trans-Alleghany country. Washington and Mason had already seen the opportunity which the lands of the new west afforded and were preparing to profit by it as well as to afford an outlet to the congested communities in which they lived.

In 1774 inhabitants of the Valley petitioned the Burgesses for permission to enter the western lands.[36] The following year Augusta County addressed a petition to the Continental Congress praying that Virginia and Pennsylvania be empowered to make treaties with the Indians. On the other hand the east tried to conserve the interests of the mother country. In this work the clergy was particularly active. Beginning with 1760 they conducted more or less systematic persecutions of dissenters until 1775.[37]

[36] *Journal, House of Burgesses* (ed. Kennedy), 1773-76, 127.
[37] James, *Struggle for Religious Liberty in Va.*, 29.

The petitions to the Burgesses also reveal a growing desire on the part of the interior for internal improvements. From the counties of the Piedmont south of the James came requests for warehouses;[38] inhabitants of the Northern Neck desired the improved navigation of the Potomac and a road from Alexandria to the Blue Ridge;[39] a petition from Frederick County suggested that the improved navigation of the Potomac from the head of tidewater "would be productive of great advantages, not only to those who are settled upon the adjacent lands, but to the whole country;"[40] citizens of Frederick and Hampshire complained that they were unable "to supply the King's troops of the western department with provisions because of the extreme badness of the roads from this government to Fort Pitt," and requested that Braddock's road be made a public highway.[41]

Differences between the east and the west perpetuated the sectional parties of 1765. Delegates from fourteen counties, lying wholly or partly in the Tidewater, did not sign the non-importation agreement of 1769, while delegates from but six interior counties did not sign it.[42] Practically the same proportion holds between the delegates of the east and the west

[38] *Journal, House of Burgesses* (ed. Kennedy), 1766–69, 218; ibid., 1770–72, 5, 124.

[39] Ibid., 1766–69, 253; ibid., 1770–72, 206.

[40] Ibid., 1770–72, 252, 258.

[41] Ibid., 1766–69, 100, 109.

[42] Ibid., 1766–69; *Int.*, XLI; Grigsby, *Va. Constitutional Convention of 1776*, 34.

INTRODUCTION

who signed the associations of 1770 and 1774. Of the sectional parties in Virginia in 1775 Grigsby said:

No error is more common than to refer the origin of party division in the Commonwealth to the present convention [1788]. Long before that time parties had been founded, not only on state topics but on those connected with the federal government. From the passage of the Stamp Act to the time when eleven years later an independent state government was formed there had been a palpable line drawn through the parties of the country.[43]

[43] Grigsby, *Constitutional Convention of 1788*, in "Va. Hist. Coll.," IX, 49.

CHAPTER II

REVOLUTION, CONFEDERATION, AND THE CONSTITUTION, 1776-90

With more tangible grievances to redress, the inhabitants of the interior were ahead of the lowlanders in the movement for independence. While the Tidewater men were deliberating on peaceful reconciliation, large numbers in the Piedmont and the Valley were being organized into military companies by such patriots as Hugh Mercer, Horatio Gates, Peter Muhlenburg, Daniel Morgan, and William Drake, who later figured as officers and generals in the Continental army. It was not until Lord Dunmore declared the colony in a state of war, offered freedom to negro slaves and indentured servants, ravaged the country by the use of armed vessels, and burned the chief commercial city, Norfolk, that the inhabitants of the Tidewater seriously thought of armed resistance to British misrule.[1] Even then, some refused to take up arms; they thought the radicals unduly aggressive. Some had sons in English colleges; others enjoyed the emoluments of office; a general spirit of pride in the mother country prevailed; and there was a strong desire to retain the commercial advantages to be derived from a dependence upon her.[2]

[1] Force, *Am. Archives,* 4th series, III, 387, 1385; Bancroft, *Hist. of U. S.,* IV, 254, 320; Hunt, *Madison,* 1.

[2] *Va. Gazette,* April 26, 1776; Frothingham, *Rise of the Republic,* 509.

When the uprising did come, however, it was general. Except in Accomac, Northampton, and Norfolk counties and in the Quaker and Mennonite communities of the interior, there were few Tories in Virginia. May 6, 1776, the House of Burgesses, assembled at Williamsburg, unanimously declared that Great Britain had subverted the ancient constitution of the colony. Accordingly the House of Burgesses was disbanded, and the last official connection with the mother country disappeared.

On the same day another body, consisting largely of the selfsame disbanded Burgesses, and declaring itself a constitutional convention, convened in the very hall of the suspended House of Burgesses. In *personnel* this body represented the two extremes of the Virginia communities. Grigsby speaks thus of it:

You mark, indeed, a variety of character in those manly faces, and in those stalwart forms a various costume. You can tell the men who come from the bay counties and from the banks of the large rivers, and who, from the felicity with which they could exchange their products for British goods, are clothed in foreign fabricks. You can also tell those who lived off from the great arteries of trade, far in the interior, in the shadow of the Blue Ridge, in the Valley, and in that splendid principality . . . . West Augusta. These are mostly clad in homespun or in the more substantial buckskin.[3]

This body had been invited by the Continental Congress to form a new state government and to consider the relations between the colonies and the mother country. The conservatives, with Robert Carter Nicholas and Edward Pendleton as principal spokesmen,

[3] Grigsby, *Va. Constitutional Convention of 1776*, 35.

were not yet ready to sever every bond of dependence. The colonial conventions of 1774 and 1775 had said nothing about independence, and they deemed an irrevocable step unwise. It was useless, however, to try to withstand the tide of popular sentiment. The delegates from the interior county of Buckingham presented the following command from their constituents: "We instruct you to cause a total and final separation from Great Britain to take place as soon as possible;" it also directed them to establish a constitution providing for "a full representation and free and frequent elections."[4] The people of West Augusta, Transylvania, and of the Holston and Watauga valleys sent similar instructions. Led by Henry, the west believed that forbearance had ceased to be a virtue and that independence was not only necessary but inevitable. The fight between the conservatives and democrats began in the very organization of the convention, when Henry's nominee, Thomas Ludwell Lee, contested unsuccessfully against Edmund Pendleton for election to the chairmanship.[5]

The crisis came on May 15, 1776, when Archibald Cary reported those famous resolutions directing the Virginia delegation in the Continental Congress to propose to that body a declaration of independence for the United States and giving the assent of Virginia to the same. Notwithstanding the fact that these resolutions passed without division, they were opposed by

[4] Bancroft, *Hist. of U. S.*, IV, 414; Hunt, *Madison*, 6.

[5] Grigsby, *Va. Constitutional Convention of 1776*, 14; Campbell, *Hist. of Va.*, 644.

a strong conservative minority. George Mason, the master spirit of the convention, later wrote Richard Henry Lee: "One thing is clear in my mind, that the three great resolutions .... were carried by the *western* vote, that is, by the vote of the members living north and west of Richmond, as were the leading measures of reform some years later."[6]

The resolution for independence was accompanied by another which proposed that a committee be appointed to draw up a declaration of rights and a plan of state government. This was carried and the committee was instructed to frame such a plan "as will be most likely to maintain peace and order in the colony and to secure substantial and equal liberty to the people." In the debates on this resolution, sectional differences became very pronounced. But the west was now handicapped; Henry, its leader, was not a constructive statesman, and his oratory availed little in constitution making. Accordingly leadership passed to a more conservative man, the celebrated George Mason, of Gunston Hall.

Mason was untouched by theories of extreme democracy. He had nevertheless a keen sympathy for the principles of English liberty as expressed in the English constitutional documents, and he was in sympathetic touch with the democratic movement in the colony. He was a sound scholar, especially well versed in the legislative and political history of his country. Unlike most of the landed aristocracy, he was free from political ambitions. He was immovable

[6] Grigsby, *Va. Constitutional Convention of 1776*, 44.

in his convictions, forceful and uncompromising in debate. He now stood between the radicals and conservatives, and his ability as a leader of men made him master of the situation.[7]

On May 27, Archibald Cary reported to the convention a Declaration of Rights drawn by Mason. It set forth the principles that all men are born equally free and independent; that all power is by God and nature vested in and consequently derived from the people; that magistrates are the trustees of the people and at all times amenable to them; that government is for the common benefit, protection, and security of the people; that elections of members to the legislature ought to be free; that all men having common interest with and attachment to the community have the right of suffrage and cannot be taxed or deprived of their property for public use without their consent; and lastly, that all men should enjoy the fullest toleration.[8]

Although founded upon political theory and evoked by abuses from abroad these declarations were, in no small degree, the product of ten years of sectional antagonism within the colony. Their sentiments were those which Henry had instilled into the minds of the frontier people; they were the principles which had mastered the minds of Jefferson and Madison, afterward their greatest exponents. *Thoughts on Government* by John Adams, and *Common Sense* by Thomas Paine had fallen upon receptive minds in the Piedmont and the Valley. Requests for freedom of elections

[7] Rowland, *Mason*, I, 235.
[8] *Ibid.*, 240.

and for general suffrage were, as has been seen, a feature of the instructions which the frontier delegates bore to the convention. Baptists and other dissenters petitioned for toleration in the new government and tried to secure the election of delegates favorable thereto.[9]

Robert Carter Nicholas feared that the Declaration of Rights would be a forerunner of civil convulsion. To him that clause which declared all men naturally free and equal was especially objectionable. Nicholas, Braxton, and Pendleton were not unfavorable to a government of monarchical tendencies. Braxton ably defended their position in an essay entitled *An Address to the Convention of the Colony and Ancient Dominion on the Subject of Government*.[10]

In the plan of government conservative principles triumphed, although the victory was not apparent at the time. The right of suffrage was restricted to those who then exercised it,[11] and each county, regardless of its size and population, was assigned two members of the House of Delegates.[12] Although not made a part of the constitution, the convention divided the state into twenty-four districts, each entitled to elect

[9] *Religious Herald*, July, 1888; Semple, *Va. Baptists*, 62; Frestoe, *Hist. of Ketocton Association*, 90.

[10] Tyler, *Henry*, 179.

[11] Persons owning twenty-five acres of improved or one hundred acres of unimproved land were admitted to suffrage together with certain artisans residing in Norfolk and Williamsburg (*Revised Code of 1819*, I, 38).

[12] Williamsburg, Norfolk, and Richmond were each given an additional delegate.

one senator. The country west of the Blue Ridge was given only four senators, and no provision was made for amending the constitution, extending suffrage, or reapportioning representation in either house.[13]

The constitution, however, was not a complete triumph for the conservatives. Members of both houses of the Assembly were made elective by the people, and elections for the most popular house were to be held annually. The legislative department was made supreme; it elected the governor and restricted his actions by associating with him an Executive Council. The higher members of the judiciary department were also made elective by the Assembly.

The reform spirit of the frontier and the general enthusiasm over the Revolution enabled the democratic element to control the first Assembly elected under the new constitution and temporarily allayed the opposition of the conservatives. The time was indeed opportune for the appearance of a constructive statesman. Mason having refused to serve his people longer as a legislator, a new leader was forthcoming in the person of Thomas Jefferson, who in order to carry forward the reform movement in Virginia had declined a re-election to the Continental Congress.[14]

Jefferson was peculiarly fitted for leadership at this time. The state was rent by differences between dissenters and conforming churchmen, but he was a believer in no creed. Educated at William and Mary and reared under the tutelage of Wythe, Tucker, and

[13] Poore, *Charters and Constitutions*, Part II, 1910.
[14] Randall, *Jefferson*, I, 195; Rives, *Madison*, I, 170.

Pendleton, he had friends and admirers among the most influential conservatives. Besides, he had had abundant opportunity to know and appreciate their conception of society and politics. Himself a member of the landed aristocracy and possessed of an infusion of patrician blood,[15] he was not at first distrusted. The secret of Jefferson's ability as a leader at this time lay, however, in the fact that he was a democrat of the frontier type. Born on the outskirts of the charmed and corrupt circle of conservatism and in the democratic air of the mountains, he loved simplicity and equality. The precocious child of a pioneer surveyor, he had the frontiersman's outlook on things, which has done so much to shape American policies and institutions. Reared on a farm devoted largely to wheat culture and under the democratic influence of the dissenters, he had little sympathy with the institution of negro slavery either practically or theoretically. He was not an agitator, however, and struck only when he knew his blows would tell.[16]

The subject of most importance before the first Assembly involved the continuation of the established church.[17] The effort to retain it met opposition from the dissenters and some Anglicans, and precipitated

[15] Jefferson's mother was Jane Randolph. Of his patrician ancestry he was accustomed to speak thus: "They [his mother's people] trace their pedigree far back in England and Scotland, to which let every one ascribe the faith and merit he chooses."—Morse, *Jefferson*, 3.

[16] See Randall, *Jefferson*, I, chap. i; Parton, *Jefferson*, chaps. i–ix; Morse, *Jefferson*, 4–8.

[17] Hunt, *Am. Hist. Asso. Rept.*, 1901, I, 165–71.

the first great sectional conflict in the state. For years Baptist associations and Presbyterian congregations had petitioned for toleration, and now their efforts were renewed with increased vigor. A memorial from the Valley reminded the Assembly "that nothing is more necessary in the present struggle than a union of mind and strength" and suggested disestablishment as a means of effecting it.[18] Numerous petitions from the west asked that the laws of the state be made to harmonize with the Declaration of Rights and the spirit of American liberty. The most significant memorial on this subject came, however, from the Hanover Presbytery. It avowed devotion to the state institutions but reminded the Assembly that "in the frontier the dissenters have borne the heavy burden of purchasing glebes and supporting the established clergy where there are very few Episcopalians either to assist in bearing the expense or to reap the advantages." It also alleged that intolerance had driven population from Virginia and reduced her to the necessity of calling in strangers to fight her battles. It ended by asking that the state laws be made to conform to the Declaration of Rights, the Magna Carta of the commonwealth.[19]

Members of the established church, residing in the Tidewater, also sent memorials. They pleaded the inviolability of the contracts by which the church held property and the efficiency of an established church in maintaining peace and happiness.[20]

[18] *Journal, House of Delegates*, 1776, 48.
[19] *Ibid.*, 24.
[20] *Ibid.*, 47.

In response to these memorials the Assembly took the initial step toward disestablishment; the salaries of the clergy were suspended for 1776, an act repeated annually until 1779. Opposition was too strong, however, to effect the whole change at once.

The reform movement of 1776 was not confined to attacks upon the established church. It was at this time that Jefferson struck the first blow at the landed aristocracy by an act abolishing entails.[21] It would be almost impossible to overestimate the effect of this law in producing democratic equality in Virginia. In 1833 Henry Clay, a native of Virginia and thoroughly in touch with the changes wrought there, said, in speaking of the effects of the abolition of entail:

> In whose hands now are the once proud seats of Westover, Cerles, Maycocks, Shirly, and others on the James and in lower Virginia? They have passed into other and stranger hands. Some of the descendants of illustrious parentage have gone to the far West, while others lingering behind have contrasted their present condition with that of their venerated ancestors. They behold themselves excluded from their fathers' houses, now in the hands of those who were once their fathers' overseers, or sinking into decay.[22]

The Assembly of 1776 also gave special privileges to the frontier county courts; increased the representation of the west by acts creating new counties; and appointed a committee to revise and amend the laws of the state.[23]

[21] Hening, *Statutes*, IX, 226; Jefferson, *Writings* (ed. Ford), II, 102.
[22] *Congressional Debates*, VIII, Part I, 290.
[23] Jefferson, *Writings* (ed. Ford), II, 116.

"The Committee on Revision" was composed of Jefferson, Mason, Wythe, Pendleton, and Thomas L. Lee, all reformers except Pendleton. It continued its labors for two years and did not make a final report until 1779. The report shows the handiwork of Jefferson. It contained his famous bill for religious liberty, which its author ranked next to the Declaration of Independence; it recommended the division of the counties into townships for the purpose of establishing free schools; and it contemplated the emancipation of the negro slaves.[24]

These radical recommendations struck the conservatives with consternation. Meanwhile, there had been a reaction against reform, and a new alignment of parties was in process of formation. The enthusiasm for the democratic principles of the Revolution had waned somewhat, and the abolition of entails arrayed against Jefferson the landed aristocracy. Chagrined at being displaced from his position as popular leader, Henry lost enthusiasm for the cause of reform and drew closer to the conservatives.[25] The transfer of the seat of war to the South also diverted attention to the matter of defense.

Under these changed conditions reform was checked. Yet an act of 1779 relieved the dissenters from the necessity of supporting the established

[24] Jefferson, *Notes on Va.* (ed. of 1801), 268, 284; Jefferson, *Writings* (ed. Ford), II, 201.

[25] This was the beginning of an irreparable breach between Jefferson and Henry (Jefferson, *Writings* [ed. Ford], II, 102; Jefferson, *Autobiography,* I, 49; Tucker, *Jefferson,* I, 97-99; Randall, *Jefferson,* I, 199-201).

church, and "to secure the equal rights of all" the capitol was removed to Richmond.[26] But further consideration of the recommendations of the Committee on Revision was postponed. Jefferson was in turn shelved by being made governor, a disposal more than once resorted to for Virginia leaders deemed dangerous in the Assembly. On the other hand, Henry returned to the House of Delegates to oppose the reforms which Jefferson had inaugurated, and to regain his popularity.[27]

As governor, Jefferson did not have smooth sailing. The constitution makers of 1776 had purposely made the executive weak and helpless.[28] Reinforced by Henry, the opposition in the Assembly soon outnumbered the followers of Jefferson. To begin with, parties had been pretty evenly divided. John Page, the conservative candidate for governor, had received 61 votes and Jefferson only 67.[29] The British invasions fell most heavily upon the conservative parts of the state, and the failure to check them caused adverse criticism to be heaped upon "the political theorist and impractical statesman," who presided in the capitol. Two days after the expiration of Jefferson's term as governor he was forced to retire from the temporary seat of government, Charlottesville, to avoid capture by the British dragoons detailed especially for the purpose of his apprehension. Notwithstanding

[26] Hening, *Statutes*, X, 85; Randall, *Jefferson*, I, 223.
[27] Tyler, *Henry*, 262, 263.
[28] *Debates, Va. Constitutional Convention of 1829–30*, 472.
[29] *Journal, House of Del.*, 1779, 29.

the facts that he was no longer governor and that a large number of the assemblymen had already fled to Staunton beyond the Blue Ridge, the censure heaped upon him was unrelenting. The Assembly appointed an investigating committee which, however, completely exonerated him from all charges of negligence.[30]

Smarting under censure and chagrined at the successes of the conservatives, Jefferson retired from public life to his plantation in Bedford County. M. de Marbois, secretary of the French foreign legation at Philadelphia, had already directed twenty-three questions to him designed to bring out information regarding Virginia. Jefferson set himself assiduously to the task of preparing answers thereto. His replies took the form of a volume entitled *Notes on Virginia*.

In this book Jefferson continued his fight for reform. Some of its chapters abound in sweeping strictures upon the constitution of 1776 and the anti-democratic tendencies in the state. To show the inequalities in representation in the Assembly he prepared the following table:

	Square Miles	Fighting Men	Delegates	Senators
Between the sea and the falls of the rivers..................	11,265	19,012	71	12
Between the falls of the rivers and the Blue Ridge of mountains...	18,759	18,828	46	8
Between the Blue Ridge of mountains and the Alleghanies......	11,911	7,673	16	2
Between the Alleghanies and the Ohio......................	70,650	4,458	16	2

[30] *Journal, House of Del.*, 1781, 37.

REVOLUTION AND CONFEDERATION 37

By this data he showed that nineteen thousand fighting men, residing in the Tidewater, were practically able to make the law and appoint the officers for over thirty thousand others.[31] The volume deals at length with the proposed reforms of 1779. He unhesitatingly attributed their defeat to the conservatives. In connection with the British invasions and the excitement which they occasioned, Jefferson intimated that a movement had been on foot to make Henry dictator, a charge which widened the breach between himself and the hero of 1765 and 1776.[32]

The west was also displeased with the conduct of the war; it did not, however, criticize Jefferson. Augusta and Rockbridge counties petitioned against the practice of drafting their residents for service in the Continental army to make good the quotas from the eastern counties and asked that soldiers be apportioned among the several counties on a property valuation basis.[33] Andrew Moore, of Rockbridge, introduced a resolution to compel the eastern counties to fill their quotas in the Continental army.[34] Berkeley and Jefferson counties petitioned against the draft system, the quartering of prisoners, and the contemplated dictatorship.[35]

In 1783 reform again became an issue. The conservative reaction had but slightly decreased the num-

[31] *Notes on Va.*, 161, 162.

[32] Henry, *Henry*, II, 144, 231; Jefferson, *Writings* (ed. Ford), VIII, 368; Randall, *Jefferson*, I, 348–52; Tyler, *Henry*, 197.

[33] *Journal, House of Del.*, 1781, 8, 18, 22.

[34] *Ibid.*, 25.   [35] *Ibid.*, 12, 27.

ber of the memorials which the dissenters were annually sending to the Assembly. In addition to relief from the necessity of supporting the established church, dissenters now desired the privilege of solemnizing marriages and a share in the use of the churches and the glebes purchased at public expense.[36] After the peace of 1783 the Episcopal church fell into greater disfavor. Some of its clergy had sympathized with the mother country and others yet rested under the charge of corruption. Accordingly the Assembly of 1783 was flooded with memorials praying for complete disestablishment. Other memorials asked for a constitutional convention, internal improvements, and administrative reform.

Jefferson, now in France, intrusted the work of reform to James Madison, who was eminently qualified for the task. He too was born and reared in the Piedmont foothills on the outskirts of conservatism. He was, however, a member of the established church. His father was vestryman of Saint Thomas parish; his mother was a devout communicant; and his cousin, also called James Madison, was president of William and Mary and later became the first Episcopal bishop of Virginia. But while at Princeton, where he studied and graduated, Madison breathed another atmosphere than that of the Virginia vestry.[37] He there became attached to the principles of complete toleration. He spoke but once in the constitutional convention of 1776, and then it was in behalf of religious liberty.

[36] *Journal, House of Del.*, 1st sess., 1783, 22; *ibid.*, 2d sess., 10, 37.
[37] Hunt, *Am. Hist. Asso. Rept.*, 1901, I, 165-71.

Although he had not protested in 1776, he was opposed to the undemocratic principles of the constitution adopted at that time. Meanwhile he had discussed with Jefferson and others both the necessity and manner of making Virginia's a true republican government. Although cold and reserved, his simple courteous manners and dignified modesty attracted strangers, who soon became friends.[38]

In the fight for disestablishment Madison was aided by the brothers, George and William Cary Nicholas, both residents of Charlottesville and intimate friends of Jefferson. Confronted by this triumvirate and conscious of the fact that the days of the established church were numbered, the Anglicans asked the Assembly to incorporate the Protestant Episcopal Church of Virginia and to pass a general assessment act. The former was to give the established church legal title to the churches, glebes, and all property whatsoever then in its possession; the latter required each and every taxpayer to contribute to the support of some church. Both bills were introduced by Henry, himself a member of the established church, and received his earnest support.[39] The decline of the established church and the increase of crime and dishonesty brought the bills into favor with Washington, Richard Henry Lee, Tazewell, and Marshall. By this time most of the conservatives were willing to admit

[38] Hunt, *Madison*, chaps. i–iii; *ibid.*, 272, 273; Rives, *Madison*, I, chap. i.

[39] Madison, *Writings* (ed. Cong.), I, 88; Tyler, *Henry*, 262; Rives, *Madison*, I, 602.

that there might be other roads to heaven, but they were sure that no gentleman would choose any other than the Episcopal.

Henry was able to secure the passage of the act of incorporation,[40] but Madison succeeded in having the final vote on the act providing for assessment postponed until the next meeting of the Assembly. Meanwhile the bill was ordered printed and distributed to enable the people to make expressions of their will. During the summer and autumn of 1785 the assessment bill was the theme of discussion in all parts of the state. At the instigation of George Nicholas, Madison prepared a remonstrance against it. This document received thousands of signatures in the interior and on the frontier. The enthusiasm called forth floods of memorials to the Assembly. Those from the vicinity of Henry's home, Henry County, and from the Tidewater were generally favorable to assessment.[41] But the Presbyterians of the Valley and the Baptists of the Piedmont denounced the proposed law as a contravention of the Declaration of Rights and the spirit of American liberty.[42] The Methodists now cast lot with the dissenters, thinning the ranks of the established church in the Tidewater and the Piedmont, where Asbury, Coke, Lee, and Jarratt had a very numerous following.

[40] As a strategic move Madison voted for the incorporation act (*Writings* [ed. Hunt], II, 88).

[41] Randall, *Jefferson*, I, 222; Hunt, *Madison*, 84, 85; *Journal, House of Del.*, 2d sess., 1785, 6, 8, 19, 29, 30.

[42] *Ibid.*, 6, 8, 9, 10, 11, 18, 19, 21, 26, 34.

In the excitement which followed this agitation the assessment bill disappeared from sight, and Jefferson's bill of 1779 was resurrected and made a law.[43] The act of incorporation which gave the Episcopalians legal title to the property then in their possession continued, however, to be a law. Accordingly petitions continued to come to the Assembly asking that it be repealed and that all church property, purchased by taxation, be sold and the proceeds converted into a public fund, or that such property be thrown open to the use of all denominations.[44] So persistent was the fight waged that the incorporation act was finally repealed. The triumph of Jefferson in 1799 brought the enactment of a law to deprive all denominations of special benefits. Thus the first great sectional conflict ended in the complete separation of the church and the state.

These years also witnessed other reform movements and sectional antagonisms. In 1784 Madison, in an elaborate speech, renewed the demand of the interior for constitutional reform;[45] Methodists and Quakers petitioned the Assembly for the abolition of negro slavery;[46] the interior secured the enactment of a law encouraging manumissions of negro slaves;[47] and

[43] Hening, *Statutes*, XII, 84.

[44] *Journal, House of Del.*, 1786–87, 13, 15, 24, 31.

[45] *Ibid.*, 1st sess., 1784, 70; Madison, *Writings*, I, 82.

[46] *Journal, House of Del.*, 2d sess., 1780, 32; *ibid.*, 2d sess., 1785, 27.

[47] Hening, *Statutes*, XI, 39.

an attempt to remove the capitol to Williamsburg was defeated.[48] The differences between the east and west were most pronounced on economic questions. The latter section secured the passage of an act restricting the number of ports of entry to five, a measure designed to afford home markets to farm products and live stock by fostering cities.[49] To secure a market for their products the western delegates also placed a duty upon imported wines, rum, cheese, beef, pork, iron, and hemp.[50] George Mason strenuously resisted these impost duties on the ground that they would make the east dependent upon the west.[51] The western counties also petitioned for time indulgences in the payment of taxes and for the privilege of paying all public dues in farm products.[52]

The first years of the Revolution mark an important period in the westward extension of Virginia's population. Following the wake of the armies which went to defend and conquer, settlers pushed into the trans-Alleghany country. The absence of hostile Indian tribes and an abundance of fertile and untimbered lands attracted the first immigrants to Kentucky. By the end of the period treated in this chapter settlers had entered northwestern Virginia in large numbers.

[48] *Journal, House of Del.*, 1st sess., 1784, 51.
[49] Rives, *Madison*, I, 548; *Va. Hist. Coll.*, X, 310, 319. The east never became reconciled to this law and soon procured its repeal (*Journal, House of Del.*, 1788, 31).
[50] Hening, *Statutes*, XII, 412.
[51] Rowland, *Mason*, II, 204.
[52] *Journal, House of Del.*, 1st sess., 1783, 32; *ibid.*, 2d sess., 1784, 95; *Va. Hist. Coll.*, X, 67, 77, 91, 204.

REVOLUTION AND CONFEDERATION 43

In 1790 the trans-Alleghany population numbered more than one hundred thousand. This unprecedented movement of population at a time when every man was a law unto himself, gave to the new frontier society an unusually intense individualistic spirit.

The first conflict of the frontiersmen was not with the eastern aristocrats; it was with the savages and with the land companies and individuals who claimed priorities to the new lands. The companies and individual claimants of large grants petitioned the Assembly for a recognition of their titles,[53] but counter petitions full of the germs of squatter sovereignty came from the individual settlers. Citizens of Botetourt County said: "We have settled in the west and defended it for years against the savage, in consequence of which we hoped to have obtained a just and equitable title to our possessions, without being obliged to contribute large sums of money for the separate emolument of individuals."[54] The officers and soldiers of the Continental army, who had received promises of land bounties, joined the pioneers in a protest against the claims of those trying to monopolize the west.[55]

Under the direction of Jefferson, the acts and resolutions passed in response to these petitions favored decidedly the individual claimants. The Indiana and Vandalia companies were informed that "no person or persons have or ever had a right to purchase lands

[53] *Journal, House of Del.*, 2d sess., 1778, 28, 42, 47, 70, 74, 92, 97.
[54] *Ibid.*, 1777, 31.
[55] *Ibid.*, 2d sess., 1778, 40.

of the Indians for themselves, and that all purchases hitherto made had inured to the state."[56] The Assembly also addressed a memorial to the Continental Congress denying the rights of the Indiana and Vandalia companies to lands within the sovereign territory of Virginia.[57] Surveys made by land companies prior to 1763 were confirmed, but those made subsequent to that date were declared invalid.[58] In response to individual requests land prices were reduced to two cents per acre, land agents and surveyors were sent to the interior, and a general land office was established. Individual enterprise was further encouraged by giving to each actual settler a "settlement right" to four hundred acres and a "pre-emption right" to one thousand acres adjoining.[59]

Virginia's liberality in granting her unoccupied lands did not prove to be good policy. True, large numbers of settlers were early attracted to the state, where they made permanent homes, but much of the land fell into the hands of speculators. Companies were formed in both Europe and America to deal in Virginia lands, which were bought up in large tracts at the trifling cost of two cents per acre.[60] This wholesale engrossment soon consumed practically all

[56] *Journal, House of Del.,* 1st sess., 1777, 39.

[57] *Ibid.,* 2d sess., 1779, 55, 84.

[58] *Ibid.,* 2d sess., 1777, 87, 88.

[59] Hening, *Statutes,* X, 35-65.

[60] *Debates of Congress,* 22 Cong., 2d sess., IX, Part I, 142. The Land Books of Kanawha County for the year 1791 record the ownership of tracts of 150,000 acres each. Joseph Mayo owned 50,000 acres valued at £2,500 and assessed at £6 5s. 5d.

REVOLUTION AND CONFEDERATION 45

the most desirable lands and forced the home-seeker to purchase from a speculator or to settle as a squatter. Added to these embarrassments were the conflicting claims regarding land titles. Under these conditions many of the later immigrants moved on to the territory beyond the Ohio. In these facts lies a possible explanation for West Virginia's retarded development.

The motives and interests which attracted settlers to trans-Alleghany Virginia were determining factors in the society and politics of that section. The only common object of attraction was the new and cheap lands. From the Piedmont of both Virginia and North Carolina came those who had been small landowners and the landless. In many instances the farmers had sold their holdings to retreat from the encroaching institution of negro slavery. The farmers of the Valley sent their sons thither to seek new homes, and the graziers of the same section pushed their holdings into the Alleghany highlands. Others, squatters for the most part, came to trap upon the large tracts of land held by foreign capitalists. The reports of rice, cotton, and tobacco grown upon Wheeling Island by Ebenezar Zane[61] and the florid descriptions of the genial climate of the new west attracted immigrants who hoped to become plantation-owners. These immigrants purchased large tracts of land and in many instances brought negro slaves to clear them.[62] In

[61] Cutler, *Cutler*, I, 410.

[62] New Englanders purchased slaves in Maryland and northern Virginia and carried them to the banks of the Ohio and the Kanawha.

the years immediately following 1790 immense clearings were made along the Kanawha and the Ohio rivers. In some instances overseers conducted this work, and in some cases the large-scale operators employed the squatters, who were not infrequently paid at the rate of one-fourth pound of gunpowder per day.

The great variety in the natural features and natural resources preserved a diversity of economic interests in the trans-Alleghany section. As has been seen, the Tidewater, the Piedmont, and the Valley possessed within themselves respectively a practical homogeneity of economic interests. They therefore tended to act as sections in political matters. But the isolation of its nuclei of settlements, the diversity of interests, and the difficulty of communication made it impossible for the trans-Alleghany country to act as a political unit. Thus, while the inhabitants of Kentucky contemplated the dismemberment of the commonwealth and a political union with either Great Britain or Spain, as a means of securing protection and commercial advantage, the inhabitants of northwestern Virginia, on the other hand, supported the movement to form a strong national government. Against foreign intrigue and Indian attacks the inhabitants of the latter section saw their salvation only in a continuation of that union which had made independence possible.

The rapid development of the trans-Alleghany section made the subject of internal improvements an important one. Commercial intercourse between the east and the west now seemed necessary to preserve

REVOLUTION AND CONFEDERATION 47

the integrity of the state and the Union. The Kentuckians found their only market on the lower Mississippi, and commercial relations were developing between New Orleans and the northwestern part of the state. In 1782 Jacob Yoder left Redstone on the Monongahela with a boat load of flour which he sold in New Orleans. With the proceeds he there purchased furs, which were sold in Havana, where he invested in sugar, which in turn was sold in Philadelphia.[63] This pioneer trading expedition was only the forerunner of numerous others soon to follow.

Washington feared that the natural commercial interests of the west would lead it to move for a dismemberment of the commonwealth, and he suggested as a remedy the construction of works of internal improvement connecting the east and the west. In 1784 he visited the trans-Alleghany country, and personally inspected the portages to and the falls in the western rivers. On his return he drew a map to show where roads and canals could be constructed in a vast scheme of internal improvements to connect the eastern and western waters.[64] A little later he wrote Arthur Lee: "There is nothing which binds one country to another but interest. Without this cement the western inhabitants, who more than probably will be composed in a great degree of foreigners, can have

[63] Winsor, *Westward Movement*, 326.

[64] Hulbert, *Washington and the West*, 32. Communication between the east and west by means of canals was first suggested by Washington in 1753. See *Washington and Lee Hist. Papers*, No. 4, p. 64; Washington, *Writings* (ed. Ford), X, 402.

no predilection for us, and a commercial connection is the only tie we can have upon them."[65]

The Assemblies of 1783 and 1784 received numerous petitions on the subject of internal improvements. They asked that the Potomac and James be made navigable above the fall line and that highways be constructed across the Blue Ridge. In 1784 Washington visited the Assembly to exert his influence in behalf of contemplated internal improvement undertakings. Under his influence and as a result of a conference with commissioners from Pennsylvania and Maryland the Potomac Company was incorporated for the purpose of improving the navigation of the Potomac and its tributaries.[66] In the same year, 1784, the James River Company was incorporated, and James Rumsey was promised an adequate compensation for any invention which would enable boats to move against the current.[67]

From a sectional standpoint the commercial interests were at this time more important than internal improvements. The towns of the Tidewater chafed under the British restrictions upon trade and desired better commercial relations between the states. Of the numerous petitions to the Assembly on these subjects that from Norfolk was, perhaps, the most significant. It claimed that the restrictions on the West India trade and the foreign commercial monopolies were produ-

[65] Washington, *Writings* (ed. Ford), X, 488.

[66] Hening, *Statutes*, XI, 510. Washington was the first president of the Potomac Company.

[67] *Ibid.*, XI, 502; *Journal, House of Del.*, 1st sess., 1784, 84.

REVOLUTION AND CONFEDERATION 49

cing injury to Virginia and asked for restriction on British trade and better commercial relations between the states.[68] Petitions of a similar tone came from Fredericksburg, Falmouth, Alexandria, and Port Royal.[69] In 1785 Madison made a speech in the House of Delegates in favor of these petitions and secured the adoption of a resolution which declared that "the relative situations of the United States have been found, on trial, to require uniformity in their commercial relations."[70] The representatives of Virginia in the Continental Congress were instructed to use their influence to bring about better commercial relations between the states.[71] James Monroe thought that Virginia's trade had never been more monopolized by Great Britain, and Washington and Henry believed that a strong government was alone adequate to remedy the situation.[72]

Simultaneously with the awakening of an interest in better commercial relations on the part of the east the subject of the free navigation of the Mississippi became an important issue in the west. As the Jay-Gardoqui negotiations became more serious the latter section developed a keener interest in national politics. Under the direction of Henry and at the earnest solicitation of the west the Assembly of 1784 resolved: "That it is essential to the prosperity and happiness of

[68] *Journal, House of Del.*, 2d sess., 1785, 22.
[69] *Ibid.*, 24, 35.
[70] *Ibid.*, 36.
[71] *Ibid.*
[72] Rives, *Madison*, I, 548; Tyler, *Henry*, 273.

the western inhabitants of this Commonwealth to enjoy the right to navigate the river Mississippi."[73]

With issues and interests shaping themselves on national questions new party alliances and alignments were formed. Although not opposed to the free navigation of the Mississippi, Madison, as has been seen, had already espoused the cause of the commercial interests of the Tidewater. Thus, just at the time when the first stage of the sectional fight over local issues was being brought to a triumph by the west, its leader, Madison, espoused the cause of those who had been his political opponents. On the other hand, Henry, never able to co-operate with either Madison or Jefferson, now returned to his first affiliation and again became the spokesman of the west. As the Jay-Gardoqui negotiations continued and the commercial questions became more acute, political parties in Virginia merged with those developing in the United States at large.

The desire for better commercial relations led to renewed negotiations with Maryland regarding the navigation of the Potomac and the Chesapeake. Accordingly commissioners met at Mount Vernon and came to agreements of mutual advantage whereby Virginia waived her right to collect duties on vessels entering the Chesapeake and was given the privilege of navigating the Potomac.[74] Gratified with the outcome of this negotiation, Maryland proposed another conference to which delegates from Pennsylvania and

[73] *Journal, House of Del.*, 2d sess., 1784, 9.
[74] Hening, *Statutes*, XII, 50.

Delaware were to be invited. Virginia did more. In January, 1786, she appointed commissioners to meet such other commissioners as might be named by all the states "to take into consideration the trade of the United States . . . . and to consider how far a uniform system in their commercial regulations might be necessary."[75] In response to this call delegates from five states met at Annapolis in September, 1786. They took no action upon the object of the call but summoned a convention of delegates from all the states to meet at Philadelphia, in the following May, to take such steps "as shall appear to them necessary to render the constitution of the federal government adequate to the exigencies of the Union."[76]

Only one month before the meeting at Annapolis Jay made the final report of his negotiations with Gardoqui to the Continental Congress. In return for a favorable commercial treaty with Spain he recommended to that body that the United States forego for a period of twenty-five or thirty years the free navigation of the lower Mississippi.[77] The desire of the seven northern states to act upon Jay's recommendations aroused interior and frontier Virginia.[78] Henry now insisted that the manifestation of sectionalism between the North and the South made a stronger union impracticable.[79]

[75] Elliot, *Debates*, I, 92. [76] *Ibid.*, I, 92.
[77] *Secret Journals of Congress*, IV, 44–63.
[78] Rowland, *Mason*, II, 195.
[79] Rives, *Madison*, II, 238, 239; Tyler, *Henry*, 273; Bancroft, *Hist. of the Constitution*, II, 397.

Nevertheless the change of sentiment on the part of many in the Tidewater and northwestern counties prevailed, and Virginia named delegates to the federal convention. Those named were George Washington, James Madison, George Mason, Patrick Henry, Edmund Randolph, George Wythe, and James Blair, all residents of the Tidewater except Henry and Madison. Henry refused, however, to attend the convention or to take any part in an effort to strengthen a government fraught with danger to the South.[80]

When the convention met, Virginia was represented by seven delegates. Before entering into its deliberations they drew up a set of resolutions embodying a plan of government. These resolutions were later called the "Virginia Plan" and became the foundation of the Constitution. This plan contemplated a government of three separate and distinct departments. The legislative department was to exercise only those powers for which the several state legislatures had proved themselves incompetent and in the exercise of which state action would not promote national interests. To make the executive and judiciary departments equal with and independent of a legislative department thus constituted was, in the minds of the authors of the plan, to create a stronger national government. That feature of the Virginia Plan of most importance as concerns the theme of interest in this monograph, however, was its contemplated division of the sovereign power between the states and the federal government. All

[80] Rives, *Madison*, II, 238.

powers not expressly delegated to Congress were to be reserved to the states. This arrangement contemplated that hardly imaginable thing, a government under which citizens were to be responsible to two sovereigns. The Virginians adhered to the principles of this plan throughout and insisted that none of the modifications later made in it vitiated its fundamental ideas.

Though dictated primarily by her representatives, the Constitution met strong opposition in Virginia. The democratic leaders of the interior declared that it sacrificed the state's sovereignty. Accordingly they made a desperate fight to secure the election of delegates pledged to vote against ratification. When the canvass was ended it was not known which side would be successful, so evenly were the friends and enemies of the new plan of federal government matched. From the Tidewater came a strong delegation favorable to ratification. It numbered among its members the most prominent characters at the Virginia bar, former sympathizers with Great Britain, and representatives of interests essentially commercial. The other delegates favorable to ratification came from the Valley and the northwestern part of the state. Most of them had seen service in the revolutionary armies and were largely under the influence of Washington. The Kentucky country and the Piedmont sent delegates opposed to ratification. The former were chiefly interested in the free navigation of the Mississippi River and were opposed to strengthening a government which might barter their commercial interests for like interests elsewhere. Recent events had taught them to look to Henry as their leader. The delegates from the Piedmont were persons who had seen much service in the Assembly; they were the old democratic file which had for years engaged the conservatives of the Tidewater.[81]

So keen was interest that a full delegation reported on the day set for the meeting.[82] The leaders of those opposed to ratification, commonly called Anti-federalists, were Henry, Grayson, and Mason; those in favor of ratification were led by Madison, Randolph, Pendleton, Carrington, and Wythe, who, except the first named, were all from the Tidewater. The talks and friendly letters of Washington, who was not a member of the convention, did much to keep those favorably disposed to ratification in line. All realized that the final result would be determined only by an intellectual battle. The prize to be fought for was the doubtful vote from some of the northern and western counties. During the course of the debate which followed each side accused the other of "scuffling"[83] for the western vote. The contest was really between the Tidewater and the Piedmont, and was in no small degree a continuation of the fight between conservatism and democracy.

The debates in the convention reveal the fact that

[81] See *Va. Hist. Coll.*, IX, 63 ff.; Elliot, *Debates*, V, 368; Madison, *Papers*, II, 1208; Henry, *Henry*, II, 340.

[82] For a complete list of delegates by counties, see *Richmond Enquirer*, September 2, 1825.

[83] Elliot, *Debates*, III, 251, 361.

the chief participants were representatives of geographical sections of the state, speaking for the interests and sentiments of their respective sections. Governor Randolph thought the Kentuckians had no better reason to hope for the free navigation of the Mississippi out of a stronger union than in it. Defeat of the movement for a stronger union, he believed, would be followed by boundary disputes and interminable wars, which would fall very heavily upon the inhabitants of the Potomac and the northwest. The Northern Neck might unite in a northern confederacy, which would aid the savages in making war upon what remained of Virginia.[84] John Marshall was certain that a strong government afforded a better agency for securing the free navigation of the Mississippi than a weak one.[85] In case the Constitution was rejected, Nicholas feared internal wars and dismemberment. He told the western delegates that they could expect no comfort from their enemies, England and Spain. He believed that the only way to bring about the evacuation of the Northwest by the British, and the consequent cessation of Indian hostilities, was by the creation of a government adequate to the task of treating with foreign nations. He encouraged the westerners to believe that the increased migrations of New Englanders to the Ohio Valley made the surrender of the Mississippi navigation improbable.[86] Those representing the commercial interests predicted war

[84] *Ibid.*, III, 72, 74, 75.
[85] *Ibid.*, 222, 223.
[86] *Ibid.*, 238 ff.

between France and England. They thought the United States should prepare for the event and then reap a harvest by becoming the neutral carrier of the commerce of the world.[87] Kentucky was promised separate statehood and encouraged to believe that she could thus protect her rights by preserving the balance of power between the North and the South.[88]

The Anti-federalists made sensational arguments designed to appeal to those interested in the free navigation of the Mississippi. Henry declared "there are no tyrants in America" and "northern Virginia has nothing to fear" because of invasion by sister republics. He did not believe the Northern Neck would secede from Virginia and insisted that, in case of the dismemberment of the Union, Pennsylvania would join a confederacy with Virginia and, if necessary, fight with her. He warned the delegates from the northwest that they would "sip sorrow .... if you want any other security than the law of Virginia."[89] Mason likewise appealed to sectional interests. He professed to see in the contemplated supreme court an instrument whereby the Fairfax heirs, the representatives of the Vandalia and Indiana companies, and individual claimants to lands in the trans-Alleghany could recover their former possessions.[90] Grayson made the ablest

[87] Elliot, *Debates,* 101, 238.

[88] *Ibid.,* III, 259, 511. During the Jay-Gardoqui negotiations many eastern Virginians became favorable to separate statehood for Kentucky. Madison thought it wise to let Kentucky become a separate state by regular and legal methods. It would, he believed, set a safe precedent (*Writings* [ed. Cong.], I, 157).

[89] Elliot, *Debates,* III, 141, 154.   [90] *Ibid.,* III, 270, 527.

argument produced by the Anti-federalists. He spoke directly for the agricultural and democratic interest of central Virginia. The North, he believed, contemplated the sacrifice of the free use of the Mississippi. It hoped thereby to increase the importance of commerce and manufacturing by retaining its population. This policy, he contended, was opposed to the true interests of the United States, whose real interest lay in agriculture. Men could not be forced to the shop and the sea, he argued, so long as they could get cheap and fertile lands. He therefore condemned the idea of making the United States the neutral carrier of the commerce of the world, as impracticable and hazardous.[91]

Grigsby, in his study of the convention of 1788, brings out some interesting facts and conditions which determined the vote of the Valley and the counties of the northwest on this occasion. "Experience in civil and military office" and "an intimate acquaintance with the wants and interests of the West" moved John Stuart, of Greenbrier County, a pioneer surveyor and soldier, to favor a stronger government. He feared that a coalition of the Indians with the foreigners might result in the "total extermination of settlement west of the Blue Ridge."[92] William Fleming "knew that so long as Spain held Louisiana and Great Britain held the Canadas Indian troubles would be frequent and that all the resources of all the states would be necessary to repel the Indians in the pay of foreign

[91] *Ibid.*, 288–92.
[92] *Va. Hist. Coll.*, X, 27.

powers."[93] Gabriel Jones, the ablest lawyer of his day west of the Blue Ridge, "had no fear of a strong government which was at the same time a republican government."[94] Expressions of similar sentiments are attributed to Andrew Moore, Ebenezar Zane, George Jackson, Isaac Van Meter, Archibald Stuart, and Thomas Lewis, delegates to the convention from the Valley and the northwest.

The masterful argument of Madison was the determining factor in favor of ratification. It was not sensational, nor did it appeal to sectional prejudices. Before the debate was ended the Anti-federalists became convinced that they had lost. Accordingly they tried to prevent immediate ratification by proposing amendments, which they insisted should be accepted by the other states as the only condition upon which Virginia would ratify the Constitution. Friends of the Constitution did not oppose amendments, but insisted that they should be made subsequently to ratification. The whole issue was accordingly reduced to the question of whether or not amendments should be made before ratification. The possibility of Virginia's being deprived of a share in putting the new government into operation made this position of the Anti-federalists untenable.

The vote on ratification was: ayes 89, nays 79.[95] The accompanying map shows practically all the lower Tidewater in favor of ratification. Only two delegates from the Shenandoah Valley and that part of the

[93] *Va. Hist. Coll.*, 40.   [94] *Ibid.*, 18.
[95] Elliot, *Debates*, III, 653-55.

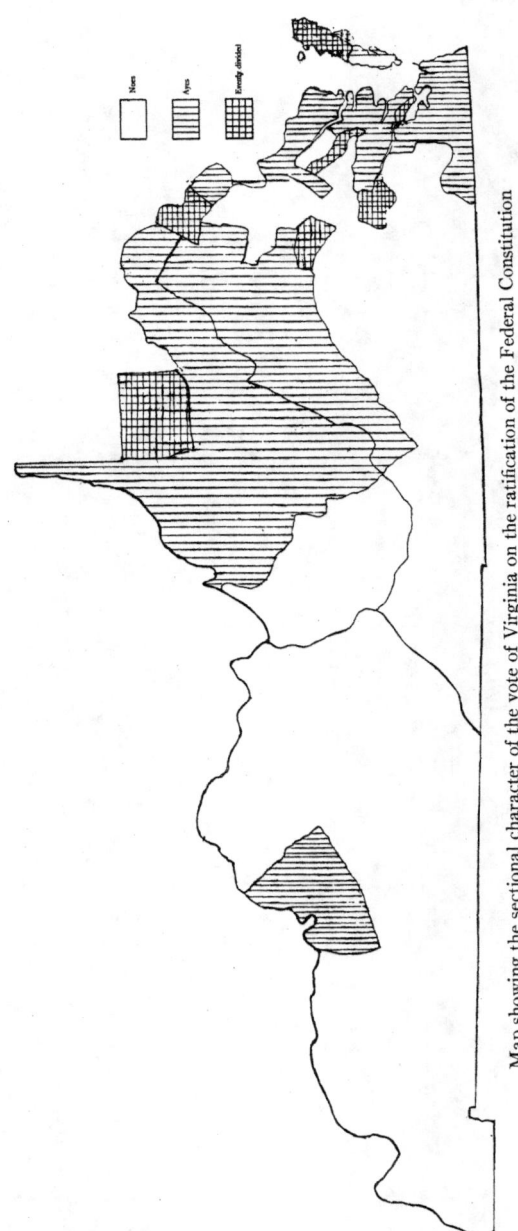

Map showing the sectional character of the vote of Virginia on the ratification of the Federal Constitution

trans-Alleghany north of the Great Kanawha voted nay. The democratic Piedmont and the Kentucky country were almost unanimous in opposition to the Constitution.

Two days after the vote on ratification George Wythe reported, as proposed alterations and additions to the federal Constitution, twenty separate amendments and a Bill of Rights. Except the amendment designed to restrict Congress to the use of requisitions in the collection of direct taxes, the report was accepted without division. The democratic element of the convention regarded the power to levy a direct tax as the most dangerous intrusted to the new government. George Mason insisted that this one power made the federal government supreme.[96] A motion to strike out the amendment requiring the use of requisitions was lost, ayes 65, nays 85. An analysis of this vote shows the Valley and the northwest in favor of striking out this amendment. Only three of the delegates from these two sections who voted for ratification were in favor of the proposed amendment. The additions to the ranks of the Anti-federalists came chiefly from the Tidewater.

Ratification did not put an end to the Anti-federalist opposition to the Constitution. During the summer of 1789 Clinton's circular letter proposing a second constitutional convention was the theme of conversation in Virginia. The Assembly of 1789–90 had been elected when the excitement over ratification was at its height and contained a large majority of Anti-federal-

[96] *Ibid.*, III, 32.

ists. Under the leadership of Henry it made a favorable reply to Clinton's letter and sent an address to the states and a memorial to Congress in support of a second convention. It also attempted to control the delegation from Virginia in the first Congress. By a sectional vote Madison was defeated for election to the Senate, and the state was districted so as to make the election of Federalists to the House of Representatives doubtful.[97] The elections of 1789 marked the passing of the Anti-federalist party in Virginia. Contrary to the expectations of many political leaders it secured only three presidential electors and three members of the House of Representatives; and Henry was forced into retirement.[98]

[97] Rives, *Madison*, II, 652; Henry, *Henry*, II, 426; Rowland, *Mason*, II, 303; Madison, *Letters*, I, 443, 444.

[98] In each case the Piedmont elected two Anti-federalists and the Tidewater one (Madison, *Writings*, I, 458; Rives, *Madison*, II, 657; Henry, *Henry*, II, 441).

CHAPTER III
FEDERALISTS AND REPUBLICANS, 1790–1816

Hamilton's plans of large powers for the new government and, in particular, his schemes for a national bank, direct taxes, heavy duties, and the assumption of the state debts were strongly opposed in Virginia on the ground not only of expediency but also of principle. It was there believed that his policy involved the creation of a stronger national government than that contemplated by the constitution makers of 1787. Even Madison, staunch Federalist as he was, believed that the framers of 1787 had created a government of delegated powers and limited jurisdiction. Besides, Virginia had paid a large portion of her revolutionary debt and was consequently averse to assuming the debts of those states which had been less prompt in meeting their obligations.

Opposition to the Hamilton programme did not, however, as some have supposed, create political unity in Virginia. Many friends of the Constitution in 1788 now favored a liberal construction of that document. These preferences were clearly manifested by the large minority vote in the Assembly of 1790 in favor of a resolution approving assumption.[1] Representatives in Congress from the Tidewater and

[1] The vote was: ayes 47, noes 88. The affirmative vote came almost wholly from those areas which had favored ratification of the federal Constitution. See *Journal, House of Del.*, 1790, 35, 36.

northern Virginia also favored parts of Hamilton's plan. Bland, who died before the final vote was taken, Lee, and White were for the assumption of the state debts. The attitude of both Bland and Lee was determined by local conditions and devotion to the principles of a strong government and not primarily by a desire to have the federal capital located on the Potomac or by political influence, which it has been alleged was brought to bear upon them. Before the understanding between Jefferson and Hamilton, whereby the former agreed to deliver enough votes to carry assumption provided the latter would use his influence to fix the temporary seat of government at Philadelphia and the permanent seat on the Potomac, both Bland and Lee were known to favor assumption.[2] They both represented districts exhausted by excessive and unscientific cropping, whence large migrations had been made to the West and to the South. They therefore favored assumption, as did others in the Tidewater and along the Potomac, as the only means whereby the newer sections of the Union could be made to pay an equitable share of the revolutionary debt.[3]

As the opposition to Hamilton's programme became more pronounced Jefferson and Madison conceived the idea of forming a strong party to resist the influence of its nationalistic tendencies. Fresh from the pre-

[2] Jefferson, *Anas,* 34; Hunt, *Madison,* 184; Maclay, *Journal,* 328; Jefferson, *Writings* (ed. Ford), I, 162, 163; V, 184; VI, 172; *Annals of Congress,* 1 Cong., II, 1712.

[3] *Ibid.,* 1 Cong., II, 1482, 1661.

liminaries of the French Revolution and imbued with the current individualistic philosophy, Jefferson was eminently qualified to become the leader of such an opposition party. Because of the predilection of some of its leaders for things French the new party was called "Republican," while the administration party continued to be called "Federalist."

In spite of the opposition of the Virginia leaders, the elections of 1793 showed unexpected Federalist strength. The party secured a large minority in the Assembly, and those sections which had favored the ratification of the federal Constitution again elected Federalists to Congress.[4]

As the next few years brought vexing questions on foreign relations, the excise, and the Jay Treaty, the Federalists lost strength locally. The westerners hoped to use French aid in checking English and Spanish intrigues and in reducing the dangers from Indian attacks; they particularly disliked the excise and went so far in their opposition as to raise liberty poles and to threaten armed resistance to the encroachments of the federal government.[5] The Jay Treaty was far from remedying the rift. From the delay in surrendering the western posts the frontier inhabitants feared a continuation of Indian attacks. In the Tidewater, although there was less love for the French,

[4] The Tidewater chose Parker, formerly elected as an Antifederalist, Lee, Page, and Griffin, and the transmontane country elected Neville, Rutherford, and Hancock (Madison, *Writings* [ed. Cong.], 255, 577; Loudoun's *Register*, April 4, 1793).

[5] *Baltimore Daily Intelligencer*, September 16, 1794; *Calendar Va. State Papers*, VII, 297, 323; V, 481.

the Jay Treaty was even more unwelcome than in the west, because it recognized the right of the British to collect debts due when the Revolution began and afforded the planters no recourse for recovering the value of negro slaves, which they alleged had been stolen by the British during the war.[6]

Other forces were at work, however, to neutralize temporarily the Republican influences. Genet's attack upon Washington and his pernicious meddling aroused resentment everywhere and especially with the planters of the Tidewater among whom Washington was even more popular than elsewhere.[7] The inhabitants of the Tidewater also had an eye upon the negro slave uprising in San Domingo and were fearful lest French influences might produce a similar upheaval in Virginia. Meanwhile the inhabitants of the west sympathized heartily with the efforts of the federal administration to defeat the Indians of the Northwest Territory. They valued protection more highly than the privilege to distil and sell whisky without paying a tax. The fact that the Federalists favored the Indian wars while the leaders of the Republican party opposed them kept many westerners loyal to the former party. They accordingly volunteered aid to put down the

[6] *Annals of Cong.*, 4 Cong., 1 sess., 1030; *Jefferson, Anas*, 78-80; Randall, *Jefferson*, II, 295; Henry, *Henry*, II, 529.

[7] Henry took advantage of this his first opportunity, under these changed conditions, to break with Jefferson and Madison. See Tyler, *Henry*, 358; Washington, *Writings* (ed. Ford), X, 562; *ibid.*, XI, 81, 82. During the most acute stage of the Genet affair both Jefferson and Madison trembled for the future of their party (Jefferson, *Writings* [ed. Ford], 338, 361).

Whiskey Insurrection and otherwise expressed devotion to nationalism.[8]

Thus while many former Federalists found abundant reasons for affiliating with the new party, others were equally attracted to nationalism. The congressional election of 1795 shows, however, a loss of Federalist strength in Virginia. Their representation in Congress fell from seven to four members.[9] For the first time an opposition member was successful in securing an election in the trans-Alleghany. George Jackson, who had been a candidate on the anti-excise ticket in 1793 and who was then defeated by six votes, was now successful in contesting the re-election of Neville.[10] The cessation of Indian hostilities and the influence of Gallatin made Republican success in the trans-Alleghany possible.

The quarrel with France, which now ensued, caused little immediate change in the party alignments. The Assembly of 1797 was, like its predecessor, in full control of the Republicans, and the congressional election of 1797 again returned four Federalists.[11] This lack of change in party strength does not, however, mean that Virginians were indifferent to the political issues of the day. Giles, for example, was strenuously opposed to war with France, while the

[8] *Baltimore Daily Intelligencer*, September 5, 13, 1794; Adams, *Gallatin*, 13; *Calendar Va. State Papers*, VII, 119, 266.

[9] The Federalists elected in 1795 were: from the Tidewater, Page and Parker; from the Valley, Hancock and Rutherford.

[10] *Calendar Va. State Papers*, VII, 289.

[11] The Federalists were: from the Tidewater, Evans and Parker; from the Valley, Daniel Morgan and James Machir.

local Federalists were pronouncedly belligerent. The Republicans, under the leadership of Giles, claimed that war was desired to perpetuate federalism, while the members of the administration party claimed that it was necessary to maintain the national honor.[12]

When it became evident that war with France was inevitable and that it was no longer the part of patriots to oppose the policy of the administration, members of the opposition party from Virginia ceased to vote on measures affecting our foreign relations. Some of them left the capitol. In April, 1798 (Congress adjourned in July), Jefferson wrote Madison: "Giles, Clopton, Cabell, and Nicholas have gone. Clay goes tomorrow. Parker has completely gone over to the war party."[13]

By 1798 war with France had actually begun; Hamilton was in control of the army and planned a coup on the lower Mississippi to incite popular enthusiasm for the government; the Federalists had a majority in both houses of Congress; and with the newly organized caucus and the confidence of the executive Pickering was in practical control of the government; the alien and sedition laws were being enforced to the discomfiture of Republican politicians; and the con-

[12] In the subsequent sessions the Virginia Federalists voted for the bills to provide means of defense, a stronger navy, the creation of the Navy Department, the suspension of commercial intercourse with France, and the increase of the provisional army. Of the four, Evans alone voted for the alien and sedition acts; Parker opposed them, and Morgan and Machir were not present when the votes were taken (*Annals of Cong.*, 5 Cong., I, 297; II, 1521, 1553, 1772, 1865, 2028, 2171).

[13] Randall, *Jefferson*, II, 387.

gressional elections of 1798 had resulted in Federalist victories everywhere. It seemed that the days of the Republicans were numbered.

The opposition in Virginia was too strong, however, to let things go by default; already John Taylor, of Caroline, had talked dismemberment;[14] and numerous mass-meetings, held during the summer of 1798 in the Piedmont and in the interior counties of the Tidewater, protested against the Federalist programme; the alien and sedition laws were special objects of attack, and Congress and the Assembly were petitioned to bring about their repeal.[15] Confronted by these conditions and supported by an enthusiastic constituency Jefferson and Madison conceived the idea of having one or more state governments protest against the nationalistic tendency of the federal government. Citizens of Kentucky had already spoken in numerous petitions, memorials, and resolutions against the constitutionality of the alien and sedition laws and the expediency of a war with France, which they feared would result in the loss of the free navigation of the Mississippi. It was accordingly decided to have Virginia and Kentucky speak in the form of resolutions from their assemblies.

Kentucky spoke first in a series of resolutions which border closely upon nullification. They made it the duty of a state to interpose to prevent federal usurpations of reserved powers. But in Virginia's case

[14] Jefferson, *Writings* (ed. Ford), VII, 263.

[15] See Anderson, "Va. and Ky. Resolutions," *Am. Hist. Rev.*, V, 46.

it was necessary to use both caution and moderation; the election of 1798 had returned a large Federalist minority to the Assembly; and, besides, both Jefferson and Madison realized that their political future was at stake. Accordingly Jefferson thought it wise to reaffirm only the essentials of the Kentucky resolutions, which he himself had drawn. On this subject he wrote to Madison, who was to draft the Virginia resolutions, that they should be left "in such a train as that we may not be committed absolutely to push the matter to extremes and yet may be free to push as far as events will make prudent."[16]

The Virginia resolutions reaffirmed the state-compact theory of the Constitution and declared that in case of a "deliberate, palpable, and dangerous exercise of power not granted by the said compact, the states who are parties thereto have the right and are in duty bound to interpose for arresting the progress of the evil," they condemned the policy of consolidating the states by degrees into one sovereignty, and declared the alien and sedition laws unconstitutional. But they did not say whether the "states" were to act through individual state legislatures or by co-operation through the medium of state legislatures or a national convention.

Although mild in expression these resolutions met the united opposition of a strong sectional minority in the state. It was led by George Keith Taylor, of Prince George County, a brother-in-law of John Marshall, and a thorough representative of the family

[16] Jefferson, *Writings* (ed. Ford), VII, 288.

and economic interests of the Tidewater aristocracy. He insisted that the resolutions invited the people of the state to arms against the federal government;[17] no other inference could be drawn, said he, from resolutions which make it "the duty" of citizens to resist the execution of alleged unconstitutional laws. He argued that the states were not the only parties, or the chief parties, to the federal compact; that the Articles of Confederation were the only real compact which had ever existed between the states, and that the effort to annul them had resulted in their destruction and in the creation of a government by the people.[18] Parts of the preamble and the fact that the people had ratified the federal Constitution in state conventions made it plain to Taylor that this is a government by the people. He denied that the alien and sedition acts were unconstitutional and insisted that they were within the prerogatives of a sovereign power. Speaking more directly for his section, the Tidewater, he ridiculed the principles of the French Revolution and protested against the further extension of republicanism in the slave-holding districts of Virginia. In this connection he pointed to the uprisings and bloodshed in San Domingo as the things which Virginia might hope to escape by casting off French influences.[19]

The opinions of the west found best expression in the speech of Brooke of Frederick County. He indorsed Taylor's theories, explaining the origin and nature of the federal government, and took advantage

[17] *Debates and Proceedings on the Res. of 1798* (ed. 1835), 81.
[18] *Ibid.*, 176.   [19] *Ibid.*, 109.

of the occasion to renew the demands of his section for a more democratic state government. He could not see the consistency of gentlemen who argued for democratic principles and voted to deprive themselves of a democratic state government. As between the government of the United States and that of Virginia, he had always favored the former, because it was more democratic. It gave every thirty thousand of its citizens a representative in Congress, while the state government, by its system of unequal representation, denied a large number an adequate voice in the Assembly. Rather than vote for the proposed resolutions he would seek an "asylum in some other region of the globe among a race of men who have more respect for peace and order, and who set a higher value upon the blessings of good government."[20] He closed his argument by proposing that the Assembly petition Congress for the repeal of the alien and sedition acts.[21]

John Taylor, of Caroline County, introduced the resolutions and led in the argument for their adoption. He professed to speak only for the principles of the federal Constitution and for public opinion. In declaring her own position and by asking the sister states to co-operate with her, he believed that Virginia was pursuing the only possible and ordinary procedure to arrest federal usurpation. Those favorable to adoption argued that "the people and the states" were parties to the federal compact.[22] Thus it was not only constitutional but necessary and right for states to

[20] *Debates and Proceedings on the Res. of 1798* (ed. 1835), 132-33.

[21] *Ibid.*, 133.   [22] *Ibid.*, 106, 165.

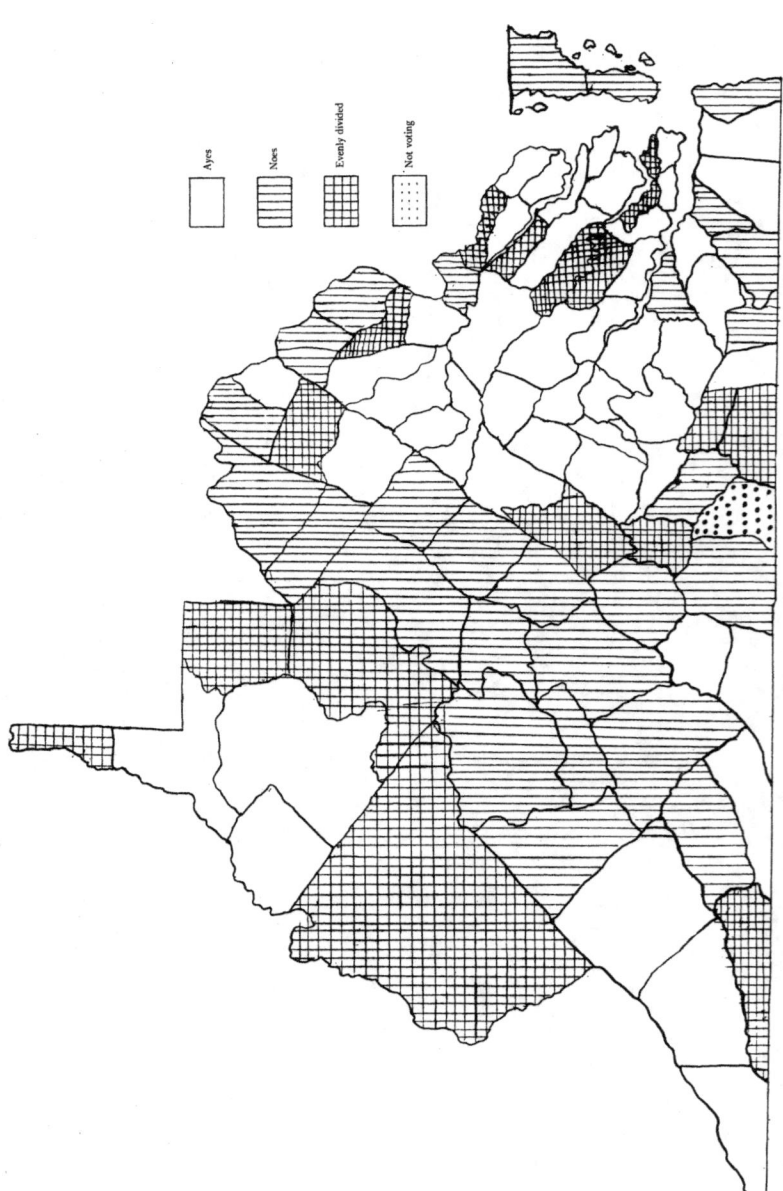

Map showing the vote by counties in the House of Delegates of Virginia on the Resolutions of 1798

arrest infractions of that compact. They insisted that the powers of the federal government were not general but that they were specifically enumerated. Usurpation of other powers were simply steps toward monarchy. Vattel and Blackstone were frequently invoked to show that aliens have rights which should be acknowledged and preserved.[23] Their opponents were frequently accused of magnifying the influence of French republicanism in San Domingo and the probable effect of its extension into the slave-holding districts of Virginia.[24]

The minority directed its chief attacks upon that resolution which condemned the nationalistic tendencies of the federal government. A motion to strike it out was, however, lost.[25]

The final vote on the adoption of the resolutions was: ayes 100, noes 63.[26] As the map shows, this vote was sectional. The Tidewater and both the northern and southern extremities of the Piedmont were almost evenly divided, while the Valley was practically a unit in the minority. The influence of John G. Jackson, a brother-in-law of Madison and a son of George Jackson, leader of the anti-excise party, and John Dawson,[27] a graduate of Yale and a close political

[23] *Ibid.*, 126, 140.

[24] *Ibid.*, 92, 109, 118.

[25] The vote was: ayes 68, noes 96 (*ibid.*, 211, 212).

[26] *Ibid.*, 212.

[27] Dawson represented the trans-Alleghany in the fifth Congress. By the time of the election for the sixth Congress he had found such favor with the eastern leaders that he was elected to represent a district east of the Blue Ridge and continued to receive elections for several years.

friend to both Madison and Jefferson, reduced the Federalist strength in the trans-Alleghany section.

In the west the discussion of 1798 brought out frequent expressions of devotion to the principles of a strong national government. A citizen of Rockbridge County wrote to his friend in Kentucky:

> The attention of the people here is principally turned to politics. The people on this side of the Blue Ridge are generally strongly in favor of the measures of the general government and determined to oppose the French and French partisans to the utmost. Most of the counties on the other side of the mountains [trans-Alleghany] are of the same mind but some are divided.
>
> We have a federal pole hoisted in Brownsburg, seventy feet high, with the colors of the United States flying on top and inscribed Independence or Death.[28]

Another citizen of the same section wrote of the Jefferson party: "Infidels hate religion, legal coercion, and all those old fashioned things."[29] Without deliberation the county court of Greenbrier County tore into pieces and trampled under foot an official copy of Madison's *Report* and the Resolutions of 1799. The acts of the Assembly establishing an armory at Richmond and requiring presidential electors to be elected upon a general ticket instead of by districts as formerly also met opposition in the Federalist strongholds. Leven Powell[30] feared that an act would be passed re-

[28] *The Palladium* (Frankfort, Ky.), October 23, 1798.

[29] *Ibid.*, January 8, 1799.

[30] See Acts of 1798-99. Leven Powell of the Loudoun-Fairfax district had voted against Jefferson for the presidency in 1796 (Randall, *Jefferson*, II, 315; *The Palladium*, February 6, 1800).

quiring representatives in Congress to be elected in the same manner.[31]

The following extract from a letter of General Daniel Morgan, then in Congress, to General Benjamin Biggs furnishes a clue to the attitude of the Revolutionary soldier of the West toward the proceedings of the Virginia assemblies of 1798 and 1799:

> Our political situation [said he] appears to have arrived at that crisis where every friend of his country should declare himself, and both by word and deed take a decided part in favor of a government under which we might live free, happy, and respectable were it not for the intrigues of designing men and the factions of party.
>
> You have doubtless seen the resolutions from Kentucky and the Address from the Virginia Legislature—My God! Who could have thought? that the Legislature of a State which ought to be the most respectable in the Union instead of devoting their exertions to the mere regulation of their State and the happiness of their constituents, were employed in fabricating division in our country and in influencing the people against our government founded by them or their constituents, and which for its justice and moderation is the Envy and Wonder of the surrounding Worlde. It is difficult to conceive what these people would be at, but I verily believe should their designs succeed, it will give a vital Stab to our political Happiness. Instead of an extensive, united nation, respectable among all the people on the Globe, we shall dwindle into a number of petty divisions, an easy prey for domestic Demagogues and foreign Enemies, having besides a moral certainty of external divisions and internal broils.
>
> Under the circumstances, my Dear Sir, it is indispensably

---

[31] *J. P. Branch Papers*, No. II, 234. The Federalists also resented the act whereby the public printing was given to a Republican.

necessary for every friend of his country to exert himself at the ensuing and future elections, as well for Congress as the State Legislature, to put in men of principle and integrity, men unbiased by any foreign interest, who are good federalists and will consult only the Honor, the advantage and Dignity of the United States government. You may rely on it Sir, it is time to know each other; faction shall raise its head and without firmness and decision that beautiful structure the Federal Government is no more! Leading men in our state talk openly of dividing the Government! In the name of Heaven! are their Views honest? I think not—a part can not contain more Wisdom and Virtue than the whole. Does it not appear that these people disappointed at not being elevated in the civil Government, wish to cut it to pieces, in order that they may rule and tyranize over a part.

I wish you to mention my sentiments to all my old friends in your Quarters, Colonel Zane, Strecker, McGuire H.—Tell them they are the sentiments of an old acquaintance who has interest but in common with his fellow citizens who is just returning to domestic life with a sincere wish to spend the remainder of his days in retirement from public life.

As to Mr. Machir and Haymond I shall be happy if either is elected, being both friends of the country; Mr. Machir will have a powerful interest on the east of the mountains. I hope you will not step between the two and suffer an enemy to our country to succeed. When I speak of two good men I wish to give no preference, but in justice to Mr. Machir's services heretofore I must say that for Talents, Gentlemanlike conduct and true federalism he is worthy of respect.

I am Sir with real Esteem and Attachment—Sir, your friend,

DANIEL MORGAN [32]

[32] Draper MSS (*Biggs Papers*), NN., V, p. 116. For practically the same statements see *Columbian Mirror*, April 18, 1799. Daniel Morgan resided in the Valley of Virginia; General Biggs in the extreme northwestern part of the state.

During the winter of 1798–99 national politics took a new turn. The peace policy prevailed and, to the great surprise of both Pickering and Hamilton, Adams nominated William Vans Murry to be minister to France. The nomination was confirmed, and a breach in the Federalist party followed. The disruption did not, however, strengthen the Republican following in Virginia. Already John Marshall had become the active leader of the Federalists in that state. His opposition to the alien and sedition laws and support of the peace policy adopted by Adams rallied about him the Federalists of 1788. Washington and others of the older school came to his aid.

Under the leadership of Marshall the Federalists determined to campaign for a majority in the Assembly of 1799 and to repeal the Resolutions of 1798. They had reason to be encouraged in this undertaking. In many states the congressional elections of 1798 had been decidedly anti-Republican and the Virginia Resolutions of that date had not aroused great enthusiasm in their behalf either at home or in the country at large. The Federalists put forth their most prominent leaders for the Assembly. At the solicitation of Washington, Henry became a candidate for election to that body. Marshall became a candidate for Congress in the Richmond district against a tried Republican, John Clopton. The Federalists claimed that the Union was in danger and that their success at the polls was necessary to preserve it. Their position was set forth in *The Address of the Minority in the Virginia Legislature to the People of the State concerning a Vindi-*

cation of the Constitutionality of the Alien and Sedition Laws, and in an address entitled *Plain Truths*. The latter was written by a resident of Westmoreland County; it denied the state-compact theory of the Constitution and insisted on the sovereignty of the people.

The Federalist platform is more clearly set forth, however, in Marshall's answer to five questions propounded to him by "A Freeholder." In substance these questions were: (1) Are you attached to the sentiments of the Constitution as sanctioned by the people? (2) Is the true interest of America dependent upon any foreign alliance? (3) Do you advocate any other relations with Great Britain than those agreed upon in 1794? (4) Is the war with France necessary? (5) Are you an advocate of the alien and sedition laws? To these inquiries Marshall's reply was that he regarded the Constitution, "as sanctioned by the people, as the rock of our political salvation, which has preserved us from misery, division, and civil war;" following the advice of Washington's farewell address, he declared himself opposed to all alliances with foreigners; he thought the Treaty of 1794 with Great Britain should be preserved and that it might even be necessary to make temporary arrangements with her to secure aid against France; he was opposed to the alien and sedition laws, because, said he, "they are useless and calculated to create unnecessary discontent and jealousies."[33]

[33] *The Spectator*, October 13, 1798. This letter was written when it was known that Marshall would be a candidate for Congress in 1799.

The Republican platform consisted of the Resolutions of 1798. Contrary to the generally accepted opinion, the leaders of this party were not contending mainly for principles; they desired practical results. They disavowed all thought of dismemberment and made persistent efforts to break down the Federalist strongholds. For this purpose political pamphlets were freely distributed in the Valley, and Republican leaders there were promised liberal rewards. The most prominent leaders in the party offered themselves for election to Congress or to the Assembly; Madison became a candidate for election to the latter. So keen was public excitement in Richmond that the final poll was accompanied by riots.[84]

The results of the election were a surprise to both parties. The transmontane country elected fewer Federalists to the Assembly than at previous elections and but one member of that party to Congress. On the other hand, the Federalists gained a marked victory in the Tidewater, where they increased their representation in the Assembly and secured the election of four representatives in Congress.[35] Nicholas, a Republican, was elected by a district in the Tidewater by a bare majority.

Contemporary comments upon the election of 1799 show the surprise which the results created among party leaders and the sectional character of the contest.

[84] *Debates, Va. Constitutional Convention of 1829-30*, 425.

[35] The successful Federalists were Parker, Marshall, Lee, and Evans. Powell of the Loudoun-Fairfax district was also elected as a Federalist.

Jefferson wrote: "The Valley between the Blue Ridge and the North mountain, which has for some time been much tainted and which has given me more serious uneasiness than any other part of the State, has come solidly around."[36] The Federalist victories in the Tidewater were attributed to the heavy vote cast by the merchants and "Tories." Of the election of Lee and the close run given Nicholas, Jefferson said: "It marks a taint in that part of the State which I have not expected." He insisted, however, that the Federalist successes were due to "an accidental combination of circumstances" and that they were only temporary.[37]

When the Assembly of 1799–1800 met, Madison's *Report,* made in answer to the sister states opposed to the Resolutions of 1798, was received and adopted. The Republicans accepted this report and the resolutions which later accompanied it as a vindication of the Resolutions of 1798 and as a conclusive answer to all arguments raised against them. The *Report* was not adopted, however, without strenuous opposition. The vote was: ayes 100, noes 63.[38] An analysis of this vote shows a Federalist loss of strength over the preceding year in the Valley and a gain in the trans-Alleghany and the Tidewater.

The Federalist showing in the elections of 1799 made the results of the election in the following year uncertain. Accordingly further efforts were made to

[36] Jefferson, *Writings* (ed. Ford), VII, 380.
[37] *Ibid.,* VII, 380.
[38] *Debates and Proceedings 1798 and 1799,* 223.

break down the sectional strongholds of the minority. Jacob Koontz, a Jefferson lieutenant in the Valley, "left no stone unturned among his fellow citizens, the Germans."[39] Numerous political pamphlets were distributed in an effort to advance the cause of Republicanism. Thomas Claiborne, of Monongalia County, wrote his chief, Governor Monroe, thus discouragingly of the prospects in the trans-Alleghany:

> The present temper of the inhabitants of this country, being federal, not much is to be expected of them toward republican works—in some owing to the personal influence of a few old residents, grown into the character of federalism by habit and premeditation and perhaps not just reasoning, and in others from a want of literature and a perusal of instructive publications.[40]

The presidential election of 1800 was a landslide for the Republicans. Practically complete returns gave Jefferson a majority of 13,363 votes in a total of 20,797. Loudoun and Augusta were the only counties which gave majorities to Adams, though several counties of the lower Tidewater and the Shenandoah Valley gave him large minorities. The vote in the eastern towns and cities was also almost evenly divided.[41]

In Congress the Virginia Federalists continued to fight the ascendency of Republicanism. They opposed the election of Jefferson to the presidency and gave

[39] *Calendar Va. State Papers*, IX, 121, 131.
[40] *Ibid.*, IX, 111.
[41] *The Palladium* (Frankfort, Ky.), December 12, 1800.

five votes to Burr;[42] they voted for the Judiciary Act of 1801 and against the reduction of the army;[43] they also opposed the repeal of the alien and sedition laws. But the congressional election of 1801 was a severe rebuke to their course; only one Federalist, John Stratton, of Accomac County, secured an election from Virginia.

The elections of 1801 were followed by a subsidence of party strife. The Republicans had undisputed control of the Assembly, and Monroe, who did Jefferson's bidding, was governor. The congressional election of 1803, however, showed a decided reaction in favor of Federalism. Jefferson had not yet accomplished his master-stroke, the purchase of Louisiana; Democracy seemed to be running to excess; and rumors of Jefferson's alleged religious skepticism made unfavorable impressions on the pious Presbyterians, Methodists, and Baptists. Accordingly the old sectional parties again showed signs of a revival. Four Federalists were successful in the congressional contest of 1803: the Tidewater elected Thomas Griffin, the Valley Thomas Lewis[44] and James Stephenson, and the Loudoun and Fairfax district Joseph Lewis. The minority party in the Assembly was reinforced to such an extent that it was able to make effective demands for administrative reform and successful attacks upon

[42] *National Intelligencer*, February 13, 1801; *Niles Register*, XXX, 433.

[43] *Annals of Cong.*, 6 Cong., 2d sess., 836, 915.

[44] Andrew Moore successfully contested the election of Thomas Lewis.

the partisan administration of Monroe.[45] In Congress the Virginia Federalists, elected in 1803, opposed the Louisiana purchase and voted against the appropriation to make it effective.[46]

The popularity of the Louisiana purchase temporarily submerged Federalism in Virginia. In the Valley the treaty with France was made the occasion for numerous mass-meetings and public orations. On March 4, 1804, Chapman Johnson addressed the citizens of Staunton, the Federalist stronghold of all Virginia, on the "Late Treaty with France." Of the breakdown in party lines which the Louisiana purchase was bringing about he said:

The clouds which accompanied the tempest [1798] are not yet scattered from the horizon; but I see them fast disappearing under the influence of the new planet. Party animosity is forgotten, whilst all denominations of politicians concur in rejoicing at our late acquisitions. This is the first distinguished occasion on which both parties have rejoiced together.[47]

The Louisiana purchase, as a harmonizing factor, was aided by the prevalence of unusual economic prosperity, especially in the Piedmont and the Valley. These sections became the great flour-producing areas for the demands created by the European wars. Of his observations at this time on a trip through Albemarle County Thomas R. Joynes wrote: "On every side large verdant wheat fields meet and cheer the

[45] *Va. Argus,* March 14, 1809.

[46] *Annals of Congress,* 8 Cong., 1 sess., 442, 546.

[47] *Oration on the Late Treaty with France,* 16. This oration may be found in the Library of the Historical Society of Wisconsin.

traveler."[48] Hundreds of flour mills sprang up along the Piedmont and Valley rivers.[49] In 1807 two thousand coal boats plied annually from Richmond to Philadelphia, New York, and Baltimore.[50] This is also the period when the timber lands of the Piedmont and the Tidewater were being exploited. Timber, heading, staves, and poles were being shipped to the West Indies and to foreign countries in large quantities. Hundreds of vessels sailed annually from Norfolk, Bermuda Hundred, and Alexandria with flour, wheat, and other products of the interior. The improved navigation of the James and the Potomac made it possible for the planters of the interior to bring their products to the shipping centers at the head of tide.[51]

These years mark also an important period in the industrial development of the trans-Alleghany. The treaty of 1795 with Spain encouraged the western farmers to plant on a larger scale and gave renewed activity to commerce on the Ohio, while the peace of Fort Grenville, of the same year, removed the Indians as a restraining influence. It was during these years that the cattle-raisers of the Valley gave their lands up to wheat-raising, to find new pastures in the "Glades" of the Alleghany Highlands.[52] At the same time the

[48] *William and Mary Coll. Quarterly*, X, 148.

[49] Single counties contained as many as seventy flour mills. See *U. S. Census of 1810*, on "Manufactures."

[50] *State Papers*, 14 Cong., 1st sess., Doc. No. 19 (Gallatin's Report).

[51] Jefferson, *Writings*, IV, 464; VII, 292; X, 227; *Baltimore Daily Advertiser*, February 11, 1796.

[52] *Richmond Enquirer*, February 2, 1820.

small farms on the Monongahela and the upper Ohio became the source of supply to the New Orleans markets for flour, potatoes, apples, and pork.[53] The renown of the flour made on the upper Ohio was so great that it commanded one dollar more per barrel than that produced in other sections. Cattle-raising also became an important industry in the Ohio Valley. Thence large numbers of grain-fed cattle were driven into the Glades where they were pastured for two or three months and then driven on to Baltimore and Philadelphia.[54] Wool-growing also became an important industry in this section, and smelting furnaces were erected on the Monongahela and in what is now the Northern Panhandle of West Virginia.[55] So important did the commerce on the upper Ohio become that Charlestown, now Wellesburg, West Virginia, was made a port of entry by act of Congress.[56]

It was, however, the manufacture of salt which began to emancipate the west from the east. After this industry became important it was no longer necessary for a pioneer to spend weeks upon the back of a pack-horse carrying a bag of salt from the eastern markets. Consequently he did not return so frequently to the east to renew his political faith at the hearthstone of the fathers and to contribute of his coon skins

[53] *The Palladium*, May 26, 1801. In 1801 $332,343.70 worth of farm products passed Louisville in two and one-half months.

[54] Cutler, *Cutler*, 90, 103.

[55] See Acts of Assembly, 1813–14, 55; *Am. Daily Advertiser*, July 10, 1810; *Richmond Enquirer*, February 2, 1820.

[56] *Annals of Cong.*, 8 Cong., 1st sess., 483.

for a part of their luxuries.[57] In 1797 Elisha Brooks set up the first salt furnace on the Great Kanawha.[58] In 1807 the Ruffner brothers improved the method of manufacture and increased the quantity of the Kanawha product. Soon the "Kanawha Salines" became known far and near for the excellent quality of salt produced. Hundreds of people became dependent upon the salt-making industry for a livelihood. Some built keel-boats and distributed the manufactured product along the Ohio and its tributaries; others made barrels and found employment in drawing the salt brine from the wells and evaporating it. In 1814 the Kanawha Salines produced 600,000 bushels annually, supplying the western markets at prices of seventy-five cents to one dollar per bushel.[59]

The industrial development of the trans-Alleghany and the Piedmont was accompanied by a large increase in their population. During the two decades from 1790 to 1810 the population of the former increased from 41,219 to 114,195. These settlers found homes along the bottom lands of the Ohio and its tributaries. During the same period the increase in the population of the Piedmont was more than ninety thousand, more than half of which was negro slaves. As the small farmers of this section sold their holdings and pushed farther westward, the lands were engrossed and

[57] See Doddridge's *Notes* (bound with Kercheval's *History of the Valley*), 344.

[58] Hale, *Salt* (a pamphlet).

[59] At this time salt was selling at five dollars per bushel in the Atlantic ports.

slavery became more important. The total population of the Tidewater and the Valley remained practically stationary.

The great development of the trans-Alleghany prior to 1807 was not accompanied by pressing demands for internal communications with the east. The river valleys, along which the people were settled, were the highways and led to the only market, the lower Mississippi. The salt produced there did not more than supply the internal demand. At this time the western people were more interested in the construction of mill-dams, ferries, and smelting furnaces, as the numerous acts of the Assembly attested,[60] than in communication with the coast. In its final form, John G. Jackson, the representative of the trans-Alleghany, did not vote for the bill to lay out and to construct the Cumberland Road.[61]

Internal improvements continued, however, to be an important interest to the inhabitants east of the Blue Ridge. John Dawson and T. M. Randolph, representatives of districts in northern Piedmont, gave the only votes from Virginia for the Cumberland Road Act. The east looked upon the James and Potomac river-improvements as the beginning of larger undertakings eventually to connect the east and the west. Gallatin's report of 1807 aroused little enthusiasm in the west but was received with great favor in the east.

[60] See Shepherd, *Statutes at Large*, III (years 1804, 1805, and 1806), 44, 54, 158, 171, 238, 245, 246, 272, 275, 301, 302, 303, 334, 349, 401, 403.

[61] *Annals of Cong.*, 9 Cong., 1st sess., 840.

The Richmond coal operators were especially interested in it, for the canal system, which it contemplated, would have brought Richmond into closer proximity with Philadelphia and New York.[62]

The semi-nationalistic policy pursued by Jefferson as president gave rise to two opposition parties in Virginia. They were the "Tertium Quids" and a rejuvenated Federalist party. The rise of the "Quids," as the opposition party east of the Blue Ridge is commonly called, was due largely to the eccentric character and the uncompromising attitude of John Randolph and to the presence of a large number of ardent strict constructionists. The occasions for the formation of this party lay in the congressional discussions over the Yazoo claims[63] and the relations with Spain, and in the unsuccessful outcome of Monroe's negotiations with England.[64] Randolph and his followers opposed the payment of the claims and favored war with Spain and peace with England. Madison, the leader of the administration party and the heir apparent to the throne, favored the payment of the Yazoo claims. Meanwhile Jefferson publicly professed to be with Randolph, who had ambitions for the presidency, but at heart he was unfriendly to war with any country. Randolph's opposition to the payment of the claims was heightened by the fact that he had been in Georgia when the Yazoo scandal was being aired and by a

[62] *Annals of Cong.*, 9 Cong., 2d sess., 83, 84.

[63] Haskins, "Yazoo Land Co.," in *Am. Hist. Asso. Rept.*, 1891.

[64] Garland, *Randolph*, I, 218, 240-64; Randall, *Jefferson*, II, 146-50.

conviction, then formed, that most persons in any way connected with it were rascals.

The Quids never became a factor in local politics. When the group was first formed it included practically all the congressmen east of the Blue Ridge. But when Jefferson and his foreign policy became involved, a large part of Randolph's following deserted him. In addition to a few outside of the state, those who continued to adhere to the Quids, more or less consistently, were Giles, Gray, Clay, and Garnett, who with Randolph claimed to be the only surviving Republicans of the school of 1798.[65]

The new Federalist party was in many respects a revival of the old Federalist party, but, unlike the Quids, it found its chief source of strength west of the Blue Ridge. It owed its origin largely to the opposition to the Jefferson-Madison policy of war by commercial restriction. That policy had early deprived the farmers of the Valley and the interior counties of the Piedmont of a market for their wheat, flour, and other products. In 1812 they were able with difficulty to secure four dollars and fifty cents per barrel for flour,[66] which under more favorable commercial conditions could have been sold for more than twelve dollars.

The effect of the embargo upon local politics did not begin to be felt until after the elections of 1807. Consequently the Federalists made little showing then in either the state or the congressional elections,[67] but

[65] See Monroe, *Writings* (ed. Ham.), IV, 486.

[66] *Niles Register*, V, 41.

[67] Joseph Lewis of the Loudoun-Fairfax district was re-elected.

the election of the following year showed a decided reaction in their favor. A large Federalist minority was elected to the Assembly.

Under the leadership of Daniel Sheffey and in alliance with the Quids, the Federalists in the Assembly of 1808-9 began a movement for reform. The armory established in Richmond in 1798, when Republicanism was in the ascendant, had always been an eyesore to the supporters of a strong national government. In 1808 it became currently reported that the armory was being used for the private emolument of its managers and that it was turning out an inferior product. Consequently Sheffey found little difficulty in securing the appointment of a committee of "backwoodsmen" to investigate it. The report sustained the rumored charges and went so far as to accuse the governor of being an accomplice. Accordingly the west again asserted itself; a law to deprive the executive of the power to appoint officials for the armory was enacted and the payment of money from the state treasury was surrounded by restrictions. This airing of mismanagement and inefficiency brought the Republican party into great discredit in the west.[68]

The Quids made a determined stand in the presidential election of 1808. With the co-operation of the Federalists they hoped to defeat Madison, whom Jefferson had designated as his successor.[69] They

[68] *Debates, Va. Constitutional Convention of 1829-30*, 480; *Journal, House of Del.*, 1808-9, 108-14; *Va. Argus*, March 14, 1809; *Revised Code of 1819*, 130.

[69] *Va. Argus*, March 9, 1809; Randall, *Jefferson*, III, 253.

selected as their candidate James Monroe, a staunch strict constructionist of the east Virginia school and an earnest advocate of peace with Great Britain, who had temporarily broken with Jefferson over British relations.

The contest between Monroe and Madison for the presidency was confined to Virginia. It began in the Assembly, in January, 1808, when a legislative caucus favorable to each candidate was held. The caucus favorable to Madison's election was attended by one hundred and nineteen delegates and senators, representatives, for the most part, of Piedmont and transmontane counties. The Monroe caucus was attended by sixty-seven delegates and senators who came mostly from the Tidewater and Valley counties.[70] As there were only about forty senators and delegates who did not attend either caucus it is fair to presume that some of the Federalists co-operated with the anti-administration forces. Later the fight was carried into the congressional caucus which the Virginia Quids and Federalists favorable to the nomination of Monroe refused to attend.

Practically complete returns gave Madison 12,451 votes, Monroe 2,770, and Pinckney 435.[71] The vote by counties shows that some counties normally Federalist supported Monroe. Such were Loudoun and Frederick which Monroe carried by large majorities, whereas Pinckney did not receive a single vote in either.

[70] *Va. Argus*, January 26, 1808; *ibid.*, January 29, 1898; Stanwood, *Presidency*, 90.

[71] *Va. Argus*, November 22, 1808.

The counties of the central Valley gave their opposition vote to Pinckney. Monroe's chief source of strength, however, was in the Tidewater counties, of which twelve gave him more than one-half of his total vote. Accomac gave Monroe 397 votes, whereas Madison received only 30, and Northampton gave 121 to Monroe, to 9 for Madison. The large anti-administration vote in the Tidewater makes it clear that Jefferson's policy of commercial restriction was unpopular there and that the section was anti-Jefferson rather than anti-strict construction.

In the elections of 1809, the first congressional elections since the embargo, the Quids and Federalists showed surprising vigor and strength. Randolph, Clay, and Gray were re-elected to Congress, as was Joseph Lewis, a Federalist from the Loudoun-Fairfax district. But to the great surprise of all, the Valley became as solidly Federalist as it had been in 1800 and 1803. Four members of that party, Daniel Sheffey, James Breckenridge, Jacob Swoope, and James Stephenson, were elected to Congress. The Federalist minority in the Assembly was also greatly increased.

The Federalists and the Quids elected to Congress in 1809 united to oppose the administration. The events of that year caused the tide to turn in favor of war, but these men consistently opposed war; they also tried to procure the repeal of the non-intercourse act, and voted against providing a more adequate defense and the dismissal of the British minister.[72] Sheffey

[72] *Annals of Cong.*, 11 Cong., 3d sess., 865; *ibid.*, 2d sess., I, 1152.

admitted that American commerce suffered most from Great Britain, but, said he, "the reason is the tyrant of Europe has not power to execute his wishes." He was unwilling to trust any man with such a "shady" past as Napoleon.[73]

Although the Quids generally co-operated with the Federalists in their attempt to recharter the United States Bank, they were not enthusiastic over it. The attitude of the Virginia Federalists in this attempt deserves, however, special attention. Sheffey was their spokesman. He defended the constitutionality of the bank on the ground that Congress possessed all power "necessary and proper" to carry into execution the delegated powers. "Congress," he said, "possesses all the attributes of sovereignty," and he insisted that the occasion for the exercise of this power rested alone with the representatives of the people. He admitted that there might be flagrant wrongs done to the rights of the minority in this feature of our government, but he insisted that "there never can be any usurpation." The charter of a national bank and kindred subjects, said he, "must always be a question of sound discretion guided by the interests of the Union and not a question of power."[74]

The congressional election of 1811 sustained the course pursued by the Federalists and the Quids. Randolph, Clay, and Gray were re-elected; and furthermore the area of Federalist strength was greatly increased. Three members of that party, Sheffey,

[73] *Ibid.*, 1st sess., I, 401, 402.
[74] *Ibid.*, 3d sess., 733–35.

Breckenridge, and Baker, secured election from the Valley. Lewis was re-elected from the Loudoun district, and the trans-Alleghany returned a Federalist for the first time since 1793. The Federalist minority in the Assembly was at the same time greatly increased.

In the twelfth Congress, 1811-12, Sheffey and Randolph earnestly resisted the new war party. In opposition to war the former spoke for the economic interests of his section. He opposed war because it would cut off the market in the West Indies and elsewhere for beef, pork, flour, and lumber. He was opposed to war with Great Britain, because that country was the only nation with whom we had a profitable commerce. He showed that, when the embargo went into effect, we exported annually to France goods valued at only $2,700,000, while our exports at the same time to Great Britain amounted to $28,000,000.[75] The Virginia Federalists and Quids voted aye on a resolution to postpone a declaration of war,[76] and when war was declared, they opposed the manner in which it was conducted,[77] an increase in the military forces,[78] and an appropriation to pay the war debt.[79] In the Assembly many delegates from the western counties voted against the bill to provide a more adequate defense for the coast towns.[80] In fact, the opposition of the interior counties of Virginia to the

[75] *Annals of Cong.*, 12 Cong., I, 622, 623.
[76] *Ibid.*, II, 1682.
[77] *Ibid.*, 1056.
[78] *Ibid.*, 1813.   [79] *Ibid.*, 1798.
[80] *Debates, Va. Constitutional Convention of 1829-30*, 136.

War of 1812 was excelled only by that of the New England Federalists.

The congressional elections of 1813 resulted in the complete disappearance of the Quid party from Virginia. Randolph went down in defeat before J. W. Eppes, a war Republican. He was possibly never more unpopular in his native state than during the War of 1812. From Washington he wrote: "By my old neighbors and my new, I have been entirely neglected."[81] On the other hand, this election shows that the Federalists were again thoroughly and securely intrenched within the state. The redistricting of 1812 produced some change in the sectional character of the opposition strength, but numerically it did not lose a representative. With the disappearance of the Quids from the Tidewater, Bayley, Federalist, secured an election from the Accomac district. Lewis, of the Loudoun district, Sheffey, and Breckenridge were re-elected and Francis White succeeded Baker, each chosen to represent districts in the Valley. In the northwestern district John G. Jackson again came to the assistance of his brother-in-law, Madison, and secured an election as a Republican. But Hugh Caperton, Federalist, was elected from the new trans-Alleghany district composed of counties along the Great Kanawha.[82]

This period of threatened Federalist ascendency in the west was accompanied by a reform movement. The things most desired were internal improvements,

[81] *Letters to a Young Relative*, 118.

[82] *Niles Register*, VIII, 192; *Debates, Va. Constitutional Convention of 1829–30*, 511.

state banks, a greater representation in the Assembly, and white manhood suffrage. The census of 1810 gave the west 312,626 white inhabitants and the east 338,827. In the Senate the former section had only four members, the latter twenty, while an apportionment on the basis of the white population would have entitled the west to nine. The unequal representation in this body had resulted in the successive defeat of several bills providing for the call of a constitutional convention,[83] and threats of dismemberment were current. A writer from Dumfries suggested that the state be divided into northern and southern Virginia by a line passing up the Rappahannock, thence to the junction of the Greenbrier and the New rivers, thence along the New and the Great Kanawha to the Ohio.[84] A writer in the *Alexandria Herald* suggested Winchester for the seat of government of the proposed new state.[85] Numerous mass-meetings passed resolutions demanding suffrage for all taxpayers and militiamen.[86] A meeting held at Harrisonburg, Rockbridge County, reiterated, in the form of a resolution, that portion of the Bill of Rights, which describes the qualifications of those entitled to suffrage.[87]

The movement finally took form in the Staunton Convention. This body met August 19-23, 1816, and

[83] *Debates, Va. Constitutional Convention of 1829-30*, 258, 259, 421.

[84] *Alexandria Herald*, August, 1816; *Richmond Enquirer*, April 13, 1816. A similar proposition had been made in 1796. See *Baltimore Daily Advertiser*, June 30, 1796.

[85] *Alexandria Herald*, March 8, 1816; *ibid.*, March 20, 1816.

[86] *Ibid.*, July 21, 1816.   [87] *Ibid.*, July 21, 1815.

was attended by sixty-five delegates representing thirty-five western counties. Congressman Breckenridge was president. The convention discussed at great length the grievances of the west and ended its labors by addressing a memorial to the Assembly. This document showed how it was possible for 204,766 white inhabitants residing in the small counties east of the Blue Ridge, a number 72,183 less than one-half the total white population of the state, to control the action of the Assembly. This condition it attributed to "unnatural and accidental" circumstances. It asked that a constitutional convention be called empowered to remedy all the defects in the government. Six delegates, however, opposed a convention with such extensive powers and insisted that it should be called to make amendments to the constitution of 1776.[88]

The persistent and concerted efforts of the reformers aroused sympathy and alarm in the east. It was on this occasion that Jefferson came forward with his famous letter of July, 1816, to Samuel Kercheval. This letter later became a text for the preachers of reform. It outlined the early reform movement of 1779 and suggested many changes in the fundamental law. It favored the introduction of the New England form of local government, equal representation based on white population, free white suffrage, and the election of the governor, judges, jurors, and sheriffs by popular vote. Jefferson ignored the conservative idea that

[88] *Niles Register*, XI, 17–24; *Alexandria Herald*, September 2, 1816.

the constitution of 1776 was the best that could be made and that it should be preserved out of veneration for the fathers.[89] Ritchie, of the *Richmond Enquirer,* warned the conservatives that they courted danger by running counter to public opinion. To the Assembly of 1816-17 he said: "If you refuse it this winter, think you that the representatives of the people will arrest their clamors and complaints? No.` The defects in the constitution must be amended. Bow, then, to the destiny which awaits you; for it is inevitable."[90]

The conservatives would not vote for a constitutional convention. They did, however, consent to a compromise whereby the west obtained a representation in the Senate based upon white numbers in exchange for a law equalizing land values for purposes of assessment.[91] This compromise and the changed conditions following 1816 caused a temporary suspension of the reform movement, the sectional and political character of which had doubtless prevented the most desirable results. Breckenridge and Sheffey, its master spirits, were Federalists. Their denunciations of Virginia's institutions and political leaders were frequently interpreted by the east as demonstrations of disloyalty and as the mutterings of voices in sympathy with the Hartford Conventionists.

The elections of 1815 marked a decline in the Federalist strength in Virginia, as elsewhere. By

[89] Randall, *Jefferson,* II, 650; Jefferson, *Writings* (ed. Ford), 37-45.

[90] *Richmond Enquirer,* October 2, 1816.

[91] *Debates, Va. Constitutional Convention of 1829-30,* 258.

1817 the party had practically disappeared. The Hartford Convention and the successful termination of the War of 1812 brought that party into disrepute. By the election of 1815 the minority in the Assembly was greatly reduced, and Joseph Lewis was the only Federalist to secure an election to Congress from a district east of the Blue Ridge. The trans-Alleghany again became solidly Republican, but the Valley remained Federalist.[92]

Although their action may seem inconsistent the Virginia Federalists, elected in 1815, in their opposition to the recharter of the United States Bank and an increase in the tariff measures, at the time deemed necessary by the administration to restore credit and to protect American industries, spoke for their constituents and were not acting in the main as an obstructing minority in Congress. They represented farmers and graziers, who had no interest to conserve by an increase in the tariff, and a section interested in the incorporation of state banks. The delegates of the eastern counties had already defeated a movement on the part of the west for the incorporation of fifteen state banks.[93]

But on the subject of internal improvements the west showed its truly nationalistic tendencies. The War of 1812 and the events leading thereto made this subject an important one to the transmontane

[92] *Niles Register*, IX, 280. Sheffey and Breckenridge were reelected and Magnus Tate was elected to succeed White.

[93] *Niles Register*, X, 90; Jefferson, *Writings* (ed. Ford), X, 2; *Alexandria Herald*, September 2, 1816.

people. Commercial restrictions, dangers to ocean commerce, and the great internal development caused trade and immigration to seek an overland route across the Alleghanies. In 1815 both cotton and wheat were being transported by wagons from Wheeling and Pittsburg to the eastern cities.[94] The remnant of the Federalist party had already become the leaders in the movement for a better means of communication between the east and the west. Marshall and Breckenridge had been the dominating power on the commission, appointed by the Assembly in 1812, to view the western rivers and to suggest plans for their improved navigation.[95] The report of this commission, which recommended vast schemes of internal improvements and suggested the expediency of securing a federal appropriation to aid in their construction, was adopted by the Assembly of 1814–15 by the united vote of the west against the east. The same Assembly, as well as the following, requested the representatives of the state in Congress to request "the legislature of the Union to manifest an interest in internal improvements."[96]

Thus the representatives of the west, both Republicans and Federalists, were prepared to support Calhoun's Bonus Bill. In behalf of this measure Sheffey spoke for the interests of the transmontane country. He believed that the implied powers were sufficient

---

[94] *State Papers*, 14 Cong., Doc. No. 75.

[95] *Proceedings of the Board of Public Works*, I, 6, 28; *Report of the Committee on Roads and Int. Imp.* (1831–32), 3.

[96] *Ibid.*, 5.

guarantee to Congress for passing the bill, and that the sovereign people, speaking through their representatives, should interpret the Constitution to meet the exigencies of the times.[97] In opposition to the individualistic theory of the Constitution, at this time so ably set forth by P. P. Barbour,[98] he insisted that the people through their representatives in Congress assembled were supreme.

With one exception each of the representatives of districts west of the Blue Ridge voted for the Bonus Bill. It received also the support of the representative from the Norfolk district. In many respects this affirmative vote of the west was the last expression of Federalism, as such, in the state. Sheffey, Breckenridge, and Tate, old-line Federalists, were the chief supporters of the bill; but the Republicans of the trans-Alleghany and the Norfolk districts were not yet so thoroughly imbued with the principles of strict construction as to warrant them in voting against a measure of such vital interest to their constituents.

[97] *Annals of Cong.*, 14 Cong., 2d sess., 886.
[98] *Ibid.*, 893 ff.

CHAPTER IV

THE ERA OF GOOD FEELING AND THE RISE OF THE NATIONAL REPUBLICAN PARTY, 1817-28

As in national politics, so in Virginia, the period following the second British war was one of accord, giving place, as years passed, to one of clashing sectional interests. In the congressional election of 1817 nationalism made no stand in the state, except in the districts along the Potomac and the projected Cumberland Road; in the former section C. F. Mercer and Edward Colston and in the latter James Pindall, all orthodox strict constructionists, except that they believed in the constitutionality of federal appropriations to works of internal improvements, were successful candidates. Each of these candidates urged his election on the ground that he stood for what the state had desired in 1815 and 1816, when the Assembly had asked the federal government to aid it in improving the communication between the James and the Kanawha rivers.[1]

The efforts to defeat Mercer in 1817 show the determination with which the young school of Virginia

---

[1] *Debates, Va. Constitutional Convention of 1829-30*, speech of C. F. Mercer. Pindall's opponent was J. G. Jackson, who had already proposed an amendment to the Constitution to give Congress power to appropriate money to works of internal improvement (*State Papers*, 13 Cong., 2d sess., Doc. No. 20). Jackson was again defeated by Pindall in 1819 (*Northwestern Gazette*, May 19, 1819).

politicians set about to unify the state in its reaction against Jeffersonian Republicanism. To effect the "complete republicanization" of the Old Dominion General Armistead T. Mason resigned his place in the United States Senate to contest the election of Mercer to the House of Representatives. Both Mason and Mercer had extensive and influential family connections in the Loudoun-Fairfax district. Mason was of the family of George Mason; Mercer of that of General Hugh Mercer of revolutionary fame. With all the earnestness which the younger school of Virginia politicians were able to command, Mason stood for the ideas of strict construction so ably enunciated by his illustrious ancestor. On the other hand, Mercer was true to the nationalistic teachings of the revolutionary soldier. After a hotly contested election Mercer was successful by a scant majority. The bitterness which grew out of the contest led to a duel between Mason and his cousin, J. M. McCarthy, in which the former was killed.[2]

The election of 1817 brought a sweeping change in the *personnel* of Virginia's congressmen. Young men of but medium talents generally replaced the more illustrious representatives. Among the new men were P. P. Barbour, John Floyd, John Tyler, R. L, Garnett, and C. F. Mercer, each of them, except Mercer, set against the Clay-Calhoun policies of nationalism and ambitious to restore the fallen prestige of Virginia. The change in the current of Vir-

[2] *Alexandria Herald*, May 9, 1817; *ibid.*, May 24, 1817; *ibid.*, February 6, 18, 1819; *Va. Hist. Coll.*, X, 265.

ginia politics was evidenced by John Randolph's restoration to public favor, he being re-elected to Congress.

Immediately following 1817 there were many local as well as national conditions of importance from a sectional standpoint, which contributed to make state unity and strict construction popular in Virginia. The Federalist party was practically dead; the west had been conciliated by reforms and promises; the zeal of the young leaders tended toward accord; and a group of issues, including the federal Supreme Court decisions, internal improvements, and slavery agitation, furthered these tendencies.

In 1816 the chief topic of discussion in northern and northwestern Virginia was the decision of the federal Supreme Court in the case of *Martin* v. *Hunter, Lessee.* In 1782 the Assembly had confiscated the claims of the Fairfax heirs, having previously declared the Vandalia and Indiana companies' claims invalid. In 1789 David Hunter was given a patent for lands which had formerly belonged to Fairfax, and being refused possession, he later brought suit in the District Court of Shenandoah County. Failing to sustain his claim there he appealed to the Supreme Court of Virginia, which reversed the decision of the lower court. Meanwhile Fairfax died, bequeathing his right in the disputed property to David Martin, who appealed from the decision of the Supreme Court of Virginia to the United States Supreme Court. In 1813 the federal court handed down a decision to sustain the lower court of Virginia and issued a mandamus to compel its execution. The decision remained unexecuted, however, and in 1815 the Supreme Court of Virginia, under the direction of Judge Spencer Roane, took under consideration the mandamus of the federal court. The bench was unanimous in the opinion that the mandamus should not be obeyed and that such appeals from the decisions of the state courts to the federal were unconstitutional.[3] In 1816 the federal court, under the direction of Chief Justice Marshall, reaffirmed its decision and ordered the marshal of western Virginia to execute its command.[4] This decision did much to diminish nationalistic sentiment in the Northern Neck and the northwest, its former strongholds. The decision was an issue in the contest between Mercer and Mason, when George Mason's objections to the ratification of the federal Constitution were brought very cogently to mind.[5] Besides, those landowners who had received grants or made purchases since the confiscation of the Fairfax, Indiana, and Vandalia claims now had material reasons for becoming strict constructionists. Spencer Roane, who lost no opportunity to take advantage of these favorable conditions, became popular in the west as well as in the east.[6]

The decision in the case of *McCullough* v. *Mary-*

[3] *Va. Reports*, 4 Mumford, 12.

[4] 1 Wheaton, 304; see also Dodd, "Chief Justice Marshall and Virginia," in *Am. Hist. Rev.*, XII, 776–87.

[5] See chap. ii, p. 56.

[6] See *Richmond Enquirer*, February, 1816; *Branch Papers*, II, 1, 131; Jefferson, *Writings* (ed. Ford), IX, 530–53.

land was also unpopular in all sections. The east opposed it because of the political principles involved;[7] the west because of the devotion there to state banks, two of which it had finally succeeded in getting.[8] The western press made copious extracts from the attacks of "Amphictyon" and "Hampden"[9] upon nationalism, and the *Northwestern Gazette,* published at Wheeling, praised the action of Ohio in collecting a tax from the branch of the United States Bank located at Chillicothe, and insisted that the charter to the federal bank was unconstitutional.[10] About the same time Pindall presented petitions from sundry citizens of Ohio and Brooke counties asking permission to pay internal revenue dues in state bank notes. It is significant that the west united with the east in the Assembly of 1819 to pass a resolution directing the Virginia senators in Congress to oppose the United States Bank.

Those interested in securing better means of internal communications came now to rely more upon state aid. Alarmed at the renewed activity of New York and Philadelphia to direct trade thither they became concerned for the future of Richmond. The veto of the Bonus Bill had temporarily dashed the

[7] *Richmond Enquirer,* January 22, 1819.

[8] The Assembly of 1817 incorporated the Bank of the Valley, located at Winchester, and the Bank of Northwestern Virginia, located at Wheeling.

[9] Pseudonyms over which Judge Roane wrote (*Richmond Enquirer,* January 22, 1819).

[10] February 4, 1819; see *ibid.,* April 23, 1818; June 13, 1819; October 28, 1819.

RISE OF NATIONAL REPUBLICAN PARTY 105

hope of assistance from the federal government. Accordingly the east and the west united to create the Board of Public Works[11] and a permanent fund for internal improvements.[12] The proceeds of the internal improvement fund were to be appropriated by the Board of Public Works to such approved companies as should have previously provided three-fifths of the capital stock necessary to complete their proposed undertakings.

The inadequacy of the income from the internal improvement fund and the proverbial inactivity of the Assembly, however, came near causing a political reaction in the transmontane country, where private enterprise was unable to avail itself of the benefits of the fund, and no important works could be commenced. Accordingly its representatives in Congress, although elected as strict constructionists, frequently showed a disposition to favor federal internal improvements. Thus the representatives of the trans-Alleghany voted for the bill of 1818 to make further appropriations to the Cumberland Road, as did those of the Valley, who recorded their vote. Still doubtful of the course of the state and federal government, Ballard Smith, of the Kanawha River district, proposed to amend this appropriation bill by the addition

[11] The board was composed of thirteen members: the governor, treasurer, and attorney-general, members *ex officio,* and ten other persons, elected annually by joint ballot of the Assembly. The elective members were to be distributed as follows: the Tidewater, 2; the Piedmont, 3; the Valley, 2; the trans-Alleghany, 3.

[12] In 1816 the fund amounted to $1,462,140.61. Acts of 1815-16, 35, 57; *Niles Register,* IX, 429, 451.

of a clause to authorize the federal government to subscribe two-fifths of the capital stock of any company which Virginia might incorporate to effect a communication between the James and Kanawha rivers.[13] Tucker, who represented a district in the Shenandoah Valley, proposed a similar amendment to aid internal improvements in that section. At the same time sundry persons, residents of counties between the Kanawha and the James, petitioned Congress to aid the state in the construction of works of internal improvement.[14]

The necessity for political union and for the accomplishment of some material results made further delay on the part of the conservatives impossible. Accordingly the Assembly of 1819 authorized the purchase of the rights of the James River Company and assumed the responsibility for continuing the James and Kanawha river-improvements at the expense of the state. The stockholders of the James River Company were to receive 12 per cent. per annum on the par value of their stock for twelve years, after which they were to receive 15 per cent. The actual work of construction was left to the management of the company, but the Board of Public Works was authorized to spend annually $200,000, in addition to the income from the permanent fund.[15] An act of 1820 further appeased

[13] *Annals of Cong.*, 15 Cong., 1st sess., II, 1660.

[14] *Richmond Enquirer*, January 23, 1818; *Niles Register*, XIII, 125, 126.

[15] Acts of 1818–19, 39; *Twenty-sixth Annual Report of the James River and Kanawha Co.*, 665.

the west by placing the management of the works on the Kanawha and of the proposed turnpike connecting the Kanawha and the James under the control of two commissions, each composed of persons residing west of the Blue Ridge.[16] At the same time efforts were made to purchase the rights and interests of the Potomac Company, and surveys were authorized to determine the best means of connecting the waters of the Potomac and the Ohio.[17] During the years immediately following 1819 many thousands of dollars were expended on the James and Kanawha river-improvements and the turnpike connecting them.

Strange as it may at first seem, the representatives of western Virginia in Congress were for the extension of negro slavery into Missouri. Both Pindall and Smith argued that extension did not necessarily increase the evils of negro slavery, or the number of those in bondage, and that it permitted diffusion, which brought intimate relations between master and slave, to the great advantage of the latter.[18] Virginia gave no vote to exclude slavery from all territory or from the proposed state of Missouri,[19] and the compromise by which Missouri was finally admitted received only four affirmative votes, but one of which came from west of the Blue Ridge.[20]

[16] Acts of 1820–21, 49.

[17] *Alexandria Herald*, August 8, 1821; *Niles Register*, XVII, 440.

[18] *Annals of Cong.*, 16 Cong., 1st sess., I, 996, 1000, 1268–72.

[19] *Ibid.*, 1316, 1572.

[20] *Ibid.*, II, 1572, 1587; *Richmond Enquirer*, March 7, 1820.

The east feared that agitation on the subject of negro slavery would endanger the existence of the institution and array the North against the South. In such agitation as the Missouri issue occasioned, Jefferson heard "a fire-bell in the night—the death knell of the Union."[21] The blow given state rights was, however, the chief objection raised in that section to the Missouri Compromise. In it Roane saw the cause of a future war to restore the rights of the states; Andrew Stevenson was opposed to any compromise with constitutional principles; and Linn Banks, Epps, and Ritchie unhesitatingly denounced the compromise as a breach of the Constitution.[22]

In 1820 temporary conditions made a large and powerful element in the west favorable to the extension of negro slavery. The belief had not yet become general there that negro slavery was an economic evil and that it was then preventing the material development of the country. True, most of the inhabitants disliked the institution, but they disliked the negro more. They knew just enough about him to banish from their minds exalted opinions of the possibilities of his race. Besides, sectional agitation of negro slavery was in their minds the greatest menace which could befall the Union.[23] The larger portion of the inhabitants knew but little about negro slavery and

---

[21] *William and Mary College Quarterly*, X, 7; Jefferson, *Writings* (ed. Ford), X, 157.

[22] *Ibid.*, 7-15.

[23] *Western Spy*, June 22, 1820; *National Intelligencer*, September 13, 1820.

RISE OF NATIONAL REPUBLICAN PARTY 109

less about its worst features. Except in small areas along the Kanawha and in the Valley, slavery was more or less paternal. Few thought of deriving incomes from slave labor or offspring, and overseers were unknown.

A few communities of the west, however, had a material interest in slaves. Following the War of 1812 much of the land, which had formerly been devoted to wheat culture, was given up to tobacco-growing, and negroes were purchased to assist in the new industry. The total increase in the slave population of the Valley during the decade from 1810 to 1820 was quite marked.[24] This was also the period when a large number of slave-owners found homes in the Kanawha Valley. For the most part they were persons emigrating to the Missouri country, who were stopped on the route by the cheapness of lands and the opportunity for hiring their negro slaves to the salt-makers for cash wages. Some owners were able to hire out as many as fifty negroes annually. Soon the emigrants became attached to the country and took up permanent residences.

This is also the period when most intense feeling existed in the west over the escape of fugitive slaves. The humane societies of Pennsylvania and Ohio were then doing much to encourage runaways and to intimidate masters trying to apprehend them.[25] In some instances masters were thrown into prison on the charge of kidnaping, while in others they en-

[24] *Debates, Va. Constitutional Convention of 1829–30.* 260–90.
[25] *Va. Northwestern Gazette,* August 20, 1820.

countered mob violence.[26] So intense did feeling in western Virginia become that Pindall introduced in Congress a resolution to amend the fugitive slave law of 1793 so as to make it the duty of the federal government to apprehend and return runaway slaves.[27] The press of Wheeling denounced the humane societies of Ohio as "inquisitorial tribunals," which "rob the master of his legal property to put it into the hands of an illegal master." It also insisted that the enthusiasm of the abolitionists made the condition of the slave worse, because it made a breach of friendship and confidence between him and his master, and brought the consequent sale of the slave to the southern dealer to prevent financial loss.[28]

But this peaceful period of political unity and apparent homogeneity of interests was marked by a divergence of industries and interests which were unconsciously working toward the destruction of the local era of good feeling. Beginning with 1818 and extending on through the '20's the east experienced a great industrial decline and loss of population.[29] The Indian land cessions opened up the Northwest and the Southwest, and the cultivation of short staple cotton, rendered profitable by the use of the cotton gin, had extended the plantation into the uplands of

[26] *Va. Northwestern Gazette*, November 30, 1820.

[27] *Journal, House of Rep.*, 15 Cong., 1st sess., 197.

[28] *Va. Northwestern Gazette*, August 18, 1820; *National Intelligencer*, September 13, 1820.

[29] Prize essay on "Agriculture," in the *Lynchburg Virginian*, July 4, 1833; *Niles Register*, XLIV, 411; Garland, *Randolph*, II, 318; Collins, *Domestic Slave Trade*, 26.

Georgia and South Carolina and into the Gulf states. Meanwhile the tobacco-growers were selling their plantations to become pioneers on the western frontier or cotton-planters in the new South.[30] Excessive emigration not only reduced population but also threw vast areas of worn-out lands upon the local markets; prices fell; and many hundreds of acres were given up to briars, broom-sedge, and pines.[31] In the '20's various travelers wrote of the gloomy depression with which they were filled at the sight of the "red-gullied and turned-out lands" of Virginia. In this period John Randolph predicted that the day would come when the master would run away from his negroes and be advertised by them in the public prints.[32] From 1820 to 1830 the total increase in the white population in the Piedmont and the Tidewater was only 26,524. In the Assembly of 1831–32 Thomas Marshall asserted that at that time the agricultural products were worth no more than they had been eighty years prior when the population was only one-sixth as large.[33] Charles F. Mercer estimated that the land values in 1817 had been $206,000,000 and that they had fallen in thirteen years to $90,000,000.[34] In 1817 Virginia exported goods valued at $8,212,860, but the exports amounted

[30] *Annals of Cong.*, 16 Cong., 1st sess., II, 1392; *Niles Register*, XII, 336, 359, 400; *ibid.*, XIII, 35.

[31] Madison, *Writings* (ed. 1865), III, 614–16; *Lynchburg Virginian*, July 4, 1833.

[32] Collins, *Domestic Slave Trade*, 26.

[33] *Richmond Enquirer*, February 2, 1832.

[34] *Debates, Va. Constitutional Convention of 1829–30*, 178.

to only $3,340,185 in 1828.[35] This was the period when Madison was unable to get a loan he wanted from the United States Bank, because of the poor security he had to offer;[36] when Jefferson mortgaged his home to make good the financial failures of friends;[37] and when Monroe sold his beautiful home at Oak Hill and became dependent upon friends and relatives in New York City.

The superior quality of her tobacco and the possession of a surplus of negro slaves were the chief economic resources which eastern Virginia possessed at this time.[38] The demand for "Virginia leaf" and the sale of the surplus negroes to the southern cotton-planters enabled the inhabitants to keep the wolf from the door and to maintain a semblance of their former hospitality. Petersburg, Lynchburg, Richmond, Norfolk, and Alexandria each contained two or three slave-dealers who made a regular business of supplying the southern markets. The press of these cities spoke enthusiastically of the new South. "It creates," said the *Alexandria Herald*, "a new demand for the slaves of the southern states, and increased demands raise prices."[39] During the year 1829 Amistead and Franklin, dealers doing business at Alexandria, are believed to have cleared $33,000 in the domestic slave traffic.[40]

[35] DeBow, *Review*, II, 402.   [36] Hunt, *Madison*, 380.
[37] *Journal, House of Del.*, 1829–30, Doc. No. 20.
[38] *Richmond Enquirer*, February 2, 1832; Hunt, *Merchants' Mag.*, VI, 473.
[39] September 22, 1833.
[40] Tremain, *Slavery in the District of Columbia*, 236.

RISE OF NATIONAL REPUBLICAN PARTY 113

By 1829, however, this traffic suffered a temporary decline. The southern states were passing laws to restrain or prohibit the trade, and the fall in the price of cotton after 1825 decreased the demand for negro slaves. Many planters feared that their negroes, under these changed conditions, would become as valueless a species of property as their exhausted realty.[41]

The new tobacco lands of the West and the Southwest, together with the constant draining of wealth and population from the Piedmont, prevented the uplands of Virginia from undergoing that economic transformation which the cotton industry effected in the uplands of the South.[42] True, the plantation did become more firmly established in portions of the Piedmont during this period.[43] As the small farmer had moved to the West and the South the plantation-owners had increased the size of their holdings and the number of their slaves. By 1828 the negro population was as dense in portions of the Piedmont as in the Tidewater, but the amount of tobacco produced was not so large as formerly. The impetus given the tobacco industry in the Valley following the War of 1812 proved only temporary.

The inhabitants of the east tried various experiments to retrieve their fallen fortunes. Under stress

[41] *Debates, Va. Constitutional Convention of 1829–30.*

[42] In 1818 Louisiana exported 24,138 hogsheads of tobacco, and Virginia's exports for same time were only 24,736 hogsheads (*Alexandria Herald,* March 29, 1819).

[43] *Debates, Va. Constitutional Convention of 1829–30,* 62.

of necessity Edmund Ruffin began the use of marl, or calcareous fertilizing;[44] in 1816, and afterward, numerous agricultural societies were organized in the Tidewater and the Piedmont;[45] an effort was made to establish a chair of agriculture in the University,[46] but the movement was defeated by the west, which did not appreciate the needs of the east and took this opportunity to strike at the hated University; and premiums and rewards were offered for good crops and well-kept farms. John Taylor deplored "the morbid aversion" to writing on subjects pertaining to agriculture,[47] and Madison, upon retiring from public life, became president of the Albemarle Agricultural Society and devoted much attention to its work.[48]

In their desperation many planters tried to devote their lands to cotton-growing. The high price of cotton and the consequent prosperity of the South caused many to look forward to the day when the cotton plant should be the staple in Virginia also.[49] They hoped that it would be especially adapted to the worn-out lands of the Tidewater; Madison entertained this delusion.[50] Enthusiastic letters were written on the possibilities of the cotton industry in Virginia.[51]

[44] *Farm Register*, I, 108.   [45] See Acts of Assembly, 1816–26.

[46] *Niles Register*, XXIII, 203.

[47] *Western Spy*, August 8, 1818.

[48] Madison, *Writings* (ed. 1865), III, 63–95.

[49] *Niles Register*, XXVII, 3, 115; XXIX, 147, 243.

[50] Madison, *Writings* (ed. 1865), III, 86.

[51] See *Richmond Enquirer*, August 5, 1826, *ibid.*, December 19, 1825; *Richmond Compiler*, November 25, 1825; *Charleston (S. C.) Gazette*, December 1, 1825.

RISE OF NATIONAL REPUBLICAN PARTY 115

As an article of commerce [wrote a correspondent to the *National Intelligencer*] cotton is far less fluctuating in value and more to be relied upon than tobacco or bread-stuffs. Cotton may decline from fifteen to ten cents, but it can hardly be so faithless as flour has proved to be in falling from fourteen to less than four dollars a barrel in a period of less than three years.[52]

So long as the price of cotton remained distinctly high Virginia continued to produce it. During the early '20's it was the chief staple in Southampton, Sussex, Greenesville, and Nansemond counties. At the same time many experiments in cotton-growing were made on the upper Potomac and James. The decline in prices in the later '20's, and the unfavorable climatic conditions, by reason of the short growing season, made it impossible to extend the cotton-growing area in the state. In a few years cotton ceased to be grown except in a few counties along the Roanoke.[53]

Other attempts to reclaim the worn-out lands of eastern Virginia and to rejuvenate her industries were generally unsuccessful. Consequently the inhabitants attributed their failures to the operation of the American System; they would not tolerate the idea of giving

[52] *National Intelligencer*, May 16, 1820.

[53] The following table shows the rise and decline of the cotton industry in Virginia:

Year	Pounds produced
1801	5,000,000
1811	8,000,000
1821	12,000,000
1826	25,000,000
1834	10,000,000

—See Turner, *Rise of the New West*, 47.

up agriculture for manufacuring. The agricultural societies became semi-political organizations and devoted much time to passing resolutions against the protective tariff. In vain did Madison and others point out the fact that excessive migrations from the state were responsible for many of its calamities. But those who remained at home refused to see in the efforts of friends and relatives to seek new homes and fortunes the cause of their undoing. They continued, therefore, to support John Floyd,[54] one of the greatest of the early American expansionists, and to attribute the cause of their fallen fortunes to the American System.

Meanwhile the west was undergoing economic change. The manufacture of iron became an important industry in several localities in the Valley and in the northwest;[55] the Jackson works on the Cheat River were among the most productive in the western country. Sheep-raising also became a profitable industry in the counties on the upper Ohio and on the Monongahela, and even extended to the Valley.[56] Wheeling rolled one thousand tons of iron annually and cut three hundred tons of nails;[57] it had two cotton and two woolen mills, each of which employed several hundred men. The application of steam to water navigation increased the importance of the salt

[54] Floyd was made governor in 1829.

[55] *Journal, House of Rep.*, 15 Cong., 1st sess., 182; Martin and Brockenbrough, *Hist. of Va.* (ed. 1835), 310, 320, 330, 357, 389, 390.

[56] *Ibid.*, 320, 330, 362, 390.   [57] *Ibid.*, 406.

RISE OF NATIONAL REPUBLICAN PARTY 117

industry and improved the facilities of the manufacturing towns on the Ohio and the Monongahela.

Meanwhile the northwestern part of the state was being settled by persons who had no sympathetic touch with the east. Thither came many New Englanders and Germans. For the most part they settled in communities of their own and lived apart politically. The largest German settlement was of some five hundred souls, and was located in Preston County near Mount Carmel.[58] It did not tolerate slavery. The largest settlement of New Englanders was on French Creek in Lewis County. It numbered about four hundred persons, and was divided into five school districts, each with a common school.[59]

As compared with eastern Virginia the west, within the state, was progressing.[60] But the development was not what settlers of a new country of boundless resources had reason to expect. Both in wealth and population the West beyond them was advancing more rapidly. In 1830 the larger part of western Virginia was inhabited by from two to six persons to the square mile. At the same time it was bounded on the north and west by a semicircle of free white population, which numbered from forty-five to ninety souls to the square mile.[61] It was with chagrin that the inhabitants looked upon the immigrant wagons that passed over the Cumberland Road and down the

[58] *Ibid.*, 421. Many Germans also found homes in Wheeling.
[59] *Ibid.*, 385.
[60] *Niles Register*, XLIII, 146.
[61] Census Map, 1890, XX.

Kanawha to the more prosperous trans-Ohio West. In 1829 a resident of the Kanawha Valley wrote: "They go on careless of the varying climate and apparently without regret for the friends and relatives they leave behind, seeking forests to fell and new countries to settle."[62] Some western Virginians, indeed, joined the caravans and moved on into the farthest West; others remained to fight the battle of reform and nationalism.

When the inhabitants of western Virginia compared their condition with that of their neighbors in the free states, they were made conscious that their development was being retarded. At this time of vast expenditures for roads and canals, it was only natural for them to attribute the cause of their misfortunes to the inefficiency of the state as an agent for such purposes. Accordingly they again came to look upon the federal government as a better agent than the state government for effecting communication between the east and the west, and in time they espoused the whole of the American System.

In 1818 citizens of Shenandoah and Frederick counties had petitioned Congress for an increase in the duty on bar, pig, and cast iron, but the Virginia west in general showed little interest in the tariff bill of 1820. On the other hand, the east was actively opposed to the bill of that year, the agricultural societies taking the lead. A memorial from the united societies insisted that the embarrassment to American manufacturers was not due to inadequate protection

[62] *National Intelligencer*, November 4, 1829.

but to a desire to realize returns on fictitious capital.[63] Thomas Newton, of the Norfolk district, alone voted for the bill, and all the other Virginia congressmen opposed it.

Meanwhile western Virginia began to develop a sentiment favorable to the protective system. In 1821 citizens of Hampshire County memorialized Congress for a general increase in the tariff.[64] Later, citizens of the Valley sent petitions praying protection for iron manufacturers, and the wool-growers of the northwest asked it for wool.[65]

As the sentiment for a protective tariff increased in the North, eastern Virginia became more bitter in its denunciations of the American System. In its attack thereon the *Richmond Enquirer* pointed to the country north of the Potomac as the place where the people were losing interest in the preservation of the Constitution; where the public expenditures were being made; where the United States Bank sat in majesty; where the spirit of mercantile cupidity was enveloping itself in the mantle of monopoly and privilege; and where the people wished to enthrone the federal government and debase that of the states.[66] Jefferson, regarded by some as the father of the American System, now thought it unsound policy and unfair to tax agriculture for the purpose of promoting manufactur-

[63] *Annals of Cong.*, 16 Cong., 1st sess., II, 2323. See Appendix, *ibid.*, 2296.

[64] *Journal, House of Rep.*, 16 Cong., 2d sess., 178.

[65] *Ibid.*, 18 Cong., 1st sess., 134, 174, 194, 212.

[66] August 8, 1821.

ing.[67] The agricultural societies continued to petition Congress against any further increase in the tariff duties.[68] It was at this time that many strict constructionists began to question the constitutionality of a tariff for protection.

The representatives from eastern Virginia argued at great length against the tariff bill of 1824. They were most opposed to the increased duty on woolens, that on "napt cotton," a coarse woolen cloth used in making clothing for negro slaves, being the most obnoxious. A memorial from Richmond and Manchester contained data to show that such a duty would be equivalent to a direct tax of at least twenty-four thousand dollars annually upon Richmond and its vicinity.[69] With the exception of the representative of the extreme northwestern district, who voted for the bill, the solid delegation of Virginia voted against the tariff of 1824.[70]

The tariff of 1824 produced a storm of indignation in the east. Jefferson, now bent with the infirmities of age, came forward to denounce it. He wrote the veteran Giles, the "younger recruits who, having nothing in them of the feelings or principles of '76, now look to a single and splendid government of an aristocracy, founded on banking institutions, and

[67] Jefferson, *Writings* (ed. Ford), X, 8, 285; *Niles Register*, XXXVIII, 294.

[68] *Journal, House of Rep.*, 16 Cong., 2d sess., 30, 32, 69, 95; *ibid.*, 17 Cong., 1st sess., 69, 138, 162, 200; *ibid.*, 18 Cong., 1st sess., 243, 245, 304.

[69] *Ibid.*, 18 Cong., 1st sess., II, 3098.

[70] *Ibid.*, 18 Cong., 1st sess., II, 1921.

moneyed corporations."[71] Madison was much milder in his criticism; he did not deny the constitutionality of a protective tariff, but doubted its expediency. He recognized that it was difficult to protect the interests of a minority in a government based on the rule of the people, but he insisted that the Supreme Court was adequate to the duty of determining the constitutionality of laws.[72] The press and the political leaders accepted the ideas of Jefferson, and were enthusiastic to return to the principles of 1798.

The increased demand for greater protection to articles of woolen manufacture added new strength to the anti-protection sentiment in the east. Fewer memorials and petitions were sent to Congress, but resolutions denouncing the principles of the American System were passed annually by the Assembly. On the other hand, the west became more desirous of protection. The salt manufacturers on the Kanawha and Holston rivers were beginning to feel the effect of competition of the salt from the West Indies, imported by way of New Orleans. Meanwhile the wool-growers and manufacturers were increasing the scale of their industries.[73] Petitions praying an increase in the tariff duties continued to come in increasing numbers from the transmontane people. Northwestern Virginia sent two delegates to the Harrisburg Convention of 1827. Except those from Kentucky, there were no

[71] Jefferson, *Writings* (ed. Ford), X, 356.
[72] Madison, *Writings* (ed. Cong.), III, 483, 507; see also Madison, *Cabell Letters*.
[73] *Journal, House of Rep.*, 20 Cong., 1st sess., 419.

other members of that body from states south of the Potomac.[74]

The debates on the Woolens Bill and the tariff of 1828 brought out no new features in the position of either the east or the west. The representatives of the west said nothing, but voted for the tariff. Map I shows practically all the area now embraced in West Virginia voting for the tariff of "Abominations," while the east was as solidly against it. Those voting aye were: Leffler, Armstrong, and Maxwell, all National Republicans.[75]

When the state had assumed the responsibility for the construction of works of internal improvement, the west had expected results; but they were not forthcoming, and a decided return to nationalism followed.[76] Already its representatives in Congress had voted for the bill of 1822 to provide for the preservation of the Cumberland Road.[77] In 1817 Madison's veto of the Bonus Bill had been readily acquiesced in by the inhabitants of western Virginia; but in 1822 they were highly incensed at Monroe's veto of a similar bill, and their representatives in Congress voted to pass it, over the president's veto.[78]

During the spring and summer of 1823 numerous mass-meetings were held along the Potomac and in the northwest to encourage internal improvements by

[74] *Niles Register*, XXXII, 388, 417.
[75] *Reg. of Cong. Debates*, IX, Part II, 2472.
[76] *Alexandria Herald*, January 9, 1822.
[77] *Annals of Cong.*, 17 Cong., 1st sess., II, 1734.
[78] *Ibid.*, 17 Cong., 1st sess., II, 1874.

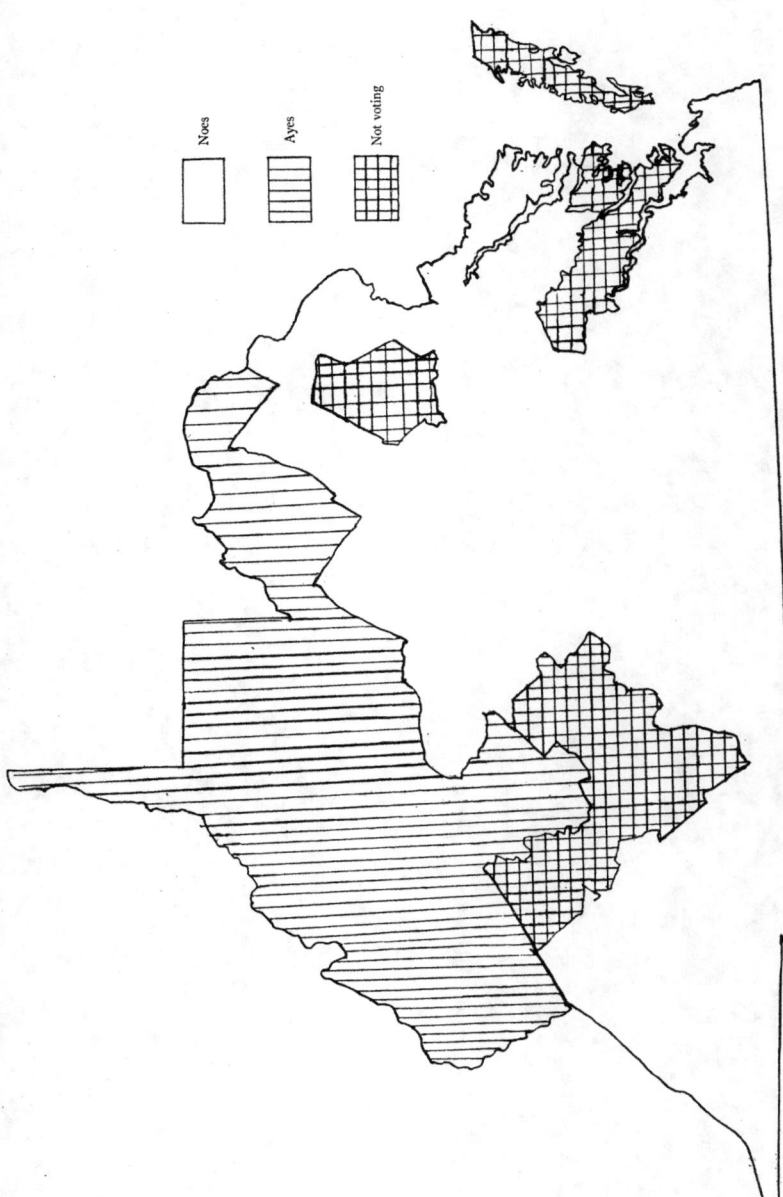

MAP I.—Showing the sectional character of the vote of Virginia on the tariff of 1828

RISE OF NATIONAL REPUBLICAN PARTY 123

the federal government. So pronounced was public opinion that Monroe began to feel doubtful of the wisdom of the position he had taken in the veto message of 1822.[79] This popular movement led to the surrender of the rights and interests of the Potomac Company, and to the incorporation of the Chesapeake and Ohio Canal Company. Notwithstanding the fact that this proposed canal was to be constructed in part by funds derived from the federal government, the influence of western and northeastern Virginia in the Assembly was sufficient to secure the ratification of the act to incorporate the new company and an appropriation to it.[80] For a time the Assembly showed a disposition to abandon the internal improvements on the James and Kanawha rivers.

The vacillation of the Assembly increased the jealousy of sections. Appropriations continued to be defeated, and efforts were made to rescind the Chesapeake and Ohio Canal Company's charter.[81] To counteract this attempt an appropriation was made to be used in constructing a canal, commonly known as the Blue Ridge Canal, around Balcony Falls where the James breaks through the Blue Ridge.[82]

[79] *J. H. U. Studies*, XVII, 490.

[80] Later some of the strict constructionists tried to explain their action on this occasion by insisting that Congress had aided the Chesapeake and Ohio Canal in the capacity of the local legislature of the District of Columbia (*Debates, Va. Constitutional Convention of 1829–30*, 146).

[81] *Richmond Enquirer*, January 23, 1823.

[82] Pamphlet, *Report of the Committee on Roads and Int. Imp.* (1831–32), 25; *Niles Register*, XXVI, 16.

The encouragement contained in the document, "Views on the Subject of Internal Improvements," which accompanied Monroe's veto message of 1822, called forth the General Survey Bill of 1824, so popular in western Virginia. This bill gave the President power to make surveys for such roads and canals as he deemed of national importance for commercial, military, and postal purposes. In the minds of its supporters it contemplated a system of national internal improvements. For this reason it met strenuous opposition in eastern Virginia. John Randolph declared that its enactment into law implied the possession of sufficient power by Congress to emancipate every slave in the Union.[83]

Map I, showing Virginia's vote on the tariff of 1828, serves also for a map of her vote on the General Survey Bill.[84] The districts voting aye are in each case the same, although those not voting are not quite identical. As has been shown, but one representative voted for the tariff of 1824. This vote, when compared with that on the General Survey Bill, shows what was undoubtedly true of western Virginia, namely, a greater interest in internal improvements than in other features of the American System.

Meanwhile the steam railway became a factor in internal improvements, which now became more complex than ever in Virginia. In 1826 the Baltimore and Ohio Railroad Company was incorporated. Immediately it appealed to Virginia and Pennsylvania for

[83] *Annals of Cong.*, 18 Cong., 1st sess., I, 1296–1311.
[84] See *ibid.*, 18 Cong., 1st sess., I, 1468.

the privilege of constructing its proposed lines across their territory. The request was granted by Virginia, but only after a severe sectional contest.

To avoid competition with the Erie Canal and the Pennsylvania lines of improvement the Baltimore and Ohio Company desired to reach the Ohio by the most southern route possible. Accordingly it asked permission to construct its lines along the Shenandoah to the headwaters of the Kanawha, thence by that stream to the Ohio.[85] The inhabitants of the Valley and the Kanawha section heartily indorsed the scheme. The western press was full of letters and editorials designed to influence the action of the Assembly. Unwilling to make the west the backyard to Baltimore and to injure the possibility of Richmond as a commercial city, the Assembly refused the request and restricted the western terminus of the proposed road to such a point as the company might select north of the mouth of the Little Kanawha.[86] There was considerable sentiment in the east favorable to keeping the road out of the state entirely,[87] and later an effort was made to repeal the act whereby permission had been given it to construct its lines across Virginia territory.[88]

When strict construction became more popular in the east and when it became certain that the Chesa-

[85] *Niles Register*, XXXIII, 163.

[86] Acts of Assembly, 1826–27, 77–84; *Report of Committee on Roads and Int. Imp.* (1831–32), 35; *Niles Register*, XXXII.

[87] *Virginia Advocate*, May 3, 1828.

[88] *Richmond Enquirer*, December, 1829.

peake and Ohio Canal would be largely a national enterprise under the direction of Adams, Virginia began to oppose the scheme for connecting the Potomac and Ohio rivers by a canal.[89] In 1826 the state engineer reported that a canal connecting the James and the Kanawha was practicable, but he suggested that the work be not undertaken until it was known whether or not the Chesapeake and Ohio Canal would be constructed. For a brief period the Assembly remained friendly to this recommendation, but the necessity for a greater demonstration against nationalism caused a reaction. Ten days after Adams threw the first spade of dirt from the proposed Chesapeake and Ohio Canal, the east Virginians held an internal improvement convention at Charlottesville. The object was to revive interest in the scheme of connecting the James and the Kanawha by a continuous canal, now a rival scheme to that of the federal government on the Potomac.[90] The Assembly of 1828 also defeated a bill to make further appropriations to the capital stock of the Chesapeake and Ohio Company.[91]

Delays and changes in plans heightened the discontent of the west and made the national plan more popular. The presence of several corps of surveyors tended to keep the subject of internal improvements

[89] *Debates, Va. Constitutional Convention of 1829-30*, 148.

[90] *Niles Register*, XXXIV, 345; *Debates, Va. Constitutional Convention of 1829-30*, 143. Madison, Marshall, Monroe, James Barbour, Mercer, and Professor Dew, of William and Mary, were members of this convention.

[91] *Debates, Va. Constitutional Convention of 1829-30*, 127.

RISE OF NATIONAL REPUBLICAN PARTY 127

continually before the inhabitants. In 1828 the west was overrun by three corps of engineers, one in the employ of the state, another in the employ of the federal government, and still another in the employ of the Baltimore and Ohio Company.[92] The incessant discussion between the advocates of the sluice and dam system, of continuous canals, and of railroads respectively did not contribute to political unity and accord.

The presidential elections of 1824 and 1828 are important from a sectional standpoint, as the various issues involved in each were the tariff, internal improvements, and local reform. Before the state became divided sectionally on these subjects it would have been difficult to tell which of the two favorites in 1824, Crawford or Adams, had the stronger following.[93] James Barbour, United States senator, favored the election of Adams, and John Taylor, United States senator for a few months of the year 1824, was, for a time at least, not unfriendly to it. By most persons Adams was then regarded as a good Republican of the Jefferson type; his character was above reproach; he was the heir apparent to the throne; and domestic tranquillity seemed to demand his election, since the North had not had a president in a quarter of a century. Besides, his official conduct had not made him unpopular.[94] On the other hand, Crawford's

[92] *Niles Register*, XXXIII, 163; *Washington and Lee Hist. Papers*, No. 5, p. 63; *Register Cong. Debates*, 19 Cong., 2d sess., III, 1565; *Report of Com. on Road and Int. Imp.* (1831–32), 32.

[93] *Richmond Enquirer*, January 26, 1822.

[94] *Ibid.*, January 26, 1822; *Alexandria Herald*, May 5, 1823.

business methods and executive ability were not above criticism. He also had supported the "infamous régime" under John Adams, and the recharter of the United States Bank. By the strict constructionists he was frequently dubbed "one of the tribe of South Carolina Federalists."[95]

In the early stages of the contest of 1824 the support given the less popular candidates, Jackson, Clay, and Calhoun, was more sectional in character than either the Adams or Crawford following. Jackson had a following in the counties of the southwest; Clay was popular in the counties along the Cumberland Road;[96] and the internal improvement interests of the west were not unfriendly to Calhoun. Not one of these candidates was seriously mentioned in the east. Calhoun was especially objectionable to the young school of state-rights politicians.[97] By them he was regarded as a "sort of prodigy, *nigro simillimus cygno.*"[98] A letter to the *Richmond Enquirer,* in 1824, gives a fair estimate of the popular conception then entertained in the east regarding Calhoun.

He has no friends [said the writer] in Virginia who will rally on the hustings in any of her districts. His kindly manners and fine genius may attract a few stragglers here and there to his banners, but no considerate Virginian who values the constitution of his country will lend himself to the care of an ultra politician of the federal school.[99]

[95] *Richmond Enquirer,* January 22, 1822; *ibid.,* January 27, 1822; *Alexandria Herald,* January 11, 1823; *ibid.,* January 26, 1823.

[96] *Richmond Enquirer,* January 22, 1822.

[97] *Ibid.,* January 26, 1822.

[98] *Ibid.,* December 19, 1822.

[99] *Ibid.,* February 12, 1824.

RISE OF NATIONAL REPUBLICAN PARTY 129

As the interest in internal improvements and the tariff discussions became intense the Adams and Crawford followings became more sectionalized.[100] Crawford's open declaration of devotion to the principles of strict construction won friends in the east. On the other hand, Adams' refusal to commit himself gave his supporters there no position to maintain, and a large number ultimately deserted him. By 1823 the *Enquirer* had espoused Crawford's candidacy and was earnestly pressing the Adams supporters for a statement of principles.[101] None came, and the extreme state-rights advocates began to doubt the orthodoxy of the favorite son of Massachusetts. They went so far as to criticize Adams for deserting his state in 1807.[102] Meanwhile Crawford's nationalistic tendencies were forgotten; his assailants were refuted as calumniators and liars; "his firmness of character and his disinterested patriotism of 1816," when he readily acquiesced in the election of Monroe to the presidency, took precedence of all other considerations.[103] The west preferred Adams with no statement of political principle to Crawford resting his candidacy upon a platform which they did not like.

Meanwhile Jackson's candidacy increased in popularity in the west and detracted from the Adams strength there. Jackson and reform struck a responsive chord in those parts of the state which had long been

[100] *Ibid.,* May, 1823.
[101] *Ibid.,* May 5, 1826; *ibid.,* October 29, 1823.
[102] *Alexandria Herald,* October 10, 16, 29, 1823.
[103] *Richmond Enquirer,* May 5, 1824; *ibid.,* July 4, 1823.

contending with conservatism. In April, 1824, the Jackson supporters held several mass-meetings in the western counties. That of Warrenton,[104] Fauquier County, appointed committees of correspondence, and inaugurated a systematic campaign. The east refused to consider Jackson seriously; Ritchie was even severe in his criticism of him. He feared Jackson would become the tool of designing politicians, and that his impetuous temper would thoroughly disqualify him for the position of chief executive.[105] When the congressional caucus for nominating presidential candidates became an issue in the campaign, Jackson's popularity in the west increased. In January, 1824, members of the Assembly held a convention to discuss the New York letter favoring a continuation of the caucus method of nomination. Out of a total of 236 delegates and senators, 168 attended. Few of the western counties were represented in this meeting by their full delegation in the Assembly. Some were not represented at all; others by only one delegate.[106] At this time Ritchie was in favor of the continuation of the congressional nominating caucus. He believed it was a choice between an election by the people and an election by the House of Representatives. In the latter alternative he feared a deadlock and the promotion of Calhoun to the presidency.[107]

[104] *Alexandria Herald*, April 23, 26, 1824.

[105] *Ibid.*, September 17, 1824; *Richmond Enquirer*, March 2, 1824; *ibid.*, March 19, 1824.

[106] *Ibid.*, January 6, 13, 22, 1824.

[107] *Ibid.*, February 12, 1824.

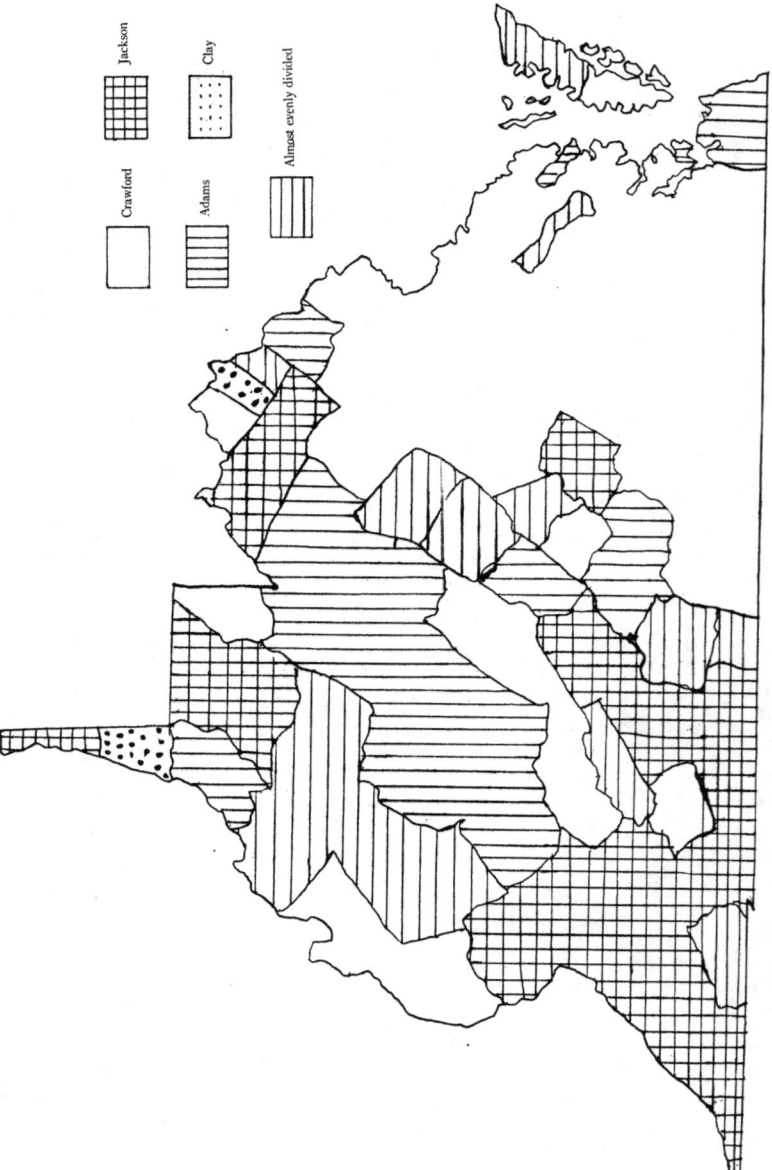

Map II.—Showing the sectional character of the vote of Virginia in the presidential election of 1824

RISE OF NATIONAL REPUBLICAN PARTY 131

Notwithstanding the fact that the congressional caucus, which placed Crawford in nomination for the presidency, was largely a New York, North Carolina, and Virginia affair, most of the representatives of the transmontane country in Virginia did not attend it.[108] Immediately following Crawford's nomination members of the Assembly met in a convention to name electors for the Democratic ticket. One hundred and sixty-three members, mostly from the counties east of the Blue Ridge, attended. Of this number 139 voted for Crawford electors, 7 for Adams, 6 for Jackson, and 5 for Clay. The *Enquirer* estimated that the 73 members who did not attend were about evenly divided between Jackson and Adams.[109]

In the summer of 1824 efforts were made in the west to induce the supporters of Clay and Adams to unite against the Crawford party in favor of Jackson, but without success. Accordingly the popular vote went to four candidates, viz., Clay, Jackson, Adams, and Crawford. There was, however, little enthusiasm in the election, not half of the full vote being polled.[110] Returns practically complete gave Clay 418 votes, Jackson 2,850, Adams 3,389, and Crawford 8,408.[111]

The accompanying Map II gives the vote of Vir-

[108] The trans-Alleghany was not represented (*ibid.*, January 15, 1824; February 19, 1832).

[109] *Ibid.*, February 24, 1824; *ibid.*, January 6, 1824; *ibid.*, February 24, 1824.

[110] *Ibid.*, August 6, 1824.

[111] Complete returns may be gathered from the *Richmond Enquirer* following November 5, 1824.

ginia by counties in the presidential election of 1824. It shows those counties interested in internal improvements and predisposed to nationalism voting for Adams and Clay. Jackson's largest vote came from the southwestern part of the state where the interest in internal improvements was not strong. Crawford carried isolated counties in the west, but his chief vote came from the Piedmont and the Tidewater. The vote for both Jackson and Clay was purely sectional, neither receiving more than a few votes east of the Blue Ridge. On the other hand, Adams received a strong minority vote in most of the eastern counties, as did Crawford in the western.

When the presidential election was taken to the House of Representatives, Powell, who represented the district on the lower Shenandoah, voted for Adams. A representative from the southwestern part of the state voted for Jackson, but the remaining vote was given to Crawford.[112]

In the presidential election of 1828 internal improvements played the important part. Under the provisions of the General Survey Act, Adams had kept a corps of surveyors employed almost constantly in those districts of the state where their presence would be most conducive to nationalism.[113] So long as

[112] The vote of the electoral college was for Nathaniel Macon for vice-president.

[113] At this time James Barbour of Virginia was secretary of war and did much to aid Adams in his effort to nationalize Virginia.

Adams operated under the provisions of the Survey Act, the strict constructionists were not in a position to interfere. But in 1826 a resolution was introduced in the House to appropriate $30,000 to be used in making surveys not provided for by the act of 1824. A debate which throws much light upon Virginia politics ensued.

W. C. Rives, spokesman for the east on this occasion, denounced the General Survey Act and the proposed appropriation as the *modus operandi* of an extensive system of internal improvements to be undertaken by the federal government. The influence of the proposed appropriation, he argued, could be measured only as the compound ratio of the whole sum necessary to complete the works contemplated by the surveys which it would make. He believed that a concerted effort was on foot to melt down the political scruples of Virginia "in the crucible of mercenary interest" and that "reconnaissances and surveys were to be the powerful menstruum by which the solution was to be effected." "Political engineering" and "topographical arguments," he alleged, were being used to smother out Jackson majorities along the Cumberland Road.[114]

Most of the representatives from the transmontane districts felt personally called upon to answer Rives. The chief refutation was made, however, by Mercer of the Loudoun district. He reviewed the internal

[114] *Register of Cong. Debates*, III, 1262–78.

improvement history of Virginia in an effort to show that he and his colleagues from the west had not departed from the principle entertained by the state in 1815 and 1816.[115] Joseph Johnson, of the northwestern district, assured Rives that notwithstanding "literal construction" and "construction construed," favorite expressions of John Taylor, of Caroline, eastern Virginia knew absolutely nothing of the feelings and interests of the west.[116] Powell denied that the inhabitants of western Virginia were disciples of the strict construction school, and assured the east that they would vote for no candidate for the presidency who denied the power of Congress to make appropriations to work of internal improvements.[117]

The election of 1828 was the most hotly contested which had yet taken place in Virginia. It was really the first election since that of 1800 to be participated in by two clearly defined and well-organized parties. In the absence of a more orthodox candidate the east accepted Jackson. Adams had a strong following there, but his greatest following was in the west. The total popular vote was 38,859,[118] which was almost two and one-half times the total vote of 1824. Of this vote Adams received 12,107, which was four-fifths of the total vote given all four candidates in 1824. The increased vote came largely from the western counties

[115] *Register of Cong. Debates*, III, 1285.
[116] *Ibid.*, III, 1320.
[117] *Ibid.*, III, 1312.
[118] *Richmond Enquirer*, November 28, 1828.

MAP III.—Showing the vote by counties in Virginia in the presidential election of 1828

and was called forth by the increased interest in reform and internal improvements.[119]

Map III of this chapter shows the vote of Virginia by counties in the election of 1828. Most counties in those sections intensely interested in internal improvements gave either majorities or large minorities for Adams. On the other hand, those counties where the sentiment for strict construction and the desire for local reform were strongest gave majorities for Jackson.

This election does not, however, show clearly the sectional character of political parties in Virginia, because the issues were too complicated. Many nationalists voted for Jackson, because his congressional record in favor of internal improvements and a tariff appealed to them. Jackson's personality is also an element which must be reckoned with in trying to account for his political success. The results of the congressional elections of 1825 and 1827 and the votes taken in the House of Delegates on federal relations afford a much better basis for a judgment of the status of political parties than does the presidential election

[119] The following table shows the increased popular vote in some of the western counties:

County	Year	
	1824	1828
Botetourt	138	469
Frederick	440	1083
Montgomery	105	452
Ohio	296	761
Harrison	72	728

of 1828. In the contest of 1825 the Valley returned three National Republicans, namely, A. H. Powell, Benjamin Estil, and William Armstrong. At the same time all those Democratic-Republican representatives, from the trans-Alleghany and from the districts along the Potomac, who believed in the constitutionality of federal appropriations to works of internal improvement, were re-elected.[120] In the election of 1827 the National Republicans made further gains. Notwithstanding the fact that Joseph Johnson and William Smith, the representatives from the trans-Alleghany, had voted for federal appropriations to works of internal improvements, they went down to defeat in an effort to secure a re-election. Their successors were Lewis Maxwell and Isaac Leffler, pronounced Clay men. Practically all the delegates from the counties west of the Blue Ridge voted against the resolutions on federal relations, adopted annually by the House of Delegates for several years following 1825.

[120] They were: Mercer and Taliaferro from districts along the Potomac, Newton from the Norfolk district, and Johnson and Smith from the trans-Alleghany.

CHAPTER V

THE CONSTITUTIONAL CONVENTION OF 1829-30

The constitutional convention of 1829-30 was the result of a half-century of conflict between the east and the west over representation, suffrage, and abuses in the state and local governments. In 1828 the House of Delegates consisted of two hundred and fourteen members; the Senate of twenty-four. Of this number the transmontane country with a total white population of 254,196 had only eighty delegates and nine senators, while the cismontane country with a total white population of 348,873 had one hundred and thirty-four delegates and fifteen senators. An apportionment on the basis of white population would have made little change in the representation of either section in the Senate, but it would have entitled the west to ninety delegates and the east to one hundred and twenty-four. Such a reapportionment would have involved a sacrifice of political power on the part of both the Tidewater and the trans-Alleghany. Accordingly these sections were not anxious for such a change or overenthusiastic for a constitutional convention.

An extension of suffrage was a subject only secondary in importance to that of reapportionment of representation. The law regulating this privilege had remained from 1776, except that the number of acres of improved land, the possession of which entitled one to a vote, had been reduced from fifty to twenty-five.

The estimates, generally accepted in 1829, fixed the number of those who could vote then at 45,000.[1] At least 31,000[2] men of legal age and taxpayers, several thousand paying on realty, were then excluded from the right of suffrage. Merchants, mechanics, and others, unattached to the soil, had been petitioning the Assembly for this right for more than a quarter of a century.

Meanwhile grave abuses had arisen in the exercise of suffrage in the western counties. There it was an easy matter to secure enough unimproved land to entitle one to the privilege. Mountain land was as cheap as "mountain dew," and much of it was used for the same purpose, namely, to carry elections. The barren lands of some counties were shingled over with patents held for the sole purpose of entitling their owners to suffrage.[3] The demands for a greater electorate were general, but were loudest in the east. Cheap lands were not so abundant there, and the eastern cities contained many landless artisans.[4]

Much dissatisfaction had also arisen over the conduct of the legislature. The prolonged discussions on federal relations did not receive a hearty response west of the mountains. Reformers believed that thousands of dollars might be saved annually by trimming down the legislative expenses and that this expenditure might be applied to better purposes upon roads and canals.

---

[1] *Debates, Va. Constitutional Convention of 1829–30.*

[2] This number did not include 22,000 men who worked the roads and performed military service (*ibid.*, 423, 424).

[3] *Ibid.*, 757.

[4] *Ibid.*, 692.

CONSTITUTIONAL CONVENTION, 1829-30 139

Accordingly they proposed to limit the Assembly both in membership and in the frequency and duration of its sessions.

In the west grave dissatisfaction was felt over the existence and character of the governor's council and the reputed abuse of its powers in connection with the internal improvement and literary funds. Accordingly the people desired a more responsible executive and the abolition of the Privy Council.

The county courts were also a source of much dissatisfaction. In many counties these bodies had become close corporations. The members were appointed by the governor, but only on recommendation of the sheriff, who was himself generally in close personal touch with the court. Persons receiving the appointment as sheriff were, as a rule, members of the county court, and generally returned to it when their term of office as sheriff had expired. The court combined the executive, legislative, and judicial functions in the county government; it appointed civil officers and all military officials below the rank of brigadier-general; it laid the county levy; in many cases the offices of honor and profit, even the petty positions, were bestowed either upon its members or their relatives. New families and those long excluded from a participation in public affairs were hostile to this institution and anxious to bring it and the whole official system to an elective basis.

The reformers also wanted to wipe out the abuses which had developed in many of the older localities in the sheriff's office. This office was usually appropriated by members of the county court who accepted it to compensate their gratuitous services as judges. It was passed on from one member of the court to another, and was in each case usually farmed out to a deputy. In some cases the privileges of the office were sold at public auction.[5] The opportunity for peculation and extortion which the office afforded was so great that deputies frequently paid as much for its privileges as the legal fees from it amounted to. In some counties the sheriff's office remained for years in the hands of professional "paper shavers."[6]

Had conditions been such as to involve no other questions than the reform of these abuses and practices, it is not at all likely that the reform movement would have encountered opposition from any quarter. But there were other and very practical reasons why the conservatives should oppose it. A constitutional convention, the only means of remedying the evils complained of, was almost sure to take political power from the east. This section was thus confronted by the very practical proposition of whether or not it would surrender to the west, which desired greater revenues to construct roads and canals and to maintain free schools, and the power to tax the worn-out lands and slave property of the east. Thus the reform movement became complicated by problems of taxation, internal improvements, and even of negro slavery.

Already the east was complaining of excessive taxation. In 1829 the west drew annually for the purposes

[5] *Debates, Va. Constitutional Convention of 1829-30*, 486.
[6] *Ibid.*, 486-503.

of ordinary administration more from the treasury than it contributed.[7] Efforts to equalize the burden by imposing a tax upon "neat cattle" had resulted in failure. The excessive tax upon realty constituted a genuine grievance in the east, which paid on an arbitrary valuation made in 1817. Then the east was in the height of prosperity; good markets for produce and the prevalence of a speculative fever inflated values of all kinds. In consequence realty had been valued at very high rates. On the other hand, the absence of state banks and the isolation of the country had checked the speculative spirit in the west. Consequently values had remained stable and realty had been rated very low. In 1829 the average valuation upon which each section paid taxes was per acre: for the trans-Alleghany, 92 cents; for the Valley, $7.33; for the Piedmont, $8.20; and for the Tidewater, $8.43.[8] B. W. Leigh estimated that the east paid $3.24 taxes for every dollar paid by the west.[9]

But the crux of the issue was that the east possessed a large amount of slave property, while the west was practically non-slaveholding. At this time there were east of the Blue Ridge 397,000 negro slaves subject to taxation and only 50,000 west thereof, and slave property contributed almost one-third of the entire state revenue. Monroe was of the opinion that, "if no such thing as slavery existed, the people of the Atlantic border would meet their brethren of the

[7] *Ibid.*, 214.
[8] *Ibid.*, 258, 661; *Richmond Enquirer*, February 22, 1830.
[9] *Debates, Va. Constitutional Convention of 1829-30*, 153.

west, upon the basis of a majority of the free white population."[10] Madison entertained a similar opinion.[11]

In 1822 the reform movement, suspended during the local era of good feeling, was again set in motion. In its first stages it met favor in all sections. In 1824 several eastern counties, quite independently of the Assembly, took polls to determine the sense of the people upon the call of a constitutional convention and gave majorities for it;[12] Jefferson again came from his retirement to advocate reform;[13] both Ritchie and Pleasants of the *Richmond Enquirer* and *Whig*, respectively, spoke for it; the advisability of reform was debated on the public square at Richmond;[14] and petitions came from all parts of the state asking for a new constitution. Under this pressure the House of Delegates of 1824–25 passed a bill to take the voice of the people upon the question of calling a constitutional convention, but it was defeated in the more conservative Senate.[15]

Unfortunately the reform movement became complicated with national politics. The conservatives began to oppose it on the ground that a constitutional convention would endanger the representation accorded slave population in the national government and the rights of the minority. Fewer delegates from

[10] *Debates, Va. Constitutional Convention of 1829–30*, 149.

[11] Madison, *Writings* (ed. Cong.), IV, 60.

[12] *Richmond Enquirer*, May 16, 1824; *Niles Register*, XXVI, 179.

[13] *Richmond Enquirer*, April 27, 1824.

[14] *Ibid.*, April 16, 1824; *Niles Register*, XXVI, 117.

[15] *Richmond Enquirer*, February 8, 10, 1825.

the east voted for the call of a constitutional convention in 1826 than had voted for it in 1825, and the opinion became current in the west that the strict constructionists were opposed to reform. By an analysis of the vote in the House of Delegates, by which the bill to submit the call of a constitutional convention to the people was finally agreed upon, the editor of the *Winchester Republican* showed that ninety-nine of the one hundred and twenty-six state-rights men in that body had voted against it.[16]

On the other hand, the reform movement fell more and more into the hands of those out of sympathetic touch with the political leaders of the east. The Staunton Convention of July, 1825, called to promote the call of a constitutional convention, was composed almost entirely of such delegates, and was representative of the western part of the state only. Mercer had been the moving spirit in bringing it about, and Sheffey and Breckenridge, the old Federalist leaders of 1816, were its most active members. It took up the cause of reform where the partisan leaders of 1816 had left off. But in addition to a resolution favoring an equalization of representation, it resolved that the privilege of suffrage should be extended to all white male citizens above the age of twenty-one, that the local and state administrations should be reformed, and that the membership of the Assembly should be reduced.[17]

[16] *Niles Register*, XXXVI, 65.

[17] *Debates, Va. Constitutional Convention of 1829-30*, 420-23; *Richmond Enquirer*, August 2, 1825.

The popular vote on the call of a constitutional convention, taken in 1828, was: for it, 21,896, against it, 16,646. The map shows the geographic distribution of this vote. A comparison of this map with a map of the vote of the House of Delegates of 1828–29 upon the resolutions on the federal relations reveals striking similarities.[18] The affirmative vote came chiefly from the large populous counties in the Valley, along the Potomac, and in the northwest. The democratic counties of the Piedmont foothills, which were slightly nationalistic, also gave majorities for the convention,[19] as did the old Federalist stronghold, Accomac County. An analysis of the vote shows seven-eighths of the voters in the Tidewater opposed to it; the Piedmont almost equally divided; the Valley practically unanimous for it; and one-fourth of those in the trans-Alleghany opposed to it.

Although the convention had carried by a large majority, it was with difficulty that the Assembly of 1828–29 agreed to call a constitutional convention. The west made a determined effort to have a census and to base the representation in the proposed convention upon the white population. After weeks of debate, in many ways a preliminary to that of the convention, it was decided to permit each of the twenty-four senatorial districts to elect four delegates. Theoretically this arrangement was a concession to the reformers; but practically it was their defeat, because the Senate

[18] See chap. iv, p. 136.

[19] The counties were Albemarle, Amherst, Campbell, Fluvanna, Henry, Nelson, and Pittsylvania.

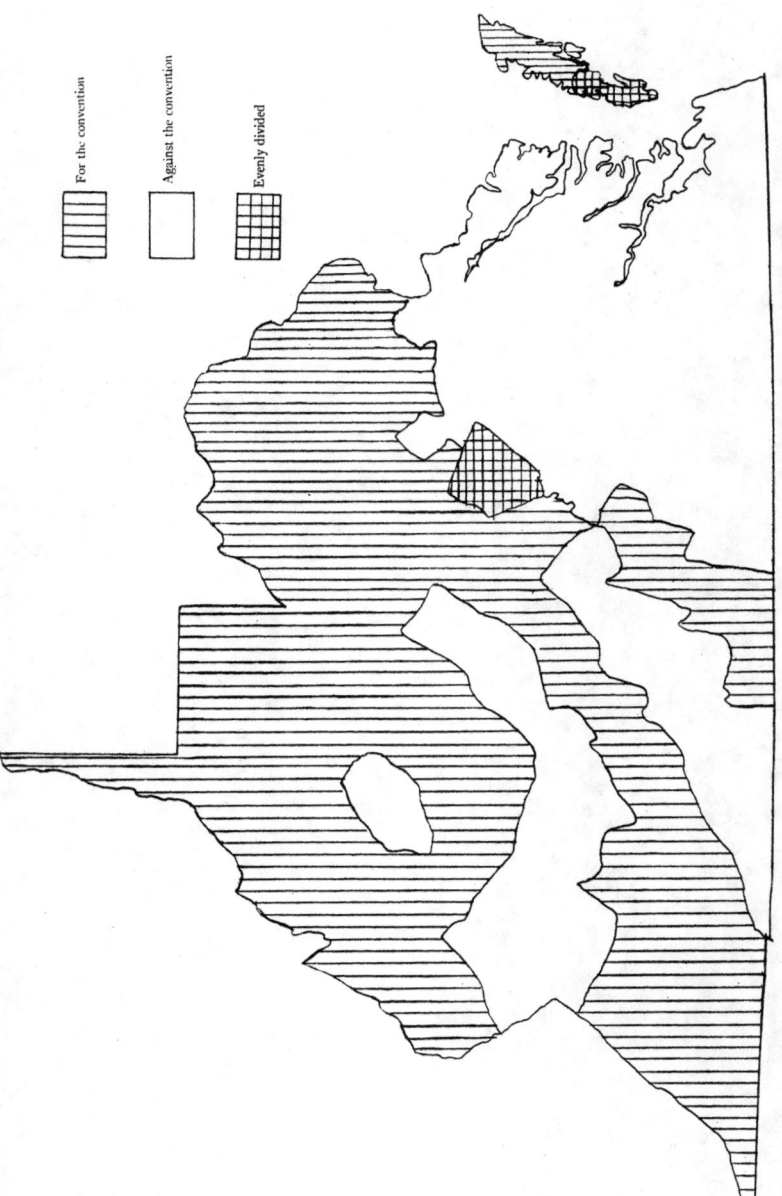

Map showing the sectional character of the vote for and against a constitutional convention, 1828

was elected upon a basis of the white population as determined in 1810. Only qualified electors for members of the most numerous branch of the Assembly were permitted to vote, but no restriction, either as to the office which the candidate held or the place of his residence, was imposed upon the voters in their choice of delegates to the convention.

The liberal provisions regulating their choice and the importance of the occasion caused the voters to appeal to the best in character and talent. Among those chosen as delegates were two ex-presidents, Madison and Monroe; the chief justice of the United States Supreme Court, John Marshall; Governor W. B. Giles; two United States senators, John Tyler and L. W. Tazewell; eleven representatives in Congress, of whom the most prominent were John Randolph, C. F. Mercer, P. P. Barbour, and Philip Doddridge; Judges Dade, Green, and Upshur; and B. W. Leigh, Chapman Johnson, and Lewis Summers, each favorably known at the state and federal bar.[20] In *personnel* the convention was of national reputation; from the east came those who had played a large part in shaping the Virginia school of political thought and in directing the affairs of the nation; while from the west came those who had long been buried beneath the "weight of their obnoxious federalism."

As the time for the meeting of the convention

[20] On the *personnel* of the convention see *Southern Literary Messenger*, XVII, 298; Grigsby, *Va. Constitutional Convention of 1829-30*, in "Va. Hist. Coll.;" *Niles Register*, XXXVI, 285, 300, 410.

approached, its far-reaching importance became more pronounced. Hezekiah Niles believed that the effects of its deliberations would not be confined to Virginia alone. Indorsing the opinion of another writer, he said, "The greatest question before the Virginia convention is the perpetual duration of negro slavery or the increase of a generous and free white population."[21] The editor of the *Charleston* (S. C.) *Mercury* looked with alarm upon the proposed free discussion of negro slavery. "Already," said he, "do the advocates of abolition rejoice even at the agitation of the subject and confidently predict the day of triumph." He believed, however, that Virginia could not be suicidal to herself, nor traitorous to her sister states similarly situated. "Sectional interests may clash," said he, "local jealousies may jar; eastern and western Virginia may contend warmly and even fearfully, but we have no apprehension for the result."[22] It was at this time that Thomas Ritchie, of the *Enquirer,* found more frequent occasion than usual to make use of his choice expression, "The eyes of the world are upon us." Young men, embryo politicians, realized the importance of the convention and repaired to Richmond to hear the debates, while distinguished strangers, foreign ministers, and travelers came to drink of Virginia eloquence on the native heath.[23]

[21] *Niles Register*, XXXVII, 145.

[22] *Richmond Enquirer*, October 27, 1829.

[23] T. F. Marshall, *Speeches and Writings, 7*; Grigsby, *Va. Constitutional Convention of 1829-30,* 5; *Richmond Enquirer,* October 17, 1829.

The convention met at Richmond, October 5, 1829. After organization[24] four committees, composed of one delegate from each of the twenty-four senatorial districts, were appointed, one each on the Bill of Rights and the legislative, executive, and judicial departments of the government. Each committee was instructed to consider and report what amendments, if any, should be made to the particular part of the constitution of 1776 committed to it.

The committees on the Bill of Rights, the executive, and the judicial departments soon reached conclusions favorable to the conservatives, but that on the legislative department found greater difficulty in agreeing upon a report. The reformers controlled twelve of its twenty-four members, and the conservatives eleven, while Madison, the twenty-fourth member, refused to concede to the extreme demands of either side. The reformers, led by Doddridge, stood out for the white basis of representation in both houses and for a general extension of the suffrage. The conservatives, led by B. W. Leigh, favored a basis for both houses to be determined by a compound ratio of white population and direct taxes. Madison favored the white basis for one house but opposed it for both.[25] Accordingly Doddridge proposed two resolutions: one to provide for the white basis for the House; the other to provide the same basis for the Senate. Madison's vote carried the first but tied the committee on the second resolu-

[24] James Monroe was made president of the convention.

[25] *Richmond Enquirer*, October 15, 1829; *ibid.*, October 22, 1829.

tion.²⁶ Accordingly the committee recommended that "in the apportionment of representation in the House of Delegates regard should be had to the white population exclusively," and said nothing about a basis for the Senate. It also recommended a reduction in the membership of the House of Delegates and an extension of the suffrage.²⁷

Fearing to accept the Bill of Rights as a basis for continuing their work, the conservatives desired to pass that part of the constitution by until the more practical parts could be agreed upon. Avowing their intention to begin where the framers of 1776 left off, the reformers favored adopting the Bill of Rights as a preliminary to subsequent work. Some desired to go even farther and to amend the declaration of 1776 by the addition thereto of clauses to provide for equal representation for all voters and for manhood suffrage. Robert B. Taylor, of Norfolk, made a long speech in favor of such an amendment.²⁸ The conservatives prevailed, however, and the report of the committee on the Bill of Rights was temporarily laid on the table. The attitude of the most radical reformers on this procedure can be shown by an extract from the speech of Alexander Campbell, of Brooke County.

> We set sail [said he] without compass, rudder or pilot. So anxious were some gentlemen here to put to sea, that when we called for the compass and the pilot, they exclaimed: "Never mind, we will get the compass and the

²⁶ *Richmond Enquirer*, March 26, 1830.
²⁷ *Debates, Va. Constitutional Convention of 1829–30*, 40.
²⁸ *Ibid.*, 46–50.

pilot when we get to port." We are now a thousand miles from land. Gentlemen are making fine speeches upon the elements of the ocean and now and then upon the art of sailing. It will be well, if the *rari nantes in gurgite vasto* apply not to us.[29]

Immediately the committee of the whole passed to the consideration of that part of the report of the committee on the legislative department, which recommended "that in the apportionment of representation in the House of Delegates, regard should be had to the white population exclusively." Judge Green moved to amend this report by striking out the word "exclusively" and adding in lieu thereof the words "and taxation combined." The debate which followed involved questions of political theory as well as practical politics. Because of their subsequent importance some space will here be given to a discussion of the political theories advanced by the different sections.

There were three clearly defined classes of political thinkers in the convention, viz., the reformers and the old and new school of conservatives. The reformers drew their political theories largely from the Declaration of Rights and the teachings of 1776, which, they contended, contained "eternal truths." Practically all the members of this class were favorable to the rule of the majority in both the state and the national government. They made frequent use of those parts of the Declaration of Rights which declare that all men are naturally free and independent, that they have inalienable rights, that power is derived from the people, that

[29] *Ibid.*, 117.

government was instituted for the common benefit, and that a majority of a community have a right to amend or abolish any government when it becomes inadequate for the purposes for which it was created. These were, said the reformers, the teachings of Locke and Milton and the products of the English struggle for liberty. Upon these hypotheses they defended the natural right of numbers to rule. The only prerequisite for the exercise of political power which they admitted in their own case was a "common interest with and attachment to the country," which they claimed to have shown repeatedly.

The older and more numerous class of the conservatives, led by Madison, Monroe, Randolph, Tazewell, and Giles, were also devoted to the teachings of 1776. But they were strict constructionists, admirers of the works of the fathers, and intensely fearful of the increasing power and prominence of the west.

The smaller class of the conservatives, and subsequently the more important one, was led by young men, such as B. W. Leigh and Abel P. Upshur. They accepted the doctrines of strict construction, but were rapidly departing from the teachings and principles of 1776. They had formed their conception of the proper relation between the states and the national government during the period of conflict between state rights and the American System and were strenuously opposed to nationalism. The representatives of a section which had become impoverished while the surrounding states became wealthy, they were concerned in the protection of minority rights and interests and, with their more powerful leader, Calhoun, were beginning to discredit the contract theory of government. They were the political forerunners of such men as R. M. T. Hunter, H. A. Wise, James A. Seddon, John Y. Mason, and Roger A. Pryor. The debate of the convention resolved itself largely into a contest between them and the reformers.

Upshur and Leigh attacked the theoretical arguments of the reformers. They each insisted that the constitution of 1776 was the only sane and practical application of Mason's Bill of Rights. They either repudiated as "metaphysical subtleties" the arguments advanced by the reformers, or accused them of intentionally misapplying the provisions of the Declaration of Rights. That all men are not born equally free and independent, they argued, is obvious, because slaves are men born daily into bondage. They insisted that the majority did not possess the right to reform or abolish a government, unless such change be "most conducive to the public weal," a condition imposed by the Declaration of Rights itself, and that no such rights were recognized in practical government. They frequently called attention to the fact that the reformers omitted from their quotations from the Declaration of Rights that part which expressly enumerated the right "to acquire and possess property" as an inalienable right.[30]

The older school of conservatives differed farthest from Leigh and Upshur on questions of political

[30] *Debates, Va. Constitutional Convention of 1829–30*, 72–88, 151–74.

theory. But, in their practical conclusions, they did not differ much from the younger leaders, even on these subjects. Wm. B. Giles, a leader in Congress during the stormy days of the French Revolution, would not agree with Upshur that a state of nature had never existed, but he willingly accepted his conclusion that a majority did not possess a natural right to rule a state.[81] Although Leigh and Upshur denounced the Bill of Rights as a compilation of "metaphysical subtleties," Randolph desired to go on record "as subscribing to every word" of it.[82]

In defense of the rights of property to a share in the law-making body, Upshur insisted that it was necessary to consider two majorities, viz., a majority of numbers and a majority of interests. He believed that physical strength, intrepidity, and skill had always been the ruling power in states and that numbers did not always possess these requisites. He admitted, however, that in most governments power could safely be intrusted to a majority of the legal voters, because they usually possessed identical interests. But Virginia, he maintained, was an exception to this general rule. There it became necessary for the slave-owner to possess political power to be able to protect his "peculiar" property against unjust taxation and fanatical assault.[83] Leigh argued that property had potential power to protect itself in all well-regulated governments and insisted that the lawmakers should acknowledge this practical fact by giving it representation. He believed

[81] *Debates, Va. Constitutional Convention of 1829-30*, 151-74.
[82] *Ibid.*, 317.   [83] *Ibid.*, 72-88.

that it was possible, by force or fraud, to separate property and political power for a time, but he insisted that as soon as the separation was felt property would either purchase power or power would destroy property. Accordingly he asked the lawmakers not to establish a basis of anarchy or corruption by refusing property a voice in the government.[34]

Here again the older school of conservatives differed somewhat from their young leaders. Giles did not base his claim to representation for negro slaves alone on the fact that they were property. He claimed representation for them on the ground that they were persons with rights which the master must protect. The slave, he argued, cannot be put to death; he must have humane treatment; and he cannot be illegally imprisoned.[35]

Because of the representation given economic interests by the English system of government, the younger school of conservatives professed great admiration for that system. Leigh had "no hesitation in saying, in the face of the whole world, that the English Government is a free Government, and the English people a free people."[36] The conservatives claimed to be the only true followers of Locke and Milton and repeatedly insisted that the reformers were tainted with the principles of the French Revolution.[37] Giles believed that the combinations of the northern majorities to oppress the South and to deprive it of the rewards of its labor had caused the political ideas

[34] *Ibid.*, 156.
[35] *Ibid.*, 248, 306.
[36] *Ibid.*, 157.
[37] *Ibid.*, 135, 157.

of the fathers to remain dormant there and had forced the minority to return to the English system of practical government.[38] John Randolph and other conservatives had become admirers of Burke and exponents of his political theories.[39]

The reformers objected strenuously to having the raw head and bloody bones of the French Revolution passed so frequently before them.[40] But they were careful to remind the conservatives that the political upheavals in France were not due to the rule of a majority, but to the rule of a privileged minority. They also contended that, however dear the price, the French Revolution was a good thing in its results because it brought a limited monarchy, a free press, a republican assembly, and the trial by jury.[41] They denied the assertions that there are no fundamental principles in government and maintained that man's social instinct, love of country, and religious feelings were fundamental to all government.[42] Alexander Campbell, of Brooke County, insisted that, if Upshur's argument be carried to a logical conclusion, it would be necessary to consider more than two majorities, a majority of numbers and of property. It would be necessary then to consider a majority of intellect, of physical strength, of scientific skill, and of general literature; interests as

[38] *Debates, Va. Constitutional Convention of 1829–30*, 237.

[39] Garland, *Randolph*, I, 52, 56, 58; Goode, *Speech in Va. Assembly 1831–32* (pamphlet), 13.

[40] *Debates, Va. Constitutional Convention of 1829–30*, 143, 425.
[41] *Ibid.*, 143. [42] *Ibid.*, 116, 124.

important and as dear to some men as the possession of negro slaves was to others; interests which the slaveholding aristocracy had proven itself unable or unwilling to protect and encourage in the non-slaveholding population. He believed a Joseph Lancaster, a Robert Fulton, or a Benjamin Franklin worth infinitely more to any society than a man whose chief merit was the ownership of a hundred negro slaves.[43] The reformers also argued that property, of whatever variety, had intrinsic qualities which had always enabled it to protect itself, and that added power, expressly conferred upon it, had always deprived individuals of their rights and liberties.[44] They believed that the man who brought a large family of intelligent children, or the section which brought a large population into the social compact, was entitled to as much, if not more, power, than he who brought only property. The latter was perishable, the former was the hope of the society.[45]

As the debate proceeded it became more practical, much time being given to a discussion of taxation. Taking "the exactions of the federal government and the state government together," Leigh doubted "whether there is a people on earth more heavily taxed than the slave-holding planters of Virginia."[46] He argued that the white basis, if adopted by the convention, would cause representation "to rise in the mountains and to overflow and drown the lowlands; while taxation rising in the lowlands, and reversing the course of nature, will flow to the mountains and

[43] *Ibid.*, 123, 124.
[44] *Ibid.*, 88, 128.
[45] *Ibid.*, 123.
[46] *Ibid.*, 154.

there spend, if not waste, its fertilizing streams over every narrow valley and deep glen."[47] Upshur scorned the argument that the west was rapidly becoming slave holding and that it would soon possess a homogeneity of interest with the east.

> There exists [said he] in a great portion of the west a rooted antipathy to this species of population—the habits of the people are strongly opposed to it. With them personal industry, and a reliance on personal exertion is the order of society. They know how little slave labor is worth, while their feelings as free men forbid them to work by the side of a slave. And besides, Sir, their vicinity to non-slaveholding states must forever render this sort of property precarious and insecure.[48]

The reformers admitted they did not pay as much taxes as the conservatives, but insisted that the reason lay in the fact that they did not possess as much property. Notwithstanding the almost conclusive arguments of Upshur, they insisted that negro slavery was increasing in the west and that it would continue to do so. The laws against the domestic slave trade and the extension of internal improvements, they argued, made such an extension inevitable. In proof of their position they pointed to the fact that the construction of the Blue Ridge Canal in 1825 had carried the plantation system into Botetourt and adjacent counties and increased the negro slave population there.[49] They also insisted that it would be impossible for political power, on the white basis, to pass to the west before

---

[47] *Debates, Va. Constitutional Convention of 1829–30*, 155.
[48] *Ibid.*, 76.   [49] *Ibid.*, 282.

1850, by which time they predicted that the Valley would be thoroughly slave holding.[50] They denied the assertion that the internal improvement schemes were intended to enrich the west and impoverish the east. Internal improvement schemes, they argued, had been handed down from the fathers and promised and re-promised almost annually by the Assembly. It was frequently pointed out that the great variety of interests made it almost impossible for two or more sections to combine their interests so as to oppress other sections by excessive taxation.[51]

The conservatives made a further defense of the rights of property to a share in the government on the ground that those who possessed it had never misruled and that in some instances their rule had been a positive blessing to the west. It was frequently asserted that a "wise and conservative minority" had spared the west the evils of excessive banking. On the other hand, the reformers believed the rule of the property classes had not always been "wise and benevolent." They could not believe that the law which exempted all persons who owned more than two negroes from service upon the public highways, and imposed such service upon all persons who owned less than that number was just. They also pointed out that the poorer whites were subject to military duty, personal taxes, and poor levies, which in some counties amounted to more than the tax contributed by property.[52] They doubted the wisdom and benevolence of a policy which made all the public

[50] *Ibid.*, 209, 281.
[51] *Ibid.*, 286. [52] *Ibid.*, 128-33, 201.

expenditures for internal improvements east of the mountains and denied foreign capital the privilege to construct a railroad where it would accommodate the largest numbers of citizens of the west.[53] Summers, of Kanawha, also showed that the Assembly had not hesitated to authorize numerous branch banks east of the Blue Ridge, while it practically denied the west the privileges of banks in any form.[54]

The conservatives also condemned the white basis on the ground that it would set a precedent which might endanger the power of Virginia in the national councils.[55] They deemed it inexpedient to repudiate a principle whereby the state was entitled to one-third of its power in the House of Representatives. "Be assured," said Leigh, "that fanatics are at work, and that the political power to which the possession of negro slaves entitles the South hangs in the balance."[56] It was alleged that on a former occasion Doddridge, the spokesman of the west, had favored the white basis for representation in Congress.[57]

The answers to these arguments were direct. You ask too great security for slave property, said the reformers; there is danger of making it odious in the sight of the west; of clothing it in the shirt of Nessus.[58] Greater security, they claimed, would be assured by admitting the white basis than by rejecting it.

[53] See chap. iv, p. 125.
[54] *Debates, Va. Constitutional Convention of 1829-30*, 658.
[55] *Ibid.*, 136, 243, 250, 317.
[56] *Ibid.*, 125, 163, 173.
[57] *Ibid.*, 135.   [58] *Ibid.*, 86, 99, 219.

CONSTITUTIONAL CONVENTION, 1829-30   159

Let it once be openly avowed as a principle [said Chapman Johnson] that the price which the western people must pay for the protection of your slaves, is the surrender of their power in the government, and you render that property hateful to them in the extreme, and hold out to them the strongest of all possible temptations to make war upon it, to render it of no value to you, and to induce you to part with it.[59] It will never do [said he] to put the people of the west under the ban of the Empire.[60]

Gordon, of Albemarle County, was certain that no better security for slave property could be established than that which lay in "the composed, silent, but tremendous power which resides in the free white population of the state; that power which defends all and without noise, or apparent effort, keeps all things still in Virginia."[61]

Leigh professed to believe that the convention had been called "to overturn the doctrine of state rights" and to remove the barrier which Virginia opposed to works of internal improvement by the federal government. Such purposes, he declared, had been avowed to him, and he had himself noticed that when "the Federal Government points a road along the Valley, or along the foot of the Blue Ridge, or across the country at the head of tidewater—state rights fall or tremble at the very sight of the tremendous ordinance."[62] The answers to these arguments were not convincing. Johnson and Mercer thought it unfair to introduce the demon of party spirit when an effort was being made to relay the fundamental law. Others made as feeble

[59] *Ibid.*, 283.   [61] *Ibid.*, 141.
[60] *Ibid.*, 283.   [62] *Ibid.*, 154.

efforts to show devotion to the doctrines of strict construction.

To reconcile the east to the white basis, some reformers proposed constitutional guarantees for the protection of slave property. Some were willing to make all taxes *ad valorem* and on a fixed ratio between personal and real property;[63] while others were willing to accept the federal ratio for the Senate.[64] The conservatives spurned with contempt the proposal of "a paper guarantee." P. P. Barbour was unwilling to accept any guarantee which the west had both the interest and power to violate.[65] Upshur believed there could be no guarantee for the protection of slave property except that which came from the possession of political power by its owners.[66]

After almost three weeks of discussion, Green's amendment[67] was defeated: ayes 47, noes 49.[68] But the reformers did not dare to demand a final vote on the report of the committee on the legislative department, because the basis of representation for the Senate and the provisions regulating suffrage had not yet been settled. Meanwhile the conservatives began to talk compromise and various plans to that end were proposed.[69]

---

[63] *Richmond Enquirer*, October 15, 22, 1829; *Debates, Va. Constitutional Convention of 1829-30*, 497.

[64] This proposition was defeated: ayes 43, noes 49 (*ibid.*, 148).

[65] *Ibid.*, 135.

[66] *Ibid.*, 177. [67] See chap. v, p. 149.

[68] *Debates, Va. Constitutional Convention of 1829-30*, 321.

[69] *Richmond Enquirer*, November 19, 1829.

CONSTITUTIONAL CONVENTION, 1829-30

Unable to agree upon a basis of representation, the committee of the whole proceeded to consider the proposed extension of suffrage. In behalf of a general extension the reformers frequently quoted from Jefferson. They also called the Declaration of Rights into use and made efforts to defend free white suffrage as a natural right. In reply the conservatives said: "We are not to be struck down with the authority of Mr. Jefferson."[70] Randolph denied that Jefferson was authority on any subject, except it be the mechanism of a plow. The conservatives claimed that suffrage was a conventional right and that it could be exercised only in the highest orders of society. Most of the arguments for and against an extension of suffrage were, however, very concrete. The reformers frequently referred to the fact that twenty-two of the twenty-four states had general suffrage and that New York and North Carolina permitted free negroes to vote.[71] Nativity, long residence, and military service, they contended, were as good proofs of "common interest with and attachment to the community" as the possession of real estate.[72] They attributed the emigration from Virginia to the non-participation of her citizens in government.[73] Morgan, of Monongalia, argued that an extension of suffrage would afford greater security to slave property. He believed that the states of the new South (Alabama and Mississippi) had felt this fact and

[70] *Debates, Va. Constitutional Convention of 1829-30*, 557, 571, 716.

[71] *Ibid.*, 366, 379, 417.

[72] *Ibid.*, 386.   [73] *Ibid.*, 353, 374, 381.

tried to make the white man as free and independent as it was in the power of government to make him. "The time is not far distant," said he, "when not only Virginia, but all the southern states, must be essentially military, and will have military governments. . . . . We are going to such a state as fast as time can move. The youth will be taught not only in the arts and sciences but they will be trained in arms." He accordingly believed it necessary to call forth "every free white human being and to unite them in the same common interest and government."[74]

Many conservatives favored an extension of the suffrage,[75] but Leigh, Upshur, Giles, and others feared that it would be followed by a transfer of political power to the west. Leigh classed general suffrage with the other plagues: the Hessian fly, the varioloid, etc., which had arisen in the north and later spread to the south, "always keeping above the fall line in the great rivers."[76] The conservatives opposed to extension argued that the possession of realty furnished the only evidence of permanent common interest with and attachment to the country. They insisted that an extension of suffrage had always preceded democratic revolution, to which they professed to believe the United States was then drifting.[77] In brief, they voiced a protest against the Jacksonian Democracy which was then sweeping the country.

[74] *Debates, Va. Constitutional Convention of 1829-30*, 382.

[75] Marshall presented an elaborate memorial from the non-freeholders of Richmond in favor of an extension of suffrage (*ibid.*, 26, 27, 31, 32).

[76] *Ibid.*, 407.   [77] *Ibid.*, 397.

CONSTITUTIONAL CONVENTION, 1829-30

Finally the convention turned to a consideration of the various plans of compromise. The reformers proposed the white basis of representation for the House of Delegates, the federal numbers for the Senate, and a reapportionment on this basis every ten years.[78] The thing most desired was the white basis for the House, the one point which the conservatives were most unwilling to yield. Four other plans were placed before the convention. That by Gordon of Albemarle, a white-basis man, although unauthorized by the reformers, became the basis of the plan which was finally agreed upon. It ignored the basis question entirely and simply attempted an equitable distribution of representation.[79] Upshur's plan, which met with next favor, was based on an average of the white basis, the federal numbers, and the mixed basis, and had the advantage of recognizing a principle in the apportionments.[80] Leigh's plan was based on an average between the white numbers and the mixed basis, while Marshall's plan favored a basis formed from an average of the white population and the federal numbers, according to the census of 1820. After modifications, which raised the number of delegates to one hundred

[78] *Ibid.*, 497. This is known as Cooke's plan.

[79] *Ibid.*, 455. Gordon's plan proposed a Senate of 24, 10 from the west and 14 from the east; and a House of 120, 26 from the trans-Alleghany, 24 from the Valley, 37 from the Piedmont, and 33 from the Tidewater. This would have given the east 24 majority on joint ballot.

[80] *Ibid.*, 494. Upshur's plan provided for a Senate of 30, 13 from the west and 17 from the east; and a House of 120, 48 from the west and 72 from the east. This plan gave the east 28 majority on joint ballot.

and twenty-seven and the senators to thirty-two, Gordon's plan was adopted: ayes 49, noes 43.[81]

The reformers' chief opposition to Gordon's plan was that it contained no basis or principle for a reapportionment. They had come to the convention to fight for "principles," but this plan recognized none. They denounced it as "a mere makeshift, a temporary expedient," and threw out the warning that failure to adopt a constitutional basis would mean another convention in the near future and a continuation of sectional strife in the meantime.[82] Doddridge announced that he was thinking of leaving the convention; John Randolph had proposed a *sine die* adjournment; and there was talk of the western delegates retiring in a body.[83]

Accordingly other efforts were made to agree upon some basis for future reapportionments. Doddridge favored a reapportionment after each census to be made, for the House, on the white basis, and for the Senate, on federal numbers, while Upshur insisted upon regular reapportionments for both houses based upon an average of the white population and federal numbers. Another plan proposed to submit the question of reapportionment to a vote of the people, and still another proposed to submit the white basis alone to a vote of the people.[84] The committee of the whole

---

[81] *Debates, Va. Constitutional Convention of 1829–30*, 574. Marshall voted aye, Madison and Monroe nay. Both Madison and Marshall favored the federal numbers (*ibid.*, 537, 538, 573, 574).

[82] *Ibid.*, 570, 571.

[83] *Ibid.*, 492, 570–72.   [84] *Ibid.*, 570, 573–75.

finally agreed upon Upshur's plan of reapportionment, which with Gordon's plan was submitted to a vote in the convention. Gordon's plan was adopted, ayes 50, noes 46, but the plan for a reapportionment was so thoroughly distasteful to the reformers that its advocates did not dare to push it.

The adoption of Gordon's plan sounded the death knell to the white basis of representation. A combination of circumstances had operated to bring about its defeat. Discussion in the convention had been followed by a democratic reaction in those parts of the east favorable to reform. By instructions the voters of the Norfolk district compelled Robert B. Taylor, the only delegate from the Tidewater favorable to reform, to leave the convention, and they replaced him by a conservative, Hugh Blair Grigsby. Both Madison and Marshall, at first regarded as neutral, gradually became more favorable to the conservatives,[85] who, following the introduction of Gordon's plan, had swamped the convention with other and similar plans until an impression had been created that compromise was inevitable. Besides, Gordon's plan was very attractive to the delegates of the large and populous counties of the Piedmont foothills and the Valley, which sections had led in the movement for reform. It gave to most of the counties of these sections two delegates and to some three,[86] whereas only a few counties in the other sections received more than one delegate each in the House.

[85] Monroe had left the convention because of ill-health.
[86] Shenandoah, Frederick, and Loudoun counties received three delegates each.

But the cause which contributed most to the defeat of the white basis was the disloyalty, approaching treason, which manifested itself in the ranks of the reformers. Cooke, of Frederick County, and Henderson, of Loudoun County, both representatives of counties which would profit largely by Gordon's compromise, secretly agreed to support it and then went into caucus with those favorable to the white basis. On the nomination of Henderson, Cooke was elected to represent the white-basis men in their conferences with the conservatives.[87] That he did not push their claims as Doddridge would have done is evident.

Talk of dismemberment characterized many debates in the convention. In the first stages of the debate, before the Gordon compromise had been agreed upon, the eastern delegates indulged most freely in such expressions. The preservation of the commonwealth was only the second wish to Leigh's heart,[88] and Morris, of Hanover County, said that an emancipation act or a heavy tax upon negro slaves "would cause a sword to be unsheathed which would be red with blood before it found the scabbard."[89] Monroe thought the dismemberment of Virginia would be followed by the dismemberment of both Georgia and South Carolina,[90] and W. B. Giles said: "The forceful separation of Virginia must and will lead to the separation of the United States, come when it will." He also added "that in

---

[87] Doddridge, circular letter in *Richmond Enquirer*, March 26, 1830. See also *ibid.*, April 2, 1830.

[88] *Debates, Va. Constitutional Convention of 1829–30*, 164.

[89] *Ibid.*, 116.   [90] *Ibid.*, 148.

the event of disunion among ourselves, the future destinies of the United States must be determined by the physical force of foreign nations."[91]

In turn the western delegates and their constituents were even more emphatic in their talk of dismemberment than the conservatives had been. Citizens of Wheeling held a mass-meeting at which resolutions were adopted calling upon the western delegates to secede in case the convention rejected the white basis.[92] At Harrisonburg, Rockingham County, the effigy of B. W. Leigh and a copy of his speech made in the convention were burned together in the public square.[93] There are few issues of the *Richmond Enquirer* for the month of December, 1829, which do not discuss the probabilities of the western delegates retiring from the convention to make a constitution of their own.[94] Later Doddridge acknowledged that they had contemplated such a course.[95] Baldwin of Augusta believed that a successful attempt to force representation for slave property would result in dismemberment, and Moore of Rockbridge assured the conservatives that the west had been settled by the Wallaces, Graemes, and Douglasses, and that if the struggle came to Bannockburn, they would all be there and old Kirkpatrick among the rest.[96]

[91] *Ibid.*, 254.
[92] *Richmond Enquirer*, December 25, 1829.
[93] *Niles Register*, XXXVII, 225.
[94] See also *Richmond Enquirer*, January 16, 1830.
[95] *Ibid.*, March 26, 1830; *ibid.*, April 2, 1830.
[96] *Debates, Va. Constitutional Convention of 1829-30*, 542.

After the adoption of Gordon's plan of compromise, the conservatives retained practical control of the convention. The reformers made a desperate effort to extend the franchise to all taxpayers, but were not successful; a resolution for that purpose was defeated by the close vote: ayes 44, noes 48.[97] Suffrage was extended, however, to leaseholders and house-keepers, but the number of men of legal age, who remained excluded, amounted to more than thirty thousand.

The central executive power was vested in a governor to be elected for a term of three years by joint ballot of the Assembly. He was given greater power than former executives, but the Executive Council was retained, although reduced in membership. The vote on Doddridge's resolution to elect the governor by popular vote was a tie and was decided in the negative by the chairman.[98]

The judicial power was vested in a Supreme Court of Appeals, such inferior courts as the Assembly might from time to time establish, the county courts, and the justices of the peace. The judges of the higher courts were made elective by joint ballot of the Assembly, but the justices of the peace, who held the county and justice courts, remained appointive by the executive. Marshall's influence was exerted in behalf of the maintenance of the established judicial system. "There is no state in the Union," he argued, "which enjoys more internal quiet than Virginia;" a condition which he

[97] *Debates, Va. Constitutional Convention of 1829–30*, 441.
[98] *Ibid.*, 485.

attributed "to the practical operation of the county courts."[99]

The last sectional conflict in the convention was occasioned by a renewed effort to adopt some constitutional basis for future reapportionments of representation. The west insisted upon the white basis, but finally agreed to accept the white basis for the House of Delegates and the federal numbers for the Senate to take effect after 1840.[100] Finally Madison proposed that the

> General Assembly, after the year 1841 and at intervals thereafter of not less than ten years, should have authority, two-thirds of each house concurring, to make re-apportionments of delegates and senators throughout the commonwealth so that the number of delegates shall not at any time exceed one hundred and fifty, nor of senators thirty-six.[101]

Notwithstanding the bitter opposition of the reformers this provision became a part of the constitution.[102]

Thus with the chief issue between the east and the west unsatisfactorily settled and with no provision in the new constitution for amendments, the question, "Shall this constitution pass?" was put. The vote was: ayes 55, noes 40.[103] Cooke of Frederick was the only

[99] *Ibid.*, 505.

[100] *Ibid.*, 681. [101] *Ibid.*, 849, 854.

[102] The plan of representation finally agreed upon provided for a House of 134 delegates and a Senate of 32 members. The trans-Alleghany was given 31 delegates; the Valley 25; the Piedmont 42; and the Tidewater 36. The counties west of the Blue Ridge were to have 13 senators; the east 19. The apportionment was practically upon the basis of the white population according to the census of 1820.

[103] *Debates, Va. Constitutional Convention of 1829–30*, 882.

member from west of the Blue Ridge who voted aye. Thirty-nine of the forty votes in the negative came from counties west of the Blue Ridge and from the Piedmont foothills. The other vote was given by Stanard, who represented a district located in the northeastern part of the state and composed of counties lying both in the Piedmont and the Tidewater.[104]

The constitution of 1830 did not settle the differences between the east and the west. It simply transferred the center of discontent and reform from the large populous counties of northern Piedmont and the Shenandoah Valley to the trans-Alleghany. Henceforth sectionalism was more largely a contest between the areas which are now Virginia and West Virginia.

The trans-Alleghany went into the reform movement of the '20's with few grievances; it came out deserted by its allies, robbed of political power, and shackled in its efforts to obtain redress. Its delegates had not long retired to their homes before echoes of discontent began to resound through the mountain valleys and occasionally to reach the lowlands. The inhabitants were determined to defeat the ratification of the new constitution when it should be submitted to a vote of the people. A writer in the *Wheeling Gazette* suggested that "the west call a convention of the west" and that commissioners be appointed "to treat with the eastern nabobs for a division of the state—

[104] Doddridge was not present when the vote on the adoption of the constitution was taken.

peaceably if we can, forcibly if we must."[105] Citizens of Ohio County resolved, "That a constitution characterized by and composed of such ingredients is unfit for the government of a free people."[106] An editorial comment in the *Wheeling Compiler* said:

> Should the victory turn out in favor of our opponents, the declared enemies of equal rights and practical republicanism, we still have, provided the entire west will move unanimously with the counties in this section of the state, *one chance left*, and that is *Separation*. This will not prove an impractical matter. If the people of the west will it, it is effective.[107]

While the west was tense with excitement over the ratification of the new constitution, Doddridge, now a member of Congress from northwestern Virginia, sent his famous circular letter[108] to the western counties. In it he laid before the people his version of how Cooke and Henderson had betrayed the west into the hands of the eastern aristocracy, and did not spare the venerable Madison the opprobrium of his cutting epithets. He narrated the part which the trans-Alleghany had in bringing the convention about and the story of its betrayal, and concluded that the price she must now pay for it all is "the unconditional surrender of ourselves and our posterity to practical vassalage under the yoke of an eastern oligarchy."

The effort to defeat ratification was unsuccessful.

[105] *Wheeling Gazette*, April 6, 1830.

[106] *Ibid.*, March 12, 1830.

[107] *Compiler*, March 10, 1830.

[108] *Richmond Enquirer*, March 23, 1830; *ibid.*, March 26, 1830; *ibid.*, April 2, 1830.

The total vote was: for ratification, 26,055, for rejection, 15,566. The accompanying map of the vote by counties on ratification shows every county east of the Blue Ridge for it, except Warwick and Lancaster. These were small counties which had been combined with other counties to constitute delegate districts. In most cases the minority vote in the eastern counties was insignificant. Madison County gave no vote for rejection and 256 for ratification. The largest votes for ratification came from the counties of northern and western Piedmont and of the Shenandoah Valley. But two of the twenty-six counties in the trans-Alleghany gave majorities for ratification. These counties were Washington and Lee, each located in the extreme southwestern part of the state and more or less interested in negro slavery.[109] Most of the trans-Alleghany counties gave insignificant minorities for ratification. Out of a total vote of 646, Ohio County gave only 3 votes for ratification. Brooke County, the home of Campbell and Doddridge, gave no vote for ratification, and Harrison gave only 8 for it in a total vote of 1,128.[110]

Although the new constitution was ratified by more than ten thousand majority, the trans-Alleghany people would not be reconciled to it, and continued to talk dismemberment. During the autumn of 1830 a series of essays, favoring the formation of a new state west of the mountains, appeared in many of the western

[109] Many negroes were employed in the salt works in Washington County.

[110] *Debates, Va. Constitutional Convention of 1829–30*, 903.

Map showing the vote by counties for and against the constitution of 1830

prints over the signature, "Senex."[111] The writer of these articles took the position that nothing but dismemberment could bring relief to the west. He believed that future reforms were practically impossible and that western Virginia had the natural resources which would enable it to become a self-sufficing and prosperous commonwealth. On October 1, 1830, the citizens of Wheeling called a mass-meeting to consider the expediency of taking measures to annex northwestern Virginia to Maryland.[112] They contemplated adding that part of Virginia's territory which lay north of a straight line from the southwestern corner of Maryland to the mouth of the Little Kanawha River. Speaking of this move, the *Winchester Republican* said:

We are not at all surprised and are prepared to see it persisted in until it is crowned with success. In politics there is an utter contrariety of sentiment between the people of these counties and their eastern brethren, while with their neighbors of Maryland they harmonize exactly. Were the cession to take place, the Baltimore and Ohio Railroad would unquestionably extend to Parkersburg or some point on the Ohio near that place.[113]

It was not "as patriots of Virginia" but "as patriots of America" that the editors of the *Wheeling Compiler* favored dismemberment.[114]

The following extract from the *Winchester Re-*

[111] See *Kanawha Banner*, September 17, 1830; *ibid.*, October 1, 1830; *ibid.*, October 8, 1830.

[112] *Ibid.*, October 29, 1830.

[113] *Winchester Republican*, October 15, 1830.

[114] *Kanawha Banner*, November 15, 1830.

publican[115] shows the change of attitude which the Valley was assuming toward the trans-Alleghany country after the constitutional convention of 1829-30, and it also afforded a clue to the various schemes of dismemberment which were on foot in Virginia at the time it was written:

The Virginia Legislature will convene on Monday. To the proceedings of this body we look with intense interest. Matters of great moment will come before it, and the discussions will be as interesting as those of the late convention. The preservation of the state we believe will depend upon this Legislature. Dispute the claims of the Trans-Alleghany counties to what they may deem a proper share of the fund for internal improvements and a *division of the state must follow*— not immediately perhaps, but the signal will be given for the rising of the clans, and *they will rise*. It is not worth while now to speculate on the mode and manner in which the government will be opposed. Sufficient unto the day is the evil thereof. But a crisis is approaching. The northern counties demand to be separated from the state with a view of attaching themselves to Maryland or Pennsylvania; the southwest counties go for a division of the state into two commonwealths. Should the latter be effected, what will be our condition in the Valley? Infinitely worse than the present. The mere dependency of a government whose interest and whose trade would all go westward, we would be taxed without receiving any equivalent; and instead of being chastened with whips, we should be scourged with scorpions. Of the two projects spoken of, that which would be least injurious to the Valley and the state at large, would be to part with the northwestern counties. Let them go. Let us get clear of this disaffected population. Then prosecute the improvements called for in the southwest, and that portion of our state, deprived of its northern allies, would give up its desire for a separation.

[115] December 3, 1830; see also the *Kanawha Banner*, December 17, 1830.

CHAPTER VI

INTERNAL IMPROVEMENTS, NEGRO SLAVERY, AND NULLIFICATION, 1829-33

The internal improvement schemes urged by advocates of the American System and the railways in process of construction westward from Baltimore were the important factors in shaping the internal improvement policies in Virginia during this period. Her legislators yet believed it possible to make Richmond a commercial rival of Baltimore, Philadelphia, and New York. Accordingly they again sought to revive interest in the proposed water communication between the James and the Kanawha rivers and took every precaution to prevent the west from becoming tributary to Baltimore by means of either the railway or canal.

During the first years of this period the chief discussion, especially in the west, was to determine the policy of the Jackson administration on the subject of internal improvements. The constitutional convention of 1829-30 taught the west to expect little of the east in the way of roads and canals. Its inhabitants, therefore, hoped for a continuation of the Adams policy, which Jackson's inaugural address and first message had led them to believe might be adhered to.

The proposed Buffalo and New Orleans turnpike, to be built by way of Washington, thence through the Valley, aroused keen interest in western Virginia. The representatives from that section argued for it on the ground that it was necessary to promote the general welfare,[1] and to comply with the provisions of a contract between the federal government and Alabama and Mississippi, whereby the former had agreed to use a portion of the proceeds of the land sales within those states to construct works of internal improvement.[2] Craig favored using the proceeds of the sales of the public lands upon works of internal improvement as the only means whereby they could be returned to the people. Another argument advanced by these representatives was that the proposed road would expedite the transfer of the mails, and afford an easy and necessary means of communication in time of war.

Archer, P. P. Barbour, and Bouldin spoke for the east in opposition to the proposed road. Barbour insisted that the circumstances surrounding the construction of the Cumberland turnpike, deemed necessary to comply with a contract between the federal government and Ohio, were not identical with those advanced in behalf of the Buffalo and New Orleans turnpike; in the former case Ohio had demanded the road, while in the latter both Alabama and Mississippi were opposed to it. He professed to see in the proposed undertaking the beginning of appropriations designed to continue the national debt and the obnoxious tariff.[3] In reply

[1] The chief market for the Valley, even to the Tennessee line, was Baltimore (Seward, *Seward*, I, 268).

[2] *Register of Cong. Debates*, 21 Cong., 1st sess., VI, Part II, 674, 696, 711.

[3] *Ibid.*, 696, 739, 743, 772.

SLAVERY AND NULLIFICATION

to the inquiry which Archer said had been repeatedly put to him, namely: "Will Virginia nullify the law providing for the road?" he answered, invariably and promptly, "no!" for that would be to "refuse obedience to the laws of the Union." He insisted, however, that the proposed road was unnecessary, unconstitutional, and bad precedent.[4]

The importance and uncertainty of the sectional conflict then on in the state was attested by the frequent references made to it, in the course of this debate, by speakers other than Virginians. Some believed the proposed road necessary to prevent the dismemberment of Virginia and possibly of the Union.[5] Irwin of Ohio, a native Virginian, believed that "the signs of the times" pointed to a revolution in the Old Dominion, and that the day was not distant when she would concede all that the friends of internal improvements desired and regard C. F. Mercer as her greatest benefactor.[6]

The bill to provide for the Buffalo and New Orleans turnpike was defeated on engrossment for a third reading: ayes 88, noes 105. The representatives of trans-Alleghany Virginia voted aye, as did Craig of the Valley and Mercer of the Loudoun district.[7] The bill was finally laid on the table in order to take up instead the bill to appropriate money to the Maysville, Washington, Paris, and Lexington Turnpike Company.

Jackson's veto of the Maysville appropriation and

[4] *Ibid.*, 745.   [5] *Ibid.*, 670, 742.   [6] *Ibid.*, 727.
[7] Smith, of the Valley, spoke for the bill but did not vote.

his subsequent pocket veto of the appropriation to the Portland Canal Company[8] did not materially lessen his popularity in western Virginia. To be sure, the pocket veto did provoke criticism in the counties along the Ohio and the Great Kanawha, but these were largely National Republican. On the other hand, the action of the House in tabling the Buffalo and New Orleans turnpike bill relieved Jackson of the necessity of expressing himself on the subject. The inhabitants of the Valley and the Piedmont foothills had therefore little grievance against the president. They continued to insist that their schemes were national in character and to attribute the responsibility for their defeat to the strict construction leaders of the east and the lower south. Their devotion to nationalism and loyalty to Jackson thus continued.

The attitude of Jackson made it clear, however, that local schemes of internal improvement could not expect federal aid, and already those interested in such schemes had turned to the state. The Assembly of 1829–30 was flooded by the west with petitions asking the incorporation of internal improvement companies and appropriations thereto. From the Kanawha Valley they requested a public highway to the mouth of the Big Sandy, while those from the north and northwest were for the incorporation of turnpike companies. Many of these petitions requested permission to institute lotteries to promote internal improvements.[9]

[8] This was the company which constructed the canal around the falls at Louisville, Kentucky.

[9] *Journal, House of Del.*, 1829–30, 13, 15, 47, 48.

Meanwhile the railway daily became a greater factor in transportation. The west readily accepted it as the only practical solution of its difficult problems, but the east clung to the canal. During these years the merits of railways and canals were subjects of much discussion. Although opposed to the Chesapeake and Ohio Canal on general principles, the Richmond press borrowed the arguments advanced in its favor and applied them to promote the James River and Kanawha Canal. The westerners were equally loud in praise of the railway. The *Winchester Republican* believed the Baltimore and Ohio Railroad had already greatly enhanced the value of property along the Potomac and confidently predicted greater prosperity due to its influence.[10] In 1831 Winchester, a very small place, subscribed $40,000 to be used in constructing a lateral road to the Baltimore and Ohio. About the same time Lynchburg subscribed $300,000 to be used to construct a railroad between the James and New rivers.[11] The hope had not yet vanished in the west that the Baltimore and Ohio Company would eventually be permitted to construct its lines through the Valley, thence to the Ohio by way of the Great Kanawha. Some expected to see the company construct its lines from Baltimore to Harper's Ferry and from Louisville to the southwestern boundary of the state. Under these circumstances it was deemed impossible longer to deprive it of permission to cross central Virginia.[12]

[10] *Niles Register*, XL, 59.

[11] *Ibid.*, XL, 59; *National Intelligencer*, November 23, 1831.

[12] *Kanawha Banner*, August 26, 1831.

Ere long the east admitted the practical utility of railroads. Accordingly the Assembly of 1830–31 incorporated a number of railway companies,[13] but the acts of incorporation were determined largely by sectional interest. Delegates from the Great Kanawha Valley made a desperate effort to amend the act incorporating the Staunton and Potomac Company, so as to permit it to extend its proposed lines westward from Staunton by way of the Great Kanawha to the Ohio River. Summers' amendment to this act aroused great alarm in the east, which feared that the act of 1827, restricting the Baltimore and Ohio Company to the northwestern part of the state, would thereby be rendered null. The conservatives believed that the Baltimore and Ohio Company was back of the Staunton and Potomac Company and that it intended to purchase its rights and interests.[14] Accordingly the amendment was defeated by a sectional vote: ayes 53, noes 58.[15] Another blow was given nationalism and the Baltimore interests, which then expected federal aid, by so amending the act of incorporation of the Staunton and Potomac Company as to render void all its privileges in case it ever received aid from the federal government.[16]

[13] The companies incorporated were the Staunton and Potomac, the Winchester and Potomac, the Loudoun, the Petersburg, and the Lynchburg and New River (Acts of 1830–31, 167–205; *Niles Register*, XL, 91; *Richmond Enquirer*, March 21, 1831).

[14] *Kanawha Banner*, July 15, 1831; *Richmond Enquirer*, March 15, 1831; *Niles Register*, XL, 58.

[15] *Journal, House of Del.*, 1830–31, 249.

[16] *Richmond Enquirer*, March 15, 1831; *Niles Register*, XL, 58; *Kanawha Banner*, March 25, 1831.

By a combination of interests the same Assembly incorporated the Lynchburg and New River Railroad Company.[17] Should the railroad prove more practicable the east hoped to divert the trade of the west from the New York and Pennsylvania routes to the Great Kanawha and New River route, thence to the James. The delegates from the southwest favored this scheme because it contemplated a lateral line to the Tennessee boundary. It also met favor from the delegates from the southern Piedmont and the counties about Norfolk, because they expected to see the proposed line extended to the coast by way of Petersburg and Norfolk.

The Assembly of 1830-31 ended its work by rejecting a bill to appropriate two million dollars intended to aid the companies it had incorporated and internal improvements in general. Because of the scarcity of private capital in the west this defeat was a death blow to the Lynchburg and New River and the Staunton and Potomac railway companies. By an analysis of the vote on this appropriation bill the editor of the *Kanawha Banner* showed that the counties west of the Blue Ridge cast only seven votes against it.[18] Commenting upon the defeat of the proposed appropriation and Mr. Summers' efforts in its behalf Niles said: "Had the people adopted his views years ago we have no doubt that the real and personal property of Virginia would now have been worth 200 millions

[17] Acts of 1830-31, 167, 177.
[18] *Kanawha Banner*, March 25, 1831.

more than it is and her population 300,000 freemen more."[19]

This unsuccessful beginning did not end the early attempts at railroad construction in Virginia. During a large part of the year 1831 Benjamin Wright, a skilled engineer of New York, assisted the state engineer in making surveys to determine the relative merits of railways and canals as a means of continuing the James and Kanawha improvements. The conflicting report of the two engineers added new perplexities to the situation. One favored a canal from Richmond to the mountains and a railroad thence to the Ohio; the other a continuous railroad.[20]

The Assembly of 1831–32 was thus placed in an embarrassing position. Some of its members desired a railroad as the most suitable method to continue the James and Kanawha improvements; others a canal; and still others clung to the sluice and dam navigation and the use of the steamboat. A compromise was effected whereby the state surrendered its interest in the James River Canal Company and its right to superintend the work to a joint stock company, the James River and Kanawha Company,[21] which was em-

[19] *Niles Register*, XL, 58.

[20] *Journal, House of Del.*, 1831–32, 11; *Report of the Com. on Roads and Int. Imp.* (1831–32), 36. This report gives one of the best reviews to be found of the internal improvement history of Virginia prior to 1832.

[21] The James River and Kanawha Company, commonly called the "J. R. and K. Co.," superseded the old James River Company. It had an authorized capital of $5,000,000, of which the state took $2,000,000, one-half of which was to be paid by a

powered to continue the work to the Ohio by either a railroad or a canal, or a combination of both. At the same time a number of railway companies, restricted, however, to the east, were incorporated to construct lateral lines to the proposed central line of improvements.[22]

This programme did not pass, however, without sectional opposition. The act incorporating the James River and Kanawha Company received 37 negative to 75 affirmative votes.[23] Delegates from counties along the proposed route of the Baltimore and Ohio Railroad and the Lynchburg and New River Railroad, through southern Piedmont, voted against it. At the same time the most enthusiastic supporters of the new company, who came largely from counties along the Kanawha and between the headwaters of the Kanawha and the James, tried to place the construction and the expense of the work upon the state. A resolution to this effect was defeated: ayes 57, noes 67. On the other hand, those interested in the extension of the Staunton and Potomac Railway to the Ohio made a renewed fight for that privilege.[24]

transfer of the state's interest in the James River Company, and the remaining half in cash when three-fifths of the capital stock had been subscribed by individuals and corporations (Acts of 1831–32, 73–87).

[22] The railroad companies incorporated at this time were the Richmond and Turkey Island, the Richmond, the Richmond and Yorktown, the Portsmouth and Roanoke, the Fredericksburg and Potomac, and the Leesburg (Acts of 1831–32, 112–61).

[23] *Journal, House of Del.*, 1831–32, 225.

[24] *Ibid.*, 224.

The James River and Kanawha Company encountered other and more material difficulties, which postponed the commencement of its work for several years. At this time there was not enough capital at the command of individuals residing in the east to promote such an undertaking, and the banks of the eastern cities, remote from the proposed central line of improvement, refused to contribute to a scheme which would make Richmond more powerful commercially.[25] Thus the question of banking again became complicated with that of internal improvements, and the west had occasion to renew its demands for state banks and to oppose any further increase in the banking capital or the number of banks in the east.

Meanwhile the management of the Chesapeake and Ohio Canal Company had incurred the displeasure of the federal administration, an incident which attracted much attention in Virginia and elsewhere. As president of the company and representative of the internal improvement interests of his section, C. F. Mercer had become very popular along the Potomac, the stronghold of National Republicanism. Because of his antiadministration sentiments Jackson resolved to remove him from the presidency of the company. Accordingly he prepared charges against him and openly asserted that, in case of his re-election, he would veto any and all appropriations to the Chesapeake and Ohio Company. When the election came off Major Eaton superseded Mercer by the votes which the federal

[25] *Lynchburg Virginian*, May 6, 1833; *Niles Register*, XLIV, 258; see also *Lynchburg Virginian*, June 3 and 27, 1833.

government owned and controlled.[26] Thus the company was deprived of Mercer's wise counsel and personal influence and soon ceased to receive federal aid.

Discussions in the constitutional convention of 1829–30 and the abolition agitation caused the question of negro slavery to assume an alarming sectional aspect in this period. Prior to 1829 the sentiments and theories of 1776 and religious enthusiasm did much to ameliorate the condition of those in bondage. But during this period portions of the east began to defend negro slavery as a divinely sanctioned institution and as the only practical means of dealing with an inferior race. Planters began to oppose emancipations and to assume an unfriendly attitude toward those who favored them. For the public good they deemed it necessary to restrict the liberties of the slave and even of the free colored population. On the other hand, the inhabitants of the west clung to the theories and sentiments which had formerly made emancipation popular. They became more grounded in the conviction that slavery was an economic evil, and consequently continued to favor gradual emancipation and deportation. There were, however, few abolitionists of the Garrison type among them, but the abolition doctrines of Jefferson and Madison continued to be popular.

The divergence of view between the east and the

[26] Mercer received 3,740 votes; Eaton 5,054. Of the votes given Eaton 2,008 were cast by the secretary of the treasury and 2,008 by the corporation of Washington. Mercer's vote was largely from the individual stockholders (*National Intelligencer*, May 22, 1833; *ibid.*, June 6 and 8, 1833).

west on the subject of negro slavery resulted largely from economic causes. Of the slavery debate in the Assembly of 1831–32 James McDowell said: "This is not a debate involving the first and leading principles of the Republic, nor a question relating to abstract principles of morality. It is a question of self-interest on the one hand and self-preservation on the other."[27] By 1830 the Kanawha Valley counties and the southwest had acquired practically as many negroes as was needed to perform the manual labor in connection with salt working. Thus there was no economic demand for them in the west. Outstripped in the race for material gain by the new states to the north and west of them and firm in the belief that negro slavery was causing the impoverishment of the east, the westerners began to attribute their lack of prosperity to their proximity to the slave-holding portion of the state. They began to indulge in statistical comparisons wherein the numerical and material strength of Virginia was contrasted with that of the free states. Conclusions like those found in Helper's *Impending Crisis* were the invariable results. The belief became current that the natural resources of the west would attract capital and population thither, if the objectionable negroes were removed.

On the other hand, the slave-holders became standpatters. Loria's proposition that slavery is never voluntarily abolished so long as slaves are overvalued[28] never found a truer confirmation than in

[27] Pamphlet, speech of James McDowell (1831–32), 5.
[28] *La Constitutione Economic Adierno*, 779.

Virginia during the years following 1830. The domestic slave trade; improved methods of agriculture produced by the agricultural societies and by the scientific experiments of Edmund Ruffin and others;[29] better means of intercommunication, the railroad and the canal; and the employment given negro slaves upon works of internal improvement and in factories revived the economic interest in negro slaves in the east. The domestic slave trade provided capital, and the scientific agriculture and improved means of communication were restoring the worn-out lands and bringing into use uncultivated areas.

Many attributed the rise in prices and the marked increased interest in negro slaves to the ravages of the cholera, but a planter denied that this had a telling effect and offered the following explanation:

The price has gradually been increasing for several years and is known to be caused mainly by the increased demand in the South for that description of negroes which form the efficient labor of the country, say males from twelve to eighteen. Such immense numbers within these ages have within a few years been bought up for the southern markets, that there is now but few of that description for sale, hence the enormous price now given for even common field hands. Besides which Virginia has, within a few years, entered largely into the spirit of internal improvements and not a little into domestic manufacturing—all which increase the demand for labor, and the blacks being better accommodated, are preferable. Men that a few years since hired out by the year for from 35 to 40 dollars now hire readily at from 60 to 70. The tobacco factories in Richmond and Manchester alone, I presume, will give employment to from one to two thousand men and boys and

[29] *Lynchburg Virginian*, August 20, 1832.

the coal pits to nearly or quite as many more. All these causes draw from the agriculturist his most efficient labor.[80]

About the same time another planter wrote:

> We have never known of negroes selling or hiring out at so high a price as they do at present. We have heard of a carpenter selling at $1,200; a boy of fourteen selling at $400. Negroes hire also at very high rates. Is it because produce is selling so high . . . . or because hands are also wanting for tobacco factories, for internal improvements—for the settlement of new farms—for slaves to supply the place of those who have died of the cholera?[81]

The Nat Turner insurrection brought a movement on the part of the east to secure itself against similar outbreaks and on the part of the west to rid the state of the evils of slavery. Governor Floyd, who sympathized with the east, attributed the causes of the insurrection to the influence of "unrestricted fanatics" from the neighboring states and to the work of negro preachers. He recommended that the legislature silence the latter, that it enact laws to keep the negro slaves in subordination, and that measures be taken for the removal of the free people of color from the commonwealth.[82]

Meanwhile the people, in their public meetings and through their prints, had broken the long silence upon the question of disestablishing slavery. Their activity called forth numerous petitions, memorials, and resolutions on this subject. These may be divided into

[80] *National Intelligencer*, January 19, 1833.
[81] *Richmond Compiler*, January 14, 1833.
[82] *Journal, House of Del.*, 1831–32, 5–14.

three classes: (1) those asking for the removal of the free people of color from the state; (2) those asking an amendment to the federal Constitution to give Congress power to appropriate money to purchase negro slaves and transport the colored population from the United States; (3) those urging the state to devise some scheme for gradual emancipation. The first class of petitions was obviously opposed to any and all forms of emancipation and desired the removal of the free people of color to make the possession of slave property less precarious. They came only from the counties of the Tidewater and the Piedmont. The second and third classes came chiefly from the Valley and the counties of the Piedmont foothills.[83] A memorial from Augusta County, signed by three hundred and forty-three women, asked the immediate abolition of slavery. A mass-meeting in Loudoun resolved,

> That a gradual emancipation and removal of the slaves of the Commonwealth is practicable and, upon that assumption, the continuation of slavery is forbidden by the true policy of Virginia, repugnant to her political theory and christian professions; and an opprobrium to our ancient and renowned Dominion."[84]

These various memorials, petitions, and resolutions were referred to a select committee composed of twenty-one members, of whom sixteen were from counties east of the Blue Ridge. Mr. Goode, of

[83] But two petitions favorable to emancipation came from the Tidewater.

[84] *Washington and Lee Hist. Papers*, No. 5, p. 84.

Mecklenburg, the leader of the slave interests, tried to prevent consideration of the requests for abolition legislation. With this object in view he introduced a resolution to relieve the committee from the necessity of considering the petition from the Quakers of Charles City County. The resolution was defeated, however, by the decisive vote: ayes 27, noes 93. Only one affirmative vote came from west of the Blue Ridge.[35]

By dilatory tactics the committee tried to prevent discussion, but it was impossible. The public had been aroused to too intense a state of excitement. While impatiently awaiting action the *Richmond Enquirer* threw a firebrand which put an end to all silence. It said:

> It is possible from what we learn that the committee on the colored population will report some plan for getting rid of the free people of color. But is this all that can be done? Are we forever to suffer the greatest evil which can scourge our land, not only to remain but increase in its domains? "We may shut our eyes and avert our faces, if you please," writes an eloquent South Carolinian, "but there it is, the black and gnawing evil at our doors—and meet the question we must at no distant day. God only knows what it is the part of wise men to do on that momentous and appalling subject. Of this I am sure, that the difference, nothing short of frightful, between all that exists on one side of the Potomac and all on the other side, is owing to that cause alone. The disease is deep rooted—it is at the heart's core—it is consuming and has all along been consuming our vitals, and I would laugh, if I *could* laugh at such a subject, of the ignorance and folly of politicians who ascribe that to an act of government which

[35] *Journal, House of Del.*, 1831–32, 29.

SLAVERY AND NULLIFICATION

is the inevitable effect of the eternal laws of nature. What is to be done? Oh, my God, I don't know, but something must be done!"[36]

Within a very few days this editorial appeared in whole or in part in practically the entire press of the state.[37] Four days after its appearance in the *Enquirer* Goode made another effort in the Assembly to restrain the smoldering fire of abolition sentiment. After inquiring when the committee on the abolition petitions intended to report and receiving no definite answer, he moved that it be discharged from the consideration of "all petitions, memorials, and resolutions which have for their object the manumission of persons held in servitude under the laws of this Commonwealth, and that it is not expedient to legislate on the subject."[38]

This resolution gave the abolitionists an opportunity, and precipitated one of the ablest debates ever witnessed in this country on the subject of emancipation. Immediately Thomas Jefferson Randolph, grandson of Jefferson, moved to amend Goode's motion by substituting in lieu thereof the following:

That the committee be instructed to inquire into the expediency of submitting to the vote of the qualified voters in the several towns, cities, boroughs and counties of this Commonwealth the propriety of providing by law that the children of all female slaves who may be born in this state on or after the fourth day of July, 1840, shall become the property of the

[36] *Richmond Enquirer,* January 7, 1832.

[37] *Niles Register,* XLI, 369; *National Intelligencer,* January 10, 1832.

[38] *Journal, House of Del.,* 1831–32, 93.

Commonwealth, the males at the age of twenty-one and the females at the age of eighteen if detained by their owners within the limits of Virginia until they respectively arrive at the ages aforesaid; to be hired out until the net sum arising therefrom shall be sufficient to defray the expense of their removal beyond the limits of the United States.[39]

This is Jefferson's *post nati* scheme, first advanced in 1779. After three days of discussion the committee made a report to the effect that "it is inexpedient for the present to make any legislative enactments for the abolition of slavery."[40] Immediately Mr. Preston, of Montgomery, moved to amend the report by substituting in lieu thereof, "it is expedient to adopt some legislative enactment for the abolition of slavery."[41]

The general tone in the argument of the western delegates in 1831–32 was quite different from what it had been in the constitutional convention of 1829–30. Now they looked upon negro slavery as the greatest evil which could befall them. They now feared that the state laws against the domestic slave trade would divert Virginia's surplus slaves to the west,[42] and that they would soon become slave-holders in spite of themselves. In reply to these arguments the eastern delegates assured the westerners that it was not imperative for them to purchase negroes. They also insisted that slavery would continue to be confined more and more to the lower South, eventually ridding Virginia of the evil. In this connection Mr. Burr said:

[39] *Journal, House of Del.*, 1831–32, 93.
[40] *Ibid.*, 99.   [41] *Ibid.*, 99.
[42] Pamphlet, speech of James McDowell (1831–32), 21, 23.

SLAVERY AND NULLIFICATION 193

> The dark wave of negro slavery, which haunts your imagination, has rolled against the mountains for generations and has cast only a slight spray beyond. The foot of the negro delights not in the dew of the mountain grass. He is the child of the sandy desert. The burning sun gives him life and vigor, and his step is most joyous in the arid plain.[43]

The burden of the argument of the abolitionists was that negro slavery was an economic evil. "It is," said Thomas Marshall, "ruinous to the whites; retards improvements; roots out our industrious population; banishes the yeomanry from the country; and deprives the spinner, the weaver, the smith, the shoemaker, and the carpenter of employment and support."[44] They insisted that the domestic slave trade was the only thing which then made negro slavery profitable in Virginia, and that when it should cease slave prices would fall to a minimum. They frequently compared the wealth and population of Virginia with that of one of the new free states to the great disadvantage of the former. They also insisted that the presence of the negro slaves was causing the standard of living to decline. Said Marshall: "All the chief glories of Virginia style have faded; gone is the massive coach with its stately attelage of four or six; shut is the beneficent hall door; . . . . the watering-places no longer blaze with the rich but decent pomp of Virginians; and the cities rarely bear witness of her generous expense."[45] But the Virginia abolitionists, like those

---
[43] Pamphlet, speech in the General Assembly of 1831–32.
[44] *Wheeling Intelligencer*, November 28, 1859.
[45] *American Quarterly Review*, December, 1832.

elsewhere, failed or refused to consider that negroes freed would still be negroes, and as repellent to white immigration as when slaves. They busied themselves chiefly with a slave problem, while their opponents were concerned with a negro problem.

The answers to these arguments reveal clearly the change of mind which the east was undergoing. Goode denied that negro slavery was responsible for the "gullied hillsides" and "the turned-out fields." Such spectacles, he insisted, had appeared only after the planter with his negroes had deserted the land to build commonwealths in the new South. He insisted that slave-holding Virginia was being reclaimed, and that her population had not flown from the evils of negro slavery, "because," said he, "they are now found residing chiefly in the slave-holding states."[46] He believed that the energy and power of Virginia and her institutions could not be estimated with accuracy unless the new commonwealths of the Southwest were taken into consideration.

Others of the eastern delegates were not so optimistic regarding the economic benefits of negro slavery. "It is," said Brodnax, "a mildew which has blighted in its course every region it has touched from the creation of the world."[47] He was, however, opposed to Randolph's plan of gradual emancipation and laid down the following conditions as the only ones under which abolition could be effected: (1) the immediate removal of the emancipated from the state;

[46] Pamphlet, speech of W. O. Goode (1831-32), 10, 20.
[47] Pamphlet, speech of W. H. Brodnax (1831-32), 11.

SLAVERY AND NULLIFICATION

(2) private property must not be interfered with; and (3) not a single negro or any other property he possesses can be taken from its owner, *"without* his owner's consent, or an ample compensation."[48] He opposed the *post nati* scheme because it deprived the owner of his property in the child-bearing power of his female slaves, "an item of chief consideration in their sale or purchase."[49]

Many of the abolitionists insisted that there was no property right in the unborn and that an act declaring them free could not infringe the rights of private property. Others admitted that such rights would be thus impaired but insisted that the sacrifice should be made. McDowell, of Rockbridge, said: "Private property, which a state allows to be held by its citizens, must consist with the general end for which the state is created; the power to correct an evil tendency is inherent in all government, and the exercise of such power is no infringement of private rights."[50]

Randolph's plan was also opposed on the ground that it was impracticable; the state would add one more purchaser; and prices would accordingly be increased. The abolitionists were repeatedly reminded that, had abolition been practicable, the fathers who desired it so much would have devised some scheme to effect it. To this argument McDowell answered: "The difficulties in the way are not more positive than the necessity of legislation" and "you cannot canonize error because of its antiquity." Mr. Summers of Kanawha

[48] *Ibid.,* 12.   [49] *Ibid.,* 14.
[50] Pamphlet, speech of James McDowell (1831-32), 15.

suggested that the proceeds of the public lands be used to effect emancipation.[51]

Moral issues influenced only a few of the Virginia abolitionists of 1832. On this phase of the subject Marshall said: "We know that the ordinary condition of the slaves in Virginia is not such as to make humanity weep for his lot. Our solicitations to the slaveholder, it will be perceived, are founded but little on the miseries of the blacks."[52] Other reasons advanced in behalf of emancipation were: the danger of a servile population in times of war and that it was demanded by the public. To support these points it was maintained that dismemberment of the Union was not improbable and that there was danger of the slaves becoming a constant source of trouble between a northern and a southern confederacy.[53]

In reply to these arguments the pro-slavery delegates insisted that negro slaves would be a source of strength in time of war and pointed to the experience of two successful wars to prove their contention.[54] The proposition to submit the question of emancipation to a vote of the people Goode condemned as unsafe; it would then be necessary to discuss emancipation in the midst of the slaves; useless excitement and possible insurrections might follow.[55]

On the part of the westerners the argument was characterized by frequent outbursts of the principles

[51] Pamphlet, speech of James McDowell (1831–32), 6 ff.
[52] *American Quarterly Review*, December 18, 1832.
[53] Pamphlet, speech of W. O. Goode (1831–32), 18.
[54] *Ibid.*, 18.   [55] *Ibid.*, 9.

SLAVERY AND NULLIFICATION

of 1776. One of the most eloquent appeals of this nature was made by McDowell:

> You may place the slave [said he] where you please, you may dry up to the utmost the fountains of his feelings, the spring of his thought—you may close upon his mind the avenue to knowledge and cloud it over with artificial night—you may yoke him to your labor as an ox which liveth only to work and worketh only to live—you may put him under any process, which, without destroying his value as a slave, will debase and crush him as a rational being—you may do this and the idea that he was born to be free will survive all. It is allied to his hope of immortality—it is the ethical part of his nature which oppression cannot reach—it is the torch lit up in his soul by the hand of the deity and never meant to be extinguished by the hand of man.[56]

Samuel McDowell Moore, his colleague and relative, believed that—

> the autocrat of Russia does not more deserve the name tyrant for sending his hordes of barbarians to plant the blood-stained banner on the walls of Warsaw, amid the desolation of all that is near to the hearts of free men, than does the petty tyrant, who, in any quarter of the globe, is equally regardless of the acknowledged rights of man.[57]

Such utterances constituted, however, only a minor part of the debate. Most of the speakers were of a younger generation and they addressed themselves to reach a more materially minded Virginia than did even the speakers of 1829–30.

Another feature of the debates of 1831–32, not so marked a feature of prior discussions but of much

---
[56] *Wheeling Intelligencer*, November 28, 1859.
[57] Quoted in speech by W. O. Goode, 32.

subsequent importance, was the disposition of the pro-slavery men to place the western leaders in a place of discredit, to whip them into line, and to dub the most refractory with opprobrious epithets. Goode was especially resourceful in the use of these tactics. He characterized the abolition leaders as the Rufus Kings of the west; they were told that the east could expect nothing of them in the time of her calamity, should it ever come. "When our aged mothers shall call in vain for protection from their slaughtered sons," asked Goode, "will they be found leading or mingling with the black horde?" C. J. Faulkner and W. B. Preston were ridiculed for comparing the abolition movement to "a great political revolution," to the "generous efforts of the Parisian patriots." W. G. Summers was an object of suspicion because he found delight in the political theories of Thomas Jefferson. He was denominated the "Byron of the west, walking on the mountain tops and gazing on the desolation which burns in the plains below." In case abolition had diffused itself through the mountains, Goode was for immediate dismemberment, as the only alternative to the recurrence of the horrors of Saint Bartholomew.[58]

Few of the prominent western leaders ever lived down the part they took in this debate. Some did not care to do so and usually sank into political oblivion; others succeeded in placating the slave power and received political recognition. Among them were McDowell, who later became governor, and Faulkner and Preston, who became minister to France and secretary

[58] Quoted in speech by W. O. Goode, 32.

Map showing the vote of Virginia by counties in the House of Delegates of 1831–32 on a resolution declaring it expedient to legislate for the abolition of negro slavery.

of the navy respectively. But Summers could not become governor; McDowell was denied the goal of his ambition, a seat in the United States Senate; while others received only casual recognition.

Preston's amendment to the report of the select committee that, "it is expedient to adopt some legislative amendment for the abolition of slavery," was defeated: ayes 58, noes 73.[59] The accompanying map shows the sectional character of the vote in the House of Delegates. Only three delegates from the Tidewater counties voted aye, and one of them represented Henrico, which lies only partly below the fall line. The counties of the Piedmont foothills, Buckingham, Amherst, Albemarle, together gave four votes in the affirmative. The fact that the counties in the upper Potomac and the lower Shenandoah Valley voted so largely in the negative is not without significance. True, they had a large slave population, but they were a'so the counties which, as has been seen, had recently formed a political alliance with the east. The map shows the central and southern parts of the valley and the whole trans-Alleghany a unit in favor of the expediency of legislation upon the subject of emancipation.

Defeated on Preston's amendment, the abolitionists attempted another declaration of principles. Bryce, of Goochland County, proposed to amend the report of the select committee which declared it inexpedient to legislate upon the subject of emancipation, by prefixing the following preamble:

[59] *Journal, House of Del.*, 1831–32, 109.

> Profoundly sensible of the great evils arising from the condition of the colored population of the Commonwealth; induced by humanity as well as policy, to an immediate effort for the removal, in the first place, as well as those who are now free as of such as may hereafter become free, believing that this effort, while it is in just accordance with the sentiment of the community on the subject, will absorb all our present means; and that a further action for the removal of the slaves should await a more definite development of public opinion, Resolved, etc.

After strenuous opposition from the pro-slavery men this preamble was adopted: ayes 67, noes 60.[60] In addition to the counties favorable to Preston's amendment those counties marked "X" on the map favored this preamble. They were represented by delegates favorable to emancipation but opposed to immediate legislation, on the ground that the status of federal relations made it inexpedient.[61]

The House next took up a bill for the removal from the state of the free people of color.[62] It provided for their compulsory removal and for an appropriation of $100,000 to meet the first expenses thereof. The discussion of this bill turned upon whether or not coercion should be used and upon the amount of the appropriation. Delegates from the west opposed forced removals and so large an appropriation. As finally passed by the House the bill made the deportation of those already free voluntary and provided for

[60] *Journal, House of Del.*, 1831–32, 110. Thus amended the report of the select committee passed but was carried by the western vote.

[61] Slaughter, *Hist. Am. Colonization Society*, 40.

[62] At this time the free colored population numbered 47,348.

an appropriation of $35,000 to be used in 1832 and $90,000 to be used in 1833.[63]

The free discussion of 1831–32 was followed by a decided reaction against abolition. A powerful essay entitled *A Review of the Debates in the Virginia Legislature of 1831–32* by Professor Thomas R. Dew, of William and Mary College, crystallized the pro-slavery sentiment.[64] In both the abstract and the practical this essay dealt with slavery in all countries and especially with the rise and development of negro slavery in America. It clearly set forth the difficulties in deporting the slave and free colored population and the dangers to society of emancipation without deportation. It deprecated the idea of a successful slave uprising so long as the whites constituted a considerable portion of the total population, and pointed out the dangers to property and society of permitting young and inexperienced legislators freely to discuss so momentous a question as emancipation.

Jesse Burton Harrison[65] answered Professor Dew in an essay entitled *A Review of the Speech of Thomas Marshall in the Virginia Assembly of 1831–32*.[66] It was simply a reiteration of the arguments

[63] *Journal, House of Del.*, 1831–32, 158. The bill was defeated in the Senate (*National Intelligencer*, February 21, 1832; *ibid.*, March 15, 1832).

[64] This essay can be found in the *Political Register*, II, No. 5, and in pamphlet form. It was also published in *Pro-Slavery Argument* (Charleston, 1852), 287–490.

[65] Slaughter, *Hist. Am. Col. Society*, 64.

[66] *American Quarterly Review*, December, 1832; *African Repository*, IX, No. 1.

advanced to prove negro slavery in Virginia an economic evil. It met with little favor, and for a long time the authorship of the essay was kept anonymous.

Madison also made a brief answer to Dew's essay.[67] He insisted that in his explanation of the depressed condition of Virginia, Dew had given too little importance to the presence of negro slavery and to emigration, and that he had emphasized too strongly the influence of the tariff laws. This protest is interesting as an expression of the attitude of the old school of conservatives.

As wool-growing and manufacturing became more important in the west devotion to the American System increased.[68] Petitions continued to come to Congress from that section for protection and appropriations for works of internal improvement.[69] Of the conditions there Niles said: "The western and middle counties are even now favorable to the system, though yet embarrassed by the *politics* of the 'junto' at Richmond."[70]

The subject of most interest to the west was the preservation of the salt industry. In 1830 Benton introduced a bill in Congress to abolish entirely the duty on salt. By numerous depositions and letters he attempted to show that the salt-makers on the Kanawha

[67] Madison, *Writings* (ed. Cong.), IV, 277, 278.

[68] The census of 1840 gave more than one-half million sheep in western Virginia (Howe, *Hist. Coll.*, 161, 162).

[69] *Journal, House of Rep.*, 21 Cong., 2d sess., 120, 162.

[70] *Niles Register*, XLV, 242.

SLAVERY AND NULLIFICATION 203

and Holston maintained a monopoly of the salt trade; that owners were annually paid large amounts to keep their salt wells idle; and that unfair means were used to prevent foreign competition.[71] On the other hand, the salt-makers claimed to be the benefactors of the country. By elaborate memorials to Congress they showed how their enterprise had reduced the price in the interior from twelve, eight, five, and three dollars successively, to seventy-five cents cents per bushel, and denied that a monopoly existed.[72] Since the application of steam to river navigation had enabled the West India salt, carried to New Orleans as ballast, to compete with home manufacturers, they insisted that increased protection was needed instead of the proposed reduction.

The final abolition of the protective duty on salt made the administration very unpopular in the Kanawha and Holston valleys. Accompanied by severe editorial comments, Benton's speeches on the salt tax appeared in the western prints, and mass-meetings were held to denounce their author.[73] "That a measure calculated to destroy the only considerable manufacture in the state," said the editor of the *Kanawha Banner*, "should meet the support of almost the entire representation from Virginia presents a strange anomaly. More than one million dollars worth

[71] *Cong. Debates*, VIII, Part III, 3314, 3469; *ibid.*, VII, 127, 131, 136.

[72] *Ibid.*, VII, Appendix, cxxv; *Journal, House of Rep.*, 21 Cong., 2d sess., 162.

[73] *Kanawha Banner*, November 12, 19, 26, 1830; *ibid.*, February 4, 18, 25, 1831.

of property, actually invested, is thus sacrificed on the altar of political consistency."[74] The policy of retaining the duty upon sugar and repealing that upon salt was denominated "an attack upon the free citizens of the country." "We hold," said the editor of the *Kanawha Banner*, "that the owner [slave-owner] can never rightfully so regulate the country by law, as to give a value to slave labor over that of the free, hardy, and enlightened sons of the republic."[75]

The accompanying map shows the vote of Virginia in the House of Representatives on the tariff of 1832.[76] But one representative from west of the Blue Ridge voted against it. The compromise feature of this tariff gained votes for it in the slightly nationalistic districts of the Tidewater and along the Potomac.[77] The affirmative vote from the district lying immediately southwest of Richmond was determined largely by the desire of the coal operators of Chesterfield and Powhatan counties for a duty on coal.[78]

In the congressional elections of 1829 and 1831 not wholly unsuccessful efforts were made by the National Republicans to carry the congressional districts in the west.[79] These attacks upon this vulnerable spot in the strict construction phalanx and the agita-

[74] *Kanawha Banner*, December 31, 1830.
[75] *Ibid.*, January 7, 1831.
[76] *Journal, House of Rep.*, 22 Cong., 1st sess., 1023.
[77] *Lynchburg Virginian*, September 3, 10, 1832.
[78] *Journal, House of Rep.*, 22 Cong., 1st sess., 234, 290.
[79] In 1829 the transmontane districts elected Doddridge, Craig, Maxwell, and Armstrong, all National Republicans. They were reelected in 1831.

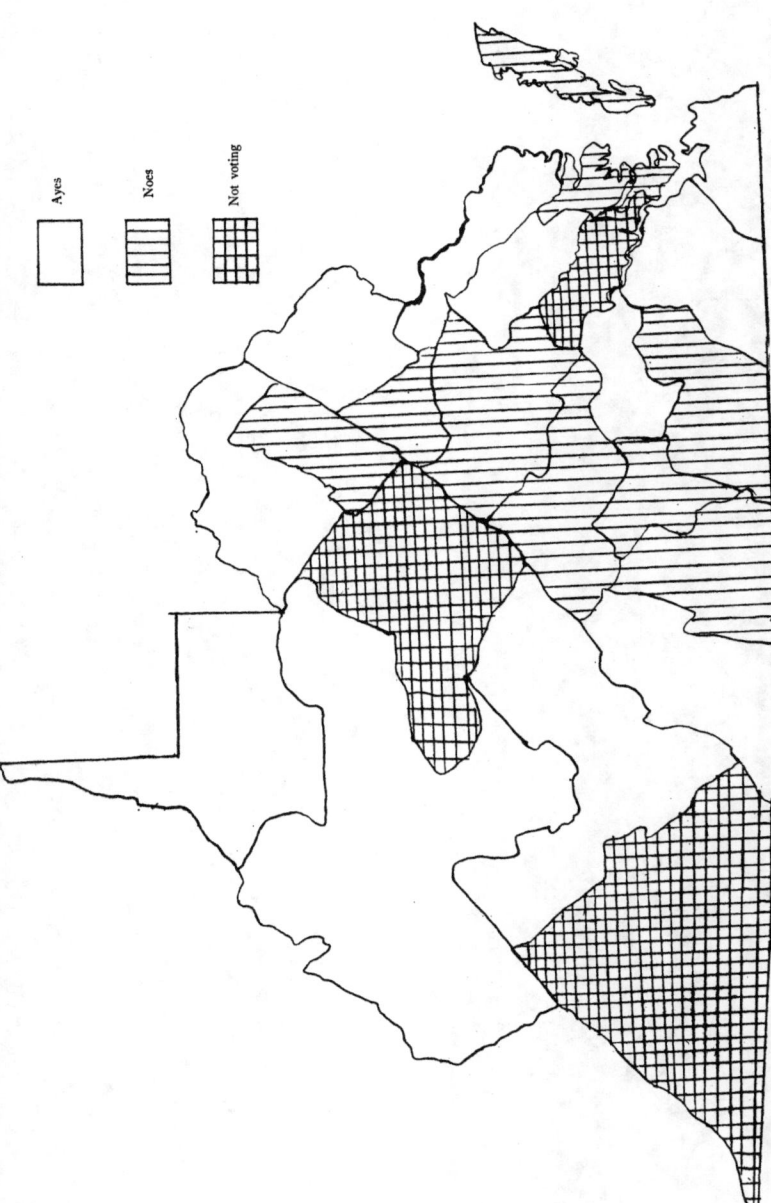

Map showing the vote of Virginia in the House of Representatives on the Tariff Bill of 1832: Ayes 12; Noes 8; not voting 3

SLAVERY AND NULLIFICATION

tion for a protective tariff called from John Tyler the following: "I know that the effort is working to sever, in sentiment and feeling, eastern and western Virginia. . . . . I have even heard something said about a division of the state. I have but a single sentiment to express upon this subject, and it is Virginia now and forever."[80]

The result of the presidential election of 1832 was more important from the standpoint of sectionalism than a map of the vote would indicate. By safe majorities Jackson carried every county in the state except seven. Clay's strength was isolated and confined to small areas more or less interested in internal improvements.[81] But the issue in the election of 1832 in Virginia was not so much specific items of the American System as the general policy of strict construction. Convinced that they could not succeed and satisfied with the attitude of Jackson toward the nullifiers the National Republicans of the west forfeited the election.[82] It is not without significance that Jackson's largest vote came from the Valley; that the old nationalist strongholds, Augusta, Greenbrier, and Kanawha counties, gave him majorities; and that the vote in the east, despite the fact that a large number had been recently admitted to the rights of suffrage, was small. Already many political leaders and most of the aristo-

[80] *Cong. Debates*, VIII, Part I, 360.

[81] He carried Ohio, Jefferson, Berkeley, Loudoun, and Princess Anne counties (*Richmond Whig*, November 19, 1832).

[82] *Lynchburg Virginian*, September 3, 1832; *ibid.*, November 15, 1832.

cratic planters were revolting against the absolutism which reigned in the White House and the whoop and hurrah methods which gave it sanction.[83] Many voters in the east accepted Jackson in 1832 as the lesser of two evils.[84]

As a sectional contest the campaign for the election of the vice-president was more important than the presidential election. Led by Thomas W. Gilmer the ardent strict construction wing of the Democratic party, for the most part confined to the counties east of the Blue Ridge, opposed the election of Van Buren and put P. P. Barbour forward as their choice. Barbour was an ardent strict constructionist; he opposed Nullification, but defended the right of a state to secede.[85] At first an effort was made to secure the nomination of the Baltimore convention for him. In this attempt the state-rights men of Virginia co-operated with others of the same political faith in South Carolina, North Carolina, and Alabama. Their combined efforts gave Barbour, however, only forty-nine votes.[86]

Chagrined at their defeat and distrustful of Van Buren's nationalism and political methods the Barbour party in Virginia resolved to turn the electoral vote to

[83] *Alexandria Gazette*, August 8, 1832; *William and Mary College Quarterly*, XXII, 87; *Niles Register*, XLI, 227; *National Intelligencer*, September 14, 1831.

[84] *Cong. Debates*, VI, Part II, 732.

[85] *Niles Register*, XLIII, 124, 125; *Lynchburg Virginian*, October 11, 1832.

[86] The vote for Barbour was: Virginia, 23; South Carolina, 11; North Carolina, 6; Alabama, 6; Maryland, 3 (*Niles Register*, XLII, 235).

their candidate. With the co-operation of other southern states they hoped to throw the election of the vice-president into the Senate and thus to defeat Van Buren. At first an effort was made to secure a pledge from the electors on the Democratic ticket to support Barbour in case the popular vote should name him as the choice of the state.[87] The Jackson–Van Buren electors refused to commit themselves,[88] and a Jackson-Barbour electoral ticket was nominated.[89] As finally launched, the opposition party professed devotion to Jackson, applauded the bank veto, and denounced the tariff. The election of Barbour, its adherents insisted, would break up the "nest of harpies" which were hovering about the federal capital, teach Jackson that he could not impose the political practices of New York upon Virginia, and allay the nullification excitement.[90]

Led by Rives, Ritchie, and McDowell the thoroughgoing Jackson Democrats remained loyal to Van Buren. The followers of McDowell and Rives, confined for the most part to the counties of the Piedmont foothills and the west, were Democrats of the Madison type. They believed in the constitutionality of a bank and a protective tariff but doubted their expediency.[91] They claimed that the defeat of Van Buren meant the

[87] *Lynchburg Virginian,* September 17, 1832.

[88] *Ibid.,* September 24, 1832.

[89] *Ibid.,* October 15, 1832.

[90] *Ibid.,* September 20, 1832; *ibid.,* October 8, 1832.

[91] See Madison, *Cabell Letters;* also "Letters to C. J. Ingersol," in *Niles Register,* XL, 352; Madison, *Writings* (ed. Cong.), IV, 183. Rives was possibly Madison's closest political friend during the last years of his life.

election of Sargent, the National Republican candidate,[92] and that Clay and Calhoun had combined to defeat Jackson and Van Buren.[93] McDowell, the leader of the western wing of this party, opposed the election of Barbour on the ground that he was a nullifier. "It is not enough," said he, "to say that Mr. Barbour is no more of a nullifier than any state-rights man in Virginia."[94]

Immediately after Van Buren's public declaration of opposition to an oppressive protective tariff, to works of internal improvement by the federal government,[95] and to the recharter of the national bank, Barbour withdrew from the contest. The necessity of party unity, he said, demanded his withdrawal.[96] Members of the opposition party alleged, however, that threats from Richmond and promises from Washington prompted his action.[97] The National Republican press was pretty well agreed that Barbour would not have received more than one-half the votes given Sargent.[98] Accepting this estimate and considering the fact that the Barbour party was almost exclusively confined to the east, there can be little doubt that a poll for their candidate would have shown a large

[92] *Lynchburg Virginian*, September 3, 1832.

[93] *Ibid.*, September 3, 1832.

[94] *Washington and Lee Hist. Papers*, No. 5, p. 113. McDowell was a brother-in-law of Thomas H. Benton.

[95] *Lynchburg Virginian*, October 25, 1832.

[96] *Ibid.*, November, 1832.

[97] *Ibid.*, November, 1832. Barbour was later appointed associate justice of the Supreme Court.

[98] Sargent and Clay received about 12,000 votes.

number of the counties in the Tidewater and lower Piedmont opposed to Van Buren.

When the Assembly met, one month after the election of 1832, there was every indication that the union between the Barbour and Van Buren factions was permanent. With only six dissenting votes W. C. Rives was elected to the United States Senate.[99] The press commented upon the political union and the blow given Nullification by the election of Rives.[100]

But South Carolina's ordinance of Nullification and the President's Proclamation soon caused the discordant factions of the Democratic party to part company. Led by Rives and McDowell the western party joined the National Republicans to form a Union party, while the seceders and nullifiers in the east united and formed a State-Rights party. True, no hard-and-fast sectional line can be drawn between these parties. The Union party had supporters in the east; the State-Rights party found a following in the Valley and along the Kanawha; Ritchie of the *Enquirer* remained with the former; while Pleasants of the *Whig*, the former National-Republican organ, joined the latter.

Already the position of the east and the west upon the subject of federal relations had been pretty definitely determined. A majority of the leaders in the former section were opposed to Nullification but in-

[99] The dissenting votes were given, two to Barbour, three to Randolph, and one to Floyd (*Journal, House of Del.*, 1832–33, 22).

[100] *Lynchburg Virginian*, December 17, 1832; *Washington and Lee Hist. Papers*, No. 5, p. 110.

sisted on the right of a state to secede. How far this position was determined by the practical difficulties which then confronted the nullifiers is difficult to determine. There were, however, many state-rights men in Virginia who believed in McDuffie's contention that Nullification was based upon the doctrines of 1798.[101] Representatives Gordon, Davenport, Bouldin, and J. S. Barbour "hobnobbed" with the nullifiers in Washington and considered their re-election in 1831 as a triumph for their cause.[102] Governor Floyd was considered friendly to Nullification;[103] the *Richmond Whig* co-operated with southern leaders in behalf of a southern convention;[104] leaders in the lower Piedmont (quite probably Bouldin and Davenport) were thought to be in alliance with the nullifiers;[105] and the *Petersburg Jeffersonian* edited by Crallé was an ardent Nullification sheet.[106]

On the other hand, the westerners had refused to accept either Nullification or Secession as the shibboleth of their party or to raise state sovereignty above that of the nation.[107] Accepting Madison's interpretation of the Resolutions of 1798, they insisted that the states possessed only a part of the sovereign power and that no one of them could nullify a federal law.[108] Nu-

[101] *Register of Cong. Debates*, VIII, Part I, 290.
[102] *Lynchburg Virginian*, August 23, 1832.
[103] *Ibid.*, August 23, 1832.
[104] *Ibid.*, September 10, 27, 1832.
[105] *Register of Cong. Debates*, VIII, Part III, 3170.
[106] *Lynchburg Virginian*, February 11, 25, 1833.
[107] *Washington and Lee Hist. Papers*, No. 5, pp. 106–12.
[108] Madison, *Writings* (ed. Cong.), IV, 61, 289, 409; Wise, *Seven Decades of the Union*, 121–25.

merous essays, letters, and editorials had already appeared in the western prints and the *Richmond Enquirer* to show that the South Carolina doctrines were not those of 1798. The most important contributions of this nature were the series of essays by "Agricola," which appeared in the *Enquirer* in August and September, 1832. Inhabitants of the west believed that South Carolina's course had been determined by the reverses of designing and ambitious politicians; they accordingly refused "to parcel out the Empire."[109] South Carolina out of the Union was pictured as "the most wretched place on the globe." "She would be," said the editor of the *Lynchburg Virginian,* "an ally contemptible to a foreign nation and would be forced to sell her independence as the price of protection." Even before the election of 1832 numerous mass-meetings had been held in the western counties to condemn the Nullification programme. Citizens of Amherst County denounced it as a fallacious delusion opposed to the Resolutions of 1798.[110] At a meeting in Nelson it was resolved: "That we consider any immediate opposition to the tariff law by the forceful interposition of a state as unsafe, impolitic, unwise, and highly dangerous to the best interests of the nation."[111]

The ordinance of Nullification, the Proclamation, and the subsequent discussions in Congress and the Assembly aroused the west to take a firmer stand for the Union. The resolutions passed by the various mass-meetings there and the letters written on federal

[109] *Richmond Enquirer,* August 23, 1832.
[110] *Ibid.,* October, 1832.   [111] *Ibid.,* September 10, 1832.

relations would fill a good-sized volume. They represent the final sentiment in the contest of the west for nationalism. They are very similar in content, and it will be necessary to note only a few of them here.

Citizens of Augusta were of opinion that no state had a right to resist federal laws; that their only recourse lay in constitutional amendment or in the Supreme Court; that the action of South Carolina was "a plain and palpable violation of her constitutional obligation to the other states;" they looked with pity rather than anger upon her rashness and asked executive clemency; they insisted that—

if South Carolina has a moral right to overthrow the government, when it becomes intolerably oppressive, Virginia and the other states of the Union have, in addition to the right of union and security conferred upon them by the federal compact, the moral right of self-protection; and in the spirit of justice, and of enlightened liberty, of preserving by force, if necessary, that government upon which they believe the strength, the freedom, and the happiness of these United States depends.[112]

Citizens of Nelson resolved that the sovereign power, both state and national, resided in the people; that power did not belong to the majority of a single state, a small part of the total population, "to alter or abolish the government established for the collective and united benefit, safety and happiness, by nullifying the laws of the United States or destroying by secession the compact entered into for the mutual benefit of all;" that the action of South Carolina was anarchic;

[112] *Lynchburg Virginian,* January 7, 1833.

SLAVERY AND NULLIFICATION

and that force should be used, if necessary, to compel obedience to federal laws.[113]

A mass-meeting in Smyth County expressed devotion to the Union, denounced Nullification as political heresy, opposed the Proclamation, and asked that the tariff be reduced.[114] Of the vacillating attitude of the state-rights men in the Assembly it said:

> Its [their] doctrines are temporizing and puerile, calculated to draw this commonwealth into the vortex of Nullification. .... For we hold that Virginia Secession and South Carolina Nullification do most necessarily lead to the same results; and it is with unutterable regret and the deepest indignation that we see the legislature of Virginia spending days and weeks in impossible debates to determine whether she will give up our whole Union into the hands of demagogues and frenzied political aspirants.[115]

Moore, the doughty old Federalist of Rockbridge, believed that—

> when the star spangled banner is unfurled upon the top of one of our lofty mountains, and the inhabitants are told that the Union is in danger, every valley, glen and dale will pour forth its population prepared to conquer or die beneath the flag that has so often led their fathers to victory.[116]

Moore's neighbor, William Taylor, wrote James McDowell:

[113] *Ibid.*, January 31, 1832. For similar resolutions, see *ibid.*, December 25, 1832; January 10, 21, 31, 1833; February 11, 25, 1833; *National Intelligencer*, January 7, 8, 10, 1833; *Niles Register*, XLIII, 318.

[114] Many, if not most, of the resolutions passed at these mass-meetings favored a reduction in the tariff.

[115] *Lynchburg Virginian*, February 11, 1833.

[116] *Ibid.*, December 25, 1832. Moore later joined the Confederate army.

The President's Proclamation meets general approval. The Clay men are loud in its praise. The *Union* [the local paper] thinks it ought to be placed along side of the Declaration of Independence.[117]

Later he wrote of the mass-meeting held in Rockbridge:

There was great unanimity and a fixed determination to sustain the President. All were against Nullification although there would have been a difference of opinion on the subject of state rights, if any attempt had been made to give an analysis of the principles of our government. This exciting subject was, however, prudently avoided.

I was sorry to see the strong sentiment expressed against Carolina by some of the people. I believe volunteers could have been obtained at once to go out against her.[118]

About the same time Archibald Graham wrote:

The old General's Proclamation seems not to have been relished much by the Virginia politicians. In this region [the Valley] it has been received with loud and almost universal applause. The old federal and Clay parties hail it as the harbinger of better times that are to settle forever the principles they have been contending for. The Jackson party receive it favorably because it is *Jackson's*. A few, and a very few, cannot swallow its high-toned federal doctrines. . . . . There is a strong feeling in this county against Nullification and a very general disposition to put it down *vi et armis*. I believe a strong volunteer company could be raised at a moment's warning to march against them.[119]

At first few mass-meetings were held in the lower Piedmont and the Tidewater counties, but the dis-

[117] *Washington and Lee Hist. Papers*, No. 5, pp. 110-15.
[118] *Ibid.*, No. 5, p. 110.
[119] *Ibid.*, No. 5, pp. 110-15.

SLAVERY AND NULLIFICATION

cussion of the Force Bill made feigned indifference on their part no longer possible. John Randolph threw away his bed and crutches and appeared on the political stage for the last time as the advocate of state rights. Under his direction citizens of Charlotte and other counties resolved that Virgina was a free, sovereign, and independent state; that, although necessity had made it convenient to delegate certain powers to a confederacy, she had parted with no portion of her sovereignty, and that she had never parted with her right to withdraw her delegated powers to secede from the confederacy. These resolutions condemned Nullification as weak and mischievous and denounced the nationalistic tendencies of Jackson's Proclamation and the Force Bill.[120]

A few days after the meeting of the Assembly of 1832–33 Governor Floyd communicated to it official information of the Nullification ordinance and the President's Proclamations.[121] Immediately a select committee of twenty-one was appointed to take under consideration the federal relations; to determine the course which Virginia should pursue and the propriety of a general convention of the states; and to make a declaration of opinion on "the present fearful crisis." After much debate in the committee of the whole, the select committee, controlled by the State-Rights party, reported a long list of resolutions. They expressed a desire for union by means which would keep the federal and state governments within constitutional limits;

[120] *Lynchburg Virginian*, February 11, 14, 25, 1833.
[121] *Journal, House of Del.*, 1832–33, 30.

deemed it unwise to make an exposition of Virginia's well-known political creed; denounced the tariff as contrary to the spirit and intent of the Constitution; praised South Carolina's resistance but deplored her methods; denounced the Proclamation as a departure from the spirit of the Constitution and the Resolutions of 1798; deplored the use of arms by either the federal government or South Carolina; recommended a general convention in case Congress did not take action to reduce the tariff; and suggested that commissioners be appointed to convey the resolutions of the Assembly to South Carolina.[122]

Marshall, of Fauquier County, moved to substitute for the report of the committee a resolution asking the proper authorities in South Carolina to rescind the ordinance of Nullification, or at least to suspend it until after Congress should adjourn.[123] Whereupon Boone, of Hanover, moved to amend the proposed substitute by adding thereto a series of resolutions which declared it the duty of Virginia to prevent disunion, denounced Nullification as untimely and opposed to the Resolutions of 1798, admitted the right of the President to enforce the laws but condemned his Proclamation, and requested that he revise it and countermand his military orders.[124]

Although somewhat milder than the report of the select committee, Boone's resolutions did not conciliate the Union party, as it was hoped they would. The

[122] *Journal, House of Del.*, 1832–33, 79. B. W. Leigh was later sent to South Carolina to offer friendly mediation.

[123] *Ibid.*, 79. [124] *Ibid.*, 79.

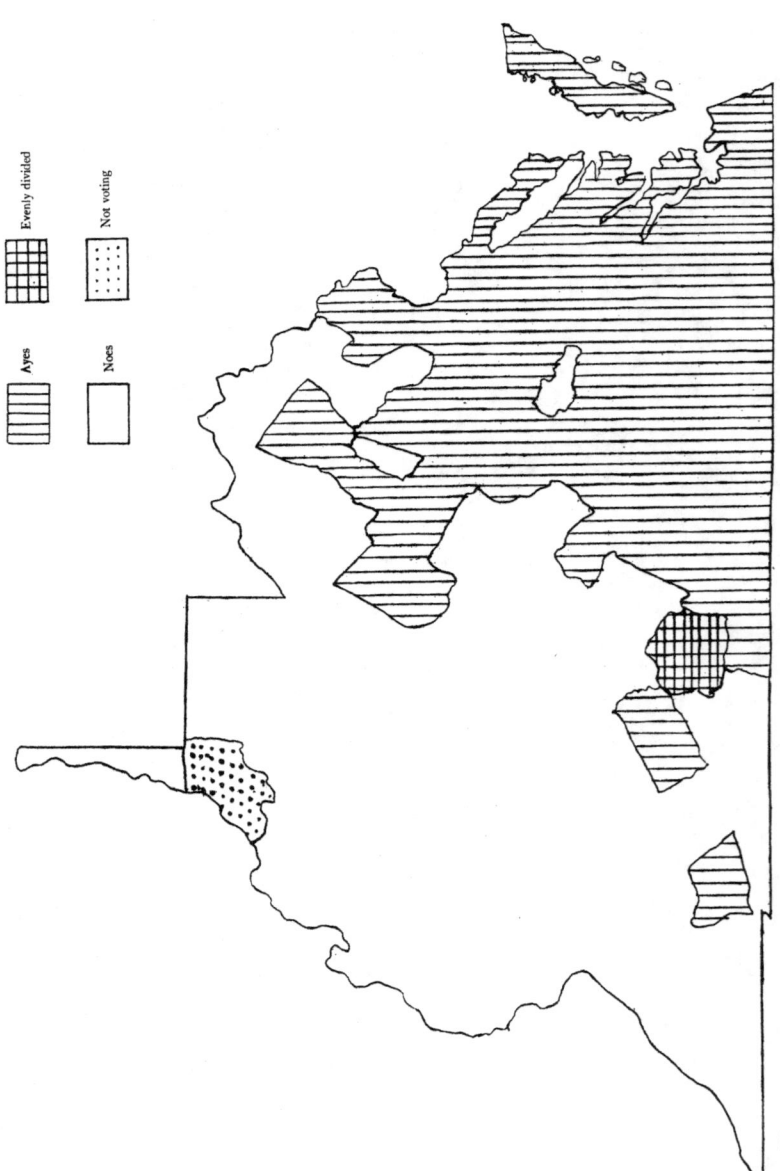

Map showing the sectional character of a vote in the House of Delegates of Virginia on a resolution mildly approving the course of South Carolina on Nullification: Ayes 43; Noes 59.

SLAVERY AND NULLIFICATION

vote on amending Marshall's substitute by adding Boone's resolutions to it was: ayes 73, nays 50.[125] The accompanying map of this vote shows practically all the delegates from counties west of the Blue Ridge opposed to it.

When it became evident that the State-Rights party was in control of the Assembly, the Union men made a desperate effort to strike from the report of the select committee that resolution which censured Jackson. A motion to this effect was decided in the negative: ayes 61, nays 70.[126] A map of this vote would show practically the same counties opposed to censuring Jackson as had opposed Boone's resolutions.

The resolutions finally adopted by the Assembly were in sentiment the same as those originally proposed by the select committee. The great change which had taken place in Virginia politics during the session of the Assembly of 1832–33 was shown in the result of the election of a United States senator to succeed John Tyler. In the first days of the session, Rives, an ardent administration man, was elected without opposition; in the last days Tyler, who sympathized with Nullification and cast the only vote in the United States Senate against the Force Bill,[127] was reelected. The vote for senator in the House was: Tyler 63, McDowell 53.[128] An analysis of this vote shows

[125] *Ibid.*, 82.   [126] *Ibid.*, 88.

[127] The vote of Virginia in the House on the Force Bill was: ayes 7, nays 13. But one delegate from west of the Blue Ridge voted nay.

[128] *Journal, House of Del.*, 1832–33. In the House Leigh also received 7 votes, Tucker 2, Randolph 1, and Daniel 1.

the same delegates voting for McDowell as opposed the State-Rights party on the resolutions on federal relations.[129]

The State-Rights and Union parties contested the congressional and state elections of 1833.[130] The former secured a majority in the Assembly and elected nine out of twenty-one representatives in Congress. East of the Blue Ridge and south of the Rappahannock River the nullifiers and seceders, names applied to the State-Rights party, elected every representative except Andrew Stevenson from the Richmond district and George Royall from the Norfolk district. In the east the Union party was successful only in those sections where the National Republican party had been strong and where the influence of Ritchie extended.[131] On the other hand, the districts west of the Blue Ridge, without exception, sent members of the Union party to represent them in Congress.

[129] Commenting upon the election of Tyler the *Lynchburg Virginian* of February 21, 1833, said: "So that John Tyler whose sentiments border so closely on Nullification as that heresy does on Secession was re-elected by a majority of two votes. This is a rather singular result, when we recollect that the same body, not many weeks ago, by an almost unanimous vote, elected W. C. Rives to the same office."

[130] *Lynchburg Virginian*, April 11, 1833; *ibid.*, May 16, 1833.

[131] *Ibid.*, May 2, 1833; *National Intelligencer*, May 7, 1833; *Niles Register*, XLIV, 162.

CHAPTER VII
PARTIES IN THE WHIG PERIOD, 1834-50

The compromise tariff and the attempt to distribute the proceeds of the sales of the public lands increased Clay's popularity in the west, but they brought confusion in the ranks of the Union party. The tariff satisfied the desire for protection, and the nationalists hoped to use the income from the land sales to promote works of internal improvement. Many citizens of the west refused to believe the rumor that Clay had formed a corrupt coalition with Calhoun and insisted that his surrender of the American System was a "magnanimous offering on the altar of peace."[1] Jackson, "the impersonation of the Union," was in a measure superseded by Clay, "its real preserver."[2]

Preparatory to the election of 1834 the administration party, again called Democrat, made a desperate effort to prevent union between the followers of Clay in the west and members of the State-Rights party in the east. To this end Rives made a campaign in the west. Though it was generally recognized that nullification and secession were no longer issues, he praised the heroic Union party of South Carolina; expounded the Resolutions of 1798 to show wherein they were unlike the Nullification doctrines; justified his course

[1] *Lynchburg Virginian,* March 4 and 14, 1833; *ibid.,* February 28, 1833.

[2] *Ibid.,* March 4, 1833.

in support of the Force Bill; and drank toasts to the President, "who has given effect to the sentiment 'the Union, it must be preserved.' "³

About the same time Mercer made a trip to the west in behalf of the Clay party, and Clay himself found it convenient to tarry among the mountaineers on his way to and from Washington. The people, however, would not be wrought up by appeals to nationalism or other general principles. They were turning again entirely to the practical questions of their locality. The following toast to Mercer shows the sentiment which was uppermost in their minds: "Western Virginia! The feeling is awake; the canal boat shall bear away the product of our industry, where a little while ago, the mountain deer trod with trim step."⁴

Meanwhile Jackson's arbitrary conduct in the removal of the deposits had widened the breach within the Union party and increased the zeal of the opposition. Although opposed to the recharter of the United States Bank, the east did not sanction executive usurpation;⁵ and many state-rights politicians had come to regard "a United States Bank" as a necessary evil.⁶ In many counties of the east mass-meetings denounced the removals as dangerous to the business interests of the country and as an executive usurpation.⁷ In his

[3] *Niles Register*, XLIV, 61, 78.
[4] *Ibid.*, XLV, 131.
[5] Wise, *Seven Decades of the Union*, 136.
[6] *Niles Register*, XLVIII, 249.
[7] *National Intelligencer*, January 2 and 30, 1834; "Calhoun Correspondence," *Am. Hist. Asso. Rept.* (1899), II, 335.

annual message to the Assembly, Governor Tazewell condemned them as a scheme intended to promote the banking interests of New York and to make the South dependent thereon.[8] In the Assembly the nationalists and state-rights delegates united to pass resolutions declaring the removals "a dangerous and alarming assumption of power" and asserting the right of Congress to a voice in policies of general finance;[9] and they requested their representatives in Congress and instructed their senators to bring about the restoration of the deposits and to adopt measures to remedy the evils occasioned by their removal.[10]

Rives refused to obey these instructions and resigned his place in the Senate. Again the nationalists and state-rights delegates united to elect his successor, B. W. Leigh.[11]

Despite the efforts of the Democrats, the coalition had been made between the opposition factions and the name Whig adopted by the whole. The election of 1834 returned a large Whig majority in the Assembly, and the coalition held a formal jubilation over this, its first victory in the state. Letters of congratulation from Clay, Calhoun, Preston, Ewing, and Poindexter were features of the occasion. Of this election Calhoun said: "The result has given joy and confidence to

[8] *Journal, House of Del.*, 1833-34, 9.

[9] *Niles Register*, XLV, 388, 410.

[10] *Journal, House of Del.*, 1833-34, 100, 167.

[11] The vote in the House was: Leigh 69; P. P. Barbour 56 (*Journal*, 1833-34, 214). One-half of the vote given Leigh came from west of the Blue Ridge. See *Washington and Lee Hist. Papers*, No. 5, p. 109.

those who supported the side of constitutional liberty."[12]

The accompanying map shows the party affiliations of the delegates elected to the House of Delegates of 1834–35. The union between the state-rights voters and the nationalists enabled the opposition to carry an unbroken line of counties from the Atlantic to the Ohio along the James and Kanawha rivers. Apparently the nationalistic wing of the Whig party was the stronger; almost one-half of the Whig delegates came from west of the Blue Ridge, and a large portion of the other half came from counties strongly nationalistic. For the most part the mountain districts of the west elected Democrats, as did those counties of the east which were under the influence of able leaders of the administration party. The Democratic counties in north-central Piedmont were in the bailiwick of P. P. Barbour, W. C. Rives, Thomas Ritchie, and Andrew Stevenson.[13]

It was with difficulty, however, that the large Whig majority secured the re-election of Leigh to the United States Senate.[14] The conflict between the incongruous elements in the party, which continued through its whole lifetime, first manifested itself on this occasion. Leigh's ardent devotion to state rights and his record in the constitutional convention of 1829–30 rendered him unpopular in the west, where some Whig counties

[12] *National Intelligencer*, July 10, 1834.

[13] This map is made from data taken from the *National Intelligencer*, May 31, 1834.

[14] The vote on joint ballot was: Leigh 85; Rives 81 (*Journal, House of Del.*, 1834–35, 110).

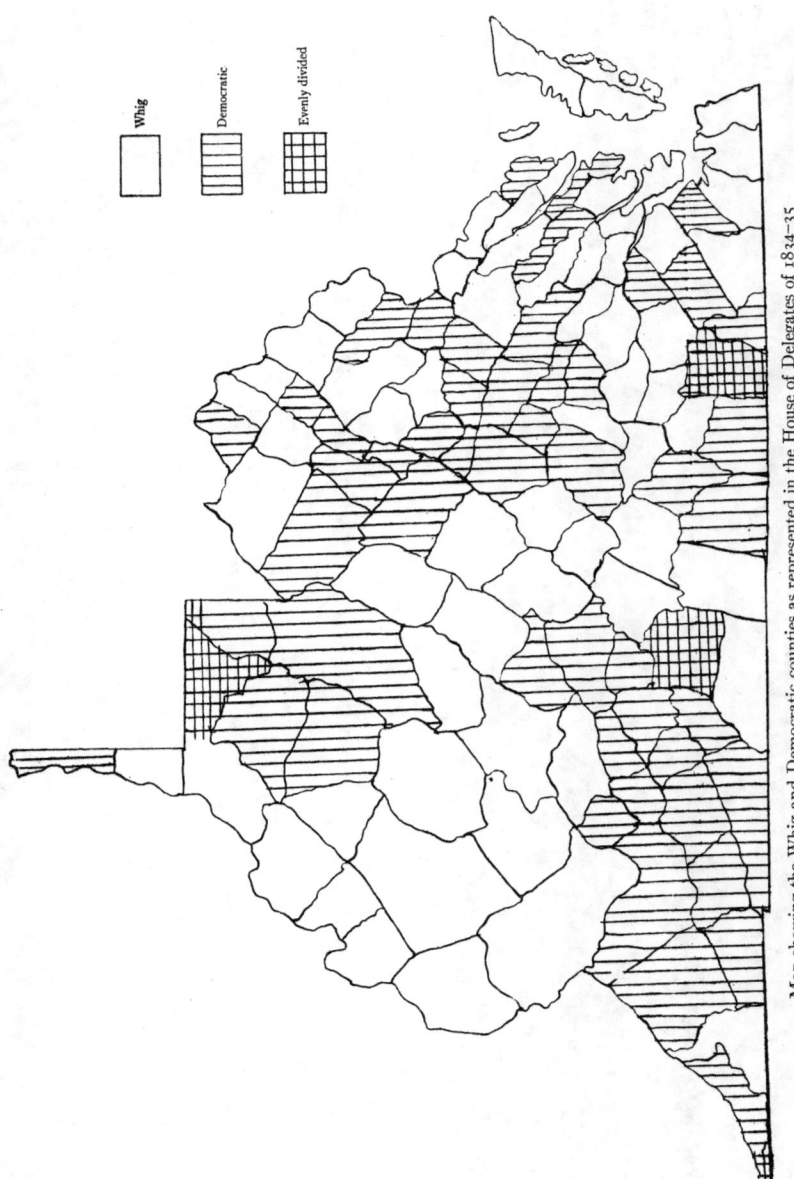

Map showing the Whig and Democratic counties as represented in the House of Delegates of 1834–35

instructed their delegates in the Assembly to vote against his re-election.[15] To defeat him an effort was made to refer the choice of a senator to a vote of the people. Of the efforts to re-elect Leigh, James McDowell, of Rockbridge County, said: "The election was a bitter one and gave rise to a far deeper resentment than I have ever seen in the Legislature."[16]

The differences within the Whig party made its rule short. It had not yet wrought its conflicting elements into a working party. In vain the *Richmond Whig* praised "the ever memorable and blessed family compact which gave quiet to South Carolina, preserved the peace and integrity of the states, and tempered the harsh operation of the tariff; in vain it insisted that the Whigs are agreed in an ardent attachment to the institutions of our country and in a deep devotion to the Union."[17] The zealous efforts of Rives, Ritchie, and McDowell, the dissatisfaction of the west with the election of Leigh to the United States Senate, and the abolition agitation brought defeat to the Whig party in the elections of 1835. The Democrats elected a large majority to the Assembly and seventeen of the twenty-one representatives in Congress. This election

[15] *Niles Register*, XLVIII, 130. In answer to the objections raised to his re-election Leigh said: "The charge of aristocracy has been raised against me, founded I am quite sure on no other ground than the course I took in the convention of 1829–30." See *National Intelligencer*, September 9, 1835.

[16] *Washington and Lee Hist. Papers*, No. 5, p. 119; *National Intelligencer*, February 21, 1835.

[17] *National Intelligencer*, March 24, 1835. This quotation is from an "Address of the *Richmond Whig* to the People of Virginia."

marked the first appearance of the "Tenth Legion" of the Valley, the German "invincibles," as a factor in Virginia politics.[18]

The Democrats retained power three years, and completely reversed the Whig policy. Ejected officials were restored to their places; resolutions censuring the President for the removal of the deposits were rescinded; and Tyler and Leigh were instructed to vote for the expunging resolutions.[19] Tyler refused to obey, resigned, and was succeeded by W. C. Rives. Leigh, however, refused to resign until the fight over the expunging resolutions was ended and then did so only because of business reasons.[20] His course met disapproval among state-rights Whigs, who believed in the right of instruction, aroused the west, and doubtless did much to increase the strength of the administration party throughout the state.[21] Leigh was succeeded by Judge R. E. Parker, a Democrat.

The year 1835 witnessed the beginning of the movement for the abolition of slavery and the slave trade in the District of Columbia. From the first both parties in the east, and especially the Whigs, opposed the abolition agitation. During the summer of 1835 most of the counties east of the Blue Ridge held one or more mass-meetings to denounce the abolition-

[18] The Whigs elected no representatives to Congress from west of the Blue Ridge (*National Intelligencer*, May 15, 1835; *Niles Register*, XLVIII, 186).

[19] *Journal, House of Del.*, 1835–36, 26, 37, 55, 100.

[20] *Ibid.*, 1836–37, 18.

[21] Wise, *Seven Decades of the Union*, 138; Tyler, *Letters and Times of the Tylers*, I, 536–38.

ists, to memorialize the Assembly regarding them, and to protest against the abolition of negro slavery in the District of Columbia.[22] These memorials insisted that negro slavery was not the cause of Virginia's industrial decline, but that unscientific cultivation and excessive migrations had produced her "turned-out" land and "gullied" hillsides. The agricultural societies advised the state to foster its "peculiar institutions" and asked that a chair of agriculture be established in the State University.[23] It was at this period and on this issue that a number of young men, most prominent of whom were: Henry A. Wise, R. M. T. Hunter, and John Y. Mason, came into prominence in the east as the defenders of negro slavery and as disciples of John C. Calhoun. "Slavery interwoven with our political institutions," said Wise, "is guaranteed by our Constitution, and its consequence must be borne by our northern brethren as resulting from our system of government, and they cannot attack the institution of slavery without attacking the institutions of our country, our safety, our welfare."[24]

On the other hand, members of both parties in the west were at first inclined to criticize the attitude of the extreme state-rights men toward the abolitionists. Opposition to the pro-slavery agitation caused many western Whigs to join the administration party, con-

[22] No such memorials were sent to the Assembly from counties west of the Blue Ridge (*Journal, House of Del.*, 1835-36, Doc. No. 12, pp. 1-25).

[23] *Ibid.*, Doc. No. 30.

[24] *Register of Cong. Debates*, XI, 1399. See also "Calhoun Correspondence," in *Am. Hist. Asso. Rept.* (1899), II, 356.

tributing to its victory of 1835. Many voters in the west believed that Calhoun was bent upon "picking a quarrel with the North about negroes." The *Lynchburg Virginian*, the chief organ of the Whig party in that section, insisted that the nullifiers and seceders had accepted the Compromise Tariff, "not for the purpose of establishing peace and tranquillity but with the design of changing their weapon of attack," and "that the subject which they are now wielding, in aid of their settled purpose to dissolve the Union and erect a southern confederacy, is slavery."[25] The western press opposed any and all attempts to call a southern convention to devise means of co-operative action against the abolitionists.[26]

But when the abolition agitation began to endanger the perpetuity of the Union, the sentiment in western Virginia toward the abolitionists changed. With the inhabitants of this section, as with those of Massachusetts, who destroyed the abolitionist printing-presses and dragged Garrison through the streets of Boston, and those of Illinois, who murdered Lovejoy, the Union was sacred and not to be endangered by fanatics. Under these conditions the Democratic party, which Jackson had made to stand for the Union, and the southern leaders who had committed themselves against abolition, increased in popularity in the west. Leaders like James McDowell, C. J. Faulkner, Jr., W. B. Preston, and G. W. Summers now tried to right themselves with the east on the subject of slavery and

[25] *Lynchburg Virginian*, April 29, 1833.

[26] *National Intelligencer*, quoting the *Lexington* (Va.) *Gazette*.

to dispel the alarm occasioned by their utterances in the constitutional convention of 1829-30 and the slavery debate of 1831-32. It now became possible for such leaders to defend the Union in the same breath that they denounced the abolitionists. This largely explains the Democratic strength in western Virginia. The following from an address, delivered at Princeton College, New Jersey, in 1838, by James McDowell, shows the position which these leaders were taking upon the question of slavery: "Leave slavery to the wisdom of those upon whom the providence of God and the constitution have cast it. Furious and mad philanthropy will bring destruction; a stop should come before it is impossible."[27] In this frame of mind the west voted with the east to suppress incendiary publications, for the "gag resolutions," and against the abolition of slavery and the slave trade in the District of Columbia.

The abolition agitation and local differences prevented the union of the Whig party in the presidential election of 1836. The eastern wing favored Hugh L. White, of Tennessee, who was not a Whig, for president, and John Tyler for vice-president. Thus no concession was to be made to the west which desired either Harrison or Clay, preferably the latter, for president, and was not enthusiastic over Tyler for the second place. Finally an unsatisfactory compromise was agreed upon whereby an electoral ticket, pledged

[27] *Washington and Lee Hist. Papers*, No. 5, p. 126. McDowell was an alumnus of Princeton. His speech on this occasion was entitled "West Augusta."

to support either White or Harrison and favorable to Tyler, was placed in the field.[28]

The Democrats, however, were scarcely more united. Ritchie and other leaders of the eastern wing were not enthusiastic over Van Buren and bitterly opposed Johnson for the second place, but a more satisfactory solution than that reached by the Whigs was agreed upon. After a vain effort to commit Van Buren on the subject of abolition, the east indorsed him for president and the west agreed to support William Smith of Alabama for vice-president. This was a mutual concession, whereas the opposing wings in the Whig party had not reached accord.

After a dull campaign Van Buren carried the state by seven thousand majority.[29] His vote was unusually large in counties west of the Blue Ridge, especially those of the Tenth Legion where the German element rallied to his support. Only seven counties west of the mountains gave majorities against him. The Whig defeat was attributed to a falling-off in their vote in the west and the Northern Neck.[30]

The financial panic of 1837 and the legislation intended to restore a healthful currency brought a breach in both the Whig and Democratic parties in Virginia. Rives and his "conservative" following refused to support Van Buren's scheme for an independent treasury and continued to favor a regulated system of

[28] *Niles Register*, XLIX, 290; Wise, *Life of Wise*, 66; *National Intelligencer*, October 5, 1836.

[29] *Niles Register*, LIX, 229.

[30] *National Intelligencer*, November 19, 1836.

deposits in the state banks. Rives believed that the general government ought to aid the states in maintaining a sound currency and an efficient banking system; that currency good enough for the people was good enough for the government; that the public purse should not be intrusted to the custody of the chief executive; that the separation of the federal government from banks and banking would impair the coöperation between it and the states; and that an independent treasury would eventually lead to a recharter of a national bank.[81] For some time the conservatives maintained a *quasi*-independent attitude, and there was much talk of a third party. The *Madisonian* founded at Washington in August, 1837, was thought to be the intended organ of the proposed new party.[82] But the northern conservatives, under the leadership of Tallmadge of New York, soon joined the Whigs, and Rives and his following in Virginia did likewise. On the other hand, R. M. T. Hunter, W. F. Gordon, L. W. Tazewell, and others of the strict construction wing of the Whig party followed their idol, Calhoun, into the administration party, which was daily growing into greater harmony with the South on the subject of abolition.[83]

These changes in issues and party alignments made union and success possible for the Whigs. They swept

[81] See his letter, signed "Camillus," in *National Intelligencer*, August 16, 1837.

[82] *Ibid.*, August 23, 1837.

[83] *Niles Register*, LVI, 411; "Calhoun Correspondence," *Am. Hist. Asso. Rept.* (1899), II, 436.

the state in the election of 1838,[34] and retained control of the Assembly for four years. Wise dates the formation of the Whig party in Virginia from the year 1838.[35]

The Whig rule worked a continuation of the sectional differences. Rives's term as United States senator expired March 4, 1839, but the west desired his re-election, while the east, led by B. W. Leigh, F. W. Gilmer, and W. S. Archer, desired the more orthodox Whig, John Tyler, to succeed him. The contest between Rives and Tyler was waged for two years, and for that period Virginia had only one senator in Congress. Mr. Wise to the contrary notwithstanding,[36] it ended only after Tyler's nomination to the vice-presidency. On several occasions Rives was near a re-election, but just enough of the leaders remained aloof from him to prevent it. Although he refused to attend a reconciliation dinner Leigh commended Rives's independence in repudiating Van Buren, but he insisted that it was only a partial atonement for his errors in supporting the expunging resolutions and the removal of the deposits. He also believed that Rives should commit himself to the support of the Whig candidate for president, in 1840, before he could expect that party to return him to the Senate.[37]

Both parties went into the election of 1840 with

[34] *National Intelligencer*, May 3, 1838.
[35] *Seven Decades of the Union*, 157.
[36] *Ibid.*, 174.
[37] *Niles Register*, LVI, 66.

greater unity than in 1836, though not with entire harmony between the sections. The eastern Democrats reluctantly supported the renomination of Van Buren but refused to support R. M. Johnson for the vice-presidency. They put forward James K. Polk, of Tennessee, for that office and ceased to support him only when he declined to be a candidate.[38] On the other hand, the eastern Whigs were willing to vote for Clay, the choice of the west, for the presidential nomination, provided the west would support Tyler for the vice-presidency.

The poll called forth an unprecedented vote in which Van Buren had a bare majority.[39] He owed his success to the heavy vote in the counties west of the Blue Ridge, which gave him more than three thousand majority.[40] A map of this vote by counties would be strikingly similar to the map of the Democratic and Whig counties as represented in the Assembly of 1834–35. It would also show the areas of Whig strength when the party was most powerful in Virginia.

Tyler's opposition to the Whig programme of 1841 caused his following in Virginia to desert the party. For some time they tried to maintain a third party, the *Madisonian* becoming the party organ, but their inability to rally a following to Tyler and his

[38] *Richmond Whig*, August 7, 1840.

[39] The total vote was 84,223. Van Buren's majority was 1,413 (*Niles Register*, LIX, 229).

[40] *Ibid.*, LIX, 294.

ultimate repudiation by the Whigs drove Wise, Gilmer, and their colleagues into the Democratic party.

The rank and file of the Virginia Whigs, however, stood fast. The nationalists of the west were exasperated by Tyler's vetoes. They had expected and petitioned for an increased duty on iron, salt, and woolens.[41] The tariff of 1842 received seven affirmative votes from Virginia, only three of which came from east of the Blue Ridge,[42] and the Whig representatives in Congress were not unfriendly to the recharter of a national bank. That the course of the eastern representatives in support of the tariff was determined by factors other than the desire to oppose the Democrats is evident from the popular support they received. Twenty-two hundred citizens of Richmond and vicinity signed a petition to Congress praying for an increase in the tariff.[43] It is evident that the eastern wing of the Whig party became more nationalistic as the eastern wing of the Democratic party became more strongly attached to state rights.

The political readjustments of 1841 and 1842 enabled the Democrats to regain control of the Assembly[44] and to reverse completely the course pursued by the Whig assemblies. They refused to receive any more of the surplus from the sale of the public lands, an act which provoked severe criticism in the Whig

[41] *House Journal*, 27 Cong., 2d sess., 532, 611, 617, 680, 793, 810, 854.

[42] *Ibid.*, 27 Cong., 2d sess., 1107.

[43] *Niles Register*, LXII, 288, 302; DeBow, *Review*, X, 542.

[44] *Niles Register*, XLVI, 112, 176.

counties of the Kanawha Valley;[45] some favored instructing Rives and Archer out of the Senate;[46] and others encouraged the use of hard money.

By 1843 most of the prominent leaders residing east of the Blue Ridge had become Democrats,[47] but the rank and file of that party continued to reside west of the mountains. Notwithstanding these conditions Hunter and his political friends inaugurated a movement to make Calhoun president in 1844 and the Democratic party of Virginia a strictly state-rights and pro-slavery party. Hunter's political biography of Calhoun was scattered broadcast, and there was talk of establishing a Calhoun paper in Richmond. That such a movement met with opposition goes almost without saying. Ritchie remained true to the west, which had enabled him to gain so many political victories, and continued to favor the renomination of Van Buren and the cause of local reform. He was frequently accused of keeping Virginia attached to the tail of a northern alliance with "demagogues" when "she should be the head of a southern state-rights party."[48] On the other hand, the Calhoun party was accused of treason to the regular Democratic party and of a desire to dissolve the Union. The following comment by the *Washington Globe* upon the Calhoun party was indorsed by the *Enquirer* and the

---

[45] *Kanawha Republican*, March 19, 1842.

[46] *Journal, House of Del.*, 1842-43, 90.

[47] Wise, *Life of Wise*, 103-5.

[48] "Calhoun Correspondence," *Am. Hist. Asso. Rept.* (1899), II, 527, 536, 602.

western prints: "Some of the would be leaders may kick out of the traces and give us some trouble, but they will soon be run over rough shod to rise no more in political preferment."[49]

These differences in the Democratic party enabled the Whigs to gain a majority in the House of Delegates elected in 1844, but the holdovers in the Senate prevented them from controlling the Assembly on joint ballot. The prospect of defeat in the presidential election was not a sufficient incentive to produce immediate union in the Democratic party. As the presidential canvass continued, Van Buren's renomination became generally conceded. Accordingly his friends tried to allay the opposition to him in Virginia by securing an agreement from the Calhoun men to support the nominee of the national convention. "Harmony," they agreed, "is necessary to defeat Clay." But the followers of Calhoun openly declared that Van Buren's nomination would necessitate an independent ticket in Virginia. Their tenacity was a determining factor in the nomination of Polk instead of Van Buren.[50]

The slogan "Polk and Texas" reunited the Democratic party and enabled it to carry the presidential contest in the state by almost six thousand majority.[51] Ritchie, who now drank toasts to "Calhoun, the president in 1848," went to Washington to become editor of

[49] Quoted in the *Kanawha Republican*, August 26, 1843.

[50] "Calhoun Correspondence," in *Am. Hist. Asso. Rept.* (1899), II, 896, 915.

[51] *Niles Register*, LXVI, 160, 176; LXVII, 276.

the *Union*[52] and Calhoun himself believed that the day of southern supremacy had returned. He wrote: "The great difficulty has heretofore been with Virginia, under the guidance of Mr. Ritchie. His policy has been to act in concert with the party in Pennsylvania and New York, as the most certain way of succeeding in the elections; and for that purpose to concede something of our principles to secure their co-operation. The effect has been to detach Virginia, in great measure, from the south."[53]

The elections of 1845 wiped out the Whig majority in the House of Delegates and returned only one Whig to Congress.[54] The political union between the east and the west was almost as perfect as it had been in 1835, when the Democrats had carried everything. The Assembly of 1845–46 elected Isaac Pennybacker, the choice of the west, to succeed Rives in the United States Senate.[55]

The opposition of the Calhoun men to war with Mexico brought a breach in the administration party and general readjustments in Virginia politics, which manifested themselves in the hotly contested elections of 1847 for United States senators to succeed Pennybacker[56] and Archer. The Whigs wanted to re-elect

[52] Hudson, *Journalism in U. S.*, 238; "Calhoun Correspondence," in *Am. Hist. Asso. Rept.* (1899), II, 637, 650, 652.

[53] *Ibid.*, 663.

[54] The previous Congress contained six Whig representatives from Virginia.

[55] *Journal, House of Del.*, 1845–46, 20. Pennybacker received 87 votes; all others 43.

[56] Pennybacker had died a short time after his election.

Archer; the administration party favored Governor Wm. Smith, and the Calhoun men favored R. M. T. Hunter. On the first ballot Archer received 57 votes, Smith 50, and Hunter 19. After much balloting the eastern Whigs united with the eastern Democrats and elected Hunter.[57] To succeed Pennybacker the Whigs desired G. W. Summers, the administration party James McDowell, and the Calhoun men J. M. Mason, all residents of the west. The first ballots gave much the same vote as the first ballots in the other contest, but the same elements which had elected Hunter eventually united to elect Mason.[58] The election of Hunter and Mason marks the first triumph of Calhoun in Virginia politics. Henceforth the sentiment for a united South gradually gained ground. McDowell, whose great ambition was to reach the United States Senate, attributed his defeat on this occasion to his enthusiasm over the war with Mexico and to his stand for abolition in the slavery debate of 1831–32.[59]

This readjustment and the general opposition to the war with Mexico again threatened the Democratic rule in the state. The Whigs gained in the east and held their own in the west. The elections of 1847 resulted in a tie on joint ballot in the Assembly and in the election of six Whigs to Congress, four of whom came from east of the Blue Ridge.[60] But the termina-

[57] *Journal, House of Del.*, 1846–47, 84–86.

[58] *Ibid.*, 94–100.

[59] *Washington and Lee Hist. Papers*, No. 5, p. 145; *Niles Register*, LXXII, 144.

[60] *Ibid.*, LXXII, 160, 280, 386.

tion of the war with Mexico and the agitation over the extension of the slave territory, which followed, drove the eastern leaders into closer affiliation with the Democratic party, enabling it to recover and retain control until the Civil War.

The instability of party organization made the presidential election of 1848 uncertain. The eastern Whigs made an effort to retain in control the Calhoun element of the Democratic party, with which they had been co-operating during the war with Mexico. Taylor's record as a slave-holder and a non-partisan made him popular in eastern Virginia. Accordingly the administration Democrats made a special effort to increase their strength in the west.[61] In this effort they were aided materially by the fact that Cass had intermarried with a family of large and influential connections in northwestern Virginia. This was possibly the determining factor in enabling Cass to carry the state. The majority given him was only 1,473,[62] and the larger part of his vote came from the western counties. The tendency to divide the state politically into two sections, the western to be Democratic, the eastern to be Whig, was more marked in this election than in preceding contests.

During the early years of the period for which the political narrative has been given in this chapter, the subject of banks was a source of political and sectional strife. The west desired the incorporation of additional independent state banks; the east desired an

[61] *Richmond Enquirer*, June 16, 1848; *ibid.*, July 21, 1848.
[62] *Niles Register*, LXXV, 108.

increase in the capital stock of the banks already existing and the establishment of branch banks. To support its claims the west argued that independent banks were necessary to aid internal improvements, to supply the necessary banking facilities, and to prevent monopoly.[63] The east argued that banks were not a panacea for all commercial and industrial evils; that the mountains could not be leveled by the use of paper currency, and that the Bank of Virginia at Richmond should be encouraged to take the place of the United States Bank in maintaining a stable currency and a wholesome restraint upon the other banks. It prevailed in the Whig Assembly of 1834–35; its banking capital was increased; and a number of branch banks were established in the eastern cities.[64]

When the Democrats came to power in 1835 they did not at first depart from the policy of their predecessors on the subject of banking. The eastern delegates were again able to unite and defeat the demands of the west for independent state banks. But the panic of 1837, the discussion over specie payment, and the inability of the west to procure such institutions for itself brought hostile feelings on the part of the Demo-

[63] *Journal, House of Del.*, 1833–34, Doc. No. 23.

[64] In 1834 Virginia had four state banks with an aggregate capital of $6,145,000. The Bank of Virginia, located at Richmond and incorporated in 1804, had a capital of $3,245,000; the Farmers' Bank, located at Richmond and incorporated in 1812, had $2,000,000 capital; the Northwestern Bank, located at Wheeling and incorporated in 1817, had $360,000 capital; and the Bank of the Valley, located at Winchester and incorporated in 1817, had $600,000 capital. See *Journal, House of Del.*, 1834–35, 144.

cratic assemblies, which were largely composed of delegates from the west, toward state banks. Accordingly the representatives from west of the Blue Ridge united to strike the eastern monopoly; the banks and branch banks were subjected to rigorous investigations; talk of abandoning them entirely was current; requests for further increases in their capital stock were denied; they were required to pay specie on a fixed date or close their doors; and they were forbidden to declare dividends so long as specie was refused.[65]

The Whig legislatures following 1838 were, however, more friendly to the state banks. New banks were incorporated in the west; issues of smaller denomination than five dollars were authorized; requests for investigations were refused; state bank notes were made a legal tender in the payment of taxes and state debts; the acts of the Democratic assemblies, declaring bank charters forfeited and imposing other penalties, were repealed; and schemes to incorporate a state bank with twenty million dollars capital stock and with power to aid in the construction of works of internal improvement met with favor.[66] With the establishment of the Independent Treasury and the failure to recharter a national bank, the subject of banking ceased to be of importance.

The subject of internal improvements was an im-

[65] *Niles Register*, LIII; *Journal, House of Del.*, 1837–38, Doc. No. 43.

[66] See Acts of Assembly of 1840–41; *Niles Register*, LIV, 3; LVI, 149; Tyler, *Letters and Times of the Tylers*, II, 28.

portant one from a sectional standpoint during this period. The James River and Kanawha Company received the fostering care of the Whig Assembly of 1834–35. Loans were made to it; an effort was made to use all the income from the internal improvement fund in its behalf; and petitions from Democratic strongholds for the incorporation of companies which might jeopardize its interests were denied.[67] This policy aroused opposition in districts remote from the James and Kanawha rivers and thus contributed to the Whig defeat of 1835.

The internal improvement policies pursued by the Democratic legislatures from 1835 to 1838 were determined largely by a desire to conserve party interests. The James River and Kanawha Canal Company received little attention and less material assistance, and greater interest was given to the construction of railroads and turnpikes. During this period sixteen turnpike companies were incorporated to carry on works in the west;[68] $200,000 was appropriated to the Lynchburg and Tennessee Railroad; the Baltimore and Ohio Company was again denied the privilege of constructing its lines through the Whig counties of central Virginia but was promised an appropriation of $1,-368,520 provided they were constructed through the northwest, a Democratic stronghold; and almost two millions were appropriated to aid in the construction of railroads intended to connect the eastern towns and

[67] *Journal, House of Del.*, 1834–35, 103, 181.

[68] Only a few internal improvement companies had been incorporated in the west before this time.

cities.⁶⁹ It is not without significance that practically all the appropriations to internal improvement companies were made to promote works located in sections strongly Democratic.

The hard times following 1837 made it impossible for either party to pursue an aggressive internal improvement policy. But a return to good times and the expiration of the charters to the Baltimore and Ohio Railroad Company and the James River and Kanawha Canal Company brought the subject before the Whig Assembly of 1844–45. Already a largely attended convention, held at Lewisburg, had revised the project of connecting the James and the Kanawha by a continuous canal;⁷⁰ and their scheme again found favor with the Assembly. But the Democratic majority in the Senate made it impossible to procure an appropriation for that purpose. On the other hand, the numerous petitions from the northwest praying that the Baltimore and Ohio Railroad Company be permitted to construct its lines by way of Clarksburg and Parkersburg to the Ohio were rejected. Instead, the western terminus was fixed at Wheeling and the appropriations authorized by Democratic assemblies were declared void because of failures to comply with stipulated conditions.⁷¹

⁶⁹ See *Fourth Biennial Report of the Board of Public Works*, 502; Acts of 1836–37 and 1837–38; *Niles Register*, LII, 115; LIII, 352.

⁷⁰ *Journal, House of Del.*, 1844–45, Doc. No. 7; *Kanawha Republican*, August 13 and 27, 1844.

⁷¹ *Journal, House of Del.*, 1844–45, Docs. Nos. 13 and 22; *ibid.*, 1845–46, Doc. No. 14; Acts of 1844–45, February 19.

The Democratic legislatures following 1845 completely reversed the policies and acts of the Whigs. They appropriated to the James River and Kanawha Company, it is true, but the appropriations were to be used to construct a canal no farther than Buchanan, a town in the Valley. Thence railroads were to be constructed to the Tennessee border and to the Ohio River. The Baltimore and Ohio Railroad Company had refused to accept the restrictions imposed by the Assembly of 1844–45 and continued to fight for the privilege to strike the Ohio at a point farther south than Wheeling. The citizens of the northwest, except those in the Panhandle, generally favored the company in its fight and held numerous mass-meetings to memorialize the Assembly in its behalf.[72] Some of these meetings favored disunion in case the request of the company was not granted.[73] The fact that it was a large Democratic constituency which spoke and that it was the Whig policy to keep the Baltimore and Ohio Railroad as far north as possible made it necessary to conciliate the northwest. Accordingly the Act of 1845 was amended, and the company was permitted to construct its lines to a point near Fairmont, thence by Grave, or Fishing Creek, to the Ohio, provided, however, that it should build a lateral line to Wheeling. Later an independent company, which soon became a part of the Baltimore and Ohio Company,

[72] *Niles Register*, LXVIII, 68, 254; *Journal, House of Del.*, 1845–46, Docs. Nos. 1, 12, and 22; *ibid.*, 1846–47, Docs. Nos. 1 and 13.

[73] Some of these meetings were attended by more than one thousand delegates.

was incorporated to build a road from Grafton to Parkersburg over practically the same route that the Baltimore and Ohio Company had desired for its main line.[74]

The Democratic legislatures from 1847 to 1850 were very liberal in appropriations for works of internal improvements, which were frequently made, however, to secure party unity and strength. Ardent pro-slavery men, such as Wise and Hunter, desired to conciliate the west by granting many of its requests. More than two millions were appropriated to the Virginia and Tennessee Railroad; and other lines, both in the east and the west, received actual or promised aid. More turnpike companies, with power to construct roads in western Virgina, were incorporated during these years than had been incorporated during the period of Democratic rule from 1835 to 1838.[75]

Liberality to the west aroused opposition in the extreme east. Speaking of the appropriations which the west was receiving the *Norfolk Herald* said:

> Laying aside all other considerations and looking only to the future commercial elevation of Norfolk, her annexation to North Carolina is certainly a consummation devoutly to be wished; for while North Carolina has the ability to build up Norfolk and would take a pride in doing it—it is not now in the power of Virginia to make her of much greater commercial importance than she now is.[76]

[74] Acts of Assembly of 1850–51, 69.

[75] See *Forty-first Report of the Board of Public Works*, 302; *Niles Register*, LXXIV, 206.

[76] *Richmond Whig*, April 17, 1849.

The most important sectional issue in Virginia during this period, however, was that which arose out of the movement for a united slave-holding South. Although the Virginia congressmen united to oppose the Wilmot Proviso, the abolition of the slave trade, and abolition of slavery in the District of Columbia,[77] leading citizens of western Virginia were at the same time trying to devise means to rid that portion of the state of negro slavery. Dr. Henry Ruffner, Samuel McDowell Moore, John Letcher, and others came forward with a scheme which proposed gradual emancipation, by which all the slaves in the state were eventually to be confined to counties east of the Blue Ridge. This scheme was first debated in the Franklin Society at Lexington in 1847. It then took form in a pamphlet entitled, *An Address to the People of West Virginia by a Slave-Holder of West Virginia.*[78] The purpose of the pamphlet was to show that slavery is injurious to the public welfare and "that it may be gradually abolished without detriment to the rights and interests of slave-holders." Like the contemporary writings of Cassius M. Clay and Thomas F. Marshall, both of Kentucky, it contained elaborate comparisons wherein the slave-holding were pitted against the non-slaveholding states to prove that slavery was an economic evil.

[77] *Journal, House of Del.,* 1848–49, 171, 174; *ibid.,* 1849–50, 147, 220, 221; *Niles Register,* LXXV, 73.

[78] Dr. Ruffner, president of Washington and Lee, was the author of this pamphlet. It is commonly spoken of as the "Ruffner pamphlet."

Of the movement Dr. Ruffner at a later time said:

> No one, so far as I remember, took the abolitionist ground that slaveholding is a sin and ought for that reason to be abolished. With us it was merely a question of expediency and was argued with special reference to the interest of West Virginia.

Of his pamphlet's reception he said:

> When the scheme was circulated by mail and otherwise through West Virginia, we soon perceived that most of the editors and publishers in the Valley would not embark with us on an enterprise of doubtful success. They objected to our movement as ill-timed while northern abolitionism was raging. .... West of the Alleghenies the pamphlet was better received; but in East Virginia some papers denounced it as abolitionist.[79]

The movement for an extension of slave territory took quite a different form in eastern Virginia. While various plans for limiting and restricting slave territory were being discussed in Congress and elsewhere many citizens of that section engaged in talk of secession and the formation of a southern confederacy. In 1850 the Assembly, under the control of the east, passed resolutions which recommended that the state send delegates to the proposed Nashville Convention and that the people assemble in district conventions to elect delegates, intrusted with sovereign power, to a general convention of the southern states.[80] Of the conditions there the *Richmond Enquirer* said:

> The two great political parties have ceased to exist in the southern states so far as the present slavery issue is concerned.

[79] *Kanawha Valley Star*, August 3, 1858.
[80] *National Intelligencer* (weekly), February 16, 1850.

United they will prepare, consult, combine for prompt and decisive action. With united voices, we are compelled to make a few exceptions, but they will, we hope, soon cease to be so counted[81]—with united voices they proclaim in the language of the Virginia resolutions, passed a few days since, "the preservation of the Union if we can, the preservation of our own rights if we cannot." This is the temper of the South; this is the temper becoming the inheritors of rights acquired for freemen by the blood of freemen. "Thus far shalt thou come and no farther," or else the proud waves of northern aggression shall float *the wreck of the Constitution.*

The only Union we love is a confederacy of equals; for as equals we entered the Union; we will remain in it on no other condition. This is the deliberate conclusion of the Southern people. There is no hesitancy, no reservation, no escape.[82]

When the Nashville Convention met, Judge Beverly Tucker, professor of constitutional and common law at William and Mary, addressed it in behalf of disunion and the formation of a southern confederacy.[83] For the first time the masses of the east united with their leaders to defend negro slavery as an economic good and to assert their constitutional right to carry slave property into any and all territory. Numerous southern rights associations were organized, and many counties held mass-meetings to encourage the call of a southern convention and the formation of a southern confederacy.[84]

[81] Many Whigs in the east did not support this extreme view. See *Richmond Whig,* February 14, 1850.

[82] Quoted in the *National Intelligencer* (weekly), February 16, 1850.

[83] *Petersburg Intelligencer,* July 27, 1850. See also *National Intelligencer,* August 3, 1850.

[84] *Richmond Whig,* May 17, 1850; *ibid.,* January 15 and 29, 1850; *ibid.,* February 1, 1850.

As the danger of secession became imminent western Virginia took practically the same stand it had taken when Nullification was at its zenith. Had secession come in 1850, there can be little doubt that this part of Virginia was then ready to take the same step it took in 1861. The union sentiment there in 1850 can be determined from a few quotations from the leading newspapers. The *Harrisonburg Republican* believed that "the best possible means . . . . for security to the peculiar institutions of the South are to be found in the Constitution of the United States."[85] "The proposed southern convention we look upon," said the editor of the *Leesburg Washingtonian,* "as a dangerous movement fraught with more serious danger to the prosperity of our glorious Union than almost anything now agitating our country."

"It would be mainly composed of 'Hotspurs' of the South, from whose hasty and rash action nothing but evil can result."[86]

The editor of the *Kanawha* (Kanawha County) *Republican* asked: "What good has resulted to the State or the Union from all the resolutions upon federal relations passed by our legislature from '98 to the present time?" and added, "Had the time and attention devoted to the affairs of the General Government . . . . been devoted to devise means of developing the resources of the state and educating the people, we would not say that she would not now occupy the first rank among the states of the

[85] *Harrisonburg Republican,* February 16, 1850.
[86] Quoted in the *National Intelligencer,* March 2, 1850.

Union," and the *Martinsburg Gazette* asked those who contemplated secession to "go to the battle fields of Bunker Hill, of Bennington, of Saratoga, and of Yorktown, to visit the blood stained plains of Brandywine, to stand before the tomb of Washington, to call up the spirit of the Marions, Sumters, and Pinckneys, and listen to the united voice of all, saying in the tones of thunder, 'Liberty and Union.' "[87]

Many western counties held mass-meetings, in which party lines were broken down, to protest against secession and to indorse the action of those who opposed it. Many such assemblies met on the anniversary of Washington's birthday and quoted copiously, in the resolutions passed, from his farewell address.[88] Citizens of Mason County resolved,

That, as a portion of the people of the 14th congressional district, a part of West Augusta, on whose mountains Washington contemplated, if driven to extremities, to make his last stand and plant his last banner in defense of the liberties of his country, we are prepared in conformity with the parting advice of that same Washington to stand by the Union; and living in the line between slaveholding and non-slaveholding states, which makes it certain that in the event of the dissolution of the Union, we shall be placed in the position of borderers exposed to the feuds and interminable broils, which such a position would inevitably entail upon us, a regard for the safety of our firesides, not less than the high impulses of patriotism, the glorious recollection of the past, and the high anticipations of the future, will induce us to adhere unswervingly to this resolution.[89]

[87] See *National Intelligencer* (weekly), March 2, 1850.
[88] *Ibid.*, February 16, 1850; *ibid.*, March 2, 1850.
[89] *Ibid.*, March 19, 1850.

The patriotic devotion of the west to the Union did much to produce moderation in the east in 1850. Calhoun's agent, Mr. Crallé, who made a visit to the west to determine its sentiments, wrote as follows: "McDowell . . . . reflects but too faithfully the sentiment of the west generally."[90] Mr. Ruffin, of the Albemarle Southern Rights Association, opposed Virginia's sending delegates to the proposed Nashville Convention, because "the recommendation of the Legislature had not been responded to by a single county west of the Blue Ridge except Jefferson."[91] "Beyond the mountains," said the *Richmond Whig,* "both parties have but one voice. The *Parkersburg Gazette,* the *Kanawha Republican,* the *Lewisburg Chronicle,* the *Harrisonburg Republican,* and the *Martinsburg Republican* are strongly opposed to it.[92] The latter paper, Democrat, observes 'this move has not originated with the people, and to say the least of it . . . . it is an imprudent step.' "[93]

When the compromise of 1850 was agreed upon most eastern Democrats united with the Whigs to observe the short truce which it declared. Judge Tucker's speech before the Nashville Convention was severely criticized;[94] the *Richmond Enquirer* vied with

[90] "Calhoun Correspondence," *Am. Hist. Asso. Rept.* (1899), II, 1200, 1201.

[91] *Richmond Whig,* May 17, 1850.

[92] The Nashville Convention.

[93] *Richmond Whig,* January 29, 1850.

[94] *Petersburg Intelligencer,* July 27, 1850; *National Intelligencer,* August 3, 1850.

the *Richmond Whig* in its professions of devotion to the Union;[95] with only one or two dissenting voices the Assembly of 1850–51 disapproved the movement in South Carolina for a southern convention, and, while it acknowledged that "a diversity of opinion existed in Virginia on the compromise measures, yet it deemed it a duty to tell South Carolina that the people were unwilling to take any step to destroy the integrity of the Union."[96]

[95] *Richmond Enquirer,* March 27, 1851.
[96] *Ibid.;* Acts of Assembly of 1850–51, 201.

CHAPTER VIII
THE REFORM CONVENTION OF 1850-51

During the two decades following 1830, population and wealth increased rapidly in western Virginia. The construction of turnpikes and railroads in the trans-Alleghany and the projection of still more of such improvements attracted thither immigrants and aroused the interest of speculators in her cheap lands and rich natural resources. Eastern and English capitalists purchased large tracts of land there and encouraged settlers to purchase and occupy them.[1] So intense was the land craze at times during this period that associations, similar to those organized in Wisconsin and elsewhere at the same time, were formed to prevent land buyers from overbidding each other and to treat those who offended their regulations to tar and feathers and rail rides.[2] Meanwhile capitalists from the middle and New England states established small manufactories in the trans-Alleghany, and immigrants from those states either found employment therein or became teachers and farmers. By 1850 the value of the lands in the transmontane country had risen until it amounted to only $15,000,000 less than the cash value of the lands east of the Blue Ridge.[3]

---

[1] *National Intelligencer*, June 2, 1835; *Niles Register*, XLVII, 234; LXXIII, 71; LXXIV, 228.

[2] *Ibid.*, LXII, 387.

[3] DeBow, *Review*, XIII, 194.

During these years several colonies of Germans found homes along the Little Kanawha, in the Northwestern Panhandle, and in Doddridge and Randolph counties.[4] So important an element did the Germans become in the trans-Alleghany population that resolutions were introduced in the constitutional convention of 1850–51 to have its documents printed in their language.[5] The census of 1830 gave the counties east of the Blue Ridge 57,012 white inhabitants more than those to the west; but the census of 1840 showed 2,172 more whites in the west than in the east, and the census of 1850 raised this majority to 90,392.

The following from the *Richmond Enquirer* shows that the east was not wholly ignorant of the changes which were taking place in the west and of its own declining power:

> The section below Tide-water, which was once populous, is in many places almost deserted. The property and wealth are shifting to other divisions. The section beyond the Alleghany, once the resort of the wolf and the bear, is fast filling up with an industrious, high-souled, thriving population whose wealth is rapidly accumulating and whose rich resources are being daily more and more developed.[6]

Under these conditions the west, especially the trans-Alleghany, naturally continued its fight for a greater share in the government. So long as the east

[4] *Va. Advocate*, August 30, 1843; *Kanawha Republican*, September 9, 1843; *Parkersburg Gazette*, August 23, 1843. The largest and most important of these settlements was the Santa Clara in Doddridge County.

[5] *Journal*, 100, 106, 110.

[6] July 22, 1845. See also DeBow, *Review*, XII, 35.

had had a large white population and paid taxes on greater land values than the west, it could consistently refuse the latter's claim; but, when the balance was turned, a further refusal could be defended only on the very dangerous ground that slave property, because of its peculiar character, was entitled to a greater voice in the government than free white inhabitants.[7]

As has been seen, the constitution of 1830 gave the Assembly power "after the year 1841, and at intervals thereafter of not less than ten years, ... two-thirds of each house concurring, to make reapportionments of Delegates and Senators throughout the Commonwealth." In view of its great growth in wealth and population, the west fully expected the Assembly of 1841-42 to reapportion representation on a more equitable basis. Immediately prior to the meeting of that Assembly there was scarcely a western print which did not repeatedly publish editorials condemning that arrangement whereby the west with a total white population of 271,000 had only ten senators and fifty-six delegates and the east with only 269,000 had nineteen senators and seventy-eight delegates,[8] and that apportionment whereby 44,097 voters residing east of the Blue Ridge were entitled to fourteen congressmen and 42,270[9] west thereof were given only seven. Some of the numerous memorials from the western counties threatened that—

[7] *Journal, House of Del.*, 1841-42, Doc. No. 8.
[8] *Niles Register*, LXII, 387.
[9] *Journal, House of Del.*, 1841-42, Doc. No. 8, p. 14.

if the remedial action of the General Assembly should be withheld, if our appeal to your honorable body is destined to bring us to the melancholy that we are without relief in the mode provided in the Constitution; that our eastern brethren "feeling power have forgotten right," we shall then be prepared to hold solemn council with our fellow citizens sharing with us our political degradation.[10]

A special committee of the Assembly of 1841–42 reported for a reapportionment of representation on the suffrage basis,[11] that is, on the qualified voters of the state; but a minority report made by eastern members advocated the mixed basis, on the ground that "persons and property are alike subjects of legislation and entitled to like protection."[12] To the great disappointment of the western delegates, who manifested their feelings by placing in the *Journal of the House of Delegates* a protest signed by fifty of their number, the matter was postponed indefinitely.[13] The western delegates then tried to force the call of a constitutional convention but were again defeated by a sectional vote.

Defeat only redoubled the determination of the westerners. When news of the action of the Assembly reached them, a large public meeting composed of delegates from ten counties in the northwest assembled at Clarksburg. By a series of resolutions it expressed surprise at the refusal of the legislators to

[10] *Journal, House of Del.*, 1841–42, Doc. No. 8; *Kanawha Republican*, December 4, 1841; *Richmond Enquirer*, January 6, 18, 22, and March 1, 1842.

[11] *Ibid.*, January 27, 1842.

[12] *Ibid.*

[13] *Ibid.*, March 10, 1842; *Niles Register*, LXII, 32, 80, 87. The vote was: ayes 68, noes 56.

REFORM CONVENTION OF 1850-51 255

exercise their constitutional power to reapportion representation and asked that a poll be taken in the trans-Alleghany to determine the sense of the people on calling a constitutional convention.[14] Talk of dismemberment was current, and the separation of Maine from Massachusetts was looked to as a precedent. Some deemed it impossible, however, to secure the admission of western Virginia as a separate state as long as Tyler was President. It was currently reported that he had exercised diligence in sending federal troops to aid the governor of Rhode Island in putting down insurrection there, because he expected soon to be called upon to render a similar service to his native state.[15] The editor of the *Kanawha Republican* thought the advantages of separate statehood to West Virginians were many and insisted that Virginia should not oppose the scheme, because two additional senators would thereby be added to the South from the new state, "Appalachia."[16]

A public meeting at Charleston, Kanawha County, appointed a committee of correspondence and called upon the people of the western counties to send delegates to a convention to meet at Lewisburg. This meeting suggested also that the west should unite politically; that it should, independently "of the Richmond Junto, of the Lowland Whigs, of the Democratic leaders," place a ticket in the field for state

[14] *Kanawha Republican*, May 7, 1842.
[15] *Ibid.*, June 18, 1842.
[16] *Ibid.*

officers; and that James McDowell should be named by the west as its candidate for governor.[17]

The proposed Lewisburg Convention met August 1, 1842. Twenty counties were represented by about eighty delegates. A state ticket was not placed in the field, but animated addresses were made, and resolutions were adopted asking the Assembly to pass a bill, submitting to a vote of the people the question of a constitutional convention to equalize representation on the white basis.[18]

But by a strictly sectional vote the Assembly of 1842–43 again defeated a proposal to call a constitutional convention. With this defeat the west ceased to make a united fight for reform; western Whigs and Democrats engaged in mutual recriminations; and the reform movement ceased to excite alarm in the east. The breach in the camp of the reformers was due largely to the political acumen of eastern leaders. When talk of dismemberment and a united west was at its height, Ritchie gave the following warning to his henchmen in the west:

> We beg leave to recommend to our republican friends in that region to put down every use that may be made of the question [representation], as a political engine. Some designing men may stir it up for party effect—and as a friend from the Valley writes us "these men may employ it as a fire-brand with which they expect to divide the members of the Democratic party in the two great divisions of the state, and at length to divert their attention from the great issues which are

[17] *Kanawha Republican*, June 4, 1842; *ibid.*, June 18, 1842.
[18] *Ibid.*, August 6, 13, 1842.

now placed before the country in connection with national politics."[19]

When reapportionment again became an issue in the west, in 1845, Ritchie and other eastern leaders espoused the cause of reform,[20] but took great care to keep control of the movement. They deemed it better for their own political well-being to control affairs than to permit the voters of the west to unite into an organization independent of either national party. Accordingly the "Tenth Legion" of the Valley was conciliated by making James McDowell governor, and the northwest, the other Democratic stronghold, by electing Isaac Pennybacker to the United States Senate. As has been seen in a previous chapter, these sections were also favored at this time by appropriations to work of internal improvement and acts incorporating internal improvement companies.

After the alliance between the eastern and western Democrats the national parties in the west found it more difficult to act in harmony. The Whigs of the Great Kanawha Valley attributed their political vassalage and inability to secure appropriations to works of internal improvement to the fact that the Democratic strongholds of the Valley and the northwest persisted in voting with the Richmond Junto. Consequently they refused to vote for a constitutional convention, when it was favored by Democrats or when there was danger of the Democrats making political capital of it. Both the bill of 1846–47 and of 1847–48

[19] *Ibid.*, August 6, 1842, quoting the *Enquirer*.
[20] *Richmond Enquirer*, July 22, 1845.

to take the sense of the people on the call of a constitutional convention received only a few votes from the western Whigs.[21]

Believing that reform was inevitable and confident of ability to direct it, the constitutional convention movement soon became popular with the eastern leaders. They did not desire a change in representation but believed that an extension of suffrage and reforms in the judicial and executive departments of the state government were necessary to remedy existing abuses.[22] Under that ruling whereby persons were permitted to vote in any county where they owned a freehold worth twenty-five dollars, it had become customary for residents of eastern cities to purchase small tracts in the surrounding counties and to control their politics. In important and close contests residents of Richmond frequently collected at Cold Harbor and controlled the choice of delegates from Hanover County. It is said that by similar means Richmond also controlled the choice of delegates from Henrico and Chesterfield counties; Fredricksburg, those in Stafford and Spottsylvania; Alexandria, those in Fairfax; and Norfolk City, those in Norfolk and Princess Anne counties.[23] Besides, the indefiniteness of the constitutional provision regulating suffrage occasioned frequent and long-drawn-out contested elections, mak-

[21] *Journal, House of Del.*, 1846-47, 114, 115; *ibid.*, 1847-48, 378.

[22] See Governor Floyd's message to the Assembly (*Journal, House of Del.*, 1849-50, 20).

[23] Chandler, "Hist. of Suffrage in Va.," *Johns Hopkins University Studies*, XIX, 312.

ing a more definite law on the subject almost imperative.[24]

Moreover, the eastern Whigs, being a minority and, as such, having no control over the election machinery, favored an extension of suffrage. They frequently attributed Democratic successes to fraudulent votes and the efforts of corrupt election officials. In an important election in Hampshire County they alleged that 295 votes had been cast by men who had contracted for small holdings, paid no money on them, and surrendered their titles to them as soon as the election was over. The *Richmond Whig* insisted that an extension of suffrage meant increased strength for the minority party.[25]

Although actuated by different and in some cases conflicting interests the eastern leaders, regardless of party, were always able to unite in an effort to control the movement for a convention.[26] Had the west, which desired the white basis for its organization, been willing to accept the mixed basis instead, it could have had a constitutional convention in 1846.[27] But a majority of the western delegates then preferred no convention to one organized on any other than the white basis, while many eastern delegates declared that, rather than accept such a basis, they would move

[24] *Journals of the House of Delegates* for the sessions from 1830 to 1850 devote much space to contested elections.

[25] *Richmond Whig*, May 22, 1849; *ibid.*, February 8, 1850.

[26] *Ibid.*, May 21, 1850; *ibid.*, March 19, 1850.

[27] *Journal, House of Del.*, 1845-46, 143-44; *Richmond Enquirer*, January 31, 1846; *ibid.*, February 20, 1846.

for the dismemberment of the state.[28] The next legislatures contained majorities favorable to a convention, but they could not agree on a basis for its organization.[29]

At length the lack of harmony which prevailed in the west enabled the eastern leaders to have their way.[30] Some of the western delegates held out to the last for the white basis for its organization, but the convention bill, which finally passed in 1850, provided for the election of its members on the mixed basis. The proposed convention was to consist of one hundred and thirty-five members to be elected one each from every 13,151 white inhabitants and every $7,000.24 taxes paid into the state treasury.[31] This apportionment gave the east 76 delegates and the west 59. Had an apportionment been made on the white basis, the east would have received 61 delegates and the west 74.

When the convention bill was submitted to the people for ratification the trans-Alleghany made a desperate effort to defeat it, 29 of its 43 counties giving majorities against it. It is significant that no county in the Valley voted against it and every eastern county except two gave majorities for it. In the east the voters were urged to support the bill on the ground that the west could not control the proposed convention and that it was then a good time to secure needed reforms and to settle the basis question.[32] The Valley

[28] *Richmond Enquirer*, February 20, 1846.
[29] *Ibid.*, January 30, 1847; *ibid.*, January 21, 1848.
[30] *Ibid.*, December 4, 14, 21, 28, 1849.
[31] Acts of Assembly of 1849–50, 9 ff.
[32] *Richmond Enquirer*, April 18, 1850.

favored the convention because it had nothing to lose by either the white or mixed basis, had hopes of controlling it and an earnest desire for reform. Almost three-fourths of all the votes cast were given for the bill.[33]

The election for delegates to the convention took place in August, 1850, and the issue in practically every case was the basis of representation. Henry A. Wise, of Accomac County, was the only candidate who secured an election from a district east of the Blue Ridge as a white-basis delegate. This distinction brought him great popularity in the west and the ill-will of his eastern associates, who branded him "the modern Jack Cade."[34] Although many western counties had given majorities for a convention to be organized on the mixed basis, each and every one of the western districts now elected white-basis men to the convention.

The convention, which is known as the "Reform Convention of 1850–51," met at Richmond in October, 1850, but adjourned after a few days to await the census of that year. It reassembled January 6, 1851, and remained in continuous session until August 1.

The basis of representation occupied almost the entire time from the middle of February to the middle of May. The committee appointed to determine the proper basis was unable to agree, twelve of its members holding to one basis and twelve to another.

[33] Complete returns for this vote are not available.

[34] *Richmond Whig,* June 1, 1850. Wise was for a constitutional guarantee to prevent the excessive taxation of slave property.

Accordingly the delegates from each section submitted propositions. That proposed by the western delegates provided for a House of Delegates of one hundred and fifty-six members to be elected biennially and a Senate of fifty members to be chosen for four years; both houses were to be elected on the mixed basis; and, in 1862 and every ten years thereafter, a reapportionment was to be made on that basis. The plan proposed by the eastern delegates provided for a House of Delegates of one hundred and fifty-six delegates and a Senate of thirty-six; both houses were to be elected on the suffrage basis; and the reapportionments were to be made on that basis in 1855 and every ten years thereafter.[35]

It soon became evident that neither of these plans nor modifications thereof could be carried. The west did not have votes enough to carry the suffrage basis; and the east did not dare to force the mixed basis, because of a fear that the western delegates would withdraw from the convention and begin anew a movement for dismemberment.[36] Indeed, it was feared that Governor-elect Joseph Johnson, of Harrison County, the first and only governor of Virginia elected before the Civil War from the trans-Alleghany, and other leaders from his section were planning to withdraw from the convention and to move for the division of the state, unless their desires were granted.[37]

---

[35] *Journal, Constitutional Convention of 1850–51.* See Appendix.

[36] *Richmond Whig*, April 9, 1851.   [37] *Ibid.*, April 9, 1851.

REFORM CONVENTION OF 1850-51

Accordingly various plans of compromise were suggested. John Minor Botts, of Richmond, proposed that for the purpose of representation the constitution should recognize two grand divisions, one east and the other west of the Blue Ridge, and that equal representation in both houses should be given to each.[38] This plan provided also for an *ad valorem* system of taxation to be levied upon every species of property, except such as might be exempt by a two-thirds vote of each house of the legislature. But Botts was forced to withdraw his plan to await the action of his constituents, who were then taking a poll on the basis question. Then George W. Summers, of Kanawha County, came forward with a proposition from the westerners, which provided that a constitution be adopted without any mention of the basis of representation and that a poll be taken to allow the people to decide between the suffrage and mixed basis.[39] This plan was rejected by the eastern members.

It now seemed certain that the mixed basis would carry, but protests and petitions began to pour in from the west in such numbers that the eastern delegates were again reminded of the danger which such action meant to the integrity of the state.[40] Accordingly attempts at compromise were again resorted to, but a comparison of the plans submitted shows that neither side conceded anything. Indeed the western delegates

[38] *Ibid.*, April 22, 1851; *Journal, Constitutional Convention of 1850-51*, Appendix.

[39] *Ibid.*, Appendix.

[40] *Richmond Whig*, May 27, 1851.

became more vehement than ever, and asserted themselves by a series of caucus resolutions, which declined any compromise, and which did not eventually provide for the suffrage basis or a vote of the people on the basis question.

To avert the impending danger of dismemberment Mr. Martin, of Henry County, a mixed-basis man, moved that a committee of eight, four from the west and four from the east, be elected by the convention to provide a compromise.[41] This proposition carried, and on May 15, the committee thus chosen reported in favor of a House of Delegates of one hundred and fifty members, eighty-two from the west and sixty-eight from the east, and a Senate of fifty, thirty from the east and twenty from the west. It also provided for a reapportionment in 1865 and for submitting both the mixed and suffrage basis to a vote of the people, should the Assembly at that time fail to agree. This plan was also rejected: ayes 55, noes 54.[42]

The proceedings now became more uncertain. Plan after plan of compromise was submitted, but each received only a passing notice and was in turn rejected. Finally Mr. Chilton came forward with a modification of the report of the Committee of Eight. The number provided therein for each house was to

---

[41] *Journal*, 206. The members of the committee were G. W. Summers, of Kanawha; Wm. Martin, of Henry; G. A. Wingfield, of Campbell; Wm. Lucas, of Jefferson; L. C. H. Finney, of Accomac; A. F. Caperton, of Monroe; Samuel Chilton, of Fauquier; and John Letcher, of Rockbridge.

[42] *Journal, Constitutional Convention of 1850–51*, Appendix.

remain unchanged; but, should the legislature in 1865 fail to reapportion representation, the governor was required to submit to the vote of the people four propositions, viz., (1) the suffrage basis, (2) the mixed basis, (3) the white population basis, and (4) the taxation basis. This plan was carried in the committee of the whole: ayes 55, noes 48, and was accepted by the convention with the following modifications, thus becoming a part of the constitution: should the legislature of 1865 fail to agree on a reapportionment, each house was required to submit a plan to the governor, who should cause a vote to be taken thereon; should the legislature neither apportion representation nor propose plans, the governor was required to submit the following propositions to the voters: (1) the suffrage basis, (2) the mixed basis, (3) the taxation basis for the Senate and the suffrage basis for the House; and should none of these propositions receive a majority of the votes cast, the two having the largest number were to be again submitted. The number of delegates was also increased from one hundred and fifty to one hundred and fifty-two, each section being granted one[43] additional.

The questions which arose in connection with suffrage, internal improvements, and the manner of electing the chief executive, the judges, and the county officials also occasioned sectional differences. The western delegates desired an extension of suffrage to every white man of the age of twenty-one and up-

[43] Poore, *Charters and Constitutions*, II, 1925.

ward.[44] While many, if not most of the eastern delegates favored a similar extension, some desired a small property qualification, and still others the freehold system as it existed prior to 1830.[45] The western delegates also favored electing the Board of Public Works, the governor, judges, and county officials by popular vote.[46] The eastern delegates did not oppose this manner of election for the governor[47] and county officials but opposed it for the Board of Public Works and judges. The convention settled these matters by extending suffrage to "every white male citizen of the commonwealth of the age of twenty-one years" with the usual exception of paupers, etc., and the members of the Board of Public Works, the governor, judges, and county officials were made elective by the voters.

Of the secondary issues, however, the most important from a sectional standpoint were those which arose in connection with taxation and appropriations. The chief motive, on the part of the eastern delegates, for refusing the white basis was the fear that the west would use its political power thus gained to impose taxes upon slave property to be used in the construction of works of internal improvements. For the purpose of raising revenue and making appropriations

[44] *Journal, Constitutional Convention of 1850-51*, 46, 310.

[45] *Ibid.*, 254; *Richmond Whig*, June 21, 1850; *ibid.*, July 30, 1850.

[46] *Ibid.*, July 30, 1850.

[47] Mr. Watts, of Norfolk County, proposed to divide the state into two gubernatorial districts, one east, the other west of the Blue Ridge, and to elect the governor alternately from them (*Journal, Constitutional Convention of 1850-51*, 295).

W. O. Goode, of Mecklenburg, proposed that the House of Delegates and the Senate be divided into two chambers each, one composed of members from east of the Blue Ridge, the other of members from west thereof, and that all revenue bills should require a majority of each chamber for passage.[48] The eastern members insisted that all property taxes should be *ad valorem* and that no one species should be taxed higher than another, but they were unwilling that slaves under twelve years of age should be taxed at all. Summers moved to strike the word "years" from the resolution exempting them and to insert instead "slaves shall be taxed at an *ad valorem* rate not to exceed that on land." This amendment was defeated by a strictly sectional vote: ayes 48, noes 61.[49]

In the west the provisions of the new constitution regulating taxation were its most objectionable features. When representation, suffrage, and general reform ceased to be issues there, as they did shortly after 1850, the subject of taxation became the chief source of difference between the east and the west. The constitution provided for an *ad valorem* tax on all property according to its value, but negro slaves under twelve years of age were exempt, and slaves twelve years old and upward were to be taxed *per capita* at not more than the tax on land worth three hundred dollars. But a capitation tax[50] equal to the

[48] *Ibid.*, 106.   [49] *Ibid.*, 328.

[50] One-half of the capitation tax was to be appropriated to purposes of education in the primary free schools. It was an effort to impose the expense of these institutions on the west which desired them most.

tax levied on land valued at $200 was to be levied upon every white male twenty-one years of age, and the legislature was given power, which it later exercised, to levy taxes on incomes, salaries, and licenses.[51] The inhabitants of the west did not object to the *ad valorem* system of taxation, but they never became reconciled to that arrangement whereby the small farmer paid taxes on his calves and colts and the plantation-owner paid nothing on his young negroes and only a small amount on his prime field hands. As slaves continued to increase in value during the years immediately preceding the Civil War the discrimination became more noticeable and more objectionable.[52]

The debates of the Reform Convention[53] repeated so many of the arguments made in 1829-30 that it is not necessary again to go into them in detail. There are, however, striking points of difference between the arguments produced on the two occasions. The reformers of 1850-51 made less use of the Bill of Rights and the precepts of the fathers; they made the increasing wealth and population of the west their chief plea for a greater voice in the government; the westerners were now able to meet the charge of radicalism with the countercharge that some of the eastern dele-

[51] Poore, *Charters and Constitutions*, II, 1928; *Richmond Times*, July 27, 1851.

[52] *Wheeling Intelligencer*, May 3, 1860.

[53] The newspapers furnish the chief source of information for these debates. The debate on representation may be had in volume form and many of the individual speeches were published in pamphlet form.

gates were "self-styled infinite radicals" bent on securing their own interests at the sacrifice of political principles and theories;[54] they now appealed to sentiments of patriotism instead of to metaphysical abstractions as in 1829–30; their speeches abound in denunciations of abolitionists and of promises of fidelity to Virginia and her "peculiar institutions" should political equality be extended to them; but most of the westerners sounded a note of warning when the mixed basis was mentioned and when it was proposed to discriminate in favor of slave property as a subject of taxation.

> Can it be expected [said Willey of Monongalia County] that men will ardently and cordially support negro slavery when by so doing they are virtually cherishing the property which is making slaves of themselves? What will be the result? It is impossible that the morbid, pseudo-philanthropic spirit of northern abolitionism should ever find a resting-place in Virginia. But will not hostility to slavery be engendered by the incorporation of such a principle into the Constitution? Your slaves, by this principle, drive us from the common place of equal rights, and usurp our place. Will the spirit of free men endure it? Never! Either the principle must be abolished, or you will excite a species of political abolition against property itself. You will compel us to assume an attitude of antagonism towards you, or towards the slave, and like the man driven to the wall, we shall be forced to destroy our assailants to save our own liberty.

The eastern leaders in this debate made even less effort than Leigh and Upshur had, in 1829–30, to follow Jeffersonian principles; they now stood out

[54] Willey, *Speech*, 5.

unequivocally for the rights of the minority in government; to them "the majority of the community" of the Bill of Rights had come to mean a political majority composed of a majority of the interests of both property and persons; in brief, the philosophy of Calhoun had displaced that of Jefferson. Although the eastern delegates frequently complained that their patience was being worn beyond endurance by the efforts of their western brethren to get possession of the purse strings of the commonwealth, their arguments are characterized by a spirit of conciliation and a feeling of fear for the future integrity of the commonwealth.

The constitution passed the convention without division;[55] but, when it was submitted to the people for ratification, voices were raised against it in the east. Its objectionable feature was the compromise plan of representation, which involved a practical surrender of the mixed basis. When the plan had been agreed upon, a little more than two months before the convention adjourned, mass-meetings were held in the eastern counties to condemn it and to move for dismemberment in case the convention refused to reconsider its action.[56] But the eastern delegates who had voted for the compromise remained firm, notwithstanding the fact that they were branded as "base Judeans" and "vile traitors."[57] There is no doubt that the east felt as intensely over the compromise of 1851 as the west

[55] *Journal, Constitutional Convention of 1850–51*, 419.
[56] *Richmond Whig*, May 30, 1851; *ibid.*, June 5 and 17, 1851.
[57] *Ibid.*, June 17 and 27, 1851.

had over that of 1830. But the constitutional provisions regulating the taxation of s'ave property, agreed upon in the last days of the convention, conciliated the east somewhat, and the new constitution was ratified by an overwhelming majority, 75,784 votes being cast for ratification to 11,063 for rejection.[58]

The quiet which followed the convention was occasionally interrupted by incidents which proved that neither the east nor the west trusted each other. The eastern prints frequently contained letters suggesting the dismemberment of the state as the only thing which would prevent the east from becoming the political appendage of the west.[59] Shortly after Governor Johnson's second inauguration an incident occurred which showed the mutual distrust of the sections upon the subject of negro slavery and the negro. In compliance with the request of numerous petitions Governor Johnson commuted to deportation the sentence of a negro, Jordon Hatcher, condemned to be hanged. This act called forth a large crowd which gathered in the governor's yard at Richmond, to vilify him and to denounce his official action. The incident aroused the west, and a resolution was immediately introduced in the Assembly to remove the state capital from Richmond.[60] The western prints, now exulting in their

[58] The vote for rejection came principally from the east, but even there only five counties gave majorities for it. All those to whom suffrage had been extended voted for ratification regardless of sectional feelings.

[59] For example see *Richmond Whig*, March 12, 1852.

[60] *Journal, House of Del.*, 1852, 448, 576. The vote in the House for removal was: noes 35, ayes 88.

newly won victory, threatened to turn "the sleeping lions of the northwest" upon the eastern aristocrats, to which threat the *Richmond Whig* replied that there were not a few in the east "who would like to see [Governor] Johnson pack for the northwest."[61]

[61] *Richmond Whig*, May 11, 1852.

CHAPTER IX

SECTIONALISM IN EDUCATION AND THE CHURCH, 1830-61

The sectional contest in educational policy was a gradual growth. It was the vote of the west which caused the state to establish the free-school system of 1796, called the "Aldermanic System,"[1] and fourteen years later to create a permanent literary fund. In 1816 the west had insisted that the total income from the "Literary Fund" should be used to establish free schools, and, in 1819, it had consented to an annual appropriation of $15,000 to the proposed university only on condition that a system of free schools should be established later.[2]

In the reform movement of the later '20's the subject of education was but a secondary issue. In the Assembly of 1828-29, and again in the constitutional convention of 1829-30 Alexander Campbell, founder of the Christian church and of Bethany College, made fruitless efforts to secure a more efficient free-school system.[3] By a sectional vote, strikingly similar to the

[1] This was the first material result of the movement initiated by Jefferson in 1779 for free schools. Under this plan each county was to be divided into districts and education was to be free to all whites (Shepherd, *Statutes at Large*, II, 3).

[2] At this time $45,000 was appropriated annually for the education of the poor white children.

[3] Acts of 1828-29, 13; *Kanawha Republican*, May 28, 1842. See also an article entitled "The Public School System," by Dr. W. H. Ruffner, in the *Richmond Enquirer*, May 12, 1876.

popular vote of 1828, on the bill to provide for the call of a constitutional convention, the House of Delegates of 1830–31 rejected a bill to increase the annual appropriation to the primary schools for the poor.[4]

When foreign immigration began to come in large numbers and when the population began to contain a large sprinkling of New Englanders, the free common schools became a subject of great concern in the west. The primary schools for the poor, maintained by the $45,000 annual appropriation from the Literary Fund, furnished the basis for a more comprehensive free-school system. The comparative absence of social distinctions and the dearth of good private schools made it convenient as well as necessary for all classes, at all desirous of attending any school, to attend the schools for the poor whites and to co-operate in the movement to change them into free common schools.[5] Accordingly the west continued to oppose the demands of the State University and the numerous colleges and academies for a greater participation in the benefits of the Literary Fund and insisted that the increased revenue should go to the free schools for the education of the poor. It even defeated an attempt to establish a chair of agriculture and an experiment station at the University and tried to cut in half the University appropriation for running expenses. It also bitterly opposed the establishment of state military schools and insisted that the revenue from the

[4] *Journal, House of Del.*, 1830–31, 283.

[5] *Richmond Enquirer*, May 12, 1876; *Report of U. S. Com. of Education* (1899–1900), I, 433, 434.

sale of forfeited lands, the chief source of income for the Literary Fund, should be returned to the counties in which the lands lay, to be used for the use of the local schools.[6]

In the '40's when the ill feeling between the east and west was very intense, the young men of the west refused to attend the University and the state military schools, even when they were given appointments and the state offered to bear a part of their expenses. Out of a total enrolment of 112 residents of Virginia attending the University in 1841–42 only 12 came from counties west of the Blue Ridge.[7] By 1845 the total enrolment from Virginia in the University had risen to 134, but the number from west of the Blue Ridge had increased by only 2. In 1839 there were twice as many residents of western Virginia attending colleges in Ohio and Pennsylvania as were enrolled in the institutions of eastern Virginia. The number attending Marietta College (Ohio) alone was 15.[8]

In 1838 Governor Campbell, a resident of southwestern Virginia, aroused many citizens of the state to an interest in behalf of the common schools. By statistics he showed that illiteracy was increasing.[9] A remarkable series of educational conventions followed.

[6] *Kanawha Republican*, December 25, 1841; *Journal, House of Del.*, 1839–40, 26, 206; *ibid.*, 1845–46, 164. Most of the forfeited lands lay in the western counties.

[7] *Ibid.*, 1842–43, Docs. Nos. 1 and 6. The *Kanawha Republican* put the number at nine, January 25, 1842; *House Journal*, 1847–48, Doc. No. 46.

[8] *Catalogue of Marietta College*, 1838–39.

[9] *Journal, House of Del.*, 1837–38, 9; *ibid.*, 1838–39, Doc. No. 1.

The first and most important of these assemblies was held in Clarksburg, now the county seat of Harrison County, West Virginia. It met September 8-9, 1841, and was attended by one hundred and thirty delegates from the northwest and the Valley. Among those attending the convention were educational workers from Ohio and Pennsylvania. Rousing addresses were made; elaborate plans for a free-school system were submitted; and enthusiastic communications were read from many of the most prominent citizens of the west.[10]

A communication from Judge E. S. Duncan was typical. He denounced that policy which denied the west federal aid for internal improvements and education, when the east had no intention of granting state aid.

> A splendid university has been endowed [said he] accessible only to the sons of the wealthy planters of the eastern part of the state and to the southern states. I have heard of only two students attending it from the northwest. The resources of the Literary Fund are flittered away in the endowment of an institution whose tendencies are essentially aristocratic and beneficial only to the very rich, and for the support of the primary schools intended for the very poor. . . . . The men of small farms are left to their own means for the education of their children. They cannot send them to the University, and they are prohibited, if they would, from joining in the scramble for the annual donation to the poor [which is scattered in the] ostentatious manner of a nabob, who throws small change among the paupers and cries, "catch who can."[11]

[10] *Report of the U. S. Com. of Ed.* (1899-1900), I, 435; *Journal, House of Del.*, 1841-42, Doc. No. 7.

[11] *Ibid.*, Doc. No. 7; *Kanawha Republican*, May 21, 1842.

EDUCATION AND THE CHURCH

The convention prepared an elaborate memorial to the Assembly and passed resolutions favoring the establishment of state free schools. The following resolution shows the importance and nature of some of the subjects considered:

Resolved, as the opinion of this committee, That the money deposited with the state by the depositary act of Congress, together with the proceeds of the public lands to which Virginia may be entitled, by the late act of Congress, depositing the proceeds of the same among the states and territories, ought to be invested in some permanent interest bearing fund and pledged by the Legislature to the support of internal improvements and common schools.[12]

The sentiment of the resolutions adopted alarmed Ritchie, of the *Richmond Enquirer*, to such an extent that he expressed to Calhoun fear that the friends of education would weaken the Democratic party in Virginia.[13]

The Clarksburg Convention was followed by numerous others of a similar nature. The most important were the conventions which met in Lexington and Richmond in October, 1842. Dr. Henry Ruffner, president of Washington College (now Washington and Lee University), was the moving spirit in the Lexington meeting, and submitted there "the most valuable document on general education issued in Virginia since the early days of Thomas Jefferson, viz., an elaborate

---

[12] *Journal, House of Del.*, 1841–42, Doc. No. 7.

[13] "Calhoun Correspondence," in *Am. Hist. Asso. Rept.* (1899), II, 839. The Democrats were opposed to receiving Virginia's share of the deposits and defeated resolutions for that purpose in the Assembly.

plan for the organization of an entire educational system of public instruction."[14] The Richmond Convention was an effort to arouse interest in the movement in the east and was controlled largely by westerners.

The Assembly responded to the educational movement by a bill, which, however, the conservatives caused to disappear from sight after its second reading. Other conventions followed, and the Assembly of 1845–46 was forced to enact a law giving to each county the authority, provided the voters desired it, to establish public free schools.[15] This act, however, was little improvement upon that of 1796. No regular state aid was given; free schools were optional; and they always encountered strong opposition even in the west, where there were enough of those who adhered to the private school and academy to cause endless trouble.[16]

Education was a subject of minor consideration in the constitutional convention of 1850–51. The western delegates desired a system of common free schools maintained by the state, and a large number of them voted for a resolution to withdraw the annual appropriation from the University.[17] The committee on education, controlled by western delegates, desired to

[14] *Report U. S. Com. of Ed.* (1899–1900), I, 437. The plan is given in full in the same report, p. 381.

[15] Acts of 1845–46.

[16] *Star of the Kanawha Valley*, February 8, 1850.

[17] *Journal, Constitutional Convention of 1850–51*, 384, 385.

make it obligatory upon the legislature to provide by law for popular education, but its report to that effect was voted down by the eastern delegates.[18]

When the Kansas trouble and the Dred Scott decision caused negro slavery again to become an issue between the North and the South, and when the latter section began to move for its intellectual, industrial, and commercial independence, Virginia led in the movement for an educational independence. Her leaders sought to make the University the intellectual center of the South, whence should emanate the orthodox teachings on the nature of the federal government. The public press was full of editorials and articles to show that the South had for more than a century been contributing largely of its means to support northern educational institutions; that her textbooks were written by northerners, who were unfriendly to her social and political institutions; and that her teachers were "Yankees."[19]

The southern commercial conventions repeatedly called attention to these facts,[20] and in 1856 and 1857 educational conventions, composed largely of college men, met in Richmond to remedy the situation. They passed resolutions favorable to making the University the intellectual center and to fostering the academies and colleges as preparatory institutions thereto. The

[18] *Ibid.*, 253. See also Appendix.

[19] *Kanawha Valley Star*, June 25, 1856; *Cincinnati Enquirer*, June 5, 1856.

[20] DeBow, *Review*, XV, 268, 273; XVI, 638.

system of primary education as it then existed was condemned.[21]

Under the influence of this movement the University of Virginia became the most prominent and important educational center in the South, and indeed, in the whole country. Its attendance rose from less than two hundred in 1848 to almost seven hundred in 1858.[22] The following editorials from a western print of strong pro-southern sentiments show the feeling which prevailed even in some parts of western Virginia:

In the last ten or twelve years Virginia has made rapid strides in the cause of education. In the session of 1846-47 the University had only one hundred and sixty-three students; now upwards of six hundred annually attend lectures at that seat of learning. . . . . Albemarle County is becoming the center of educational attraction, not only for Virginia but for the whole South. The University and preparatory schools in Albemarle now number annually one thousand students who are all being instructed in like manner, who are all being impressed with similar thoughts, with like principles, who are united by a common devotion to Southern rights, to Southern institutions, to Southern manners and Southern chivalry. In a word, the

[21] *House Documents of Virginia Legislature of 1857–58*, Doc. No. 1.

[22] In 1859 there were enrolled in the University of Virginia 624 students, only 8 of whom came from the free states. The enrolment by states was as follows: Virginia, 370; Alabama, 52; South Carolina, 35; Mississippi, 25; Louisiana, 25; North Carolina, 21; Georgia, 20; Maryland, 15; Kentucky, 14; Tennessee, 11; Texas, 9; District of Columbia, 7; Missouri, 7; Florida, 2; Pennsylvania, 3; New York, 2; Delaware, 1; Ohio, 1; Arkansas, 1; Iowa, 1; Peru 2 (*House Documents* [1858–59], Part II, Doc. No. 12).

EDUCATION AND THE CHURCH

University is shaping and molding the minds of the educated youth of Virginia and the entire South; it is uniting the young men of the South together and making them more and more attached to her peculiar institutions."[23]

On the subject of teachers and teaching the same print said:

Virginia has, however, in the last ten years undergone a great change in respect to her school teachers and to school teaching. . . . . A few years ago when Virginia was filled with indifferent Yankee school teachers, you could scarcely find a school master who occupied an influential position in society. Now, through means of the University, the Military Institute, and other Virginia colleges the profession of teaching has become one of the most important, lucrative, and respectable of pursuits. The first young men in the state in point of talent, education and respectability have turned their attention to the subject of teaching.

And this happy change has been going on so rapidly that, at the present time in East Virginia, it is almost impossible for one to get employment as a school teacher unless he was native born, raised and educated in Virginia. And this truly Virginian and Southern feeling prevails nearly to the same extent in the Valley of Virginia, and we hope the day is not far distant when it will prevail over every portion of the entire Commonwealth, and that no person will be employed to teach and instruct Virginia youths unless he be of the "Manor born." . . . . And here we will add that the influence exerted in the trans-Alleghany by Yankee teachers is entirely too great, and that it behooves every true Virginian to correct this evil. No education is better than bad education; no morals are better than bad morals.[24]

In spite of these occasional protests by ardent pro-southern men the Yankee school teachers held their

[23] *Kanawha Valley Star*, July 12, 1859.
[24] *Ibid.*, December 2, 1856.

own in the trans-Alleghany, which never co-operated in the movement to make the University the intellectual center of Virginia and of the South. E. W. Newton, editor of the most important newspaper published in the trans-Alleghany before the Civil War, the *Kanawha Republican,* and himself a former Vermont school teacher, pleaded earnestly and continuously the cause of the common free school and denounced the system whereby illiteracy was allowed to increase among the masses. It is significant that, when the total enrolment of the University had risen to 645 in 1857, and that from Virginia alone to 333, there were only 13 students enrolled from those counties now forming West Virginia.[25] In 1859 the total enrolment of Virginians at the University had risen to 370 only 17 of whom came from what is now West Virginia.[26] When dismemberment came, one of the charges brought by the westerners against the east was that they had been denied common free schools, and that their taxes had been taken to maintain a University for aristocrats.[27]

Far more important factors than even the differences between the sections over education, in shaping the antagonistic pro-southern and pro-Union sentiment in Virginia, were the struggles between the churches and the subsequent contest between the various church organizations over the subject of negro slavery. Because of the political movements which

[25] *Documents of the Assembly of 1857–58,* Doc. No. 12, p. 112.
[26] *Documents of the Assembly of 1859–60,* Part II, Doc. No. 12.
[27] *Wheeling Intelligencer,* May 3, 1860.

EDUCATION AND THE CHURCH 283

combined with them the importance of these factors have been minimized, but a careful study of any section of the Border, during the years immediately preceding the Civil War, must convince one that they were potent.

The contest within the Methodist church and between the separate church organizations which arose therefrom was the most important. The struggle in the other churches, although important, will not here be followed.

The northern and western portions of Virginia lay divided among the Baltimore, Philadelphia, Pittsburg, and Ohio annual conferences of the Methodist church. Each of these conferences comprised both slave and free territory, and each forbade its ministers to own negro slaves. The laws of the slave states prohibiting manumissions made it difficult in some cases for ministers residing therein to avoid becoming slave-owners, because they might come into possession of negroes either by marriage or inheritance and the laws of both Maryland and Virginia prohibited their manumission. When a minister thus became a slave-owner, his services were thereby rendered undesirable to congregations in the free states, and not infrequently to congregations in Virginia west of the Blue Ridge. Cases involving the possession of negro slaves by the traveling ministers had come up in the local conferences, and had arrayed the slave-holding and the non-slaveholding portions of their membership against each other.

In 1840 members of the Baltimore Annual Conference residing in Virginia petitioned the General Conference for permission to join the Virginia Annual Conference.[28] They set forth that, while they were subject to the civil law of Virginia which forbade emancipation, they were ecclesiastically under the Baltimore Conference, which refused slave-owners election to elders' orders or to the itinerary ministry, and asked for an interpretation of the church law on the subject. The General Conference directed "that the ownership of slave property in states or territories where the laws did not admit of emancipation or permit the liberated slave to enjoy freedom constituted no legal barrier to the election or ordination of ministers to the various grades of office known to the Methodist Episcopal church," thus practically nullifying the laws of the local annual conferences. It also refused the request of the petitioners for annexation to the Virginia Conference.[29]

The Baltimore Conference, however, refused to abide by this decision, and suspended one of its traveling ministers, Mr. Harding, who had become a slave-owner by marriage. Through Dr. W. A. Smith of the Virginia Conference, an ardent pro-southern man, Harding appealed to the General Conference of 1844 for reinstatement. The Baltimore Conference, through one of its ablest ministers, John A. Collins, fought the appeal. Both sides claimed to represent the true posi-

[28] *Journal of the General Conference of 1840*, 168. The General Conference of the Methodist Episcopal church met every four years.

[29] *Ibid.*, 167.

EDUCATION AND THE CHURCH 285

tion of the Methodist Episcopal church on the subject of negro slavery, and the debate waged between Smith and Collins depicted clearly the differences between the northern and southern sympathizers in the Border.[30]

Dr. Smith argued that the highest church law, that of the General Conference, permitted Harding to own negro slaves; that the action of the Baltimore Conference in suspending him was "ultra-abolitionist;" that there was danger of the church becoming embroiled in the political discussions of the day; that abolitionists had killed colonization and gradual emancipation; and finally that "slavery is a great evil but beyond our control, yet not necessarily a sin. We must then quietly submit to a necessity, which we cannot control or remedy, endeavoring to carry the gospel of salvation to both master and slave."[31]

Collins, who undoubtedly spoke the sentiment of the northern portion of the Border, said: "We are just where we always were, standing as a breakwater to pro-slavery in the South and the waves of abolition in the North." He admitted that abolition had killed colonization and gradual emancipation, but denied the justice of the contention of the South regarding the relation of church officials and ministers to negro slavery. The following statement from his argument voiced a sentiment not unpopular in Maryland and western Virginia: "We will not combine with the enemies of the African either in the North or in

[30] *Debates of the General Conference,* 1844.
[31] *Ibid.,* 28.

the South, ... abolition shall not make us pro-slavery."[32]

The case was decided against Harding,[33] and the General Conference passed to a consideration of the charges preferred against Bishop James O. Andrew, of Georgia, who, it was alleged by some of the New England conferences, had become a slave-owner. This involved a contest on a larger scale, and resulted in the division of the church into two churches, the Methodist Episcopal and the Methodist Episcopal Church, South. But before adjournment the conference accepted a "Plan of Separation" which the northern church later officially and the southern church practically repudiated.

"The Plan," as it is commonly called, provided that "should the annual conferences in the slave-holding states find it necessary to unite in a distinct ecclesiastical connection," the following rule "shall be observed" with regard to the northern boundary:

All the societies, stations, and conferences adhering to the church in the South, by a vote of the majority of the members of said societies, stations and conferences, shall remain under the unmolested care of the Southern Church, and the Methodist Episcopal Church shall in no wise attempt to organize churches or societies within the limits of the church South.

This rule was to be reciprocal, and provision was also made that it should apply only to societies, stations, and conferences bordering on the line of division, and not to "interior charges," which in all cases were left

[32] *Debates of the General Conference,* 1844, 33-39.
[33] *Journal of the General Conference of 1844,* 34.

EDUCATION AND THE CHURCH

to the jurisdiction of that church in whose territory they should be situated.[34]

The original line of separation between the two churches, in Virginia, lay through the Chesapeake Bay from the Atlantic to the mouth of the Rappahannock River; thence following that stream to its source, and continuing to the Blue Ridge Mountains, it ran along their crest to a point southwest of Lynchburg; thence it turned almost due west to the source of the Big Sandy River, which it followed to the Ohio.[35]

It was only natural for each church to try to hold all the territory and membership which it could secure along this line. But the southern church, true to the spirit of aggressiveness which then characterized its membership, soon began a campaign for members and territory in the whole slave-holding Border. The northern church was active on the defensive. It assured the Methodists in the Border that the "Discipline will remain as it is on the subject of negro slavery;"[36] the southern church was accused of secession; and interior stations and circuits, north of the line of separation, and where only a minority had adhered to the northern church, were promised ministers to conduct their services and legal aid to enable them to retain the church property.[37]

[34] *Ibid.*, 135.

[35] *Ibid.*, 93.

[36] *Richmond Christian Advocate*, August 21, 1845. The Discipline permitted members of the Methodist Episcopal church to own negro slaves.

[37] *Ibid.*, August 25, 1845.

Both churches sent agents into the Border to distribute literature and to organize their respective adherents. In both the Valley and the trans-Alleghany it was necessary for the southern church to take aggressive action to place its contentions before the people before they should be called upon to vote upon the question of adherence. Prior to 1844 the church membership in these sections had received its literature from Pittsburg, Philadelphia, and Baltimore, and it was consequently out of sympathetic touch with the South and southern sentiment. Of the situation one of the southern agents said: "I find that as soon as I cross the Blue Ridge .... the southern papers do not circulate there, or only to a very limited extent."[38]

The voting to choose between adherence to the northern or southern branches of the Methodist church occurred almost simultaneously in the belt of territory north of the line of separation. In many instances the voting was not restricted to the stations and circuits along the line of separation, as provided by the Plan, but votes were taken in "interior" stations and circuits. As a rule the minorities in such places refused to join their brethren in adhering to the southern church, and the northern conferences, true to the unofficial promises made by their members, continued to send regular ministers to them. This condition precipitated a bitter contest for church membership and church property.

The effect of these clashes of authority and conflicting views was demoralizing in the extreme. In

[38] *Richmond Christian Advocate*, August 21, 1845.

EDUCATION AND THE CHURCH

some instances two pastors tried to hold services in the same church at the same time; ministers of the northern church were forced to leave the state for fear of being summarily dealt with; church property was mutilated and destroyed; Bibles were torn and soiled; and church entrances were, in some instances, guarded with shot guns. Frequently those defeated in the voting to adhere to the northern or southern church refused to abide by the decision of the majority, claiming that it had not been fairly and accurately ascertained. A house-to-house canvass usually followed in which most conflicting results were obtained. In some of these contests members of the same family and near relatives were arrayed against each other.[39]

Resort was finally had to the courts. The grand jury of Accomac County presented the *Christian Advocate* and *Journal* of Baltimore as an "incendiary sheet tending to excite slaves to insurrection," and took steps to prohibit its circulation. The grand jury of Parkersburg, Wood County, presented the *Western Christian Advocate* of Cincinnati on a similar charge and took similar precautions.[40] Important suits involving the possession of church property arose in Parkersburg, Wood County, Charleston and Malden, Kanawha County, Harrisonburg, Rockingham County, and Salem and Rectortown, Fauquier County. In the

[39] *Pittsburg Christian Advocate,* February 11, 1846; *ibid.,* March 11, 1846; manuscripts in the Parkersburg church case, *T. A. Cook* v. *L. P. Neal;* pamphlet, the Harrisonburg church cases, *Sites* v. *Harrison,* and *Plecker* v. *Harrison.*

[40] Matlack, *Anti-Slavery Struggle and Triumph of the M. E. Church,* 185.

local courts the Methodist Episcopal church won almost invariably. But when the case went to the Supreme Court, which was composed largely of judges who resided east of the Blue Ridge, the decisions of the local courts were reversed.[41] The local courts based their decision upon "a fair interpretation of the Plan of Separation" and insisted that the original line between the churches must be accepted and that only such stations and circuits as bordered on that line had a right to choose whether or not they should adhere to the northern or southern church. The Supreme Court passed over the fact that the property in dispute belonged to "interior" societies and sustained the claims of the southern church on the ground that the realty and property in dispute had been deeded to local societies and not to the Methodist Episcopal church as a sect.[42]

The General Conference of the Methodist Episcopal church of 1848 received numerous petitions from its adherents in western Virginia asking that they be not forced to affiliate with another church; that ministers be sent to them; and that an annual conference of the Methodist Episcopal church be erected on slave territory within Virginia. Accordingly the General Conference organized the Western Virginia Annual Conference and entered upon a renewed effort to gain territory and membership within Virginia; a large force of ministers and agents was sent into the disputed territory to organize conferences and circuits; resolutions of sympathy were adopted for those who

[41] 13 *Gratt.*, 310.   [42] 13 *Gratt.*, 309.

had been deprived of the possession of church property; and the Plan of Separation was repudiated.[43]

This event was soon followed by the organization of the Western Virginia Annual Conference of the Methodist Episcopal Church, South.[44] Both churches now engaged in mutual recriminations, but interest in church propagandism soon ceased. It was not revived until the North and the South were again arrayed on the subject of the extension of negro slavery into Kansas. During the years 1854 and 1855 propagandism was at red heat in western Virginia. The southern church adopted the policy: "Carry everything up to the Mason and Dixon line." New corps of ministers and agents were sent into the Border to carry on this work. They there met agents of the northern church, and some of the joint discussions which followed were marked by all that vituperation and bitterness which usually characterize religious controversies. In many instances the inhabitants deserted their fields of labor to attend the "politico-religio" gatherings; a large portion of the public prints was given up to a discussion of the differences between the churches; and in some instances ministers were again forced to leave the country.[45]

It was at this period that the struggle between the churches did much to crystallize public opinion and to determine subsequent affiliations with either the North or the South. The adherents of the northern church

[43] *Journal of the General Conference of 1848*, 17, 73, 116, 164.
[44] This conference was organized in 1850.
[45] Pamphlet by Wesley Smith, *Defense of the M. E. Church*, 1.

now renewed their oft-repeated accusation of secession on the part of the southern church and took the comparatively new ground of champions of the Union. In this rôle they foreshadowed their policy in the Civil War. In reply to a speech made in Harrison County (now West Virginia) by Rev. Kelley of Kentucky, Rev. Wesley Smith used the following language:

> Are you prepared for a dissolution of the American Union? If you are not, then speak out in thunder tones and tell these disunionists that they shall not divide the church of the land by the line which separates the slave states from the free! Tell them that the Methodist Episcopal church shall exist on slave territory to the end of time, and that as a Heaven appointed instrumentality, ... we shall aid in preserving the integrity of the Union.
>
> That the existence of the American Methodist church, in the slave states as well as in the free, is the surest guarantee for the preservation of this confederacy. We have a constantly increasing fleet of the line of battle ships commencing with the Baltimore Annual Conference on the seaboard and embracing Western Virginia, Kentucky, Missouri, and Kansas,[46] and to these we expect to add an additional ship on slave territory every four years.[47]

It was only natural for the intense sectional rivalry between the churches to manifest itself in things purely political. The Virginia constitution of 1851 digressed from the general and fundamental to give the Assembly power to secure to societies and congregations the possession of church property. In the first gubernatorial contest decided by a vote of the people, that of

[46] These annual conferences, except that in West Virginia, were organized in 1852.

[47] Pamphlet by Wesley Smith, *Defense of the M. E. Church.*

EDUCATION AND THE CHURCH

1851, George W. Summers, the Whig candidate, was a resident of the trans-Alleghany, as was his opponent, Joseph Johnson. Summers was accused by the Democratic prints of being friendly to the Methodist Episcopal church and in this way of being affiliated with the abolitionists. Rumor went the rounds that he had permitted members of that sect to erect a church on his farm in Kanawha County where abolitionism was preached.[48] In the gubernatorial campaign of 1855, Mr. Wise, who relied for his election upon the Democratic vote of the northwest, the Methodist Episcopal stronghold, denied having ever accused the Methodist preachers of introducing Know-Nothingism into Virginia.[49] On the other hand, the Know-Nothing prints attacked the Methodists on the charge of popery. Their church government by bishops was compared to that of the pope and cardinals. This attack, together with the fact that many members of the Methodist Episcopal church in the northwest were foreigners, Irish and German, tended to keep some of them in the Democratic party.[50]

In the General Conference of 1856 the members of the Methodist Episcopal church in the Border made a determined stand against the abolitionists. At this time the New England conferences made an effort so to amend the Discipline of the church as to make slave-

[48] *Richmond Whig*, December 2, 1851.

[49] *Kanawha Valley Star*, March 21, 1856.

[50] *Ibid.*, March 28, 1855; Hambleton, *Life of Henry A. Wise*, 107.

holding a disqualification for membership.[51] Under the leadership of John A. Collins, of the Baltimore Conference, the delegates from the Border asked that the plighted faith of 1844 be kept. The arguments for and against this change show that the Border and the North had drifted almost as far apart in 1856 as had the extreme North and South in 1844. The northern conferences now denounced slave-holding and any recognition of it as a sin and accordingly refused to compromise. On the other hand, Gordon Battelle, of the West Virginia Conference, claimed that negro slavery was a national and civic institution with which the church had nothing to do,[52] and Collins assured the northerners that there was but one reason why the Baltimore Conference had not gone with the South in 1844, viz., "It did not concur with the sentiment of the South which proclaimed slavery a Divine institution."[53]

By the co-operation of the conferences in the middle and western states the Border conferences were victorious in 1856, and the Discipline remained unchanged.[54] But the abolitionists scored victory on another line, which was ultimately of much importance in shaping the anti-slavery sentiment even in the Border. By their influence the editorial staff of the various church papers and periodicals was almost com-

[51] *Journal of the General Conference of 1856.*

[52] Matlack, *Anti-Slavery Struggle and Triumph of the M. E. Church,* 222.

[53] *Ibid.,* 252.

[54] *Journal of the General Conference of 1856.*

pletely changed.⁵⁵ The conservative editors, who since 1844 had acted on a policy of conciliation and for the extension of the church in the Border, were displaced by the election of young abolitionist editors, and a resolution removing the church censorship on anti-slavery publications was adopted.

Under these changed conditions the church press, even in portions of the Border, soon became decidedly anti-slavery. Much of the Sunday-school literature used there pictured "rum-selling, cheating, and slave-owning" as temptations which the young must shun.⁵⁶ The church periodicals published letters from correspondents in which "the stench, the suffocation, and the death of slave society" were described.⁵⁷

The change in the attitude of the northern church press and its frequent attacks upon southern society and institutions called forth scathing answers from both the political and church organs of pro-southern sentiment and caused the stump and the pulpit alike to engage in excited utterances of theological dogma and political harangue. In many cases it would have been difficult to tell whether or not a given newspaper or periodical was a church or party organ. Whole issues of the trans-Alleghany and Valley newspapers were practically given up to articles and editorials written

⁵⁵ Six of the twelve editors elected in 1856 had voted for the proposition to make slave-holding a disqualification for membership in the church (Matlack, *Anti-Slavery Struggle*, 296).

⁵⁶ *Sunday School Advocate*, November 14, 1857; *Kanawha Valley Star*, January 12, 1858.

⁵⁷ *Pittsburg Christian Advocate*, August 21, 1857; *Kanawha Valley Star*, September 1, 1857.

to prove that the Methodist Episcopal church "is an abolitionist, anti-slavery, anti-South, and anti-Virginia institution," and that "it is more of a political than a religious organization."[58] Many mass-meetings were held to protest against the dissemination of sentiments "derogatory and dangerous to our institutions." The resolutions passed by a meeting at Boothsville, Marion County, are here given as typical of those passed by other gatherings and of the sentiment which prevailed among the pro-southern sympathizers in western Virginia.

1. Resolved, That, as the firm friends of the National Constitution, we pledge ourselves to oppose with manly firmness every attempt of northern abolitionists and of their coadjutors who are vainly seeking to conceal their dark purposes by fraud and disguise, to beguile our people into an alliance with Black Republicanism.

2. That the present position of the northern division of the Methodist Episcopal Church on the slavery question, the action of its general and annual conferences, the course taken by its editors and clergy, prove it to be as thoroughly abolitionist as any party organization in the country.

3. That we ask as a special favor of the Methodist Episcopal Church and any other church that may consider this country a part of their moral vineyard for the future to send among us only such ministers as have wisdom and grace enough to enable them to preach the gospel without meddling with our civil institutions.[59]

The Methodist Episcopal Church, South, took advantage of the anti-abolition sentiment in western Vir-

[58] *Kanawha Valley Star*, October 20, 1857; *ibid.*, December 8, 1857.

[59] *Ibid.*, September 15, 1857.

EDUCATION AND THE CHURCH 297

ginia to push its demand for "everything up to the Mason and Dixon line." Joint discussions, sometimes nine or ten hours in duration, were held in the Valley and elsewhere between ministers of the northern and southern church. Those friendly to the southern organization now frequently called attention to the oft-repeated prophecy, made in 1844 and 1845, that the northern church would ultimately show its true character as an abolitionist institution.[60] At the same time an effort was made to drive the northern church literature out of western Virginia, a Book and Tract Society being incorporated for that purpose.[61]

In the General Conference of 1860 the northern ministers overcame the opposition of those from the Border, who continued to "battle for the old-fashioned anti-slavery Methodism," and amended the Discipline on the subject of slavery.[62] This action disrupted the Baltimore Conference, the larger number of whose ministers met immediately at Staunton, Virginia, and passed resolutions declaring the bond which united them to the northern church sundered and established themselves as a separate and independent church.[63] The minority refused to abide by the action at Staunton, and continued to adhere to the northern church, claiming all the time to be the legal Baltimore Conference. Thus was occasioned another series of

[60] *Ibid.*, March 9, 1859.

[61] *Ibid.*, November 16, 1858.

[62] *Journal of the General Conference of 1860*, 202, 404.

[63] 32 *Gratt.*, 428. This organization maintained a separate and independent existence down to 1866 when it affiliated with the Methodist Episcopal Church, South.

suits for possession of church property. These suits pended during the Civil War and down into the reconstruction period.[64]

It is significant that the West Virginia Conference of the Methodist Episcopal church did not follow the action of the Baltimore Conference in repudiating the changes in the church Discipline on the subject of negro slavery and in establishing a separate and independent church. Its loyalty to the northern church finds a possible explanation in the fact that the southern church had in the period from 1854 to 1860, when anti-abolition was its shibboleth, extended its Western Virginia Annual Conference over practically the whole trans-Alleghany area. Although the membership of the northern church in that section greatly outnumbered that of the southern, congregations, adhering to the southern church, existed, in 1858, in a large part of the trans-Alleghany. Indeed, that church had made a much better showing there than in the Valley or the Northern Neck. Consequently those few persons in the West Virginia Conference, who desired to leave the northern church because of its action in 1860 on the subject of negro slavery, found an organized church to their liking awaiting them.[65]

The oft-repeated statement, made even to this day by many of the older residents of northern West Vir-

[64] 32 *Gratt.*, 422 ff.; 3 *West Virginia*, 102, 310.

[65] There can be no doubt that the Christian church, of which Alexander Campbell was the founder, received into its membership a large number of those who did not sympathize with the Methodist Episcopal church.

EDUCATION AND THE CHURCH

ginia, that "the members of the Methodist Episcopal church made West Virginia" is only partly true. Indeed, ministers of that church were prominent in many of the mass-meetings which opposed secession, and Gordon Battelle, one of the ablest preachers of that sect in the northwest, was prominent and influential in the conventions, which attempted to reorganize the government of Virginia and eventually brought about the dismemberment of the state and the admission of West Virginia. But the influence of other church controversies, the political and educational movements of the times, together with the natural antipathy between the sections, are factors which were of equal importance in bringing about the dismemberment of Virginia. That the struggle between the Methodist churches was a potent factor must be conceded.

CHAPTER X

HISTORY OF POLITICAL PARTIES FROM 1851 TO 1861

The years immediately following 1851 marked a brief period of political accord. In local politics the constitution of that year produced much the same effect as the compromise of the previous year had produced in national politics. Sectional controversies in the Assembly sank into insignificance; Joseph Johnson, the first governor of Virginia to be elected by a vote of the people, was selected from the trans-Alleghany; J. M. Mason, of the Valley, and R. M. T. Hunter, of the Tidewater, were elected to the United States Senate with little opposition; the state selected a practically solid Democratic delegation to Congress; and Democrats and Whigs vied with each other in their professions of devotion to the Compromise of 1850.

The co-operation of the east in the banking legislation and in the internal improvement schemes desired by the west contributed to political accord. Immediately following the adoption of the new constitution the Assembly incorporated ten independent banks in towns west of the Blue Ridge.[1] True to former Democratic policies, the James River and Kanawha Canal Company was neglected;[2] but large appropriations were made to the Virginia and Tennessee Rail-

[1] Acts of Assembly of 1851-52; *National Intelligencer* (weekly), June 10, 1852.

[2] The James River and Kanawha Company was refused an appropriation to extend its works beyond Covington in the Valley.

road, and the scheme of connecting the western terminus of the James River Canal with the Ohio River by railroad was undertaken at state expense.[3] From 1850 to 1854 more turnpikes and railroad companies were incorporated with the privilege of constructing works of internal improvement in the west than in all the years preceding.[4] Very liberal appropriations were also made to the western turnpike companies, and this caused an acquiescence by the westerners in the more generous appropriations made to the various railroad companies operating east of the mountains. Speaking of what had formerly been the most disaffected section of the state, Governor Joseph Johnson, himself a resident of the trans-Alleghany section, was able to say, in his message to the Assembly of 1855:

> The northwestern portion of the state is most happily situated. The Baltimore and Ohio Railroad terminating at Wheeling and Parkersburg places it within sixteen hours of Baltimore and still nearer to Alexandria. The Hampshire and Loudoun road, ... the Northwestern Turnpike from Winchester to Parkersburg, and the Staunton and Parkersburg turnpike connecting those points, together with the network of turnpikes not macadamized, afford all the facilities for travel and transportation the most fastidious could desire. . . . . It may truly be said that she wants little and asks less.[5]

---

[3] The Covington and Ohio Railroad was incorporated to connect the James and Kanawha river navigation (*Thirty-ninth Annual Report of the Board of Public Works*, Doc. No. 17). See also *Seventeenth, Eighteenth,* and *Nineteenth Annual Reports of the James River and Kanawha Company;* DeBow, *Review,* XIII, 525, 641.

[4] See Acts of Assembly of 1850–51; 1852–53; 1853–54.

[5] *House Documents,* No. 1, of the Assembly of 1855–56.

With the Virginia and Tennessee Railroad nearing completion the same statement could have been made of the southwest. The only dissatisfaction on account of inadequate communications existed in the old Whig strongholds along the Kanawha Valley, but the proposed Covington and Ohio Railroad was intended for relief there.

But forces were at work to terminate this brief period of activity in internal improvement and of political harmony. They first manifested themselves in national politics, when the Democratic state convention of 1852 refused to incorporate into its platform a plank declaring the Compromise of 1850 to be a permanent settlement of the questions therein embraced and adopted instead a plank declaring the doctrines of 1798 to be the fundamental principles of the Democratic party.[6] This action alienated many former Whigs as well as some Democrats, who desired to end the sectional agitation over negro slavery and to relegate the discussion of federal relations to the background. It was, however, an effort of the party leaders to keep the Democratic party from disintegration and to divert the trend of political discussion from negro slavery. Of the inconsistency of the convention's action the *Lynchburg Virginian* (Whig) said:

> The men who united in the adoption of this declaration know perfectly well they stand to each other direct antipodes in their construction of the resolutions of '98–'99, the one party maintaining that they assert the right of secession at pleasure, and without accountability to the federal government; and the

[6] *National Intelligencer*, April 8, 1852.

other contending that they point out no other redress of grievances to the separate states, than the provisions of the Constitution, and the final appeal to arms. There were men in that body who believed that the right to quit the Union exists at all times with the states, to be exercised at their discretion; there were others who deny all such right and hold that secession is treason.[7]

The action of the Democratic representatives in Congress, in refusing to vote for a resolution declaring the Compromise of 1850 to be final, drove others from their party.[8] But the Democrats were able to carry the state for Pierce by a good majority,[9] and by the aid of a gerrymander they elected, in 1853, a solid delegation to Congress.[10]

In the election of 1855 the Whigs revived under the name Know-Nothings, or Americans, who had become a powerful organization at the North during the discussions over the Kansas-Nebraska Bill. The Know-Nothings, like their predecessors, were sectional in strength, drawing their chief support from areas which had formerly been Whig. If any differences existed in the sectional strength of the two parties the Know-Nothings were more popular in the east than the Whigs had been. The slogan "Put only Americans on watch tonight" appealed to many east Virgin-

[7] *National Intelligencer* (weekly), April 10, 1852, quoting the *Virginian*.

[8] Seven out of thirteen Democrats from Virginia voted against the resolution (*ibid.*, April 8 and 17, 1852).

[9] Pierce's majority was 15,281 (*Whig Almanac*, 1852, p. 53).

[10] *National Intelligencer*, May 26 and 31, 1853; *ibid.*, June 4, 1853.

ians, who attributed their waning power in national councils to the foreign immigrants at the North.[11] Before the new organization had become powerful politically even the Democratic press of the east looked with favor upon it.

> Know-Nothingism is partly right [said the *Richmond Enquirer*]. American citizenship ought not to be made dirt cheap. The sovereignty of this republic is in the people; and every vagabond adventurer escaping from the jails and packed off from the poor houses of Europe, is not fit for sovereign citizenship in this country the moment his dirty rags and stinking carcass touch our shores.[12]

Besides, the old-line Whigs concurred in the apparent effort of the Know-Nothings to put down the agitation of negro slavery.[13]

The factors tending to preserve the former Democratic strongholds intact were equally effective. Although the inhabitants of the west contained a large intersprinkling of English families of old standing, there were many among them in whose veins ran Scotch-Irish, German, and Irish blood, who almost invariably continued to be Democrats.[14] It is significant that this was the period when Irish laborers came to Virginia in largest numbers and found homes on the cheap lands along the western railroads.[15] Al-

[11] Wise, *Seven Decades of the Union*, 245; Wise, *Wise*, 175.

[12] December 12, 1854.

[13] Tyler, *Letters and Times of the Tylers*, II, 516.

[14] Koerner, *Das deutsche Element in den Vereinigten Staaten*, 403.

[15] This is the period when the Irish settlements were made in Lewis and neighboring counties.

though the westerners were intensely Protestant, the anti-Catholic plank of the Know-Nothing party did not appeal to them. They continued to cherish the principles of the Declaration of Rights and Jefferson's Statute for Religious Liberty, each of which their ancestors had been instrumental in making effective. The prevailing tariff, though moderate, furthermore was objectionable to those voters, in both the east and the west, who desired cheap iron to be used in the construction of railroads.[16] Besides, the Democratic strongholds of the state at this time were engaged in a political "log-rolling," which had already brought good returns in the way of internal improvements and now held out flattering inducements of better things to come. Thus the northern Democrats of the west and the pro-southern Democrats of the east found it to their mutual advantage to co-operate in efforts to carry elections.[17]

In the gubernatorial election of 1855 Henry A. Wise, of Accomac County, was the Democratic nominee and Thomas S. Flournoy, of Halifax, the Know-Nothing. Flournoy secured his nomination at a conference of party leaders, but Wise was nominated by a state convention. Most of the eastern leaders opposed him, but his record in the constitutional convention of 1850–51 on the questions of internal improvements, representation, and education made him popular with the voters of the west. Prior to the

[16] *National Intelligencer* (tri-weekly), January 12, 1856; De Bow, *Review*, XVIII, 117.

[17] *Kanawha Valley Star*, February 10, 1857.

meeting of the state convention everything pointed to the nomination of Shelton F. Leake, who had a large following in the Piedmont and the Valley; but, when the trans-Alleghany delegation arrived, it was almost a unit for Wise. The trans-Alleghany and the Tidewater delegates united to secure his nomination.

The canvass was a heated one and had an important bearing upon later developments. By his brilliant oratory and winning personality, Wise, an ardent prosouthern man, gained an influence over the young leaders, especially those of the west, and was able thereby to neutralize the conservative influences of such men as John Letcher, William Smith, and Leake, who opposed his nomination and continued to oppose his pro-southern policy.[18] It is significant that Wise's majority of 10,180 came almost wholly from west of the Blue Ridge[19] and that he made his chief fight against the Know-Nothings on the ground that they were abolitionists.[20]

Wise's administration was characterized by a continuous struggle between the conservative and radical wings of the Democratic party. Under the leadership of Hunter, who had become less enthusiastic for the South after the death of Calhoun, and Letcher, the conservatives tried to keep the subject of negro slavery in the background and refused to encourage the idea, which gradually became more prevalent in the east,

[18] Hambleton, *Va. Politics, 1855, and Life of Wise*, 60 ff.

[19] Wise's majority east of the Blue Ridge was only 955 (*Whig Almanac,* 1856, 56).

[20] *Star of the Kanawha Valley,* April 25, 1855.

that dismemberment and civil war were inevitable. Under the leadership of Wise, of the surviving nullifiers and seceders of 1832, and of a corps of young politicians the radicals set about to make the Democratic party pro-southern and pro-slavery and at the same time to retain Wise's leadership in the west. For this purpose a large number of Democratic newspapers were established throughout the state, and the test of a true Democrat was made devotion to the South and her institutions. The leaders thus hoped to enlist a united Virginia in the programme then making for a united, self-sufficing, pro-slavery South.

For a brief period after the election of 1855 the differences within the administration party remained beneath the surface. The west saw in Wise "the champion of the Union-loving, indomitable Democracy of Virginia"[21] and remained loyal to him. Had he desired it, Virginia would have given him her undivided vote for the presidential nomination in 1856.[22] A united party under his leadership gave Buchanan the largest majority yet given by Virginia to any Democratic candidate for the presidency,[23] and under the

[21] *Kanawha Valley Star*, April 30, 1856.

[22] Most of the western counties passed resolutions indorsing Wise for the presidency in 1856 as did some of the eastern counties; but he had no following in other states and declined the vote of Virginia on the ground that no man from the South could be elected. Wise's influence was largely instrumental in securing the nomination of Buchanan (Tyler, *Letters and Times of the Tylers*, II, 520–26; *Kanawha Valley Star*, February 13, 20, 27, 1857).

[23] Buchanan's majority was 25,548 (*Tribune Almanac*, 1857, 51).

slogan "anti-abolitionism" the Democrats were able, in 1857, to carry every congressional district in the state.[24]

But internal changes were so rapid and diverse during these years that permanent political union between the east and the west was rendered impossible. The east sent delegates who took a prominent part in the southern commercial conventions,[25] forerunners of the southern Confederacy, and the sentiment there for southern independence daily became stronger. Edmund Ruffin and other industrial leaders now joined the politicians in the assertion that Virginia must have more slaves and better slave markets if she were to regain her fallen fortunes.[26] These leaders also condemned emancipation and colonization and favored the admission of Kansas under the Lecompton constitution. The eastern press frequently denounced the abolitionist tendencies of the west, those counties containing abolitionist colonies[27] and periodicals[28] favorable to abolition being threatened with "a long and

[24] In the congressional contest of 1857 John S. Carlisle, who had been elected as a Know-Nothing by the old Whig counties of the Kanawha Valley, was defeated (*Kanawha Valley Star*, June 2, 1857).

[25] DeBow, *Review*, XXIV, 570–84; XXVII, 94, 205, 219, 360, 468.

[26] *Ibid.*, XXVI, 418–647.

[27] The Eli Thayer colony was located in Wayne County, the Valley Mills colony in Wood County. There were few counties along the Ohio and in the northwest which did not contain abolitionist settlements.

[28] The *Wellsburg Herald* and *Wheeling Intelligencer* were Republican papers.

peaceful period of rest in which to enjoy the pleasures of negro worship." It is significant that the industrial and political leaders of the east now resumed their denunciations of "the political heresies brought from France by Thomas Jefferson."[29]

On the other hand, the west took little interest in the southern commercial conventions, the one held at Richmond being attended by only four delegates from the trans-Alleghany. Frequent utterances, of which the following is an example, were made there against the southern programme: "A union of all parties at the South for the defense of the South will produce a union of all parties at the North for the destruction of the South; and thus the two sections will be divided politically and the Union severed."[30] A large number of the inhabitants of the west continued to believe slavery an economic evil and to entertain the idea that it would be eventually abolished,[31] and the abolitionist newspapers of the northwest now denounced it as an "unmitigated curse to the soil of Virginia."[32] The westerners generally opposed the admission of Kansas under the Lecompton constitution, and the *Wheeling Argus,* a strong pro-southern paper, commented thus upon the attitude of the eastern prints upon that issue: "*The Enquirer,* the *Examiner,* and the *Richmond South* have over the intense discussion over Kansas and Governor Walker changed from the strictly

[29] DeBow, *Review,* XXIV, 584; *ibid.,* XXVI, 415 ff.
[30] *Kanawha Valley Star,* July 14, 1857.
[31] *Ibid.,* September 23, 1857.
[32] *Ibid.,* May 26, 1857, quoting the *Wheeling Intelligencer.*

state-rights sentiment to the position of one defending the administration of Buchanan and the course of the South."[33] In the west the threats of the eastern prints against the abolitionists were interpreted as declarations from the party leaders of an intention to retard the industrial development of the state by preventing northern immigration thereto.

> You know not [said the *Guyandotte Union*] the import of such a threat. You know not what it awakens in the bosoms of honest patriots! Leave Guyandotte and Cattletsburg "to the quiet and peaceful enjoyment of negro worship!" Oh! *Examiner! Examiner!* You know not how you sink the hearts of this people. "Thou hast wounded the spirit that loved thee."[34]

Although eastern and western Virginia were united upon but one thing, namely, opposition to the movement of the lower South for reopening the foreign slave trade, many editors and politicians in both sections tried to create the impression that the state was a unit politically. That their action was an incident in a party programme there can be little doubt. The ardent pro-southern newspapers, of which there were a number established in the west after 1854, were loudest in such professions. In reply to an editorial comment in the *Richmond South* to the effect that east Virginia had, by her railroads and reforms, indoctrinated the west on the subject of negro slavery and thus secured a united commonwealth, the editor of the *Kanawha Valley Star* denied that the sentiment in

---

[33] *Ibid.*, September 8, 1857, quoting the *Argus*.

[34] *Kanawha Valley Star*, October 13, 1857, quoting the *Guyandotte Union*.

favor of negro slavery was more universal east of the Blue Ridge than west of it. "The people of the west are pro-slavery from principle," said he, "and we venture the assertion that there are more abolitionists east of the Blue Ridge than west of it."[35] The transmontane editors were practically unanimous in their belief that the changes, which the east had experienced regarding negro slavery, had extended to the west.[36] The impression given by enthusiasts for the South created a false impression in the east of what might be expected of the west should the South decide to secede. To the very last many eastern editors and politicians continued to deny the rumors that the west could not be depended upon to play its part in the programme and cherished the delusion, "the union of Virginia is accomplished."

The internal improvement legislation of Virginia during Wise's administration was determined largely by the programme for a united South. With those striving for this end the completion of the Covington and Ohio Railroad, to connect the James and the Ohio rivers, became a cherished scheme. The following from the *Richmond Enquirer* furnished some idea of the spirit which actuated them:

It will be observed that two-fifths of the whole trans-Alleghany region is wholly isolated, that it has no communication with the northern frontier except a precarious one up the

[35] *Kanawha Valley Star*, August 31, 1858; *ibid.*, September 22, 1857.

[36] This is true only of those who edited Democratic newspapers.

Ohio and none with eastern Virginia. Yet this very region is the seat of a large portion of the military strength of the state, containing, as it does, a majority of the white population. *It is as if we had a citadel filled with men and outworks feebly manned, with no connection from one to the other.* The Covington and Ohio Railroad passes through the heart of this region and will when finished pour its strength either upon the Seaboard by way of Staunton and Richmond or upon the northern frontier by way of Staunton and Harper's Ferry.[37]

That this programme had supporters in the west is shown from the following from the *Kanawha Valley Star:*

We now come to the protection of our own people from the designs of our northern foes, ... the gradual preparation of Virginia for the great future struggle that every revolving year is hastening upon her. The struggle whose issue will be "State Rights and Constitutional Union" or a union of power untempered by law, unchecked by constitutional guarantees, ruled only by a fickle, irresponsible, fanatical majority.[38]

But it was not alone for the purpose of defense that the friends of the Covington and Ohio Railroad desired its completion. They hoped by this means to tap the granary of the Union, the Northwest, to divert the mineral resources of the mountains to Richmond or Norfolk, thereby creating a rival commercial city to New York and Philadelphia, and thus to aid in the programme of a self-sufficing and united commonwealth.

There were, however, many sectional interests

[37] *Richmond Enquirer,* August 10, 1855; DeBow, *Review,* XIX, 445.

[38] *Kanawha Valley Star,* February 24, 1857. For similar statements see *Speech of R. G. Morris* (pamphlet).

which opposed the completion of the Covington and Ohio Railroad. In the first place the James River and Kanawha Canal Company claimed a prior right to construct a railroad or a canal over the route designated for it. Many residents of the James River Valley and the southeast claimed that the proposed road would inevitably divert trade from Virginia to Baltimore by way of the Shenandoah, and proposed instead a railroad from some point on the Virginia and Tennessee Railroad to pass to the Ohio by way of the New and Kanawha rivers.[39] The inhabitants of the northwest and the southwest, now enjoying the benefits of the Baltimore and Ohio and the Virginia and Tennessee railroads respectively, did not wish to tax themselves to tunnel the Alleghanies. In the Assembly of 1855-56 the delegates from these sections voted against an appropriation to complete the proposed railroad.[40] These clashes of sectional interest, the financial panic of 1857, and the decline of Virginia's credit, due to the large appropriations made to the various internal improvement companies, rendered it impossible to prosecute work on the central line of improvements.

Meanwhile the inhabitants of the Kanawha Valley became interested in securing the improved navigation of the Kanawha River. The proposed Covington and Ohio Railroad was to leave the Kanawha near Charleston and pass thence to the mouth of the Big Sandy

[39] *Speech of Joseph Segar at the Internal Improvement Convention at White Sulphur Springs* (pamphlet), 8.

[40] *Journal, House of Del.*, 1855-56, 486; *Kanawha Valley Star*, April 6, 1856.

River by the most direct line. Because of the ready facilities afforded by the steamboat, the coal companies, of which there were a score or more doing business in or near Charleston, and the salt manufacturers desired to retain and even to improve the water navigation of the Kanawha.[41] As the Kanawha River was the only portion of the James River and Kanawha Canal Company's works which then paid more than the expenses of operating, the westerners insisted that the additional expenditures made upon that work should be made on the Kanawha River; the sluices and dams there were condemned as obstructions rather than aids to navigation; many suits, which the western juries almost invariably decided in favor of the plaintiff, were brought to recover damages from the James River and Kanawha Canal Company for sunken coal and salt barges; indeed, some shippers refused "to pay tribute," resorting to various devices to cheat the toll-gatherers;[42] and the public prints of the Kanawha Valley contained frequent editorial articles accusing the east of retarding the development of the west and impeaching the northwest and southwest on the charge of political logrolling.[43] On this subject one editor said: "But there is one other very important reason why central trans-Alleghany is so far behind in railroads, etc., etc. It is because the parties of this part of Virginia have in

[41] *Twenty-first Annual Report of the James River and Kanawha Co.*, 71–85.

[42] *Twentieth, Twenty-first, Twenty-second,* and *Twenty-third Annual Reports of the James River and Kanawha Co.*

[43] *Kanawha Valley Star*, February 10, 1857; *ibid.*, November 24, 1857.

years past been in direct opposition to the dominant party in the state."[44]

The movement in the Kanawha Valley led to the creation of the "Kanawha Board," which was nothing more than a subcommittee of the board of directors of the James River and Kanawha Canal Company intrusted with the improvements on the Kanawha River. But the hard times and the opposition of those interested in the Covington and Ohio Railroad and in the improvements on the James River made it impossible for the local board to negotiate loans and forced it to disband without accomplishing anything.[45]

The return of good times and the enactment of laws imposing heavy taxes restored Virginia's credit and revived interest in internal improvements. This interest was heightened by the fact that the relations between the North and the South were daily becoming more strained. The split which had occurred in the Democratic party intensified the general belief in the South that dismemberment of the Union was inevitable and increased the disposition to prepare for it. The Assembly of 1857–58, for example, made liberal appropriations for completing the Chesapeake and Ohio Railroad and incorporated numerous companies to build branch lines thereto. At the same time

[44] *Ibid.*, March 23, 1858. This was an ardent pro-southern paper and many of its editorials were written for the purpose of allying eastern with western Virginia and increasing the strength of the Democrat party.

[45] *Twenty-fourth, Twenty-fifth,* and *Twenty-sixth Annual Reports of the James River and Kanawha Co.; Kanawha Valley Star,* November 24, 1859.

William Ballard Preston was sent to France as agent of Virginia to negotiate for the establishment of a steamship line between Norfolk and Nantes.[46] Commenting upon the plans of the political leaders the *Kanawha Valley Star* said: "It is in the power of this legislature in five years to build up cities and fleets, and an immense commerce both home and foreign."[47]

But Virginia was not united in this her last great effort to develop her resources, to unite her people, and to provide an adequate defense. The conservative counties of the northwest and the southwest continued to vote against the appropriations for the central line of improvements.[48] Still more decided opposition came from those interested in the completion of a continuous waterway from the James to the Kanawha. As the necessity for union between the east and the west became more apparent, the scheme for a continuous waterway to the Ohio had been revived, receiving the support of Wise and others, who had formerly favored a railroad to the Ohio.[49] The James River Canal was denominated "a gaping wound in the heart of the

---

[46] The Assembly of 1857–58 appropriated $800,000 and that of 1859–60, $2,500,000. Almost one half-million of the appropriation of 1859–60 was used to grade the roadbed on which the Chesapeake and Ohio Railroad now runs from Charleston, West Virginia, to Huntington.

[47] January 19, 1858.

[48] Practically all the counties of both the northwest and the southwest voted against the appropriations of 1857–58 and 1859–60 (*Kanawha Valley Star*, April 6, 1858; *ibid.*, April 16, 1860).

[49] *Ibid.*, January 19, 1858; Wise, *Wise*, 221.

Commonwealth," and completion of the work was urged on the ground that a continuous canal would afford the only means whereby heavy freight, such as lumber, building-stone, and coal could be transported to the sea.[50]

As a result of this agitation the Assembly of 1859-60 guaranteed the debt of the James River and Kanawha Canal Company and vested the entire control of its management in the stockholders. It also authorized the company to borrow $2,500,000 to be used in continuing the canal.[51]

This action of the Assembly and the general revival of interest in a continuous canal from the James to the Ohio was in part the outcome of the movement for a steamship line between Virginia and France and of negotiations which Charles J. Faulkner, minister of the United States to France, had been conducting with certain French parties for the purchase by them of the rights and privileges of the James River and Kanawha Company. The Bellot family of Bordeaux and several other parties associated with them had become interested in the "Swan Lands,"[52] which the Assembly had relieved from the penalty of forfeiture and vested in John Peter Dumas to hold in trust for the heirs and

[50] *Twenty-fourth Annual Report of the James River and Kanawha Co.*, 449 ff.; *Kanawha Valley Star*, January 19, 1859. In 1858 those interested in the construction of a continuous canal published *An Appeal* in which its merits were fully set forth.

[51] The Assembly had appropriated only $2,500,000 for the construction of the Covington and Ohio Railroad.

[52] These lands included several thousand acres of the best coal and timber lands in central West Virginia.

creditors of Colonel Swan, an officer of the American Revolutionary Army. In 1859 M. Bellot and the directors of the James River and Kanawha Canal Company entered into an agreement providing for the sale of the company's property to certain French parties and for the creation of a new company to be called "The Virginia Canal Company," to have a capital stock of not less than twenty millions. The new company was to have a charter similar to that of the James River and Kanawha Company and was to complete a continuous waterway from the Kanawha to the Ohio within a specified time. A ship line was also to be established between Virginia and France.[53]

These negotiations pended during the year 1860 and were encouraged by those striving for a united Virginia friendly to the South. After the election of Lincoln and the renewal of the secession movement many Virginians, especially those residing in the west, opposed carrying the southern programme for secession and the formation of a confederacy into practice, but Governor Wise made the French negotiations a prominent reason for calling into extra session the Assembly, which took the initial step to secession on the part of Virginia. The public press and politicians in possession of party secrets held out flattering promises to the west, provided she should remain loyal to the programme for a united South, and, when the leaders were hesitating between secession and loyalty to the

[53] *Twenty-sixth Annual Report of the James River and Kanawha Co.*, 760 ff.: *Forty-first Report of the Board of Public Works*, 41 ff.; *House Documents*, No. 17, Assembly of 1859–60.

Union, the Assembly passed an act incorporating "The Virginia Canal Company" whereby the task of connecting the James and the Kanawha by a continuous canal was intrusted largely to the French persons interested.[54]

Thus the Civil War found the question of internal improvements a paramount one in the Kanawha Valley. Inaccessibility to markets, the fruitless results from public expenditures, the log-rolling of sectional political interests, and a lack of sympathy with features of the southern programme produced dissatisfaction with the east and eastern leaders. Had the James and Kanawha been connected commercially, the dismemberment of Virginia by a line passing along the top of the Alleghanies would have been rendered difficult if not impossible.

During the last years of Wise's administration the political differences between the east and the west were more pronounced than the social, industrial, and commercial differences. The gap between the radical and conservative Democrats, confined as these factions were chiefly to the east and the west respectively, became daily wider and the opposition of the anti-administration parties, also sectional, became more bitter.

In the gubernatorial contest of 1859 each wing of the Democratic party had its candidate. Wise and the radicals favored the nomination of John W. Brockenbrough, an eastern man of strong pro-southern

[54] *Twenty-sixth Annual Report of the James River and Kanawha Co.;* Acts of Assembly of 1861.

sympathy but well and favorably known in the west, where he had presided for years as judge of the western district of Virginia. The *Enquirer,* now edited by Wise's favorite son, O. Jennings, and the younger politicians and editors were loud in their praise of Judge Brockenbrough. On the other hand, the conservatives, led by Hunter, favored the nomination of "honest John" Letcher, the political idol of the Tenth Legion, the Democratic stronghold of the Valley. The Letcher boom was launched in Washington at a meeting of the Democratic congressmen from Virginia[55] and was meant to be a direct attack upon the radical policy of Wise and his followers. For this reason and because of the general belief that its outcome would determine whether or not Wise or Hunter should receive the vote of Virginia for the presidential nomination of 1860, it attracted much interest both locally and nationally.[56]

The contest between Brockenbrough and Letcher for the gubernatorial nomination marked a decided departure from the previous political contests in the state and was characterized by incidents of much subsequent political importance. Despite the fact that Virginians of all sections had persistently and consistently condemned northern politicians for bringing the question of negro slavery into politics, it now became the leading political issue within their own state. The eastern prints, especially the *Richmond Enquirer,*

[55] *Kanawha Valley Star,* October 12, 1858.

[56] *New York Tribune,* June 16, 1859; *Richmond Whig,* March 3, 1859.

denounced Letcher as an abolitionist and a freesoiler.[57] "It was in the darkest hour," said the *Enquirer,* "when the Wilmot proviso, the abolition of slavery in the District of Columbia, and the abolition of the slave trade between the states were paramount, that John Letcher was found encouraging the abolition sentiments of the Ruffner Pamphlet."[58] In fact, the Ruffner Pamphlet of 1847 and John Letcher's connection with it became the main issues in the canvass. The nature of the opposition to Letcher arrayed the western newspapers in his defense[59] and called forth long editorial articles and enthusiastic resolutions to defend his course in favor of the abolition of negro slavery in western Virginia.[60]

Of the many incidents of political consequence connected with the Brockenbrough-Letcher contest the Wise-Clemens duel was possibly the most important. When the Virginia congressmen had agreed upon Letcher, one of their number, for the gubernatorial nomination, Sherrard Clemens, who represented the northwestern district, resolved to sidetrack Brockenbrough. Accordingly he waited upon him and succeeded in getting from him a statement to

[57] *Richmond Whig,* January 7, 1858; *ibid.,* March 15, 1859; *Richmond Enquirer,* November 2, 1858; *Kanawha Valley Star,* July 6, 1858; *ibid.,* October 19, 26, 1858; *ibid.,* November 9, 16, 1858.

[58] *Richmond Enquirer,* November 2, 1858.

[59] The Republican as well as many of the Whig papers were favorable to his candidacy.

[60] *Richmond Enquirer,* November 26, 1858; *Kanawha Valley Star,* November 16, 1858.

the effect that he was not a candidate for the office of governor. Immediately Clemens wrote letters to the *Richmond Enquirer* and other papers saying that Brockenbrough had authorized him to withdraw his name from the contest. This called forth a letter from Judge Brockenbrough denying that he had authorized Clemens to speak for him and again asserting that he was not a candidate for the office of governor, but that he would accept the honor, should it be offered him. A caustic correspondence between Clemens and O. Jennings Wise, of the *Enquirer,* the leader of the Brockenbrough supporters, ensued; the lie was passed; and a duel, in which Clemens received a wound almost fatal, followed.[61]

So intense was feeling in the northwest against the Wise programme and eastern radicalism that Clemens' constituents, with whom he was very popular, took up the fight for him. The ardent pro-southerners made a fruitless effort to prevent his renomination for election to Congress, but they were unable to carry a single county against him. Travelers who passed through the northwest at this time believed that the feeling against the Wises was so intense and the "gun-powder popularity" of Clemens so great that he could have been re-elected on an independent ticket.[62]

In the light of subsequent history the Wise-Clemens duel became doubly significant. It was Clemens,

[61] *Richmond Enquirer,* September 14, and following dates; *Kanawha Valley Star,* September 21 and 30, 1858.

[62] *Wheeling Intelligencer,* February 18 and 19, 1859; *ibid.,* January 17, 1859.

yet upon crutches, who, upon the adoption of the ordinance of secession by Virginia, led the western delegates to his rooms in the Ford Hotel, where the first steps leading to the formation of West Virginia were taken.

Letcher received the Democratic nomination for governor, and William L. Goggin that of the opposition party. But the question of negro slavery continued to be the main issue in the contest between them. The fact that Goggin was an eastern man and closely identified with the slave-holding interests caused the voters of that section to rally about him, whereas the voters of the west rallied about Letcher for directly opposite reasons. Following the cue of the *Richmond Whig* the eastern prints repeated the charges of free-soilism made against Letcher, quoting copiously from the Ruffner Pamphlet; while Governor Wise and the *Richmond Enquirer* gave him only a half-hearted support, both being at times accused of favoring Goggin.[63] On the other hand, the western prints, irrespective of party affiliations in many cases, continued to defend Letcher's position on the abolition question.

The following statement from the *Richmond Whig* and the answer thereto are typical of the editorial contests which took place between the eastern and western writers at this time:

> We impeach him [Letcher] of seeking to divide this glorious old Commonwealth into two distinct and hostile parties, and we impeach him of trying to abolitionize the western half! We

[63] *Kanawha Valley Star*, May 24, 1859; *Richmond Whig*, March 24, April 22, May 25, 1859.

impeach him of warring upon the *foundation interests of the state—upon the institution of slavery itself and of endeavoring to exterminate it root and branch;*

and the reply:

It is more particularly that part of the sentence which speaks of slavery as "the foundation interest of the state" that we have singled out and it is to it in particular that we call the attention of the white working men of western Virginia. We ask them if they are disposed to enter into an opposition contest upon this issue with John Letcher. Do they for this reason also impeach John Letcher?[64]

Notwithstanding the effort of many party leaders to fight the contest on national issues, both Letcher and Goggin vied with each other in demonstrating to the east their allegiance to negro slavery and the South and in making the slavery question the paramount issue of the campaign.[65] But the record of each condemned him. By many Goggin was looked upon as the protégé of John Minor Botts of Richmond; his vote against the admission of Texas stood against him; and his devotion to the Compromise of 1850 had ceased to be a political virtue. But Letcher had only recently repudiated his abolitionist record, and his affiliation with the conservatives was regarded with suspicion.[66]

Notwithstanding the fact that each candidate stood upon a pro-slavery platform, there can be no doubt that Letcher owed his election to his former utterances

[64] *Wheeling Intelligencer,* January 15, 1859.

[65] *Richmond Whig,* June 10, 1859; *Wheeling Intelligencer,* May 9, 1859; *Parkersburg News,* April 28, 1859.

[66] *Kanawha Valley Star,* May 24, 1859.

in favor of abolition and to the anti-slavery sentiment of the west. East of the Blue Ridge he carried only two congressional districts, each of which was located in a comparatively non-slaveholding portion of the Piedmont. On the other hand, he lost only one congressional district west of the Blue Ridge, that in the southwest, which had long been largely slave holding. The two congressional districts in the northwest, which bordered on Ohio and Pennsylvania, gave him almost 4,500 majority in a total majority of 5,569.[67]

The contest between Letcher and Goggin attracted attention throughout the entire Union.[68] Many northern writers erroneously spoke of the result as a true test of the relative anti- and pro-slavery strength of Virginia and looked upon it as a probable indication of what might be expected, should the ardent southern sympathizers insist upon forming a southern confederacy. But the zealous young Democratic editors, who spoke for the southern programme in western Virginia, refused to concede that negro slavery had been an issue in the campaign and insisted that only southern rights and political theories in general had been involved.[69] The eastern Democrats of the Wise type would have been delighted with the defeat of Letcher, while the *Richmond Whig* insisted that, inasmuch as Buchanan had carried the state by almost 26,000, the

[67] *Tribune Almanac* (1860), 51; *Richmond Enquirer*, May 27, 1859.

[68] *Richmond Whig*, April 26, 1858; *ibid.*, August 5, 1859, quoting the *National Era*; *Wheeling Intelligencer*, March 24, 1859, quoting the *Ohio State Journal*.

[69] *Kanawha Valley Star*, June 21, 1859.

result of this election was equivalent to a defeat for the Democrats.[70]

That both the cause and the significance of Letcher's election were understood in the east is shown from the following editorial statements from the *Richmond Whig:*

> We repeat that Letcher owes his election to the tremendous majority he received in the Northwest Free Soil counties, and he owes his tremendous majorities in these counties to his anti-slavery record. . . . . By the vote of Virginia and Virginians William L. Goggin is today the Governor elect of the state by thousands. But the Yankeeism and Black Republicanism of the Pan Handle and other portions of the Northwest have carried John Letcher into the Gubernatorial chair, and we congratulate the eastern Democracy upon their abolition allies and the shameful triumph they have achieved.[71]

In the following manner the *Whig* recommended Letcher to the consideration of the Republican state convention to be held in Wheeling in 1860 for indorsement as a suitable candidate for the presidential nomination: "His majority comes from that neighborhood, and his Ruffner antecedents entitle him to the consideration of a convention proposed to be held where his best friends reside."[72]

The gubernatorial election found the contest between Wise and Hunter for the support of Virginia for the presidential nomination of the Democratic party well under way. Letcher's victory was generally regarded as a victory for Hunter also, but Wise's

[70] June 3, 1859.

[71] *Richmond Whig,* June 7, 1859.

[72] *Wheeling Intelligencer,* June 10, 1859, quoting the *Whig.*

devotion to the pro-southern programme and his radicalism had not yet sufficiently alienated his western admirers to make smooth sailing for his opponent. When the state convention met in 1860, neither candidate was able to control it, so evenly were their forces divided. Consequently no effort was made to instruct for either Hunter or Wise, and the several congressional districts were requested to choose between them in their selection of delegates to the Charleston Convention.[73]

In the hotly contested canvass which followed Hunter stood for Buchanan's administration, the admission of Kansas under the Lecompton constitution, and the theory of state rights as expounded in 1798. Although in favor of non-intervention on the part of Congress to prevent slave property from being carried into the territories, he thought this question should be kept in the background as no issues were likely to arise which would involve it. On the other hand, Wise had repudiated both the Buchanan administration and the admission of Kansas under the Lecompton constitution[74] and insisted on the doctrine of southern rights as opposed to state rights. He believed that the Democratic platform should assert the constitutional right of any owner to take his property, of whatever description, into any and all territory. He had already proposed to the Democratic governors of the southern

[73] *Richmond Enquirer*, February 28, 1860; Tyler, *Letters and Times of the Tylers*, II, 557.

[74] Wise was not opposed to the non-intervention doctrine, but he insisted that the Lecompton constitution did not represent the wishes of the voters of Kansas.

states a conference to take measures to protect "the honor and interest of the shareholding states."[75] To the surprise of many, Hunter received practically all the delegates from west of the Blue Ridge together with several of those from the east, who, under the unit rule, cast the vote of Virginia for him to the last in the Charleston Convention.[76]

Aside from his position on national questions there were local issues which contributed to Wise's loss of popularity in the west and to Hunter's success there. The inhabitants of that section had gradually ceased to look upon Wise as the patron of internal improvements and common free schools and had come to see in him what he boastfully considered himself, "A bold man in place, having their confidence,"[77] and thus able to effect a union of the southern people. The western prints now frequently spoke of him as "bold without discretion and generous without judgment."[78] The west hated Wise's mouthpiece, his son O. Jennings, whose record as a duelist shocked even those who did not hesitate to decide their differences on the "field of honor." Besides, Wise's copious political letters, each overflowing with vaunting ambition, were as con-

[75] Tyler, *Letters and Times of the Tylers*, II, 530–60; Wise, *Wise*, 236; Wise, *Seven Decades*, 246; *Richmond Whig*, July 9 and Sept. 30, 1859; *Kanawha Valley Star*, October 12, 19, 1858; *ibid.*, July 12, 1859; *House Doc.*, No. 1, 1857–58.

[76] The Tenth Legion elected two delegates friendly to Douglas (*Richmond Enquirer*, August 11, 13, 1860).

[77] Tyler, *Letters and Times of the Tylers*, II, 521.

[78] *Kanawha Valley Star*, August 16, 1859.

POLITICAL PARTIES, 1851-61   329

temptuously received by the westerners as by others.[79] But strange as it may seem, the west repudiated Wise's course in connection with the John Brown affair. Notwithstanding the fact that many mass-meetings held there indorsed his action in giving prompt relief to Harper's Ferry and in taking precautions to prevent similar attacks, a second thought convinced the inhabitants that they had little to fear from "clandestine raids," that Brown was a misguided fanatic, and that Wise was seeking to make political capital out of the whole affair and to complete the programme for a united South.[80] Accordingly they opposed the resolution to call a conference of the southern states[81] and the bill to establish a state armory and the bill to provide for the better organization of the state militia.[82] They also looked upon the proposed plan of boycotting the North as suicidal, some counties passing resolutions to condemn it, as well as the measures taken to arm the state.[83] That a lack of sympathy with this

[79] Tyler, *Letters and Times of the Tylers*, II, 551; *New York Herald*, July 13, 1859; *Richmond Enquirer*, November 26, 1858; *Richmond Whig*, August 16, 1859.

[80] *Kanawha Valley Star*, December 26, 1859; *ibid.*, April 2, 1860; *Richmond Enquirer*, January 6, 1860.

[81] The vote was: noes 90, ayes 42 (*House Journal* [1859–60], 413).

[82] For the purpose of defense the state was divided into five military districts, but the two composed of the trans-Alleghany and Valley counties, although more exposed and containing more free white men, had very much smaller companies than those east of the Blue Ridge (*Richmond Enquirer*, May 25, 1860).

[83] *Kanawha Valley Star*, December 29, 1859; *ibid.*, April 16, 1860; *Wheeling Intelligencer*, January 21, 23, 1860.

programme marked the decline of Wise's influence and popularity in the west the western prints furnish abundant evidence.

In the presidential election of 1860 Virginia had four electoral tickets in the field, viz., two Democratic tickets pledged to Breckenridge and Douglas respectively, the Republican ticket, and the Constitutional Union ticket. Her electoral vote went to the Constitutional Union candidates, Bell receiving, however, only about four hundred more popular votes than Breckenridge.[84] The accompanying map shows the sectional character of the vote given each candidate. The Douglas vote came chiefly from three sections, namely, two counties of the Valley within the bounds of the Tenth Legion, and the old Democratic counties, Monongalia and Cabell, the one located in the northwest, the other in the extreme southwest, but each bordering upon free territory. The votes given Lincoln came almost wholly from the counties of the northwest, the Pan Handle alone giving him almost twelve hundred in a total vote of 1,929. A large part of the other votes given him came from the Northern Neck, from Loudoun, Alexandria, Fairfax, and Prince William counties, and were given by New England abolitionists who had recently settled there and were making an effort to reclaim Virginia's worn-out lands as well as to make them free territory. Breckenridge received his chief support from the southwest, the northwest, and a belt of counties extending through

[84] The popular vote was: Bell, 74,681; Breckenridge, 74,323; Douglas, 16,290; and Lincoln, 1,929 (*Tribune Almanac*, 1861, 50).

Map showing the vote of Virginia by counties in the presidential election of 1860

the northeastern portion of the state, the old Democratic strongholds, which had been able to combine and control Virginia politics ever since 1850. It is significant that the Bell vote came chiefly from the belt of former Whig counties extending from the Atlantic Coast to the Ohio River by way of the James and the Kanawha. A comparison of this map with that of the Whig and Democratic counties in the Assembly of 1834–35 shows that a large number of the counties which voted for Bell, in 1860, were Whig at an earlier date.

The Douglas Democrats stood for the doctrine of popular sovereignty as advocated by their leader and for the principles of 1798. They were devoted to the Union and were, almost without exception, opposed to the admission of Kansas under the Lecompton constitution. They were unable to increase their ranks, largely because of the fact that they represented no sectional interest, because their leader was looked upon as responsible for the renewal of the sectional struggle between the North and the South, which was menacing the Union, and because of the custom then so prevalent in Virginia of adhering to party organization. It is significant that the votes given Douglas came largely from those counties where the local press broke the chain of political custom by supporting him. In each of the four counties carried by him, the local newspapers favored his election, and the *Richmond South*, which had formerly favored his nomination, but had ceased to be published, was largely instrumental in securing the very large vote given him in Richmond

City and Chesterfield County.[85] Had the Democratic press, which, as has been shown, was largely in the hands of pro-southern editors, given Douglas better support, thus removing the stigma of a breach of party faith and bringing his candidacy to the attention of the rural and non-slaveholding communities, there can be little doubt that he would have received a larger vote in the state. But, as it was, the Breckenridge Democrats had both the press and the political organization, which, at this time, were all-powerful in the state.

The Breckenridge Democrats professed to stand unitedly upon the doctrines of 1798. That the conservative, or western, and the radical, or eastern, wings of their party differed, however, in their respective interpretations of those doctrines there can be no doubt. They were yet divided by the same differences as had existed in the party, when Letcher and Brockenbrough, Hunter and Wise had contended for its leadership. Possible explanations of why the western wing did not desert Breckenridge and support Douglas have been attempted. In addition it should be said that, as the representative of Henry Clay's old district in Congress and as the reputed heir to much of the Great Pacificator's conservatism, Breckenridge had long enjoyed great popularity in western Virginia.[86]

The supporters of Bell acted largely in the capacity of an opposition party, and their total vote, when com-

---

[85] Richmond City gave Douglas 753 votes, Chesterfield County 588. Roger A. Prior, who had edited the *Richmond South*, had now become joint editor of the *Washington States and Union*.

[86] *Kanawha Valley Star*, July 2, 1856.

pared with that given Douglas and Breckenridge, was no greater than their usual minority poll. So bitter was their feeling against the Democrats, of whatever type, that the *Richmond Whig,* their mouthpiece, pledged the Whigs to "support Seward a thousand times sooner than any Democrat, Northern or Southern, in the land."[87] Like the Breckenridge Democrats, the opposition party was divided into an eastern and western faction, both of which were, however, more conservative than the eastern wing of the Breckenridge party. The name applied to this new party, "Constitutional Union," together with the fact that it was the heir to the Whig traditions, is almost conclusive evidence that those who supported its candidates were, regardless of location, sincere in their devotion to the Union. But that the eastern and the western wings of this party differed in their respective interpretations of the term "constitutional union" almost as widely as did those of the Breckenridge Democrats in their interpretations of the doctrines of 1798 is certain.

As is frequently the case in political contests, so in this one: the party casting the smallest number of votes was an important one. In less than one year after this election took place more than one-half of the voters in what is now West Virginia had become Republicans. Consequently some space will be given to a consideration of what the Republican party in Virginia stood for in 1860. The Republican platform, adopted by a state convention which met at Wheeling,

[87] September 30, 1859.

May 2, 1860, repudiated both the old parties. It claimed that opposition was no longer necessary or advisable and that the Democratic party, under the leadership of Toombs, Yancey, and Davis, had ceased to be the party of "Old Hickory" and had become a "Southern-British-Antitariff-Disunion party." It alleged that the cotton-planters had made war upon the manufacturing interests and that they were seeking to drive manufacturers into the production of agricultural products that slave capital might be maintained more cheaply. It also alleged that slave capital had encroached upon the personal rights of the free white men of the west, the farmers and artisans there being weighed down with capitation, income, license, and various other forms of taxes to be used for the construction of works of internal improvement in the east in order that the products of slave labor might find an easy market, while slave property was practically privileged, paying only $300,000 taxes annually when it should pay $3,000,000; that the products of slave labor, tobacco, corn, wheat, and oats were exempt from taxation, whereas the products of white labor, cattle, hogs, sheep, and horses were taxed; that whereas a negro slave under the age of twelve was regarded as privileged property, and as such exempt from taxation, colts, calves, lambs, and pigs were listed; and that whereas the slave-owner paid only $1.20 taxes annually on a slave valued at $1,200 or more, the small merchant with a capital of $600 was made to pay $60. This platform, as well as the various resolutions adopted by the local conventions of the Republicans, acknowledged the right of the slave-owner, under the laws of Virginia, to the peaceful possession of his property and pledged the Republicans to respect that right.[88] But when Francis H. Pierpoint and other Republican leaders stumped the counties of the northwest in behalf of their ticket, they carried with them tax receipts which they offered as evidence of the economic evils of negro slavery to western Virginia.[89] A casual study of the history of the formation of the Republican party in western Virginia will be sufficient to convince one that its origin was due more largely to a conflict of economic interests between the east and the west than to the existence in the latter section of theories regarding the equality of men or of feelings of love or even pity for the negro.

Neither the explanation of Mr. Rhodes, to the effect that the election of Lincoln was a triumph of the "noblest conservatism"[90] nor the other explanation more often given, and doubtless truer of the results in the country at large, that the election of 1860 resulted in a triumph for the radicals of both sections, those of the North being led by Lincoln and those of the South by Breckenridge, explains the result of the election of 1860 in Virginia. This is true, notwithstanding the fact that Virginia was in many respects a microcosm of the nation at that time. When considered from any standpoint, the election in Virginia

[88] *Wheeling Intelligencer*, May 3, 1860.

[89] *Ibid.*, April 7, 10, 1860; *ibid.*, May 22, 24, 29, 1860; *ibid.*, September 6, 1860.

[90] Rhodes, *History of the United States*, II, 502.

was a decided victory for conservatism. True, the active germs of radicalism of much the same varieties as had contested in the nation at large were present in the handful of Republicans at the northwest and in the pro-southern wing of the Breckenridge party, confined for the most part to the east. But the Republican party was small and the pro-southern wing of the Democratic party was not a much greater factor than it had been in the political contests immediately preceding the election of 1860. That the western wing of the Breckenridge party acted conservatively and out of devotion to the Union there can be no doubt, because those counties of the northwest which gave Breckenridge almost their entire vote had within less than two years almost as many soldiers in the Union army as they had polled votes in 1860. That the voters in the other leading parties were actuated by a devotion to the Union and by conservatism will hardly be questioned.

Notwithstanding the fact that the Union was a subject of important consideration and the verdict of each of the political parties was in favor of its preservation, a close study of the election of 1860 in Virginia reveals another fact, namely, that state rights was a subject of almost equal importance. The Constitutional Union party defended the Union of the fathers, the Breckenridge party the doctrines of 1798, and each of the other parties insisted that the states had powers which the federal government could not exercise. That the east and the west differed in their respective theories as to where the ultimate sovereignty resides has been repeatedly shown in this study. Doubtless the east believed the states sovereign and "in duty bound" to protect their rights and defend their territory. But the diversity of opinion as to the nature of the federal government was so great even there and the devotion to the Union so strong that the inhabitants of this section had never been able to agree upon a means for protecting their rights. Some refused to recognize that rights had been infringed in a given case, others insisted on fighting in the Union, others on the right of a state to nullify federal laws, and still others on the constitutional right of peaceful secession. But, when it came to the question of defending the state's territory, these differences of opinion immediately crystallized and the east presented a united front to defend the sovereignty of the state. On the other hand, the inhabitants of the west had never doubted the ultimate sovereignty of the federal Union. Thus when it came to a choice of allying themselves with the Union or the state in a contest to determine the ultimate sovereign, they too did not hesitate as to their course.

After Lincoln's election, the consequent secession of the southern states, and the threatened resort to force on the part of both the Union and the seceding states the east and the west, each standing for their respective theories regarding the nature of the federal Union, struggled for control of the state with unexampled vigor. The west fought for delay, opposing the proposed extra session of the Assembly and a constitutional convention, but the east held out and secured both. While these bodies deliberated, the germ of radicalism in the handful of Republicans at the northwest fed upon the discontent occasioned by the conflicts between the churches, the inadequate facilities for internal communication and education, and the burden of unjust taxation and, throughout the district already prepared by the Letcher-Goggin campaign of 1859, grew into a formidable party organization resolved to stand by the Union. On the other hand, that germ of radicalism in the eastern wing of the Breckenridge party, which had maintained a precarious existence upon the movement for a united South and the inspiration of Wise, Ruffin, and others, was now resuscitated and developed into a well-organized party of much greater vitality than its eastern prototypes of 1798, 1832, and 1850. Under the influence of later events it was impossible to prevent a clash between these two parties; but it is not the purpose of this study to enter into a discussion of the consequences, to show how the advocates of state sovereignty carried Virginia out of the Union, and the radicals of the northwest in turn dismembered the "Mother of Commonwealths."

BIBLIOGRAPHY

There are no general or local histories of much value for the study of that part of Virginia's history treated in this monograph. It is necessary to rely almost wholly upon state and federal public documents and the newspapers. The principal sources used in this study may be divided as follows:

I. GENERAL AND LOCAL HISTORIES OF VIRGINIA

1. BROWN, ALEXANDER. The Genesis of the United States. 2 vols. Boston, 1890.
2. ———. The First Republic in America. Boston, 1898.
3. BRUCE, PHILIP ALEXANDER. Economic History of Virginia in the Seventeenth Century. 2 vols. New York, 1896.
4. ———. Social Life in Virginia in the Seventeenth Century. Richmond, 1907.
5. CAMPBELL, CHARLES. Introduction to the History of the Colony and Ancient Dominion of Virginia. Richmond, 1847.
6. DODDRIDGE, REV. JOSEPH. Notes on the Settlement and Indian Wars of the Western Part of Virginia and Pennsylvania. Wellsburg, Va., 1824.
7. FOOTE, WILLIAM HENRY. Sketches of Virginia, Historical and Biographical. 2 vols. Philadelphia, 1850.
8. HOWISON, ROBERT REID. A History of Virginia from Its Discovery and Settlement by Europeans to the Present Time. 2 vols. Philadelphia, 1848.
9. HOWE, HENRY. Historical Collections of Virginia. Charleston, S. C., 1852.
10. JEFFERSON, THOMAS. Notes on the State of Virginia. Philadelphia (ed. 1801.)
11. JOHNSON, DAVID E. A History of the Middle New River Settlements and Contiguous Territory. Huntington, W. Va., 1906.

12. KERCHEVAL, SAMUEL. A History of the Valley of Virginia. Winchester, Va., 1833.

II. SPECIAL MONOGRAPHS, ARTICLES, AND WORKS

1. ADAMS, HERBERT BAXTER. Thomas Jefferson and the University of Virginia, with Sketches of Other Colleges in Virginia. Washington, 1888.
2. ANDERSON, FRANK MALOY. Virginia and Kentucky Resolutions. Printed in the American Historical Review, Vol. V.
3. CHANDLER, J. A. C. History of Representation in Virginia. Printed in the Johns Hopkins University Studies, Vol. XIV.
4. ———. History of Suffrage in Virginia. Printed in the Johns Hopkins University Studies, Vol. XIX.
5. COLLINS, WINGFIELD HAZLITT. Domestic Slave Trade in the United States. New York, 1904.
6. DODD, WILLIAM E. Chief Justice Marshall and Virginia. Printed in the American Historical Review, Vol. XII.
7. GOOCH, —. —. Prize Essay on Agriculture. Printed in the Lynchburg Virginian, July 4, 1833.
8. GRIGSBY, HUGH BLAIR. Virginia Convention of 1829–30. Richmond, 1854.
9. ———. The Virginia Convention of 1776. Richmond, 1855.
10. ———. History of the Federal Convention of 1788. Printed in the Virginia Historical Collection (New Series), Vols. IX and X.
11. HASKINS, CHARLES H. The Yazoo Land Company, 1891. Printed in the American Historical Association Papers, Vol. IV, No. 4.
12. HULBERT, ARCHER BUTLER. The Old National Road. Columbus, Ohio, 1901.
13. ———. Washington and the West. New York, 1905.
14. HUNT, GAILLARD. James Madison and Religious Liberty. Printed in the American Historical Association Report, 1901, Vol. I.
15. KUHN, OSCAR. German and Swiss Settlements of Colonial Pennsylvania. New York, 1901.
16. PARTON, JAMES. Thomas Jefferson a Reformer of Old Virginia. Printed in Atlantic Monthly, July, 1872.

17. PHILLIPS, ULRICH B. Origin and Growth of Southern Black Belts. 1906. Printed in American Historical Review, Vol. XI.
18. RUFFNER, W. H. The Public School System. Printed in the Richmond Enquirer, May 12, 1876.
19. SCHURICHT, HERMANN. History of the German Element in Virginia. Baltimore, 1898–1900. Printed in the Annual Report of the Society for the History of the Germans in Maryland.
20. SLAUGHTER, PHILIP. The Virginia History of African Colonization. Richmond, 1855.
21. STANWOOD, EDWARD. A History of the Presidency. Boston, 1906.
22. ———. American Tariff Controversies in the Nineteenth Century. Boston and New York, 1903.
23. TREMAIN, MARY. Slavery in the District of Columbia. New York, 1892.
24. WINSOR, JUSTIN. The Westward Movement. Boston, 1897.

III. PAMPHLETS AND SPEECHES

It is impossible in every case to determine the date and place of publication of pamphlets.

1. BRODNAX, WILLIAM H. Speech Delivered in the Slavery Debate of 1831–32.
2. DEW, W. R. Review of the Debates on the Abolition of Slavery, in the Legislature of Virginia, in the Winter of 1831 and 1832. Richmond, 1832.
3. GOODE, WILLIAM O. Speech in the Virginia Legislature of 1831–32. Richmond, 1832.
4. HARRISON, JESSE BURTON. Review of the Speech of Thomas Marshall, in the House of Delegates of Virginia, on the Abolition of Slavery. 1832. Printed in the American Quarterly Review (December, 1832), and in the African Repository (March, 1833).
5. JOHNSON, CHAPMAN. Oration on the Late Treaty with France. Staunton, Va., 1804.
6. MCDOWELL, JAMES. Speech in the Legislature of 1831–32. Richmond, 1832.

7. MORRIS, R. G. Speech on Internal Improvement. Delivered at White Sulphur Springs, 1854.
8. RUFFNER, HENRY. An Address to the People of Virginia by a Slaveholder of West Virginia. Reprinted, 1862, at Wheeling, W. Va.
9. SEGAR, JOSEPH. Speech Delivered at White Sulphur Springs, 1854.
10. SMITH, WESLEY. Defense of the Methodist Episcopal Church. To be found in the office of the Pittsburg Christian Advocate, Pittsburg, Pa.
11. WILLEY, WAITMAN T. Speech Delivered in the Constitutional Convention of 1850–51. Richmond, 1851. In the Library of the West Virginia University, Morgantown, W. Va.

IV. BIOGRAPHIES, MEMOIRS, AND LETTERS OF CONTEMPORARIES

1. ADAMS, CHARLES FRANCIS. Memoirs of John Quincy Adams. 12 vols. Philadelphia, 1874–77.
2. ADAMS, HENRY. Life of Albert Gallatin. Philadelphia, 1879.
3. ———. Writings of Albert Gallatin. 3 vols. Philadelphia, 1879.
4. ———. John Randolph. American Statesmen Series. Boston, 1883.
5. CALHOUN, JOHN CALDWELL. Correspondence of John C. Calhoun, edited by J. F. Jameson. Printed in the Report of the American Historical Association for 1899. 2 vols. Washington, 1901.
6. CUTLER, JULIA P. Life and Times of Ephraim Cutler. Cincinnati, 1890.
7. CURTIS, WILLIAM E. The True Thomas Jefferson. Philadelphia, 1901.
8. FORD, PAUL LEICESTER. The Writings of Thomas Jefferson. 10 vols. New York, 1892–99.
9. FORD, WORTHINGTON C. The Writings of George Washington. 14 vols.
10. GARLAND, HUGH A. Life of John Randolph of Roanoke. 2 vols. New York, 1851.

11. HAMBLETON, JAMES P. A Biographical Sketch of Henry A. Wise with a History of the Political Campaign of 1855. Richmond, 1856.
12. HAMILTON, STANISLAUS MURRAY. Writings of James Monroe. 7 vols. New York, 1898–1903.
13. HENRY, WILLIAM WIRT. Patrick Henry, Life, Correspondence, and Speeches. 3 vols. New York, 1891.
14. HUNT, GAILLARD. Life of James Madison. New York, 1902.
15. ———. Writings of James Madison. 7 vols. New York, 1900–1908.
16. MARSHALL, THOMAS F. Speeches and Writings of T. F. Marshall, edited by W. L. Barre. Cincinnati, 1858.
17. RANDALL, HENRY STEPHENS. Life of Thomas Jefferson. 3 vols. New York, 1858.
18. RANDOLPH, JOHN. Letters to a Young Friend. Philadelphia, 1834.
19. RIVES, WILLIAM CABELL. History of the Life and Times of James Madison. 3 vols. Boston, 1866.
20. ———. The Journal of Thomas Walker.
21. ROWLAND, KATE MASON. The Life of George Mason, Including His Speeches, Public Papers, and Correspondence, with an Introduction by General Fitzhugh Lee. 2 vols. New York, 1892.
22. SEWARD, FREDERICK W. William H. Seward, an Autobiography. New York, 1891.
23. SMITH, MARGARET VOWELL. Virginia, 1492–1892. A Brief Review of the Discovery of the Continent of North America with a History of the Executives of the Colony and Commonwealth of Virginia. Washington, 1893.
24. SPARKS, JARED. The Writings of George Washington. 12 vols. Boston, 1855.
25. SPOTSWOOD, ALEXANDER. Official Letters. Edited by R. A. Brock and Printed in the Virginia Historical Collections. New Series, Vols. I and II. Richmond, 1882–85.
26. TYLER, LYON G. Letters and Times of the Tylers. 3 vols. Richmond and Williamsburg, 1884–96.
27. TYLER, MOSES COIT. Patrick Henry. American Statesmen Series. Boston, 1887.

28. WIRT, WILLIAM. Sketch of the Life and Character of Patrick Henry. Ninth edition. Philadelphia, 1838.
29. WISE, BARTON HAXALL. Life of Henry A. Wise of Virginia. New York, 1899.
30. WISE, HENRY ALEXANDER. Seven Decades of the Union. Richmond, 1881.

V. PUBLIC DOCUMENTS

A. OF THE UNITED STATES

1. Annals of Congress, 1789–1824. 42 vols. 1834–56.
2. Census Reports of the United States, 1800–1890.
3. COMMISSIONER OF EDUCATION. Biennial Reports, 1893–1901.
4. The Congressional Globe, containing the debates and proceedings of Congress, 1834–73. 108 vols.
5. ELLIOT, JONATHAN. Debates in the Several State Conventions on the Adoption of the Federal Constitution. 4 vols. Washington, 1845.
6. Journals of Congress. Secret Journals of the Continental Congress and Journals, 1789–1860.
7. POORE, BENJAMIN PERLEY. Federal and State Constitutions, Colonial Charters and Other Original Laws. 2 vols. Washington, 1872.
8. Register of Debates of Congress, 1825–37. 39 vols.
9. State Papers of the Federal Congress, 1789–1860.
10. Wheaton, Reports of Decisions in the Supreme Court of the United States, 1817–28. 12 vols. Notes by R. B. Curtis. 5th ed. Boston, 1870.

B. OF VIRGINIA

1. BOARD OF PUBLIC WORKS. Annual and Biennial Reports. 1816–60.
2. Case Briefs in Church Law Suits. *Sites* v. *Plecker* and *Plecker* v. *Harrison*. Pamphlets in the Department of Archives and History, Charleston, W. Va.
3. Calendar of Virginia State Papers, 1781–1869. 11 vols. Richmond, 1875.
4. Debates and Proceedings on the Resolutions of 1798. Richmond, 1835.

5. GRATTAN, PEACHY R. Report of Cases Decided in the Supreme Court of Appeals of Virginia, 1844–60. 15 vols. Richmond.
6. Documents of the House and Senate of the General Assembly from 1789–1860.
7. JAMES RIVER AND KANAWHA COMPANY. Annual Reports, 1835–60.
8. Journals of the House of Delegates, 1776–1861.
9. Journals of the House of Burgesses, 1761–76. Edited by John Pendleton Kennedy. 4. vols. Richmond, 1905–7.
10. Journal of the Constitutional Convention of 1850–51.
11. Proceedings and Debates of the Virginia Constitutional Convention of 1829–30. Richmond, 1830.
12. MUMFORD, WILLIAM. Report of Cases Decided in the Supreme Court of Appeals of Virginia, 1810–21. 6 vols. New York and Richmond.

C. OF WEST VIRGINIA

1. HAGAN, JOHN MARSHALL. Report of Cases in the Supreme Court of Appeals. 3 vols. Reprinted, Wheeling, 1899–1900.

VI. LAWS OF VIRGINIA

1. Acts of the General Assembly, 1776–1860.
2. HENING, WILLIAM WALLER. Statutes at Large, Being a Collection of All the Laws of Virginia from the First Session of the Legislature to 1792. 13 vols.
3. Revised Code of 1819. 2 vols.
4. Code of 1849. 2 vols. Richmond, 1849.
5. SHEPHERD, SAMUEL. The Statutes at Large of Virginia from the October Session, 1792, to the December Session, 1806. 3 vols. Richmond, 1835.

VII. CHURCH HISTORIES, PAPERS, AND MONOGRAPHS ON CHURCH HISTORY

1. BEALE, G. W. Revised edition of Semple's History of the Rise and Progress of the Baptists in Virginia. Richmond, 1894.
2. Debates in the General Conference of the Methodist Episcopal Church, 1844.
3. Journals of the General Conferences of the Methodist Episcopal Church, 1832–60.

4. MATLACK, LUCIUS C. The Anti-Slavery Struggle and the Triumph of the Methodist Episcopal Church. New York, 1881.
5. MEADE, WILLIAM. Old Churches, Ministers, and Families of Virginia. 2 vols. Philadelphia, 1891.
6. SEMPLE, ROBERT B. History of the Rise and Progress of the Baptists in Virginia, Richmond, 1810.

VIII. MANUSCRIPTS

1. Biggs Papers, in the Draper Manuscripts. Historical Library, Madison, Wis.
2. Land Books of Kanawha County. In the office of the County Clerk of Kanawha County, Charleston, W. Va.
3. File of papers in the Parkersburg Church case, *T. A. Cook* v. *L. P. Neal.* In the office of the Circuit Clerk of Wood County, Parkersburg, W. Va.
4. Pay-Rolls of the Members of the General Assembly of Virginia before 1828. In the State Library at Richmond.

IX. MISCELLANEOUS

1. BANCROFT, GEORGE. History of the United States. 10 vols. Boston, 1857–74.
2. ELLIOTT, W. M., AND W. A. R. NYE. Virginia Directory and Business Register for 1852. Richmond, 1852.
3. HUDSON, FREDERICK. History of Journalism in the United States, 1690–1871. New York, 1873.
4. MACLAY, WILLIAM. Journal of William Maclay, United States Senator from Pennsylvania. Edited by E. S. Maclay. New York, 1890.
5. MARTIN, JOSEPH. A New and Comprehensive Gazetteer of Virginia and the District of Columbia. Charlottesville, Va., 1835.
6. Marietta College Catalogues, 1831–60.
7. Report of the Committee on Roads and Internal Improvements Made to the General Assembly of 1831–32.
8. Tribune Almanac and Political Register, 1856–61. New York. Published annually.

BIBLIOGRAPHY 347

9. Whig Almanacs and the United States Register, 1843–55. New York. Published annually.

X. NEWSPAPERS, MAGAZINES, AND PERIODICALS

A. FILES IN THE STATE HISTORICAL LIBRARY AT RICHMOND, VA.

1. Branch Papers. Vols. I and III. Publication of Randolph-Macon College.
2. Richmond Compiler, 1832–34.
3. Richmond Enquirer, 1804–60.

The file in the Virginia library is not complete, but it may be made practically complete when supplemented by the files in the Historical Library at Madison, Wis., and those in the Department of Archives and History, Charleston, W. Va.

4. Richmond Examiner, 1858–59.
5. Richmond South, a few numbers for 1858.
6. Richmond Times, 1850–60.
7. Richmond Whig, practically complete files 1830–60.
8. Virginia Historical Magazine, Vols. I–XIII.
9. The Virginia Magazine of History and Bibliography. Vols. I–XIV.
10. William and Mary College Quarterly, Vols. I–XVII.

B. FILES IN THE OFFICE OF THE "RICHMOND CHRISTIAN ADVOCATE"

1. The Richmond Christian Advocate, 1850–60.

C. FILES IN THE STATE HISTORICAL LIBRARY, MADISON, WIS.

1. Alexandria Daily Gazette, July to December, 1810.
2. Alexandria Herald, June, 1811, to June, 1812; June, 1815, to May, 1819; June, 1821, to May, 1824; June, 1825, to May, 1826.
3. American Quarterly Review, for 1831 and 1832.
4. Baltimore American and Commercial Advertiser, January to June, 1806; June to December, 1810; January to February, 1811; January to June, 1814.
5. HUNT, FREEMAN. The Merchant's Magazine, 1839–60. 42 vols. Published at New York.
6. DEBOW, J. P. B. Review and Industrial Resources, Statistics, etc., 1846–61. 31 vols. Published at New Orleans.

7. Federal Intelligencer and Baltimore Daily Gazette, November to December, 1794; July to December, 1795.
8. Federal Gazette and Baltimore Daily Advertiser, 1796; January to June, 1797; August to December, 1799; 1801; January to June, 1803; January to June, 1804; November to December, 1808.
9. Loudoun's Register, 1793; January to June, October to December, 1794.
10. National Intelligencer. Practically complete files, including daily, tri-weekly, and weekly, 1802–61.
11. National Republican and Ohio Political Register, 1823 and 1824; 1825–30. Published at Cincinnati.
12. Niles Weekly Register, September, 1811, to June, 1849. 75 vols. Published at Baltimore.
13. The Palladium. August, 1798, to June, 1801. Frankfort, Ky.
14. The Southern Literary Messenger, 1834–60. 50 vols.
15. The Virginia Northwestern Gazette, April, 1818, to October, 1820. Published at Wheeling, W. Va.
16. Virginia Gazette, 1775; January to September, 1775. Published at Williamsburg, Va.
17. Virginia Argus, November, 1804, to December, 1807; January, 1808, to October, 1811.
18. Washington and Lee Historical Papers, Nos. I–V inclusive.
19. Western Spy, July, 1814, to December, 1822. Published at Cincinnati, Ohio.

D. FILES IN THE DEPARTMENT OF ARCHIVES AND HISTORY, CHARLESTON, W. VA.

1. Kanawha Banner, 1830–33. Published at Charleston, W. Va.
2. Kanawha Valley Star, 1855–61. Published at Charleston, W. Va.
3. Kanawha Republican, 1841–44. Published at Charleston, W. Va.

This was possibly the best newspaper published in trans-Alleghany Virginia prior to the Civil War. It continued to be published until the Civil War.

4. Star of the Kanawha Valley, 1850–55. Published at Buffalo, Va.

BIBLIOGRAPHY

5. Wheeling Intelligencer, 1851–61.
   After 1856 this was a Republican newspaper.

E. FILES IN THE OFFICE OF THE "PARKERSBURG GAZETTE," PARKERSBURG, W. VA.

1. Parkersburg News, 1850–54.
2. Parkersburg Gazette, 1856–61.

F. FILES IN THE OFFICE OF THE "PITTSBURG CHRISTIAN ADVOCATE"

1. The Pittsburg Christian Advocate, 1852–61.

G. FILES IN PRIVATE COLLECTIONS

1. Guyandotte Chronicle, 1856. Published at Guyandotte, W. Va.
2. Harrisonburg Republican.
3. Wellsburg Herald, 1858–61.
   This was a Republican newspaper published at Wellsburg, W. Va.
4. Wheeling Gazette, 1822 and 1823.

INDEX

INDEX

Abolitionists: unpopularity of, 225; danger to the Union, 226; threatened by eastern prints, 310.

Adams, John, breach with Hamilton, 75.

Adams, J. Q.: and Chesapeake and Ohio Canal, 126; in campaign of 1824, 127; interest in Virginia politics, 132-33.

Agriculture: societies formed, 114; opposed abolition, 225.

"Agricola," essays of, 211.

American system: opposed in eastern Virginia, 115-16; attitude of the west toward, 118; opposition of east increases, 119-20; arguments against tariff of 1824, 120; denounced by the General Assembly, 121; interest of western salt-makers in, 121-22; tariff of 1828, 122; influence of Virginia statesmen, 150; effect on internal improvements, 1829-33, 175; devotion of west to, 202; surrender by Clay, 219.

Andrew, Bishop James O., a slave-owner, 286.

Anti-Federalists: arguments of, 56-57; control Assembly of 1789-90, 59; loss of political control, 60.

Archer, W. S.: arguments on internal improvements, 176; orthodox Whig, 230.

Assumption of state debts, opposed by Virginia, 62.

Augusta County, petition on abolition, 189.

Baltimore: market of the Valley, 16; commercial rival of Richmond, 175.

Baltimore and Ohio R.R. Co. *See* Railroads.

Banks: U.S. Bank favored in eastern Virginia, 220; subject of sectional strife, 237-40; independent banks incorporated, 300.

Bank of United States, desired by Federalists, 91.

Barbour, James, U.S. senator and friend of Adams, 127.

Barbour, J. S., position on Nullification, 210.

Barbour, P. P.: member of Congress, 101; member of convention of 1829-30, 145; on representation in convention, 160; speech on internal improvements, 176; candidate for vice-presidency, 206; Democratic leader, 222.

Battelle, Rev. Gordon, position of, on negro slavery, 294.

Bell, John, candidate for presidency, 330.

Bill of Rights: work of Mason, 28; opposed by conservatives, 29; attempt to amend, 148; text of reformers, 149; little considered in 1850, 268; popular in western Virginia, 255.

Blackstone: effect of, upon young men, 20; on rights of aliens, 71.

Board of Public Works: incorporated, 105; members made elective by popular vote, 266.

Bonus bill, favored by Federalists, 98-99.

353

Border states: church controversies in, 283; attitude toward negro slavery, 285.

Botts, John Minor, member of convention of 1850–51, 263.

Braxton, Carter, opposed to Bill of Rights, 29.

Breckenridge, John C.: candidate for presidency, 330; position of party in Virginia, 332.

Brockenbrough, John W., candidate for governor in 1859, 319.

Brodnax, W. H., on evil effects of slavery, 194.

Brooks, Elisha, salt manufacturer, 84.

Brown, John, effect of Raid on Virginia politics, 329.

Buffalo and New Orleans Turnpike: arguments pro and con, 175–77; bill for, defeated, 177.

Calhoun, J. C.: author of Bonus bill, 98; unpopular in Virginia in 1824, 128; influence on Virginia leaders, 150–51; letter on formation of Whig party, 221; influence on Virginians, 225–29; favored for presidency in 1844, 233; reconciled to Ritchie, 235; opposition to war with Mexico, 236; triumph in Virginia politics, 236; displaced Jefferson in east, 270.

Campbell, Alexander: speech on Bill of Rights, 148–49; on theories of government, 154–55; efforts in behalf of free schools, 273.

Cass, Lewis, popular in western Virginia, 237.

Caucus, congressional, nominated Crawford in 1824, 131.

Charles City County, abolition petition, 190.

Chesapeake and Ohio Canal Co. *See* Internal improvements.

Christian Advocate and Journal of Baltimore, indicted, 289.

Churches, and negro slavery, 282–86.

Clarksburg: reform convention of 1842, 254–55; educational convention of 1841, 276.

Clay, Henry: remarks on abolition of entail, 33; presidential candidate in 1824, 128; candidate for presidency, 1832, 205; popularity in west, 219; visits in western Virginia, 220; letter on formation of Whig party, 221; choice of west for president, 227.

Clemens, Sherrard: in duel with O. Jennings Wise, 321; popularity in western Virginia, 322.

Collins, Rev. J. A.: opposition to negro slavery, 284–85; changed attitude toward slavery, 294.

Commerce, British restrictions of, 48–49; interest of the Tidewater in, 48–49; activity in, 82.

Commercial conventions: interest in education, 279; forerunners of Confederacy, 308; unpopular in western Virginia, 309.

"Committee of Revision of 1776," *personnel* and work of, 34.

Compromise of 1850: reception in Virginia, 300; repudiated, 302.

Constitution of 1776, provisions of, 29–30.

Constitution of 1830: provisions of, 168; ratification of, 171–72; opposition to, in trans-Alleghany, 172–74; provisions for future representation, 253.

Constitution of 1851: provisions of, 264–68; opposed by east, 270; church property, 292.

Constitutional convention (Virginia), 1776: *personnel*, 25; work of, 26–27.

INDEX   355

Convention, constitutional, 1829–30: movement leading to, 137–43; popular vote on, 144; difficulty over basis of representation in, 144–45; *personnel* of, 145; national importance of, 146; met in Richmond, 147; classification of delegates, 149–51; compromise plans proposed, 163–66; *sine die* adjournment proposed, 164.

Convention, constitutional, 1850–51: bill passed, 260; first meeting, 261; debates of, 268–70; education discussed, 278.

Convention, federal, of 1787: originated in Virginia, 45–51; delegates to, 52; the "Virginia Plan," 52.

Convention of 1788: *personnel*, 53; sectional interests represented, 53; debates, 54–57; delegates from trans-Alleghany, 57–58.

Constitution, federal: interest of commerce in, 48–52; based on the "Virginia Plan," 52; interests and sections for and against, 53; ratification of, 58.

Cotton, attempts to grow, in Virginia, 114–15.

Cotton gin, effects of invention of, 110.

County courts, members of, appointed, 139.

Courts: conflict between state and federal, 103; Supreme Court of Virginia, decision in church cases, 290.

Crallé: editor of *Petersburg Jeffersonian*, a Nullification paper, 210; visits of, to western Virginia in 1850, 249.

Crawford, W. H., candidate for presidency, 127.

Cumberland Road: bill to establish, opposed in Virginia, 85; thoroughfare for immigrants, 117–18; vote on bill of 1822, 122.

Davies Samuel, pioneer teacher, 16.

Dawson, John: Republican leader in the trans-Alleghany, 71; vote on Cumberland Road bill, 85.

Declaration of Independence: interior for, 26–27; conservatives oppose, 27.

Democratic party: in 1834, 219; control of Assembly of 1835 by, 223; candidates in election of 1836, 228; breach following election of 1836, 228; in control of Assembly in 1841, 232; bank legislation, 238; internal improvement legislation, 240; strongholds, 257; convention of 1852, 302; successes of, in 1852, 303; conservatives and radicals, 306; successes in 1857, 308; campaigns of 1859–60, 319 ff.

Democratic Republican party: founded, 63; in campaign of 1798–99, 77; in control of Virginia Assembly, 80.

Dew, Thomas R., essay on negro slavery, 201.

Disestablishment. *See* Religious liberty.

Dismemberment of Union: denounced in western Virginia, 309; regarded as inevitable, 315.

Dismemberment of Virginia: proposed in 1796 and 1816, 94; talked of in convention of 1829–30, 166; movement for, in western Virginia, 167; talk of, in 1829–33, 177; slavery a cause of, 198; discussed by John Tyler, 205; threatened in 1842, 255; and Methodist Episcopal church, 298–99; cause of, 338.

Dissenters: protests against corruption in church by, 17; persecuted, 21; for religious liberty, 32; Hanover Presbytery, 32; opposed to the general assessment bill, 40.

Doddridge, Philip: member of convention of 1829-30, 145; for white basis, 147; contemplated leaving convention of 1829-30, 164.

Domestic slave trade: effects of, in 1830, 187; extent of, 194.

Douglas, Stephen A.: candidate for presidency, 330; position of party in Virginia, 331.

Duncan, Judge E. S., remarks upon university, 276.

Eaton, Major, president of Chesapeake and Ohio Canal Co., 184.

Education: influence of Princeton and Yale on, 16; founding of Washington and Lee and Hampden-Sidney, 16; "Aldermanic System," 273; free common schools, 274; conventions, 276; legislation of 1846, 278.

Elections, congressional: of 1817, 101; of 1829 and 1831, 204; of 1833, 218.

Elections, presidential: of 1800-1801, 78-80; of 1808, 88-90; of 1824-28, 127-36; map showing vote of 1824 in, 132; vote in election of 1828, 135; election of 1832, 205; of 1836, 227; of 1840, 231; of 1844, 234; of 1848, 237; of 1860, 330.

Embargo, opposed by "Quids" and Federalists, 87-88.

Enquirer, Richmond: favored Crawford's candidacy in 1824, 129; opposed Calhoun, 233; on preservation of the Union, 246, 249; on development of trans-Alleghany, 252.

Entail and primogeniture, abolished, 33.

Episcopal church: influence of, in the Tidewater, 9; decline of, 17; opposed disestablishment, 32.

Era of good feeling, effect on Virginia, 100.

Faulkner, C. J.: distrusted in eastern Virginia, 198; opposed abolition, 226; minister to France, 317.

Fauquier, Governor, influence of, 17.

Federalists: on the ratification of the federal Constitution, 54-57; Hamiltonian Federalists, 63; strength in the northwest of, 64; losses of, in the trans-Alleghany, 65; in 1798-99, 75-76; successes by, in elections of 1799, 77; opposed Jefferson, 80; opposed Louisiana Purchase, 81; opposition of, to commercial restrictions, 86-88, congressional election of 1809, 90; congressional election of 1811, 91-92; opposed to second war with Great Britain, 92; a strong party in 1813, 93; death of the party, 96-97.

Flournoy, Thos. S., Whig candidate for governor, 305.

Floyd, John: member of Congress, 101; an expansionist, 116; governor of Virginia and remarks on Turner insurrection, 188; message to Assembly regarding Nullification, 215.

Force bill, effect of, on eastern Virginia, 214-15.

France: war with, 65-68; peace with, 75; W. B. Preston agent to, 316; Franco-Virginia steamship line, 317.

Free negroes, attempt to remove from the state, 200.

French Revolution, influence of, upon Virginia, 153-54.

Fugitive slaves, feeling in western Virginia on escape of, 109.

INDEX

Gallatin, Albert: influence of, in the trans-Alleghany, 65; *Report* of 1807, 85.

General assessment bill: proposed, 39; theme of general discussion, 40–41; opposed by Madison, 40.

General survey bill of 1824, opposed by east, 124.

Genet, attack by, upon Washington, 64.

Germans: settlement of, in the Valley, 13; in the trans-Alleghany, 252; adhere to Democratic party, 293, 304.

Giles, W. B.: opposed the war with France, 65–66; member of convention of 1829–30, 145; on theories of government, 152; basis of representation, 153; remarks of, on dismemberment, 166.

Gilmer, T. W.: strict constructionist, 206; orthodox Whig, 230.

Goggin, Wm. L., candidate for governor, 323–24.

Goode, W. O.: opposed to abolition, 190; speech of, against abolition, 194; member of convention of 1850–51, 267.

Gordon, Wm. F.: on guarantee for protection of slave property, 159; plan of compromise in convention of 1829–30, 163; on Nullification, 210; a Democrat, 229.

Governor's Council, unsatisfactory, 139.

Graham, Archibald, letter of, on Nullification, 214.

Grayson, William, an anti-Federalist, 56, 57.

Grigsby, H. B.: on constitutional convention of 1776, 25; *personnel* of convention of 1788, 57; member of convention of 1829–30, 165.

Hamilton, Alexander: secretary of Treasury, 61; plans opposed by Jefferson and Madison, 62–63; war with France, 66.

Harrisburg Convention, of 1827, Virginians in, 121.

Harding, Rev. John A., suspended by Baltimore Conference, 284.

Harrison, Jesse Burton, essay of, on negro slavery, 201.

Harrison, W. H., choice of west for presidency, 227.

Harrisonburg Republican, on secession, 247.

Henry, Patrick: leader of the west, 17; member of House of Burgesses, 18–19; for independence, 26; in the convention of 1776, 27; Bill of Rights, 28; alienated from Jefferson, 34; member of Anglican church, 39; again leader of the west, 50, 54; an anti-Federalist, 56; a Federalist, 75.

Hunter, R. M. T.: influenced by Calhoun, 151, 225; became member of Democratic party, 229; favored Calhoun for presidency, 233; elected to U.S. Senate, 235–36; internal improvement policy, 243; re-elected to U.S. Senate, 300; as a conservative, 306; favored Letcher for governor, 320; candidate for presidency, 326.

Impending Crisis (Helper's), popular in western Virginia, 186.

Internal improvements: interest of the interior in, 22; means of connecting east and west, 46–48; Potomac and James River Canal companies incorporated, 48; interest following second war with Great Britain, 93–94; nationalistic tendencies of the west, 97; Virginia Asesmbly on, 98; by federal government, 105; rights of James River Company purchased by state, 106; surveys on upper Potomac, 107; interest in, along the Potomac, 122; incorporation of Chesapeake and Ohio Canal Company, 123; sectional jealousies, 123–24; interest in railroad building, 124–25; opposition in the east to Baltimore and Ohio Railroad and to Chesapeake and Ohio Canal, 125–26; surveys in the west, 126–27; influence on election of 1828, 132; activity in western Virginia, 175 ff.; railroad vs. canal, 179; James River and Kanawha Company incorporated, 182; Jackson and Chesapeake and Ohio Canal, 184; internal improvement legislation, 1833–50, 240–43; legislation following 1850, 300; legislation in Wise's administration, 311; sectional jealousies, 313; Kanawha Board incorporated, 315; appropriations in 1857–58, 315; appropriations in 1859–60, 317; Virginia Canal Company incorporated, 318; condition in western Virginia in 1860, 319. *See also* Railroads.

Irish: settlement of, in Valley, 13; adhere to Democratic party, 293, 304.

Jackson, Andrew: presidential candidate, 128–30; internal improvement policy, 1829–33, 175; veto of Maysville Turnpike bill, 177; popularity of, in western Virginia, 178; hostility of, to C. F. Mercer, 184; re-elected president, 205; proclamation of, 209.

Jackson, George: a Federalist in 1788, 58; elected to Congress, 65.

Jackson, J. G.: Republican leader in the trans-Alleghany, 71; vote of, on Cumberland Road bill, 85.

James River Company. *See* Internal improvements.

James River and Kanawha Company. *See* Internal improvements.

Jay treaty, opposition to, 63.

Jefferson, Thomas: in 1765, 20; leader of reform movement, 30–33; governor of Virginia, 35; author of *Notes on Virginia*, 36; influenced land legislation, 43; opposition of, to Hamilton, 62; Virginia and Kentucky Resolutions, 67; remarks of, on election of 1799, 77–78; elected president, 79; breach with Randolph, 86; letter of, to Samuel Kercheval, 95; on Missouri Compromise, 108; mortgaged Monticello, 112; on tariff of 1824, 120; favored constitutional convention, 142; abolition doctrines of, 185; *post nati* plan to abolish slavery, 191; displaced by Calhoun, 270; repudiated by east, 309.

Johnson, Chapman: oration of, on purchase of Louisiana, 81; member of convention of 1829–30, 145.

Johnson, Joseph: favored Survey Act, 134; governor of Virginia, 262; commuted sentence of Jordon Hatcher, 271; re-elected governor, 300; message of, in 1855, 301.

Johnson, R. M.: unpopular in Virginia, 228; opposed for vice-president in 1840, 231.

Kanawha Banner: on internal improvements, 181; salt industry, 204.

Kanawha Republican: opposed secession, 247; favored dismemberment, 255.

Kanawha Valley (Great): interest of, in internal improvements

INDEX 359

178; dissatisfaction in, 302; interest of, in river navigation, 314.

Know-Nothings: attacked Methodists, 293; factor in politics, 303.

Land companies and grants: Indiana and Vandalia companies, 43; Virginia's liberality to, 44; retarded development of west, 45; opposed to federal Constitution, 56; opposed Marshall's decisions, 103.

Land Office, established in 1779, 44.

Leake, Shelton F., candidate for governor, 306.

Lee, Richard Henry, friend to Anglican church, 39.

Leesburg Washingtonian, on secession, 247.

Leigh, Benjamin Watkins: remarks of, on taxation, 141; member of convention of 1829–30, 145; for mixed basis, 147; political theories, 151–52; condemned federal system of taxation, 155; compared general suffrage with plagues, 162; submitted compromise in convention of 1829–30, 163; remarks of, on dismemberment of Virginia, 166; elected to United States Senate, 221; re-elected, 222; resigned, 224; orthodox Whig, 230.

Letcher, John: indorsed Ruffner pamphlet, 244; candidate for governor, 320; elected, 323.

Lewis, Joseph, Federalist member of Congress, 80.

Lewisburg: convention of 1844, 241; convention of 1842, 256.

Lincoln, Abraham, candidate for presidency, 330.

Literary Fund, use of income, 273; appropriation to free schools, 274.

Loudoun County, and abolition, 189.

Loria, opinion of, on slavery, 186.

Louisiana, purchase of, 81; effect on Virginia politics, 81–82.

Loyalists, location and members, 25.

Lynchburg Virginian: on secession, 211; opposed Calhoun, 226; remarks on Compromise of 1850, 302.

Madison, James: leader of reforms, 38; and commerce, 49–50; a Federalist, 58; opposition of, to Hamilton, 62; Virginia and Kentucky Resolutions, 67; *Report* of 1799, 72, 78; hated by Randolph, 86; elected president, 89; financial embarrassments of, 112; president of agricultural society, 114; on the effect of immigrations, 116; on tariff of 1824, 121; on negro slavery, 142; member of convention of 1829–30, 145; on white and mixed basis, 147; conservative attitude of, in convention of 1829–30, 165; abolition doctrines of, 185; reply of, to Dew, 202.

Madisonian: newspaper founded, 229; organ of third party, 231.

Marion County, Boothsville Resolutions, 296.

Marshall, John: opposed disestablishment, 39; for ratification of federal Constitution, 55; leader of Federalist party, 75; commissioner to view western rivers, 98; member of convention of 1829–30, 145; submitted compromise in convention of 1829–30, 163; conservative attitude of, in convention of 1829–30, 165.

Marshall, Thomas: on industrial decline of the east, 111; on negro slavery, 193, 196; resolution of, on Nullification, 216.

Martin v. *Hunter, Lessee*, case of, in state and federal Supreme courts, 102–3.

Maryland: interest of, in commerce, 50; delegates of, in the Annapolis Convention, 51.

Mason, Armistead T.: defeated for election to Congress, 101; duel of, with J. M. McCarthy, 101.

Mason County, denounced secession, 248.

Mason, George: interested in western lands, 21; leader in convention of 1776, 27; author of Bill of Rights, 28; retired to private life, 30; opposed import duties, 42; an anti-Federalist, 56.

Mason, J. M.: elected to U.S. Senate, 236; re-elected, 300.

Mason, John Y., influenced by Calhoun, 151, 225.

Maysville, Turnpike bill for, considered, defeated, 177.

McCullough v. *Maryland*, decision in, unpopular, 104.

McGuffie, George, on Nullification, 210.

McDowell, James: on slavery, debate of 1831–32, 186; private property in unborn slaves, 195; speech of, on abolition, 197; activity of, in election of 1832, 207; member of Union party, 209; remarks of, on re-election of Leigh to United States Senate, 223; opposed to abolition, 226; suggested as governor of western Virginia, 255–56; governor of Virginia, 257.

Mercer, C. F.: for internal improvements by federal government, 100; on industrial decline of the east, 111; speech of, on behalf of Survey Act, 133; member of convention of 1829–30, 145; friend of internal improvements, 177; defeated for presidency of the Chesapeake and Ohio Canal Co., 184; political tour of western Virginia, 220.

Methodist Episcopal church: dissentions of, over slavery, 282–86; action of general conference of, on negro slavery, 284; fight of, for property and members in Border, 287–89; lawsuits of, 289–90; western Virginia, annual conference organized, 290; abolitionist agitation, 293; periodicals of, favor abolitionists, 294–95; negro slavery and Discipline, 297.

Methodist Episcopal Church, South: organization of, 286; fight of, for property and members in Border, 287–89; western Virginia annual conference organized, 291; denounces abolitionists, 295–97.

Mississippi River: free navigation of, 49; report of Jay-Gardoqui negotiations, 51.

Missouri Compromise, popular in Virginia, 107–8.

Monroe, James: and commerce, 49; governor of Virginia, 80; minister to England, 86; candidate for presidency in 1808, 89; financial embarrassments of, 112; veto of, of internal improvement bill of 1822, 122; "Views on the Subject of Internal Improvements," 124; on negro slavery, 141; member of convention of 1829–30, 145.

Moore, Samuel McDowell: speech of, on abolition, 197; on Nullification, 213; indorsed Ruffner pamphlet, 244.

Morgan, General Daniel, letter of, to General Benjamin Biggs, 73.

INDEX

Nashville Convention: delegates sent to it, 245; opposition to, 249.

National Republicans, in congressional elections of 1829 and 1831, 204.

Negro slavery: caused growth of plantations, 7; in the Piedmont, 8; failure in the Valley, 14–15; Methodists and Quakers opposed to, 41; introduced into trans-Alleghany, 45–46; attitude of west toward, in 1820, 108–9; retarded reforms, 140–41; in western Virginia, 156; a sectional issue, 185; increased interest of east in, 187; abolition movement of 1831, 189; moral issues in debate of 1831–32, 196; sectional feeling displayed in debates of 1831–32, 198; in District of Columbia, 224; a sectional issue, 244–50; factor in politics, 323.

New Englanders, for free schools, 274.

Newton, E. W.: editor of *Kanawha Republican*, 282; friend of common free schools, 282.

Newton, Thomas, for tariff of 1820, 119.

New York, commercial rival of Richmond, 175, 312.

Nicholas, George, favored religious liberty, 39.

Niles, Hezekiah: remarks of, on convention of 1829–30, 146; on internal improvements, 181; the American System, 202.

Norfolk: a commercial center, 181; control of local elections, 258; rival commercial center, 312.

Norfolk Herald, remarks of, on internal improvements, 243.

Northern Neck: location of, 11; inhabitants of, 12; conservatism of, 12–13; and the federal Constitution, 55; fears of secession of, from Virginia, 56; opposed Marshall's decisions, 103.

Notes on Virginia, written by Jefferson, 36.

Nullification: and bills for internal improvements, 177; effects of ordinance on, 209; position of eastern Virginia toward, 209–10; resolutions denouncing, 211–13; letters regarding, 213–14; and Resolutions of 1798, 216.

Page, John, defeated by Jefferson for governorship, 35.

Parker, Judge R. E., elected to United States Senate, 224.

Pennybacker, Isaac, elected to United States Senate, 235, 257.

Philadelphia, commercial rival of Richmond, 175, 312.

Piedmont: location and natural features of, 1; for revolt against England, 24; opposed alien and sedition laws, 67; wheat industry of, 81–82; decline of population in, 113; slaves and population of, in 1828, 113; interest of, in railroads, 181; opposition of, to abolition, 189; vote of, on abolition, 199; Nullification sentiment of, 214.

Plantation: beginnings of, 6–7; basis of society in east, 8; a self-sufficing institution, 11; in the Northern Neck, 12.

Pleasants, James: for local reforms, 142; member of State-Rights party, 209.

Political parties, in colonial times, 22–23.

Polk, James K.: candidate for vice-presidency in 1840, 231; elected to presidency, 234.

Potomac Company. *See* Internal improvements.

Powell, Leven, Federalist leader, 72.

Preston, W. B.: on abolition of slavery, 192; distrusted by eastern Virginia, 198; amendment of, for abolition defeated, 199; on formation of Whig party, 221; opposed abolition, 226; agent of Virginia in France, 316.

Pryor, Roger A.: influenced by Calhoun, 151; editor of *Richmond South*, 332.

"Quids": opposition party, 86; *personnel* of, 87; congressional election of 1809, 90; successes of, in congressional election of 1811, 91; defeat of the party, 93.

Railroads: Baltimore and Ohio Railroad Company incorporated, 124; effect of, on internal improvement policy, 175; enthusiasm for, in western Virginia, 179; taken up by east, 180; Staunton and Potomac Railroad Company incorporated, 180; Baltimore and Ohio Railroad Company's fight for charter, 180; Lynchburg and New River Railroad Co. incorporated, 181; Baltimore and Ohio Railroad Company's fight for a new charter, 241-42; Virginia and Tennessee Railroad, 243; influence of, on southwest, 302; Covington and Ohio Railroad, 311; route of Covington and Ohio Railroad, 313.

Randolph, John: founder of "Quid" party, 86; defeated for re-election to Congress, 93; on industrial decline of eastern Virginia, 111; admirer of Edmund Burke, 154; on Nullification, 215.

Randolph, Thomas J., for abolition of slavery, 191.

Randolph, Thomas M., vote of, on Cumberland Railroad bill, 85.

Randolph, Peyton: conservative, 20; friendly to federal Constitution, 55.

Reform movements: movement of 1765, 20-21; reforms of 1776, 30-34; reforms following peace of 1783, 38-42; movement of 1816, 94; Jefferson and, 95; following 1825, 138-43; opposed by the east, 143; following 1830, 252-60.

Religious liberty: Jefferson begins movement, 31-33; Madison's fight for, 39.

Representation: constitution of 1776, 30; increased, 33; for election of senators, 1816, 96; in 1828, 137; debate on proper basis in convention of 1829-30, 149-62; provisions of constitution of 1830, 169; dissatisfaction with, in west, 253-60; discussion of, in convention of 1850-51, 261-65.

Republican party: in Virginia in 1860, 333; platform of, 334.

Resolutions of 1798: written by Jefferson and Madison, 67; contents of, 68; opposition to, in Virginia, 68-70; vote on, 71.

Richmond: coal operators of, 86; interest of, in internal improvements, 104; commercial rivals of, 175; for tariff of 1842, 232; residents of, control county elections, 258; commercial convention of, 279; rival commercial center, 312.

Richmond Enquirer: editorial on negro slavery, 190; on secession, 211; desired a united Virginia, 311; opposition of, to Letcher, 321.

Richmond "Junto," unpopular in west, 255.

Ritchie, Thomas: reform movement of 1816, 96; opposed Jackson in 1824, 130; for local reforms, 142; remarks of, on convention of 1829–30, 146; activity in election of 1832, 207; member of Union party, 209; influence of, in election of 1833, 218; Democratic leader, 222–23; opposition of, to Calhoun, 233; editor of the *Union*, 235; rallies the west, 256; friendly to reforms, 257; alarmed at free school movement, 277.

Rives, W. C.: opposed General Survey Act, 133; activity of, in election of 1832, 207; elected to United States Senate, 209; member of Union party, 209; member of Democratic party, 219; resigned place in United States Senate, 221; Democratic leader, 222–23; re-elected to United States Senate, 224; opposed Van Buren's financial policy, 229; contest of, for re-election to Senate, 230.

Roane, Judge Spencer, opposed Marshall's decisions, 103.

Robinson, John: speaker of the House of Burgesses, 17; scheme for a public loan office, 17–18.

Royall, George, elected to House of Representatives as member of Union party, 218.

Ruffin, Edmund: began use of marl, 114; pro-slavery tendencies, 187; pro-slavery leader, 308.

Ruffner, Dr. Henry: author of the "Ruffner pamphlet," 244–45; interest of, in general education, 277.

Ruffner pamphlet: publication of, by Franklin Society, 244; factor in politics, 321.

Rumsey, James, inventor, 48.

Salt: beginning of manufacture of, in the trans-Alleghany, 83; duty on, 203; difficulties in shipping, 314.

San Domingo, slave uprisings in, 64–71.

Scotch Irish, settlement of, in the Valley, 13.

Secession: popular in eastern Virginia in 1832, 209; feeling in western Virginia, 210; attitude of western Virginia in 1850, 247–50.

Seddon, James A., influenced by Calhoun, 151.

Sheffey, Daniel: Federalist leader, 88; for United States Bank, 91; opposed to second war with Great Britain, 92.

Slave trade: domestic, 112; opposition to, 310.

Smith, Dr. W. A., defended Rev. Harding, 284.

Smith, Rev. Wesley, champion of Union, 292.

South Carolina: course of, unpopular in Virginia, 211–12; acts of, praised, 215–16.

Squatter sovereignty, in western Virginia, 43.

Stamp Act Resolutions, passed, 19.

Staunton Convention, of 1816, 94–95.

State rights: doctrine of, 68; issue of, in election of 1860, 336.

State-Rights party: formed, 209; in control of eastern Virginia, 215.

Stevenson, Andrew: on Missouri Compromise, 108; member of Union party, 218; Democratic leader, 222.

Stratton, John, member of Congress, 80.

Suffrage: constitution of 1776 on, 29; voters in 1829, 137–38; abuses in exercise of, 137; debate in convention of 1829–30, 161–62; provisions of constitution of 1851 concerning, 266.

Summers, Geo. W.: interest of, in internal improvements, 180; for abolition of slavery, 195; distrusted by eastern Virginia, 198; opposed to abolition, 226; member of convention of 1850–51, 263; candidate for governor, 293.

Summers, Lewis, member of convention of 1829–30, 145.

"Swan Lands," purchased by French parties, 317.

Tariff: bill of 1820, 118; bill of 1824, 120; bill of 1828, 122; effort to remove duty on salt in, 202; vote on bill of 1832, 204; bill of 1842, 232.

Taxes, direct: and the federal Constitution, 59; provisions of constitution of 1851 on, 267.

Taylor, George Keith, opposed resolutions of 1798, 68–69.

Taylor, John: talks dismemberment, 70; for Resolutions of 1798, 70; interest of, in agriculture, 114; friendly to J. Q. Adams, 127.

Taylor, Robert B.: speech of, on Bill of Rights, 148; forced to resign from convention of 1829–30, 165.

Taylor, William, letter of, on Nullification, 213.

Tazewell, L. W.: member of convention of 1829–30, 145; as governor opposed removal of deposits, 221; a Democrat, 229.

"Tenth Legion": a factor in Virginia politics, 224; in election of 1836, 228; factor in politics, 257.

Tidewater: extent of, 1; industrial, social, and political life of, 6; social distinction of, 8–9; in the Revolution, 24; fear of slave uprising in, 64; in presidential election of 1808, 90; decline of, 111–12; opposition of, to abolition, 189; vote of, on abolition, 199; Nullification sentiment in, 214.

Tobacco: effect upon plantation system, 7; migration of tobacco-growers to lower South, 11–12; effect of competition, of the new West, 113.

Trans-Alleghany: location and description of, 2–3; new lands in, 21; development of, during Revolutionary period, 42–43; variety of elements in population of, 45; no political and economic unity in, 46; interest of, in internal improvements, 47–48; opposed to Resolutions of 1798, 72–74; industrial development of, following 1795, 82–83; growth of population in, 84; lack of interest of, in internal improvements, 85; interest of, in federal improvements, 105–6; negro slavery in, 108–9; industrial transformation of, 116–17; German and New England settlements in, 117; center of discontent after 1830, 170–73; attitude of, on internal improvements, 177; vote of, on abolition of slavery, 199; internal development of, after 1830, 251; church controversies in, 288.

Tucker, Judge Beverly: speech in Nashville Convention, 246; Nashville speech criticized, 249.

Turner's, "Nat," Insurrection, effect of, 188.

Tyler, John, Jr.: member of Congress, 101; member of convention of 1829–30, 145; remark of, on dismemberment of Virginia, 205; re-elected to United States Senate, 217; resigned place in United States Senate, 224; candidate for vice-presidency, 227; nominated for vice-presidency,

230; repudiated by Whigs, 231; opposed to dismemberment, 255.

Union party: formed, 209; and Nullification, 216; of South Carolina, 219.

University of Virginia: movement of, for a chair of agriculture, 225; interest of, in Literary Fund, 274; unpopular in Western Virginia, 275; opposition to appropriation for, 278; intellectual center of South, 279; enrolment of 1857 at, 282.

Upshur, Abel P.: member of convention of 1829-30, 145; on Bill of Rights, 151; on theories of government, 152; on extension of slavery, 156; submitted compromise in convention of 1829-30, 163.

Valley of Virginia: location and subdivisions of, 1-2; settled by Scotch-Irish and Germans, 13; socially unlike the east, 14-15; community settlements of, 14; industrial life of, 14; theories of, regarding local government, 15; material grievances of, in 1774, 21; for revolt from England, 24; opposition of, to Resolutions of 1798, 72-74; wheat industry of, 81-82; in presidential election of 1808, 90; interest of, in Baltimore and Ohio Railroad, 125; negro slavery in, 156-57; vote of, on abolition of slavery, 199.

Van Buren, Martin: candidate for vice-presidency, 206; candidate for presidency, 228; carried Virginia in 1840, 231; candidacy of, in 1844, 234.

Washington, George: interested in western lands, 21; opposed disestablishment, 39; letter of, to Arthur Lee regarding West, 47; promoter of internal improvements, 48; influence of, on convention of 1788, 54; interested in politics of 1798, 75.

Washington Globe, opposition of, to Calhoun, 233.

Wheeling, western terminus of Baltimore and Ohio Railroad, 241, 242.

Whig party: formed, 221; candidates of, in election of 1836, 227; breach following election of 1836, 228; successes of, in elections of 1838, 229; opposed Tyler, 232; victory of, in 1844, 234; successes of, in 1847, 236; Whigs and Calhoun, 237; banking legislation, 238; internal improvement legislation, 240; opposed to reform, 257; favored an extension of suffrage, 259.

Whiskey Insurrection, political influence of, 64-65.

White, Hugh L., candidate for presidency, 227.

Whig, Richmond: pleas of, for union of Whigs, 223; denounced secession in 1850, 249; opposition of, to Letcher, 323, 326; Bell organ in 1860, 333.

Willey, W. T., taxation of slave property, 269.

Wilmot Proviso, opposition to, in Virginia, 244.

Winchester Republican, on railroads, 179.

Wise, Henry A.: influenced by Calhoun, 151, 225; internal improvement policy of, 243; member of convention of 1850-51, 261; and the Methodists, 293; candidate for governor, 305; for united Virginia, 306-7; popularity in western Virginia, 307; favored canal to the Ohio, 316; interested in Franco-Virginian steamship line, 318; candidate for presidency, 326; unpopu-

larity of, in western Virginia, 328.
Wise, O. Jennings, editor of *Richmond Enquirer*, 320.
Woolens Bill, debate on, 122.
Wright, Benjamin, engineer, 182.
Wythe, George, proposed amendment by, to federal Constitution, 59.

"Yankees": teachers, 279; teachers opposed in eastern Virginia, 281; influence of, in western Virginia, 281.
Yoder, Jacob, commercial ventures of, 47.

Zane, Ebenezar, settlement of, on Wheeling island, 45; Federalist, 58.

www.ingramcontent.com/pod-product-compliance
Lightning Source LLC
Chambersburg PA
CBHW070747230426
43665CB00017B/2274